Radical Psychology

Radical Psychology

Multicultural and Social Justice Decolonization Initiatives

Edited by
Susan O. Gelberg, Mathew A. Poteet,
David D. Moore, and Don Coyhis

LEXINGTON BOOKS
Lanham • Boulder • New York • London

Published by Lexington Books
An imprint of The Rowman & Littlefield Publishing Group, Inc.
4501 Forbes Boulevard, Suite 200, Lanham, Maryland 20706
www.rowman.com

Unit A, Whitacre Mews, 26-34 Stannary Street, London SE11 4AB

British Library Cataloguing in Publication Information Available

Library of Congress Cataloging-in-Publication Data Available

LCCN 2018945975 | ISBN 9781498553681 (cloth: alk. paper) |
ISBN 9781498553698 (electronic)

∞™ The paper used in this publication meets the minimum requirements of American National Standard for Information Sciences—Permanence of Paper for Printed Library Materials, ANSI/NISO Z39.48-1992.

Printed in the United States of America

Contents

Preface

Why Radical Psychology Now?

Susan O. Gelberg

In the American Psychological Association's (APA's) *Principles of Psychologists and Code of Conduct*, General Principle A, Beneficence and Nonmaleficence, states that psychologists strive to benefit those with whom they work (beneficence) and take care to do no harm (nonmaleficence; American Psychological Association, 2002, 2010a, 2016). Applying Principle A to cultural issues, Guideline 1 of the APA's Guidelines on Multicultural Education, Training, Research, Practice, and Organizational Change for Psychologists states: "Psychologists are encouraged to recognize that, as cultural beings, they may hold attitudes and beliefs that can detrimentally influence their perceptions of, and interactions with, individuals who are ethnically and racially different from themselves" (Manese, Croteau, Helms, & Horwitt, 2003, p. 382). Although these objectives seem straightforward, contemporary mainstream Western psychologists, counselors, researchers, and educators sometimes violate them either overtly or covertly as well as intentionally or unintentionally.

Radical Psychology: Multicultural and Social Justice Initiatives (hereafter referred to as *Radical Psychology*) explores the principles of beneficence and nonmaleficence, social justice, and multiculturalism as they relate to Euro-American psychologists and psychological institutions whose Eurocentrism can create harmful experiences for the people of other cultures or different worldviews who receive their services.

In 2006, Lisa Grayshield, PhD, graduated from a Western educational institution and became an assistant professor in a Western university. As a member of the Washo Tribe of Nevada and California, she faced conflicts between the Indigenous Ways of Knowing (IWOK) that shaped her cultural identity and the educational and professional experiences she had in Western educational institutions. Being exposed to contemporary Western psychological research principles and working in Euro-American mental health systems created strong clashes between her cultural beliefs and Euro-American psychological paradigms:

> As I contemplate the meaning behind my own work as a counseling educator, service provider, and researcher, I question its relevance. Do we continue to debate the same issues that arise from a purely Western European paradigm, issues such as racism, sexism, classism, and so on? Or do we go beyond the limits of imposed value structures that have been established by our profession to find better ways to inform our praxis. I have come to a standstill in my career, presented with an irreconcilable difference that must be addressed if this field and the praxis that underlies its basic assumptions are to be considered a viable avenue in making a better world for all. More honestly stated, from my perspective, as a tribal Indigenous person and human being on this earth, unless a radical shift in paradigm praxis takes place in the field of counseling psychology, it will remain both irrelevant and a tool for further colonization of Indigenous/tribal people.

From Indigenous ways of knowing as a philosophical base for the promotion of peace and justice in counseling education and psychology by L. Grayshield, L., & A. Mihecoby, 2010.

Why is it that Dr. Grayshield finds Western European psychology both irrelevant and harmful? How can we use the literature about culture and cognitive biases to further explore our own biases as psychologists or counselors? How can we listen to and respond to statements such as hers without having what Nagai calls *ethnocultural* and *linguistic transference* and *countertransference* (Nagai, 2009) shut down further productive dialogue because of our own ethnocultural countertransference responses of discomfort, anxiety, anger, frustration, misunderstanding, or confusion—or because of the ethnocultural transference experienced by those who receive our services?

RADICAL PSYCHOLOGY: THE ACRONYM

RADICAL is the acronym we use to refer to a set of attitudes and behaviors that reduce the likelihood of the irrelevant or inappropriate imposition of Euro-American worldviews onto psychological research, program designs, theoretical formulations, and clinical practices. We use this acronym to help psychologists keep in the forefront of their minds certain cultural competency and social justice principles that go far to prevent doing harm to supervisees, students, or clients who are hurt by Eurocentric psychological approaches. Specifically, radical psychologists:

R: Realize that there is still much that they don't know, and much that they "don't know that they don't know" (Coyhis, personal communication). These are their "blind spots" and the "unknown," two of the four quadrants of the Johari Window, which was developed by American psychologists Joseph Luft and Harry Ingham in the 1950s (Chandler & Munday, 2011). Banaji and Bhaskar state, "Memory and belief . . . operate . . . outside the actor's awareness (Banaji & Bhaskar, 2001, p. 140). Jun writes, "It is possible that some scholars, practitioners, and researchers are not aware of their ethnocentric biases or of inconsistencies between their behavior and their knowledge" (Jun, 2010, p. 5). In *Blindspot: Hidden Biases of Good People*, Banaji and Greenwald (2013), professors of psychology at Harvard and the University of Washington, use the Implicit Association Test (Greenwald, McGhee, & Schwartz, 1998), to challenge the perception, "I know my own mind. I am able to assess others in a fair and accurate way." In their challenging book, they focus on hidden biases related to age, gender, race ethnicity, religion, social class, sexuality, disability status, and nationality (Banaji & Greenwald, 2013).

A: Accept that because of their blind spots, their imposition of Eurocentric psychological worldviews and practices onto culturally and ethnically diverse individuals and groups has a high potential for being harmful to those vulnerable populations.

D: Make efforts to then decolonize (Duran, 1995) their psychological formulations, practices, theories, and research through attempts to:

I: Support the inclusion of peers, colleagues, and consultants who endorse and practice other worldviews.

C: Develop counterhegemonic (opposition to status quo) initiatives including

A: Acting to address multicultural and social justice issues, and

L: Working for the legal protection for all individuals, regardless of the diversity of culture, ethnicity, socioeconomic status, health, physical or mental ability, spiritual or religious beliefs, educational background, sexual orientation, gender identity, sexual biology, age cohort, and ancestral backgrounds.

MORE ABOUT THE BOOK TITLE

Recently, at a national multicultural conference, we, the four editors of *Radical Psychology*, met to discuss the proposal for this book. We were concerned about the still-prevailing imposition of Euro-American worldviews onto people who do not hold contemporary Western worldviews (Ivey, D'Andrea, Iver, & Simekk-Morgan, 2007).

At that conference, we talked with each other about our growing impatience with the slow progress of social justice and multicultural initiatives. [For example, the beginning of the development of multicultural counseling competencies by an APA committee began in 1981 by Division 17. It was not endorsed by the APA Council of Representatives until 2002 (Arredondo & Perez, 2003).]

We also spoke about our wish to become more radical in confronting psychologists and counselors about the impact of their own Western psychological privilege on their professional work. We discussed our wish to "go off the grid" of Western Ethnocentrism.

With that concept, the seeds of this book were planted.

CULTURALLY SENSITIVE WRITING AND PUBLICATION ISSUES

In seeking to "walk the talk" of diversity with our authors, this book reflects our hope to challenge more directly the predominant Western research methodologies and other psychological practices that are inappropriate and/or harmful for people who hold other worldviews. This includes encouraging each author to select the writing topics and styles that best represent that author's professional and cultural perspectives. For example, our Indigenous writers often use capitalization as tools to emphasize spirituality and sacred elements in their worldview. The authors' writing also differs in such factors as the types of research methodologies they use, their worldviews about mental health, how much they self-disclose, their use of humor, their choice of literal or figurative language, the directness of their language, whether they include narratives and testimonies, their sources of knowledge, how they perceive credentialing issues, the formatting of their chapter, their views of the role of spirituality in writing about mental health, the degree to which they incorporate Euro-American research into their writing, and their beliefs about mental health. The authors were encouraged to select the writing styles that would best communicate their treatises. This diversity of style encourages readers to look beyond stylistic differences in order to best comprehend the arguments within each chapter.

Early in the process of writing the proposal, in speaking with some individuals we hoped would write a chapter for a book for a Western academic press, one highly published Indigenous author turned us down, saying he was "tired of fitting into the box" of what he saw as a Eurocentric publishing process. He told us that he was planning to publish in ways that would give him more flexibility in content and style.

The authors we subsequently spoke to enthusiastically resonated with the idea of using diverse writing content and styles to challenge those who continue to rely on culturally inappropriate, outdated Western research tools, clinical formulations, and teaching methodologies when working with diverse populations. We understood that in some ways we would be diverging from standard Euro-American texts in how the chapters are organized (American Psychological Association, 2010b). Still, we would be working within the culturally sanctioned views of our professions.

The authors' hope is rather than focus on stylistic differences between standard Western psychology texts and the different chapters in *Radical Psychology*, readers might view this book as a type of immersion experience into other cultural or ethnic worldviews. They also hope that the differing writing styles and content they have used will better help readers further examine those same issues for themselves: that is, to look more closely inward using a process that includes deep self-reflection and self-scrutiny.

At the same time, we all agreed to, when appropriate, discuss Western psychological practices and writing styles that do reflect cultural sensitivity in their structures and thus have reliability and validity for people who do not endorse Western worldviews. No one wishes to "throw the baby out with the bathwater." There is much about contemporary Western psychology that has been helpful to people of all cultures, and *Radical Psychology* includes many references along that vein.

SOCIAL JUSTICE AND MULTICULTURALISM IN PSYCHOLOGY

When Eurocentric research, teaching, and therapy goes wrong for people of different ethnic and cultural groups, professional action is required in the area of increasing general cultural competence and social justice skills and actions by the offending psychologists. Many outstanding books address general cultural competence and social justice issues in great depth (e.g., Chung & Bemak, 2012; Goodman & Gorski, 2015; Ratts & Pedersen, 2014; Jun, 2010). These resources are invaluable in helping psychologists, educators, social workers, and medical professionals develop practices, teaching curricula, and research that lead to positive social, educational, medical, and psychological changes for vulnerable, underrepresented populations. These books focus in different ways on introductory social justice concepts, suggested social justice research, social justice models, the history of social justice, and strategies for practicing social justice and equality. They cover different contexts for social justice, and they describe exemplary social justice actions taken on behalf of specific underrepresented populations. They are rich sources of information, and their authors cover those topics with expertise as culturally competent psychologists and social justice activists. These references occur extensively throughout the book.

Taking a somewhat different approach, rather than offer another extensive, general, introductory coverage of multicultural justice and cultural competence, *Radical Psychology* seeks to address a number of more narrow questions about the psychology of multicultural competence and social justice through the examination of the following issues:

Colonization

What is *colonization* in psychology and how is it currently reflected in contemporary psychological theories, knowledge, and practices? How can psychologists transition into providing *postcolonial* psychological services (Duran, 2000, 2006; Duran & Duran, 1995; Duran & Firehammer, 2015; Goodman & VGorski, 2014)?

Smaller Audiences

Why is it often only within the subgroups of special interest psychological associations that there are more frequent, in-depth discussions of the imbalance of power, access, and opportunity that Euro-American biases create in Western psychology, social work, and education?

Why are these discussions of power, access, and opportunity not moving more quickly into the awareness of general Western psychologists, researchers, social workers, educators, and other mental health professionals despite APA's ethical mandates for increased social justice and multiculturalism? Why are so many in the dominant psychological culture still unaware that clients outside Euro-American treatment frameworks see their values, beliefs, and assumptions as at best, irrelevant, and, at worst, potentially harmful? Why is the literature about the potential harmfulness of the imposition of Euro-American paradigms onto marginalized cultures not more widely known by general psychologists, counselors, and social workers?

Cultural competence and social justice are still viewed by many psychologists as specializations or as options—not as mandates. Why do psychologists often avoid what are called the fourth and fifth counseling forces of psychology (Ratts & Pedersen, 2014)?

Nonexistent, Shortened, or Impaired Dialogues with Mainstream Audiences

Why is there often so little dialogue about cultural competence and social justice between those professionals who represent marginalized groups and those whose practices primarily reflect Euro-American research, teaching, or psychological practices? For example, why do professional workshops sometimes either fail to fully relate social justice and multicultural competence issues to their conference topics or give only passing references to these concepts?

Professional Backlashes

Why do psychologists who work toward multicultural competence and social justice often experience negative responses such as denial, retaliation, anger, isolation, or other kinds of backlashes from mainstream professionals or Euro-American institutions? Why is there so much resistance by some in the dominant culture to discussing social justice topics or taking action as a social justice agent? What is "White fragility" and what historical factors have created it (DiAngelo, 2011)?

Emphasis on Self-Reflection by Psychologists

What have been the positive and negative personal and professional experiences and consequences of those in the fields of mental health and education who have shown dedication to incorporating multiculturalism and social justice concepts into their professional work? How have they addressed their own cultural countertransference or the transference of others as they attempt to incorporate multicultural and social justice initiatives into their practices? How can readers learn from their experiences?

MOVING FORWARD

What psychological concepts and strategies are relevant to our professional development as social justice advocates and culturally competent psychologists? What are the future challenges for multiculturalism and social justice advocacy in the fields of education, medicine, and mental health?

SUMMARY

The goals of the authors and editors of *Radical Psychology* are to focus on the abovementioned questions in ways that encourage deeper dialogues between general psychological audiences and psychologists who have specialized in multicultural and/or social justice areas. We understand that these are controversial topics. One of our editors, Don Coyhis, summarizes the issue of controversy with a single statement: "Conflict precedes clarity" (Coyhis, personal communication).

In the end, readers decide for themselves what their approach to addressing Eurocentrism in psychology will be. We hope, however, that the concepts presented in *Radical Psychology* will help readers make more conscious decisions in following psychological and counseling ethical principles and mandates for the inclusion of multicultural and social justice considerations into their professional practices, whether they be clinical practices, community programming, research, teaching, or supervision.

REFERENCES

American Psychological Association. (2002, Sept; 2010a, June; 2016, June). Ethical principles of psychologists and code of conduct. *American Psychologist, (57)*, 1060–1073. Note: amended on February 20, 2010, effective June 1, 2010; amended again on August 3, 2016, effective June 1, 2017 (APA website, APA.org). Washington, DC: Author.

American Psychological Association. (2010b). *Publication manual of the American Psychological Association*. Washington, DC: Author.

American Psychological Association. (July 10, 2015). *Press release and recommended actions: Independent review cites collusion among APA individuals and defense department officials in policy on interrogation techniques*. PDF. Retrieved from APA website, apa.org.

Arredondo, P., & Perez, P. (2003). Expanding multicultural competence through social justice leadership. *Counseling Psychologist, 31*(3), 282–289.

Banaji, M. R., & Bhaskar, R. (2001). Implicit stereotypes and memory: The bounded rationality of social beliefs. In D. L. Schacter & E. Scarry (Eds.), *Memories, brain, and belief* (pp. 139–175). Cambridge, MA: Harvard University Press.

Banaji, M. R., & Greenwald, A. G. (2013). *Blindspot: Hidden biases of good people*. Unknown location: Delacorte Press.

Chandler, D., & Munday, R. (2011). *Oxford dictionary of media and communication*. Oxford, England, UK: Oxford University Press.

Chung, R. C.-Y., & Bemak, F. P. (2012). *Social justice counseling: The next steps beyond multiculturalism*. Thousand Oaks, CA: Sage.

DiAngelo, R. (2011). White fragility. *International Journal of Critical Pedagogy, 3*(3), 54–70.

Duran, E. (2000). *Buddha in redface*. Lincoln, NE: IUniverse.

Duran, E. (2006). *Healing the soul wound: Counseling with American Indians and other native peoples*. Columbia University: Teachers College Press.

Duran, E., & Duran, B. (1995). *Native American postcolonial psychology*. Albany, NY: State University of New York.

Duran, E., & Firehammer, J. (2015). Story sciencing and analyzing the silent narrative between words: Counseling research from an Indigenous perspective. In R. D. Goodman & P. C. Gorski (Eds.), *Decolonizing "multicultural" counseling through social justice* (pp. 85–97). NY: Springer Science + Business Media.

Grayshield, L., & Mihecoby, A. (2010, Fall). Indigenous says of knowing as a philosophical base for the promotion of peace and justice in counseling education and psychology. *Journal for Social Action in Counseling and Psychology, 2*(2), 1–16.

Grayshield, L., & Mihecoby, A. (2010). *Journal for Social Action in Counseling and Psychology, 2*(2), 3. Reprinted with permission by L. Grayshield.

Greenwald, A. G., McGhee, D. E., & Schwartz, J. L. K. (1998). Measuring individual differences in implicit cognition: The implicit association test. *Journal of Personality and Social Psychology, 74*(6), 1464–1480.

Ivey, A. E., D'Andrea, M., Ivey, M. B., & Simek-Morgan, L. (2007). *Theories of counseling and psychology: A multicultural perspective* (6th ed.). Boston, MA: Allyn & Bacon.

Jun, H. (2010). *Social justice, multicultural counseling, and practice: Beyond a conventional approach*. Thousand Oaks, CA: Sage.

Manese, J. E., Croteau, J. M., Helms, J. E., & Horwitt, S. (2003). American Psychological Association's Guidelines on multicultural education, training, research, practice, and organizational change for psychologists. *American Psychologist, 58*(5), 377–402. doi:10.1027/0003-66X.58.5.377.

Nagai, D. (2009). Ethno-cultural and linguistic transference and countertransference: From Asian perspectives. *American Journal of Psychotherapy, 63*(1), 13–23.

Ratts, M. J., & Pedersen, P. B. (2014). *Counseling for multiculturalism and social justice: Integration, theory, and application* (4th ed.). Alexandria, VA: American Counseling Association.

Acknowledgments

Since the four editors come from very different cultural backgrounds, their acknowledgments reflect different cultural writing styles. For example, Indigenous writing often includes the use of capitalized words to honor concepts that are sacred in the view of the culture of that writer.

First, we, the four editors, wish to thank Lexington Book's editors and staff for their willingness to pursue a venture that has content and a format that is "outside the box" of a standard Euro-American psychology textbook. We appreciated their willingness to understand that we, the editors, and our authors represent very different forms of professional expertise, writing styles, cited research forms, and worldviews. We understand that this book's format may be challenging for some who are not familiar with the culturally relevant writings of mental health professionals from diverse backgrounds. We have sought to challenge the status quo of contemporary psychology and are grateful that Lexington books provided a venue for us to do so. Special thanks go to Kasey Beduhnand Becca Rohnde for editorial assistance and guidance, Jayanthi Chander, and Alison Keefner for help with the latter stages of the manuscript and marketing.

As editors, we are all very grateful to the other authors who helped us develop this dream. Their professional accomplishments, consultations, writing, encouragement, and direction made this a much better and more comprehensive book. All of the authors accepted the challenge of addressing mainstream mental health professionals in honest, relevant, and supportive ways to help to further develop readers' multicultural competence and social justice activism.

Susan O. Gelberg

Many thanks to my husband, Howard; our children, Sarah and Katherine; our five grandchildren, Benjamin, Katie, Adam, and the twins, Sophie and

Diana, all of whom have supported and encouraged me to pursue a project that realized one of my lifetime passions. Howard has lovingly helped edit all of my writing, and I have greatly benefitted from his encouragement, support, and writing skills. My children's and grandchildren's ability to appreciate what I am striving for has helped motivate me more than they can imagine.

A special thanks to the three other editors—Don Coyhis, David Moore, and Mathew Poteet—who have inspired me, supported me, and challenged me in such important ways. I have admired Don's work from afar for many years and am delighted to have his visionary work as a model for this book. David has been an important mentor to me because he is a psychologist who has done outstanding cross-cultural research, developed creative culturally informed community services, and provided new paradigms for clinical services. Mathew has fully welcomed me into Indian country, and his ability to both challenge and support me has led to much personal and professional growth. Thank you, Don, David, and Mathew! In addition, Kateri Coyhis' help with the many administrative details of the book has made my life as editor so much smoother!

As I have worked over the years to understand White privilege and intergenerational trauma, Dr. Eduardo Duran's writings have changed my life as a Caucasian woman working to be a better ally to other populations. Ed has provided supervision and consultation in ways that always show kindness, insight, and spiritual power at its best. I frequently quote him in my parts of the book because his insights are so relevant to our book's vision. Thank you, Ed!

Finally, thanks also to the many friends and colleagues who have expressed interest in my work. You have helped me weather the institutional sluggishness (and sometimes difficulties) I have experienced as I have tried to instigate agency change. Thank you for sharing your own challenges with me as multicultural mental health allies and social activists!

Mathew A. Poteet

I would first like to express my deepest gratitude to the Creator for my life and my journey. It has been an amazing journey so far. My beautiful family—blood and extended (my wife, my daughter, my son, and my grandson; my mom and dad, my brothers and sisters, my grandmas and grandpas, my uncles and aunties, my nieces and nephews), many friends, and many communities—I would not be where I am today if it weren't for your continual belief in the best of me being triumphant. Thank you for your time, patience, and love.

Being a part of this book has been eye-opening, and has also been a great opportunity to give back to the people, communities, and organizations who have taught me so much. As words became pages, and a book took form, the conversations that took place between the coeditors and authors created new ideas and significant insights. So much of this has evolved throughout time, and I can't wait to see where this goes next. It has been a remarkable journey, and I am proud and honored to be included in this with them all.

Lastly, I would like to share my gratitude with the people and organizations that made my adolescent life a little more challenging than it should have been, in my opinion. You helped me become who I am today, and it may be different had you not made the choices you did.

David D. Moore

The change agent responsible for my lens on the brave new world of psychology is the fifth era of behavioral health ushered in by the DSM-5. The core of this text is the ascendance of developmental psychology within the Cultural Case Formulation. A century of norm-referenced diagnosis from clinical psychology has given way to the phenomenological force of person-centered counseling psychology. Attending counseling psychology's 1987 Georgia Conference, a new generation of researchers were born when that Division of Psychology embraced Program Evaluation Research. With support from colleagues at the Universities of Puget Sound, Washington, and Johns Hopkins, I embarked on 30 years of health prevention program evaluation.

The Community of Juneau Alaska provided 18 years of program evaluation insight carried into this text as teachings from our "JUMPP" program. The essential person for project longevity is the position of Ombudsman. They must resolve the many points of friction caused by change. Over 18 years, Elsa Demeksa has been the JUMPP Ombudsman. Elsa retired as a University of Alaska Regent and stepped into 18 years of volunteer service in the community she loves. In the rapidly changing field of health-care services, the Juneau Community Foundation's Hope Endowment Fund plays the major role in helping to maintain the mental health safety net through their support of the JUMPP program and other Juneau nonprofit mental health providers.

Juneau is home to the State of Alaska's government, as well as the Central Council of the Tlingit and Haida Indian Nations. This leadership city of innovators produced the JUMPP prevention system of integrated pediatric primary care and psychology. The pediatric leadership came from late Dr. George Brown, who taught the rest of us the great truth of family-centered health-care years before DSM-5.

Don Coyhis

First and foremost, we would like to thank the Creator for allowing us the opportunity to do this amazing work and revealing the healing power of our culture! We would like to acknowledge our Wellbriety Council of Elders, who, since 1988, have provided their leadership, wisdom, teachings, and ceremonies to help guide the Wellbriety Movement.

We would like to thank all of the Native researchers who "discovered" the connectedness between intergenerational trauma and current issues in our Native communities. We acknowledge the healing power of our culture to overcome intergenerational trauma so we stop passing it on to future generations. We can be the generation that makes the choice not to pass this trauma on and we can be the generation that initiates this healing process! When we can bring our communities back to our culture, we have found this is what works! Our Culture is Prevention!

This book is so much more than just a product of individuals who contributed. It is a compilation of energy from each author and editor who poured their hearts and passions into these pages in order to provide a different and unique perspective. This book serves as a way to enhance the healing journey and so we would like to acknowledge all of the authors and editors for providing your knowledge and experience for this project.

Introduction

Susan O. Gelberg

THE LONG-STANDING HISTORY OF DOING HARM

The professional ethical codes for psychologists and other mental health professionals (e.g., the Ethical Principles of Psychologists and Code of Conduct; American Psychological Association; APA, 2002, 2010, and 2016) were developed through the lens of contemporary, Western Euro-American worldviews. These include the following assumptions: (1) behavior can be best studied as discrete units to understand the whole; (2) compartmentalism is helpful in promoting the understanding of how humans function; and (3) it is best for individuals to be autonomous and self-reliant (Morse & Blume, 2013). These values often conflict with the values of individuals from other cultures or those who hold worldviews that differ from Western worldviews. This introduction will discuss how differing lenses of perception affect the ability of psychologists to follow the principles of beneficence and nonmaleficence.

Dr. Grayshield's comments (see Preface; Grayshield & Mihecoby, 2010) articulate some of the professional and personal dilemmas that mental health professionals face when, having trained in Western educational systems and then working in contemporary Euro-American educational institutions, research programs, or clinical practices, they seek to develop and provide culturally informed research designs, mental health services, and/or educational programs for individuals who endorse non-Euro-American cultural worldviews (Wendt, Gone, & Nagata, 2015b). A few examples of the potential harmfulness of Eurocentric biases and stereotypes follow.

Heteronormative Bias

Hudak and Giammattei (2014) write about the potential harm of the Western prevalence of heteronormativity, the Western-dominant mainstream belief that a viable family consists of a heterosexual mother and father raising heterosexual children together (Gamson, 2000). Heteronormativity still shapes psychological theory and practices involving the family (Hudak & Giammattei, 2014). Hudak and Giammattei (2014) focus on the need to shift the counseling paradigm away from a heteronormative one based on dominant Euro-American cultural values to a model that embraces all forms of sexual diversity in order to end potentially harmful heteronormative clinical practices, theory development, and research.

Collusion

Psychologists have taken actions that have resulted in condoning physical harm and torture. It is well known that psychologists were implicated in condoning torture interrogation procedures used by the United States Department of Defense. What is less well known, however, is that when an investigation was opened into the role of psychologists in justification of the use of torture (Independent Review Relating to APA Ethics Guidelines, National Security Interrogations, and Torture), some APA staff refused to cooperate with the investigations, and many APA insiders "spent the past decade obstructing and discrediting good-faith efforts to redirect the Association away from the disturbing path chosen by its leadership, a path that compromised fundamentals of human rights and the core principle of 'do no harm'" (The Steering Committee of Psychologists for Social Responsibility (PsySR), July 13, 2015). The investigation, termed the "Hoffman Report," concluded that psychologists "curried favor" with the Defense Department and enabled the government's use of abusive interrogation techniques. In response to public outcry, the APA issued a formal apology and made policy and procedural changes in order to address these ethical violations (American Psychological Association, July 10, 2015).

Torture

As early as 1991, Douglas C. Haldeman had concluded that conversion therapy techniques and reparative therapy for lesbian, gay, bisexual, and transgender clients (l/g/b/t) constituted *torture*. Reparative therapies include aversive conditioning techniques such as electric shock to the hand or genitals or the use of nausea-inducing drugs, directed at individuals who identified as gay, lesbian, bisexual, transgender, questioning/queer (g/l/b/t/q). Halderman wrote that conversion therapy not only was ineffective, but also led to shame, conflict, and fear about sexual feelings (Haldeman, 1991).

It took the APA 18 years to label these practices harmful and unethical. In 2009, the APA issued statements labeling reparative therapy and sexual conversion therapy as unethical, unsuccessful, and harmful (APA Task Force on Appropriate Therapeutic Responses to Sexual Orientation, 2009, 2011).

Biased Medical or Psychiatric Diagnoses

Historical documents exemplify the medical, psychiatric, and psychological professions' doing harm to women in the form of sexism in medical diagnoses. As early as the thirteenth century (but not documented in the literature until the nineteenth century), symptoms such as women's sexual desire and a "tendency to cause trouble" were diagnosed as female hysteria (the Greek word for "uterus"). Other symptoms of hysteria included faintness and "irritability." At that time, "normal" women were thought to be asexual, as reported by Maines (1998).

Karen Horney (1973) questioned many traditional Freudian views, such as Freud's theory of penis envy, in addition to what she saw as other instances of male bias in psychoanalytic theory. She wrote that many psychiatric concerns were primarily a reflection of male dominance and power. *The Handbook of Gender Research in Psychology* includes many citations of research that conclude that therapists' biases about gender are not always value-free, nor are they consistently based on scientific evidence (Ali, Caplan, & Fagnant, 2009). *Bias in Psychiatric Diagnosis: A Project of the Association for Women in Psychology* (Caplan & Cosgrove, 2004) also focuses on biased psychiatric diagnoses that cause potential harm to women.

Forced Medical Procedures

Biased psychiatric and psychological diagnoses create the potential for unnecessary and/or inappropriate medical procedures. In the 1960s and 1970s, the Indian Health Services (IHS) was accused of forced and coerced sterilization of thousands of Native American women. On November 6, 1976, a report released from the Government Accounting Office (GAO) stated that of the 12 IHS program areas, between 1973 and 1976 four program areas reported that 3,406 sterilizations were performed. The GAO discovered that three different types of information and reporting forms were used throughout the different program areas, and two of the forms were not complete in providing all the required information to properly inform patients of the procedures and risks. The main reasons physicians (the majority of whom were White Euro-Americans) gave for why they performed these procedures were economic and social. They believed that their actions supported society by limiting low-income, people of color from reproducing. Multiple studies showed that the IHS sterilized between 25 and

50% of Native American women in just six years (1970–76). These sterilization procedures were viewed as related to marital problems, alcoholism, drug abuse, psychological difficulties, shame, and guilt. Sterilization abuse affected the entire Indian community in the United States (Lawrence, 2000).

OTHER IMPACTS OF EUROCENTRISM AND COLONIZATION

When the literature about the harmful impacts of bias in the field of mental health is reviewed, it is evident that the potential for harm by mental health providers exists in regards to the elderly, the young, those with developmental or acquired disabilities, the g/l/b/t/q community, women, those who are diverse in their gender expression, non-Caucasians, people with poor health, non-Christians, individuals who are not viewed as physically attractive according to Euro-American standards of beauty, the sick, those experiencing poverty, immigrants, refugees, those who do not have Western educational credentials, the working class, and veterans who have unique psychological needs stemming from battlefield trauma.

These are only a few examples in which medical, psychiatric, or psychological diagnostic and treatment protocols have harmed individuals who do not share the mainstream cultural demographics or worldviews that the mental health provider may share. In addition to causing physical or emotional harm, Eurocentric faulty psychological diagnoses and treatments can have other impacts such as reducing the ability to get insurance, affecting employability, impacting child custody arrangements, reducing housing options, and impacting end-of-life decisions.

CULTURAL ASPECTS OF "DO NO HARM"

Wendt, Gone, and Nagata (2015b) point out that the concept of "harm" has important cultural components: "The history of modern medicine suggests that 'harm' does not have a straightforward, objective, or obvious meaning. Rather, harm is a social construct that is interpreted and negotiated, however informally, in relation to norms about well-being, clinical treatment, and social relations" (Wendt, Gone, & Nagata, 2015b, p. 346). Went, Gone, and Nagata (2015a & 2015b) and other writers point out that the concept of "harm" is affected by factors such as concerns about litigation, the financial status of the client, and mental health legislation (Sharpe & Faden, 1998; Wendt, Gone, & Nagata, 2015b, pp. 346–347).

THE MANY FORMS OF BIAS

Stereotypes and biases create perceptual blind spots in individuals (Banaji & Bhaskar, 2001; Banaji & Greenwald, 2013). Some biases may occur unconsciously, as in the impact of cognitive biases that affect information gathering, information processing, diagnoses, and clinical judgment. Falling into that class might be biases that are blind to the psychologist (Maccoun, 1998), such as attentional bias (Pronin & Kugler, 2007), confirmation bias (Oswald & Grosjean, 2004), and belief bias (Klauer, Musch, & Naumer, 2000). Other ethical violations may occur intentionally, as shown by the actions of the psychologists who participated in the enabling of torture (as documented by the Hoffman report (American Psychological Association, July, 2015). In part due to these biases, the effectiveness of Euro-American psychological services has been called into question as to their relevance to people from other cultures or worldviews (Wendt, Gone, & Nagata, 2015a, 2015b).

Euro-American Biases Toward Indigenous Worldviews

White Bison, Inc. is an American Indian/Alaska Native nonprofit charitable organization. Table 1 is adapted from White Bison's *The Red Road to Wellbriety* (2002, pp. 19–29) and contrasts Western thinking with Indigenous worldviews. Table 1 shows how contrasts between Indigenous mental health providers and Euro-American providers can be strong and at times oppositional to each other.

Bias and the Role of Spirituality

As seen in Table 1, one of the differing values between Eurocentric psychology and Indigenous psychology relates to the roles of spirituality and religion in psychological healing. Psychotherapy that includes a strong spiritual focus may reflect values that differ from contemporary, secular Western psychology or medicine and thus sometimes promotes referral to spiritual and/or religious professionals (Snodgrass, McCreight, & McFee, 2014). In contrast, Davis, Fitzpatrick, Garcia, Maynard, and Sultan (2016) incorporate spiritual elements into treatment models, proposing the use of a "biopsychosocial-spiritual model" for treatment.

There are many culturally informed spiritual treatments that are not sanctioned by Euro-American mental health treatment facilities. One example follows.

> Mathew Poteet: One spiritual tool that is not usually incorporated into Western psychological treatments is the Sweat Lodge. Mental health professionals are

Table 1 Indigenous vs. Euro-American Cultural Values

Indigenous Values	*Euro-American Contemporary Values*
Cooperation	Competition
Group emphasis—contributions to the group are emphasized; personal glory discouraged; modesty	Individual emphasis—competition, winning, and individual status are emphasized; self-attention
Modesty, humility	Self-important
Individual autonomy	Interference/involvement
Passivity/calmness	Activity/restlessness
Generosity	Saving
Patience	Impatience
Nonmaterialism	Materialism
Work to meet need	Puritan work ethic
Time—always with us	Time—use every minute
Orientation to present	Orientation to the future
Pragmatic, practical	Theoretical
Respect for age	Respect for youth
Right-brain orientation	Left-brain orientation
Cooperate with nature	Control over nature
Religion—way of life	Religion—segment of life
Spiritual—*Mythical*—Mystical	Skeptical
Personal caution	Personal openness
Listening/observational skills	Verbal skills
Indirect criticism—gentle teasing	Direct criticism
Extended family	Nuclear family
Cultural pluralist	Assimilationist
No/*minimal* eye-to-eye contact	Eye-to-eye contact important
Self-exploratory child rearing[a], "Planting of Good Seeds"—directing a child's thoughts and action, encouraging good behavior by acknowledging helpful traits, and use of praise to encourage positive actions	Strict discipline, four family cultures[b]: • Faithful—look to divine source for morality (20%) • Engaged progressives: virtue of personal freedom, responsibility for choices (21%) • Detached: "Let the kids be kids" (19%) • American dreamers: high levels of engagement, high hopes for children (27%)
Restitution, accountability—responsibility	Punishment, rewarding good behavior, natural consequences, logical consequences, time-outs, taking away[c]
Character = source of status	Academic degree = source of status
Bilingualism	Monolingualism
Expression of ideas and feelings through action	Expression through speech
Illness = imbalance(s)	Illness = physical issue
Belief in the unseen	Belief in the seen/proven
Respect for tradition	Progress oriented
Giving/sharing	Taking/saving

Note: Adapted from *The Red Road to Wellbriety* (White Bison, 2002, pp.19–20). Citations for revisions made appear in footnotes.

Source: White Bison (2002).

[a]BigFoot & Funderbunk (2010, August); [b]Bowman, Hunter, Dill, & Juelfs-Swanson (2012); [c]Recommended by American Academy of Pediatrics, American Association of Child and Adolescent Psychiatry, and National Mental Health Association (WebMD, undated).

> working with clients who hold shame and guilt for things they had done or things that had been done to them; some clients find it difficult to talk in group settings, even in Talking Circles. The Sweat Lodge is a healing tool that has proved to be helpful in these situations. Within the safety of the darkness, the womb of rebirth and renewal (one symbolization of the Sweat Lodge), and away from the eyes of judgment, clients feel safe enough to address their fears. Clients see that it wasn't that they feared what the dark had to show them about themselves, but instead they realized that if there is comfort in the dark, one can learn who one truly is.

It is obvious that the benefits, metaphors, and clinical impacts as described by Mathew Poteet differ from how a mental health treatment would be reported in Euro-American institutions. It is, however, a treatment that is culturally sanctioned by Indigenous psychologists and agencies such as the Society of Indian Psychologists (SIP), and it reflects many of the value differences as laid out in Table 1.

Although Euro-American psychologists are encouraged to view spirituality and psychology as separate disciplines, in *War and the Soul: Healing Our Nation's Veterans from Post-traumatic Stress Disorder* Edward Tick (2005) uses a spiritual approach to treat what he sees as soul wounding caused by war violence. He writes, "Though the affliction that today we call post-traumatic stress disorder has had many names over the centuries, it is always the result of the way war invades, wounds, and transforms our spirit" (Tick, 2005, p. 1).

In *Healing the Soul Wound: Counseling with American Indians and other Native Peoples*, Eduardo Duran (2006) proposes a spiritual focus to diagnose and treat soul wounds that have been caused across generations through exposure to Euro-American colonialism and genocide. Walker, Courtois, and Aten also write that "trauma work is inherently spiritual and must include a focus on the client's belief system" (Walker, Courtois, & Aten, 2015, p. 4).

How Biases Impact the Relevance and Validity of Western Professional Ethical Codes

What factors related to bias lead to the reduced reliability and validity of contemporary Western psychological practices for individuals who differ in some way from Euro-American views of life and healing? The editors and authors of *Radical Psychology* suggest answers that are complex and involve contrasting worldviews, diverging values, distinctly different priorities, background historical factors, current Eurocentric microaggressions, discrimination, structural violence (harm caused by social structures or social institutions; Galtung, 1969), trauma/intergenerational trauma, genocide (both physical and cultural), imposed colonization, revitalization, and characteristics within the dominant culture that often make it difficult for many professionals to grapple with these discrepancies.

TAKING ACTION: ADDRESSING THE BIASES AND STEREOTYPES BEHIND POTENTIALLY HARMFUL PSYCHOLOGICAL SERVICES

Because of this history of doing harm to vulnerable populations, medical and mental health professionals are now being asked to examine the potentially harmful biases they may have in regards to such factors as age, generational influences, developmental disabilities, disabilities acquired later in life, sex, sexual orientation, gender, race, ethnicity, culture, health, spirituality, religion, Indigenous heritage, military background, physical appearance, socioeconomic status, national origin, immigration status, refugee status, and values that do not represent the dominant cultural values held by White, heterosexual, middle-class, able-bodied, Christian Euro-Americans (Chung & Bemak, 2012; Goodman & Gorski, 2015; Hayes, 2016; Jun, 2010; Ratts & Pedersen, 2014).

Mainstream Psychology's Response to Harm and Bias

Although the general ethical codes of most mental health and educational professional associations mandate or recommend the integration of multiculturalism into professional practices, these references to multiculturalism do not usually emphasize consideration of the potentially harmful effects of Eurocentric clinical research, teaching, and clinical practices on people from other cultures or worldviews.

Special interest groups of the American Psychological Association

Special interest groups within professional associations have consistently sought to further clarify multicultural ethical guidelines in working with clients with differing worldviews. In 2013, at a national convention of the APA, representatives from the Association of Black Psychologists, Society of Indian Psychologists (SIP), Asian American Psychological Association, and National Latina/o Psychological Association discussed the relevance of the APA Code of Ethics for ethnic minorities or people with diverse worldviews. There was an agreement that "psychological societies worldwide would benefit from revised guidelines that more closely reflect their beliefs and values about community, spiritualism and relationships, as well as consider the effects of historical trauma or colonialism, than the beliefs and values incorporated into the current APA code" (Morse & Blume, 2013). Many of the APA's 54 divisions do focus on reducing harm through the reduction of biases and stereotypes in regards to specific diverse areas such as aging (Division 20), rehabilitation (Division 22), intellectual and developmental disabilities/autism spectrum disorders (Division 33), the psychology of women (Division 35), the psychology of religion and spirituality (Division 36), health psychology (Division 38), l/g/b/t issues (Division 44), and culture, ethnicity, and race (Division 45).

These special interest divisions in APA help psychologists understand the ways in which biases, negative attitudes, and stereotypes can be identified and addressed. Because some APA members may only join several divisions, however, their awareness of the biases and stereotypes they themselves may hold may be limited to the exposure they get from participation in the particular divisions to which they belong.

National Latina/o Psychological Association

APA's National Latina/o Psychological Association has as one of its goals "to seek a physical, psychological, and social environment for Latinas/os in the USA that reflects the ideals of respect for mental health, dignity, and human and civil rights" (National Latina/o Psychological Association website). Its journal, the *Journal of Latina/o Psychology*, includes a focus on addressing issues of multicultural competence, social justice, and advocacy. Some Latina/o values include family-centeredness (familism), the tendency to seek harmony in relationships (simpatia), and a preference for subtle self-expression (Dingfelder, 2005).

Guidelines for Psychological Practice with Lesbian, Gay, and Bisexual Clients

APA's publication, The Guidelines for Psychological Practice with Lesbian, Gay, and Bisexual Clients includes 21 aspirational guidelines that address the effects of stigma, discrimination, and violence (APA, 2011). It states, however, that these aspirational psychological practices are superseded by Federal and state law and "must be consistent with the current APA Ethical Principles of Psychologists and Code of Conduct."

APA recently developed a task force to reduce transphobia among psychologists (Arkles, 2015). This task force developed the first guidelines for working with transgender and gender nonconforming people (http://www.apa.org/practice/guidelines/transgender.pdf). Fifteen guidelines address the mistreatment that transgender and gender nonconforming individuals have experienced from mental health professionals. In addition, the guidelines encourage social justice activism in addressing institutional transphobia as well as in developing trans-affirmative practices. Guideline 4 states:

"Psychologists are aware of how their attitudes about and knowledge of gender identity and gender expression may affect the quality of care they provide to TGNC people and their families" (APA, 2015, p. 837). Guideline 6 states: "Psychologists strive to recognize the influence of institutional barriers on the lives of TGNC [trans gender non-conforming (gender)] people and to assist in developing TGNC-affirmative environments" (APA, 2015, p. 840). Guideline 7 states: "Psychologists understand the need to promote social change that reduces the negative effects of stigma on the health and well-being of TGNC people" (APA, 2015, p. 841). These guidelines are, however, aspirational, not mandatory. Glassgold (n.d.) discusses the APA's task force's view on appropriate therapeutic responses to sexual orientation issues.

Guidelines for Assessment of and Intervention of Persons with Disabilities

The Guidelines for Assessment of and Intervention with Persons with Disabilities (American Psychological Association, 2012) present 22 aspirational guidelines. Guideline 2 (American Psychological Association, 2012) states: "Psychologists strive to examine their beliefs and emotional reactions toward various disabilities and determine how these might influence their work." Guideline 22 (American Psychological Association, 2012) states: "Psychologists strive to recognize and address health promotion issues for individuals with disabilities." This guideline includes references to specific erroneous assumptions psychologists may make in working with people with disabilities. Psychologists may make misattributions in the diagnostic process, may over- or underemphasize disability concerns, and may have negative emotional reactions to their clients.

Dunn and Andrews (2015) discuss the harm imposed by biased language in discussing disability issues. The implication of the abovementioned is that when misattributions are made, the interventions that follow are substandard, inappropriate, or potentially harmful to persons with disabilities. When I (SOG) worked as a psychologist in a university counseling center, one of my clients was a law school student with quadriplegia. Several other psychologists commented to me that they imagined his presenting concern for counseling was a wish to deal with the stress associated with quadriplegia. They had not considered the possibility that he was close to graduation and was seeking career counseling as he began his job search.

Society for the Psychology of Religion and Spirituality

One of APA's special interest groups, Division 36, the Society for the Psychology of Religion and Spirituality, integrates a spiritual focus into clinical services. Other Euro-American counselors and psychologists see spiritual issues as separate from other psychological concerns, and clients are thus referred out

(Snodgrass, McCreight, & McFee, 2014). These authors see competence in spiritual issues as a special, not general, area of expertise. While knowing one's professional limitations is a clinical boundary issue, the assumption that spiritual issues are separate from psychological issues is a controversial assumption that is challenged by a number of the authors of *Radical Psychology*.

Association of Black Psychologists

Recognizing the differences in values between Euro-American worldviews and Afrocentric values, the Association of Black Psychologists bases its ethical guidelines on a foundation of Black/African-centered values, historical trauma, the consequences of slavery, and ongoing discrimination experienced by African Americans (Association of Black Psychologists, 2006). The association defines Black/African-centered psychology in the following way:

> Preamble: Based on a proposal submitted and accepted by the Board of Directors (BOD) of the Association of Black Psychologists, the following definitions of African-centered psychology has been adopted. It is the intention of the Committee to Advance African Psychology (CAAP) to establish a framework for content provided during the African Psychology Institute (API) that adheres to the values and principles expressed therein. In recognition of the diverse historical experiences and cultural expressions within and between peoples of African ancestry, the following is the accepted definition:
>
> Black/African-centered psychology is a dynamic manifestation of unifying African principles, values, and traditions. It is the self-conscious "centering" of psychological analyses and applications in African realities, cultures, and epistemologies. Black/African-centered psychology, as a system of thought and action, examines the processes that allow for the illumination and liberation of the spirit. Relying on the principles of harmony within the universe as a natural order of existence, Black/African-centered psychology recognizes the following: the spirit that permeates everything that is; the notion that everything in the universe is interconnected; the value that the collective is the most salient element of existence; and the idea that communal self-knowledge is the key to mental health. Black/African-centered psychology is ultimately concerned with understanding the systems of meaning of human beingness, the features of human functioning, and the restoration of normal/natural order to human development. As such, it is used to resolve personal and social problems and to promote optimal functioning (Association of Black Psychologists public website).

Society of Indian Psychologists

After a three-year process, a member of SIP published a 96-page critique of the APA Code of Ethics (Garcia, 2014). Garcia concludes that it is not possible to understand ethics separate from culture. In addition, Garcia emphasizes that mainstream psychology is not often aware of those cultural power dynamics: "The abuse of power, whether intentional or unintentional, plays a major role in the harm experienced by Indigenous people as well as other marginalized and stigmatized people. While the APA Ethics Code encourages psychologists to be aware of their own biases, values and sociocultural framework, in actual practice, this kind of awareness is rare" (Garcia, 2014, p. 15).

IMPLICATIONS FOR RADICAL PSYCHOLOGY

One intent of *Radical Psychology* is to highlight conversations about potentially harmful biases that are occurring in many professional special interest groups in order to reach the readership of researchers, educators, psychologists, counselors, social workers, and other mental health professionals who may be less aware of these imperatives because their professional work, including research, teaching, or clinical practices, is more generalist in nature and because they may not see themselves as multicultural professionals or social activists.

OTHER ETHICAL CONSIDERATIONS: SOCIAL JUSTICE IN THE HELPING PROFESSIONS

In addition to multicultural counseling consideration of the relationship between bias and the mandate to "do no harm," professionals in the fields of mental health and education have other ethical and legal responsibilities that shape their clinical, theoretical, educational, and research activities. Those ethical standards, ethical principles, and legal responsibilities are described in the ethical codes of professional associations, licensing and credentialing regulations, federal mandates, and state laws. They include social justice as a necessary component of multicultural competence and as a crucial way to address the harm of Eurocentric psychological worldviews.

In reflecting on social justice from a psychological perspective, former APA president Melba Vasquez (2012) discusses the term "justice": "Justice, in its broadest sense, is 'fairness . . . ' Sometimes treating others fairly means treating them differently . . . in proportion to their relevant differences (Kitchener & Anderson, 2011), such as is true in the application of affirmative action policies" (Vasquez, 2012, p. 338). Thus, Vasquez challenges the idea that justice always means treating individuals equally.

Social Justice Discourse in Mainstream Organizations

Psychologists

For psychologists, ethical responsibilities as specified in the APA's Ethical Principles of Psychologists and Social Conduct (American Psychological Association, 2010) include working for social justice for their clients (Principle D).

Melba Vasquez (2012) highlights the APA's commitment to social justice and its overlap with APA's ethical principles. APA's Ethical Principles of Psychologists Code of Conduct includes General Principle D, Justice.

The publications of psychological journals reflect specific topical priorities for that organization. When the topic of social justice is considered, articles that are published in mainstream professional publications may include only a brief mention of social justice issues. Lee, Rosen, and Burns (2013) surveyed multicultural literature published in the *Journal of Counseling Psychology* (JCP) between 1954 and 2009. The themes of different identities included race/ethnicity, gender/sex, religion/spirituality, sexual orientation, social status, disability, age, and intersections. Gender/sex was the most prevalent multicultural identity found in the JCP, followed by race/ethnicity. Social justice was not among the top subject themes in the literature reviewed.

National Association of Social Work

In its Code of Ethics, the National Association of Social Work (NASW) writes that its value system can be summarized in two words: "social justice." NASW's Code of Ethics states that social workers use social justice concepts to "open the doors of access and opportunity for everyone" and "social workers address structural problems in the social service agencies in which they work." The NASW encourages its members to "work within larger social and political arenas" (NASW website: socialworkers.org).

American Psychiatric Association and American Medical Association

Section 1.2. of the Bylaws of the American Psychiatric Association states: "The purposes for which the Association is organized include: (g) to promote the best interests of patients and those actually or potentially making use of mental health services; and (h) to advocate for its members" (American Psychiatric Association, 2013). Advocacy is also stressed by the American Medical Association (American Medical Association Editor, 2016) and individual authors (Patel, 2015).

American Counseling Association

The 2014 American Counseling Association Code of Ethics states in section F.11.c., Multicultural/Diversity Competence, that counselor educators include multicultural/diversity competency into their training and supervision practices. They must train students to increase cultural competencies (American Counseling Association, 2014).

National Education Association and National Association of Foreign Student Advisers

The National Education Association (NEA) mission statement, as adopted at the 2006 NEA Representative Assembly (National Education Association, 2013), states that the mission of its members is to "fulfill the promise of public education to prepare every student to succeed in a diverse and interdependent world" (NEA website: nea.org). NEA Core values include equal opportunity, respect for the worth, dignity, and equality of every individual in a diverse society and a responsibility for collective action (NEA—adopted by the 1975 Representative Assembly, amended 2010).

The Statement of Ethical Principles of the National Association of Foreign Student Advisers (NAFSA) Association of International Educators also states that educators are to respect other worldviews (NAFSA website: NAFSA.org).

Potential Harm De-emphasized

As with the concept of "do no harm," in the abovementioned ethical codes, there is usually no mention of the large body of literature that proposes that social justice is a primary way to reduce the sole reliance on Euro-American values, assumptions, and worldviews (which reflect primarily Caucasian, Euro-American, cis-male, heteronormative, Christian, able-bodied, and middle-class values and worldviews) that can be harmful to those who do not share those same worldviews (Lilienfeld, 2007; Morse & Blume, 2013; Sue, Capodilupo, Torino, Bucceri, Holder, Nadal, & Esquilin, 2007; Wendt, Gone, & Nagata, 2015(a), 2015(b)).

Social Justice and Special Interest Groups

As with the topic of multiculturalism and diversity, it is only until one considers the literature of independent special interest groups or special interest groups within those mainstream organizations that social justice topics more often include a stronger focus on the potential harm a Euro-American bias has on people of color and others who do not share certain Eurocentric worldviews.

Social Justice and Special Interest Groups of the American Psychological Association

APA has 54 divisions with special interest groups such as Rehabilitation Psychology (Division 22), the Society for the Psychology of Women (Division 35), the Society for the Psychology of Religion and Spirituality (Division 36), the Society for the Psychological Study of Lesbian Gay Bisexual, and Transgender Issues (44), the Society for the Psychological Study of Culture, Ethnicity, and Race (Division 45), and the Society for the Psychological Study of Men and Masculinity (Division 51). As was the case with the topic of multicultural counseling, the discourse within these divisions about social justice sometimes remains within the social justice interest groups of each division. Furthermore, the discussion of the topics that are top priorities for the special interest groups are not always equally highly prioritized by the general membership in that particular professional association. These special interest groups are the ones to most often highlight the harm that mainstream psychology can do. Social justice imperatives are also made by these special interest groups.

Society of Indian Psychologists

As discussed earlier, the membership of one independent special interest national professional organization, SIP recently spent three years reviewing the ethical codes of the APA and developed a 96-page document that highlights instances in which a particular APA practice may be harmful to Indigenous people and by implication to other people of color (García & Tehee, 2014). SIP recommended that the APA take social justice actions in order to address the injustices Indigenous clients experience when a Western psychological approach is imposed on them.

When we (SOG and MAP) discuss the SIP document in our psychology workshops, many Euro-American psychology audiences are initially unaware of any of the potential conflicts Native American clients might experience when exposed to Euro-American educational or treatment models. In contrast, most of the Indigenous mental health professionals that we speak to in Indian Country are well aware of SIP's document and its content. The result is that Euro-American psychologists who use contemporary Western practices with Indigenous populations continue to provide services that reflect colonization (Duran, 2000, 2006; Duran & Duran, 1995).

Several years ago, I (SOG) attended a SIP conference in which members of the APA's Ethics Committee attended by invitation. The conference was held during the time that SIP was examining the APA Ethical Code in order to determine its appropriateness and relevance for Indigenous clients or other people of color. At that conference, several SIP members told the APA Ethics

Committee members that they felt they had to "leave their culture at the front door when following the APA Ethical Codes." One APA Ethics Committee member responded with surprise at that statement. That individual had never considered the conflicts that could occur between the APA Code of Ethics and Native American culturally informed best practices.

SOCIAL JUSTICE IMPLICATIONS

In summary, the social justice elements of the impacts of power differentials, exploitation, cultural incompetence, and the injustices that Euro-American biases create are often more clearly understood by the members of special interest groups than by the general membership of a particular mental health professional organization. It is sometimes within those special interest groups that there is a greater effort to address the social justice issues related to the negative impacts of Euro-American bias on their clients. For most special interest groups social justice is a main core value.

Raising the Bar on Multiculturalism and Social Justice: Mandates vs. Aspirational Goals

In contrast to the lower priorities mainstream Euro-American psychology gives to cultural competence and social justice, cultural competence and social justice are more and more often being viewed by some professionals as being essential to all fields in mental health and education. That is, these two elements are no longer seen as specializations that are separate from general psychological competence, and they are no longer considered to be specialized professional interests. They are now viewed as two of the five main pillars of competency in psychology, social work, counseling, research, and education. That is, social justice and cultural competence are viewed as two of the five key approaches in psychology known as the "Five Forces": Psychoanalytic, Cognitive-Behavioral, Existential-Humanistic, Multicultural, and Social Justice (Ratts, D'Andrea, & Arredondo, 2004; Ratts & Pedersen, 2014). Thus, social justice is now viewed by many as essential to all practices within the fields of mental health research, education, and practice.

A Call for Action

Social justice is frequently defined more by action than by theory. Prilleltensky (1997) writes, "Discourse without action is dangerous because it creates the impression that progress is taking place when in fact only the words have changed" (Prilleltensky, 1997, p. 530). Gorski and Goodman write, "multiculturalism without a social justice framework is dangerous because it creates the illusion that our practices address the oppressions of marginalized people and the oppressiveness of hegemony, even if its attention to marginalized groups is superficial" (Gorski & Goodman, 2016, p. 2). They go on to warn against "pedagogies and practices that unintentionally reinforce and perpetuate a voyeuristic curiosity of the lives of the oppressed . . . instead of promoting individual and social responsibility for taking action with and on behalf of the oppressed" (Gorski & Goodman, 2016).

Goodman et al. (2016) stress the need for action in order to guard against the practice of what they term "passive empathy," in which the individual momentarily "feels badly for a particular individual family or group experiencing poverty, but their larger worldview and understanding of their role in the larger system of oppression is not challenged" (Goodman et al., 2016, p. 154). Other authors (Boler, 1999; Kumashiro, 2000) similarly emphasize the role of action versus discourse.

At a university teaching exercise, Cirecie West-Olatunji (2013) responded with the following scenario to students' questions about why social justice and advocacy should be incorporated into education: she instructed students to imagine encountering a client trapped on the ground under a large tree branch. She then asked them, "Which choice would you be more inclined to make? (a) Ask the client how she or he feels about being trapped under the branch. (b) Attempt to remove the branch from the client's body" (West-Olatunji, 2013, para 7). Whatever the students' response was to this question, West-Olantunji found that this scenario continued the conversation with the students about social justice, advocacy, and the importance of taking social action.

Expanding the Discussions: Unread Research, Unheard Conversations, and Untold Histories

The discussions of social justice in *Radical Psychology* will give readers many insights as to why there is often minimal social justice discussion about the harmful impacts of Euro-American worldviews on marginalized groups. It will also help explain the resistance by psychologists from the dominant culture in responding to issues of cultural competency and social justice. Whether or not professionals in the dominant culture are aware of them, historical forces still shape our current worldviews, regardless of our personal and professional demographics. We, the authors and editors of *Radical Psychology*, have found that the conflicts others may have with Eurocentric educations or mental health treatments are revealed sometimes only in private conversations that occur when dominant group members are not present. These conversations include telling the true histories of a particular group of people—stories that may differ greatly from mainstream historical statements about that group.

Dan Brown writes that history is always written by the dominant culture. He states that when two cultures clash, the dominant culture has control of how history is recorded, how minority cultures are then disparaged, and the causes of the majority are elevated (Brown, 2009).

Ronald Takaki, a historian, academic, and author whose work addresses stereotypes ascribed to non-Anglo peoples, understood that American historians do not always include the perspectives of non-Anglo peoples. In an effort to write a different view of American history from a multicultural perspective, his book, *A Different Mirror: A History of Multicultural America*, includes the voices of non-Anglo peoples including African Americans, Native Americans, Jews, Irish-Americans, Latinos, Asian Americans (Takaki, 2008). With the same intentions as Takaki, Dunbar-Ortiz' book, *An Indigenous Peoples' History of the United States* (Dunbar-Ortiz, 2014) reframes the history of the United States through the perspectives of Indigenous people.

These two books discuss the impacts of colonization, genocide, and exploitation of non-Anglo peoples. The history seen from these perspectives contradicts the historical narratives as portrayed by the dominant Euro-American culture in America. The general audience of psychologists often sees these books as multicultural, rather than general, psychology texts. The result is that many general psychologists may never be confronted with the concept that the research, education, or clinical services they provide is harmful—their lack of awareness being due to an ignorance of the biased Euro-American historical information they have accumulated.

In a documentary about the national White Bison Journey of Forgiveness undertaken by Indigenous Peoples across the United States (White Bison, no date), one of the goals of White Bison was to "tell the real story." People of color and other marginalized groups often despair of the way mainstream history has always reflected a Euro-American bias. If one only reads mainstream literature, discussions of the magnitude and extent of the acts of genocide and colonization promoted by the government and mainstream agencies are denied, minimized, or altogether omitted (Mihesuah, 2005).

At one recent university presentation on cultural competency, we (SOG and MAP) initially asked our participants, all of whom were staff and educators mandated to attend our workshop, "How does it feel to work for a university that committed genocide?" One of the attendees replied, "Genocide? We were told that our university's schools provide a free education to Native American children." They were not aware of the fact that a large number of children who attended school at that university's programs for children, by U.S. Policy, were forcibly taken from their families, died, or suffered from abuse and neglect at those schools. We then read the university's description about that "free education offered to Native American children" and discussed the fact that the authors and editors of these university statements were probably from the dominant White culture, with little or no knowledge of the atrocities that had been committed in the name of "free education." The participants were surprised to think that no Native Americans had probably been consulted before the history about their children was written.

False histories, or untold histories, as told by the dominant culture, contribute to conversations across cultures that are misinformed and harmful to both the dominant culture and underrepresented cultures. Research and academic treatises that are developed by the dominant culture intrinsically contain Western biases in research protocols, data, interpretations, and academic conclusions. The resulting distortions occur because our educational systems and social environments tend to protect and insulate Caucasians from race-based stress (DiAngelo, 2011). This insulation creates additional barriers between cultures.

As we stated in the Preface, our wish in *Radical Psychology* is to simply increase the depth and scope of conversations about multiculturalism, social justice, beneficence, and nonmaleficence. At the same time, we include many examples of Euro-American psychological research that is culturally informed and has been shown to have both reliability and validity in application to populations who hold other worldviews. We hope that readers will find it enlightening and energizing as they walk their unique paths toward increased multicultural competence and social justice.

CHAPTER SUMMARIES

The Preface and Introduction to *Radical Psychology* focus on increasing insight about historical Euro-American colonization and how it is still pervasive in relation to current psychological practices. Oftentimes we "don't know what we don't know" (Don Coyhis, personal communication, undated).

Chapter 1, "A Changing Paradigm," provides an in-depth history of colonialism as it has been experienced by consumers of services of medical and mental health professionals (including mainstream psychological organizations). The chapter suggests new conceptualizations about how social justice–savvy professionals might address this history of colonization within the profession of psychology through a deeper understanding of historical trauma, genocide, the nature of bias, the actions of mental health special interest groups, and applications of person-environment theory.

Chapter 2, "The Existential Change in Perspective in the Diagnostic and Statistics Manual, Fifth Edition (DSM-5)," includes an oral history of a time in the development of the psychological profession when the intersections among cultural factors, the development of evidence-based practices (EBPs), and the evolving *Diagnostic and Statistical Manual of Mental Disorders* (DSM, American Psychiatric Association, 1952, 1968, 1980, 1987, 1994, 2000, 2013) created conflicts among psychologists and between psychological associations and interest groups. The chapter integrates insights about integrating cultural sensitivity into services provided to ethnically and racially diverse clients. The oral history describes the major impacts cultural competency requirements have had on EBPs and the DSM formulations across revisions (American Psychiatric Association, 1952, 1968, 1980, 1987, 1994, 2000, 2013). To the editors' knowledge, this oral history has never been recorded.

Chapter 3, "The Psychologist and Allied Behavioral Health Facilitators Retrained as Humanistic Firestarters," proposes new ways to evaluate psychological practices, research, evidence-based practices, education based on traditional healing paradigms, the research the authors have done, and one of the author's roles as an Indigenous leader and visionary.

Chapter 4, "Treatment Interventions for Intimate Partner Violence in the Lives of African American Women: A Social Justice Approach" draws on the author's personal experiences, professional training, research, and peer-reviewed professional writing to relate violence to social justice initiatives.

Chapter 5, "Immigration and Social Justice," illustrates how conducting culturally informed research, developing a community outreach project, and engaging in professional leadership activities within a state psychology association work toward meeting social justice goals.

Chapter 6, "Moving Beyond Culturally Competent Services for Vietnamese Americans: Working Toward Social Justice," focuses on Asian American social justice issues. This chapter exemplifies how two people from two different backgrounds work together to develop writing that shows strong inclusivity and incorporates differing worldviews. Information about common Asian American traditional values, behaviors, and communication styles will help those from other cultures understand Asian etiquette and develop stronger rapport with clients through a deeper understanding of Asian history, communications styles, and values. It will also help researchers avoid misinterpretations of Asian American verbal and nonverbal behaviors. The case histories presented provide a deep understanding of individual, family, and cultural traumas experienced by many Asian Americans.

Beyond knowing about cultural colonization, the practice of social justice requires deep introspection by activists in order to become more aware of implicit and explicit biases and stereotypes they may hold (Boysen, 2009). Chapter 7, "Adventures in Intersectionality: The Journey of an Early Career Psychologist," illustrates the author's introspective uses of self-reflexivity, critical consciousness (Shin, 2015), and intersectionality (Shin, 2015).

Supervision issues, White fragility (DiAngelo, 2011), and identity factors (Meyers, 2016) as they affect work with diverse clientele in a Euro-American mental health agency are described.

Chapter 8, "Social Justice in Prevention Psychology: Healing with the Community Readiness Model," presents insights about decolonization initiatives as shaped by the history of the impact of Native American boarding schools and the Community Readiness Model.

Chapter 9, "The Issues of Identity, Self-Awareness, and Social Justice," focuses on social justice issues for African American males.

Chapter 10, "Decolonizing Knowledge Creation: Moving Toward the Sacred and the Liminal," documents the damage Euro-American psychologists and mental health practitioners may create when using Eurocentric thinking as a universal standard. Insights of an individual outside the system of psychology whose thinking is informed more by traditional Indigenous histories than by Eurocentric educations are shared, and the two authors' discussion of colonized knowledge creation and the need for the democratization of knowledge challenges readers to understand the perspectives of writers who have both witnessed and experienced colonization.

The Conclusion, "Moving Forward in Social Justice Initiatives," presents additional research relating to the developmental nature of social justice activism skills. Mentoring and self-efficacy are also discussed as they relate to social justice. Several social justice approaches that endorse many social justice values are also discussed.

In the Appendix, the authors of each chapter have developed a set of reflective topics to highlight the central arguments of their chapters. We hope that our research, reflections, and commentaries energize readers to begin, or walk further along, their own journeys as culturally competent, social justice advocates.

REFERENCES

Ali, A., Caplan, P. J., & Fagnant, R. (2009). Gender stereotypes in diagnostic criteria. In J. C. Chrisda & D. R. McCreary (Eds.), *Handbook of gender research in psychology: Vol. 2. Gender research in social and applied psychology* (pp. 91–109). NY: Springer-Verlag.

American Counseling Association. (2014). *ACA code of ethics*. Alexandria, VA: Author.

American Medical Association. (2016, November 15). *The code of medical ethics of the American Medical Association*. Chicago, IL: Author.

American Medical Association Editor. (2016, October). Health and social justice: The role of today's physician. *American Medical Association Journal of Ethics*, 17(1), 894–896.

American Psychiatric Association. (2013). *The principles of medical ethics* (2013 ed.). Arlington, VA: Author.

American Psychological Association. (2002, Sept; 2010, June; 2016, June). Ethical principles of psychologists and code of conduct. *American Psychologist*, 57, 1060–1073. Note: amended on February 20, 2010, effective June 1, 2010; amended again on August 3, 2016, effective June 1, 2017 (APA website, APA.org). Washington, DC: Author.

American Psychological Association. (2012). Guidelines for assessment of and intervention with persons with disabilities. *American Psychologist*, 67(1), 43–62.

American Psychological Association. (July 10, 2015). *Press release and recommended actions: Independent review cites collusion among APA individuals and defense department officials in policy on interrogation techniques*. PDF. Retrieved from APA website, apa.org.

American Psychological Association Task Force on Appropriate Therapeutic Responses to Sexual Orientation. (2011, initiated 2009, January). *Report of the task force on appropriate therapeutic responses to sexual orientation*. Washington, DC: American Psychological Association. PDF. doi:10.13140/RG2.1.3075.8004.

Arkles, G. (2015, August 11). *APA task force aims to reduce transphobia among psychologists*. Truthout. Retrieved from truth-out.org website.

Arredondo, P., & Perez, P. (2003). Expanding multicultural competence through social justice leadership. *Counseling Psychologist*, 31(3), 282–289.

Association of Black Psychologists. (2006). Licensure certification proficiency Program standards: The ABPsi ethical standards. Retrieved from http://www.abpsi.org.

Banaji, M. R., & Bhaskar, R. (2001). Implicit stereotypes and memory: The bounded rationality of social beliefs. In D. L. Schacter & E. Scarry (Eds.), *Memories, brain, and belief* (pp. 139–175). Cambridge, MA: Harvard University Press.

Banaji, M. R., & Greenwald, A. G. (2013). *Blindspot: Hidden biases of good people*. Unknown location: Delacorte Press.

Boler, R. A. (1999). *Feeling power: Emotions and education*. NY: Routledge.

Bowman, C. D., Hunter, J. D., Dill, J. S., & Juelfs-Swanson, M. (2012). *Culture of American Families executive report*. Charlottesville, VA: Institute of Advanced Studies In Culture, University of Virginia. Retrieved from http://www.iasc-culture.org/survey_archives/IASC_CAF_ExecReport.pdf.

Brown, D. (2009). *The DaVinci code*. New York, NY: Anchor Books (Knopf Doubleday).

Caplan, P. J., & Cosgrove L. (Eds.). (2004). *Bias in psychiatric diagnosis: A project of the Association for Women in Psychology*. NY: Jason Aronson (subsidiary of Rowman & Littlefield Publishing Group).

Chung, R. C.-Y, & Bemak, F. P. (2012). *Social justice counseling: The next steps beyond multiculturalism*. Thousand Oaks, CA: Sage.

Davis, H. R., Fitzpatrick, S., Garcia, D., Maynard, E., & Sultan, N. (2016, January). *Two doors: How religion and psychotherapy address suffering*. Houston, TX: University of St. Thomas.

Desportes Bowman, C., Davison Hunter, J., Dill, J. S., & Jeulfs-Swanson, M. (2012, November 15). *Culture of American families*. Charlottesville: Institute for Advanced Studies in Culture. Retrieved from http://iasc-culture.org/survey_archives/IASC_CAF_ExecReport.pdf.

DiAngelo, R. (2011). White fragility. *International Journal of Critical Pedagogy*, 3(3), 54–70.

Dingfelder, S. F. (2005, January). Closing the gap for Latino patients. *Monitor*, 36(1), 58.

Dunbar-Ortiz, R. (2014). *An Indigenous peoples' history of the United States*. Boston, MA: Beacon Press.

Dunn, D. S., & Andrews, E. E. (2015). Person-first and identity-first language: Developing psychologists' cultural competence using disability language. *American Psychologist*, 70(3), 255–264.

Duran, E. (2000). *Buddha in redface*. Lincoln, NE: IUniverse.

Duran, E. (2006). *Healing the soul wound: Counseling with American Indians and other Native peoples*. Columbia University: Teachers College Press.

Duran, E., & Duran, B. (1995). *Native American postcolonial psychology*. Albany, NY: State University of New York.

Duran, E., & Firehammer, J. (2015). Story sciencing and analyzing the silent narrative between words: Counseling research from an Indigenous perspective. In R. D. Goodman & P. C. Gorski (Eds.), *Decolonizing "multicultural counseling" through social justice* (pp. 85–97). NY: Springer Science + Business Media.

Galtung, J. (1969). Violence, peace, and peace research. *Journal of Peace Research*, 6(3), 167–191.

Gamson, J. (2000). Sexualities, queer theory, and qualitative research. In N. Denzin & Y. Lincoln (Eds.), *Handbook of qualitative research* (2nd ed.) (pp. 347–365). Thousand Oaks, CA: SAGE.

Garcia, M. A. (2014, December). *Communiqué* Implications of the Society of Indian Psychologists' (SIP) commentary on the APA Code of Ethics are many, broad, and deep. Retrieved from APA website, apa.org.

García, M. A., & Tehee, M. (2014; 2002, Amended, June 1, 2010). *Society of Indian psychologists commentary on the American Psychological Association's APA Ethical Principles of Psychologists and Code of Conduct*. Society of Indian Psychologists, OEMA Resources and Publications.

Glassgold, J. *Report of the American Psychological Association Task Force: Appropriate Therapeutic Responses to Sexual Orientation*. (PDF). Retrieved 10/12/2013. APA website: apa.org.

Goodman, R. D., & Gorski, P. C. (Eds.). (2015). *Decolonizing "multicultural" counseling through social justice*. NY: Springer.

Goodman, R. D., Williams, J. M., Chung, R. C., Talleyrand, R. M., Douglass A. M., McMahon, G., & Bemak, F. (2016). Decolonizing traditional pedagogies and practices in counseling and psychology education: A move towards social justice and action. In R. D. Goodman & P. C. Gorski (Eds.), *Decolonizing "multicultural" counseling through social justice* (pp. 147–164). NY: Springer.

Gorski, P. C., & Goodman, R. D. (2016). Introduction: Toward a decolonized multicultural counseling and psychology. In R. D. Goodman & P. C. Gorski (Eds.), *Decolonizing "multicultural" counseling through social justice* (pp. 1–10). NY: Springer.

Grayshield, L., & Mihecoby, A. (2010, Fall). Indigenous says of knowing as a philosophical base for the promotion of peace and justice in counseling education and psychology. *Journal for Social Action in Counseling and Psychology*, 2(2), 1–16.

Haldeman, D. C. (1991). Sexual orientation conversion therapy for gay men and lesbians: A scientific examination (PDF). In J. Gonsiorek & J. Weinrich (Eds.), *Homosexuality: Research implications for public policy*. Newbury Park, California: Sage Publications, Inc. ISBN 0-8039-3764-4.

Hayes, P. A. (2016). *Assessing cultural complexities in practice, assessment, diagnosis, and therapy* (3rd ed.). Washington, DC: American Psychological Association.

Horney, K. (1973). *Feminine psychology*. NY: Norton.

Hudak, J., & Giammattei, S. (2014, March). Doing family: Decentering heteronormativity in "marriage" and "family" therapy. In *Critical topics and family therapy: APTA monograph series. Family Therapy* (pp. 105–115). SpringerBriefs. doi:10.1007/978-3-319-03248-1_12.

Jun, H. (2010). *Social justice, multicultural counseling, and practice: Beyond a conventional approach*. Thousand Oaks, CA: Sage.

Klauer, K. C., Musch, J., & Naumer, B. (2000). On belief bias in syllogistic reasoning. *Psychological Review*, 107(4), 852–884. doi:10.1037/0033295X.107.4.852.

Kumashiro, K. K. (2000, Fall). Teaching and learning through desire, crisis, and difference: Perverted reflections on anti-oppressive education. *Radical Teacher*, 58, 6–11.

Lawrence, J. (2000). The Indian health service and the sterilization of native American women. *American Indian Quarterly*, 24(3), 400–419.

Lee, D. L., Rosen, A. D., & Burns, V. (2013, January). Over a half-century encapsulated: A multicultural content analysis of the Journal of Counseling Psychology, 1954–2009. *Journal of Counseling Psychology*, 60(1), 154–161. doi:1037/a0031002.

Lilienfeld, S. O. (2007). Psychological treatments that cause harm. *Association for Psychological Science*, 2(1), 53–70.

Maccoun, R. J. (1998). Biases in the interpretation and use of research results. *Annual Review of Psychology*, 49, 259–287.

Maines, R. P. (1998). *The technology of orgasm: "Hysteria," the vibrator, and women's sexual satisfaction*. Baltimore: The Johns Hopkins University Press.

Mihesuah, D. A. (2005). *So you want to write about American Indians? A guide for scholars, writers, and students*. Lincoln, NE: University of Nebraska Press.

Morse, G. S., & Blume, A. (2013, September). *Does the APA Ethics Code work for us? Members of ethnic minority associations examine the APA Ethics Code's relevance to people of color*. American Psychological Association Communiqué. OEMA Resources and Publications, September, 2013.

National Association of Social Workers (socialworkers.org). National Association of Social Workers Website (socialworkers.org).

National Education Association. (2013). Code of ethics of the education profession. Retrieved from NEA website: nea.org.

NAFSA (originally National Association of Foreign Student Advisors). (Adopted 2009). NAFSA's statement of ethical principles. Retrieved from nafsa.org.

National Latina/o Psychological Association. Retrieved from www.nlpa.ws.

Oswald, M. E., & Grosjean, S. L. (2004). Confirmation bias. [Chapter]. In R. F. Pohl (Ed.), *Cognitive illusions: A handbook on fallacies and biases in thinking, judgement, and memory*. Hove and NY: Psychology Press. doi:10.13140/2.1.2068.0614.

Patel, N. A. (2015). Health and social justice: The role of today's physician. *AMA Journal of Ethics*, 17(10), 894–896.

Prilleltensky, I. (1997). Values assumptions, and practices: Assessing the moral implications of psychological discourse action. *American Psychologist*, 52(5), 517–535.

Pronin, E., & Kugler, M. B. (2007). Valuing thoughts, ignoring behavior: The introspection illusion as a source of the bias blind spot. *Journal of Experimental Social Psychology*, 43(4), 565–578. doi:10.1016/j.jesp.2006.05.11.

Ratts, M., D'Andrea, M., & Arredondo, P. (2004, July). Social justice counseling: Fifth "force" in field. *Counseling Today*, 47(1), 28–30.

Ratts, M. J., & Pedersen, P. B. (2014). *Counseling for multiculturalism and social justice: Integration, theory, and application*. Alexandria, VA: American Counseling Association.

Sharpe, V. A., & Faden, A. I. (1998). *Medical harm: Historical, conceptual, and ethical dimensions of iatrogenic illness*. Cambridge, UK: Cambridge University Press.

Snodgrass, J. L., McCreight, D., & McFee, M. R. (2014, Dec.). To whom shall I refer? *Counseling Today*, 57(6), 54–59.

Steering Committee of Psychologists for Social Responsibility (PsySR), July 13, 2015.

Sue, D. W., Capodilupo, C. M., Torino, G. C., Bucceri, J. M., Holder, A. M. B., Nadal, K. L., & Esquiline, M. (2007). Racial microaggressons in everyday life: Implications for clinical practice. *American Psychologist*, 62(4), 271–286.

Takaki, R. (2008). *A different mirror: A history of multicultural America* (Rev. ed.). NY: Little, Brown, and Company.

Tick, E. (2005). *War and the soul: Healing our nation's veterans from post-traumatic stress disorder*. Wheaton, IL: Quest Books.

Vasquez, M. (2012). Psychology and social justice: Why we do what we do. *American Psychologist*, 67(5), 337–346. doi:10.1037/a0029232.

Walker, D. F., Courtois, C. A., & Aten, J. D. (2015). *Spiritually oriented psychotherapy for trauma*. Washington, DC: American Psychological Association.

Wendt, D. C., Gone, J. P., & Nagata, D. K. (2015a). Potentially harmful therapy and multicultural counseling: Extending the conversation. *The Counseling Psychologist*, 43(3), 393–403. doi:10.1177/00/10000/5576801.

Wendt, D. C., Gone, J. P., & Nagata, D. K. (2015b). Potentially harmful therapy and multicultural counseling: Bridging two disciplinary discourses. *The Counseling Psychologist*, 43(3), 334–358. doi:10.1177/0011000014548280.

West-Olantunji, C. W. (2013, September). Returning to our roots: Embracing social action in counseling. *Counseling Today*, 56(3), 5, 51.

White Bison, Inc. (n. d.). The journey of forgiveness. Retrieved from YouTube, www.whitebison.org. Also available by emailing info@whitebison.org for DVD.

White Bison, Inc. (2002, 2006). *The red road to wellbriety: In the native American way*. Colorado Springs, CO: Coyhis Publishing & Consulting Services.

Chapter 1

A Changing Paradigm

Susan O. Gelberg and Mathew A. Poteet

POSTCOLONIAL PSYCHOLOGY: DEPTH vs. BREADTH

It is impossible for this book to cover the full scope of the many social justice issues, multicultural counseling factors, and racial, cultural, ethnic, and intersecting identities. This chapter takes a narrow focus, highlighting the impact of a history of genocide, exploitation, and colonization on a number of marginalized, underserved, or vulnerable populations in the United States. In this chapter, we share our knowledge of the research behind, and clinical insights about, the populations with whom we have the most experience. We believe that the in-depth study of even one particular culture leads to new learning that can be applied to developing services, conducting research, or teaching people from other cultures and worldviews.

HOW PSYCHOLOGY STILL COLONIZES

In order to address the decolonization issues related to the harm that Euro-American contemporary psychology, research, social work, education, and counseling can impose on individuals who do not endorse the values of the dominant culture, professionals and other mental health professionals should be trained to recognize elements of their professional work that are based on biases that still reflect Euro-American colonization. Goodman and Gorski (2015) write that psychology is still colonizing when it

- denies culture,
- attempts to destroy culture,
- belittles and insults cultural values and practices,

- shows only a token acceptance and accommodation, or
- reflects control of expression of cultural values within the dominating structure of the colonizer.

Goodman and Gorski (2015) describe the complex relationships between postcolonial psychology and social justice. They emphasize that the goal of all psychologists should be to work toward being "multicultural social justice psychologists." In their book, *Decolonizing "Multicultural" Counseling through Social Justice*, they write that social justice and multiculturalism

- should not be separate fields of study but should instead be integrated into all disciplines and courses,
- challenges the Euro-cis-male-, Christian-, or hetero-centric norms of counseling and psychology,
- deconstructs sociopolitical and socioeconomic contexts,
- includes environmental as well as intrapsychic focuses,
- avoids simplistic identity development,
- avoids overgeneralizing,
- views clients as objects of oppression versus passivity,
- includes concepts of "white supremacy" along with "white privilege,"
- is strengths versus deficit oriented,
- is interventionist,
- is highly political, and
- informs psychological, academic, political, and ethical stances.

(Goodman & Gorski, 2015)

If mental health practitioners are to reflect the abovementioned qualities of postcolonial psychology, they must be able to recognize instances in which their Eurocentric values, beliefs, and actions are inconsistent with the postcolonial qualities endorsed by Goodman and Gorski (2015). The Introduction discussed the impact of Eurocentric biases on the effectiveness of psychology services. This is further complicated in that Banaji and Bhaskar state that "Memory and belief . . . operate . . . outside the actor's awareness" (Banaji & Bhaskar, 2001, p. 140); Jun (2010) also writes, "It is possible that some scholars, practitioners, and researchers are not aware of their ethnocentric biases or of inconsistencies between their behavior and their knowledge" (Jun, 2010, p. 5).

In *Blindspot: Hidden Biases of Good People*, Banaji and Greenwald (2013) use the Implicit Association Test (Greenwald, McGhee, & Schwartz, 1998), to challenge the perception, "I know my own mind. I am able to assess others in a fair and accurate way." In their book, they focus on hidden biases related to age, gender, race ethnicity, religion, social class, sexuality, disability status, and nationality (Banaji & Greenwald, 2013). Thus, the process of self-examination of bias becomes much more problematic if one's biases are often unconscious.

POSTCOLONIAL PSYCHOLOGY AS A PARADIGM SHIFT

In order to address the abovementioned issues, Euro-American worldviews about mental health must be seen in new ways. The term *paradigm shift* was originally used to refer to a fundamental change in the practices, beliefs, and worldviews of a particular natural scientific discipline. Paradigm shifts are types of scientific revolutions (Kuhn, 1962, 1970, 1996, 2012). In the field of natural science, the transition from theories of Newtonian gravity and Einstein's theory of general relativity exemplify paradigm changes.

The term "paradigm shift" is now used to describe profound changes in the social sciences such as the paradigm shift that occurred in psychology when it moved away from a disease model and evolved into a strengths-based model. A paradigm shift also occurred when psychology moved away from focusing solely on risk factors to placing more emphasis on the role of client resilience in mental health well-being. Social justice and multicultural counseling help professionals see that paradigm shifts should include a stronger consideration of social justice along with multicultural competence in all mainstream psychology and educational topics.

Thus, the notion that "there is only one way, the contemporary Western Euro American psychology way, to see life, mental health, and healing," is a worldview in need of a paradigm shift. In working toward that paradigm shift, the authors of *Radical Psychology* strive to describe what the world is like for a number of individuals and groups from non-Western cultures and worldviews. We are calling for a paradigm shift that includes viewing culturally approved practices as being on an equal standing with Western evidence-based practices. In order to understand the need for this paradigm shift, we first focus on the limitations of Western-based worldviews.

WESTERN EVIDENCE-BASED PSYCHOLOGICAL PRACTICES

In 2006, the American Psychological Task Force on Evidence-Based Practices published an overview of guidelines for recommended best practices from the perspective of Euro-American contemporary mainstream Western psychology

(Levant, 2005; APA Task Force on Evidence-Based Practice, 2006). In Western psychology, evidence-based practices have become key features of research, health-care systems, and health-care policies (McHugh & Barlow, 2010).

Two of the many hallmarks of evidence-based practices are, first, the reliance on Western scientific research methods; second, a clinical consensus about the efficacy and clinical utility of psychological interventions (Stout & Hayes, 2004). Evidence-based treatments often use randomized controlled experiments in order to evaluate the effectiveness of specific psychological treatments for different psychiatric diagnoses (American Psychological Association Task Force on Evidence-Based Practice (2006). A second hallmark, clinical consensus about whether or not an intervention reflects an evidence-based practice, is achieved through the judgments of individuals who hold Western-based psychological credentials and who tend to hold Western worldviews about mental health (Stout & Hayes, 2004).

Limitations and Controversies of Evidence-Based Practices

Underrepresentation and Funding Issues

As simple and clear-cut as those two hallmarks for evidence-based research seem, there are factors that complicate the application of these principles to people with nondominant worldviews. The two hallmarks described earlier best reflect services for what Heinrich, Heine, and Norenzayan (2010) describe by using the acronym *WEIRD* (Western, educated, industrialized, rich, and democratic). This acronym refers to the set of clients who hold Euro-American worldviews. McHugh and Barlow (2010) discuss the need to consider the impact of individual differences in culture, ethnicity, age, and other individual factors on the efficacy of a particular treatment.

In addition to the difficulties in integrating cultural concerns into evidence-based research, stringent Euro-American governmental, health care, funding, or educational policies about how evidence-based research is proposed, funded, and evaluated automatically lead to still more sampling biases. Furthermore, because psychological research is often conducted in university settings, the particular restrictive demographics of the university student population results in difficulties in applying the reliability, validity, and generalization of research results to nonstudent populations. Thus, much of the quantitative research normed samples backing evidence-based research may not include consideration of the worldviews of underrepresented groups.

Relevance

Referring to the complexities of imposing Western psychological worldviews on marginalized people, Norcross, Hogan, and Koocher (2008) pose the question of whether the use of evidence-based practices that have not been normed on minority or marginalized practices even qualify as being evidence based. Sloan and Toporek (2007) echo those sentiments: "We do not believe that sustaining and expanding the business of counseling and psychology as currently constituted will play a tangible role in the achievement of social justice or the construction of peace and social justice either locally or globally. Second, we are concerned that some practices associated with counseling and psychology are worse than ineffective and are, in fact, either part of the problem or do direct harm" (Sloan & Toporek, 2007, p. 1).

Credentialing Issues

A third hallmark of evidence-based practices is the requirement that evidence-based treatments are to be administered by individuals who are seen by Euro-American institutions as "clinically competent" to providing evidence-based treatments. Western professional credentials including formal training in evidence-based concepts and holding a professional credential awarded by an accredited Western educational institution (Hayes, 2005). Holding professional licensures is also viewed by Euro-American institutions as reflecting professional competence.

The abovementioned evidence-based credentials may differ from the perspectives of expertise as seen through the eyes of people who hold other cultural worldviews. For example, Thomason (2011) surveyed mental health professionals who worked primarily with Native American clients. Half of the participants stated that Native counselors were more effective with Native American clients than were non-Native counselors. Thus, the cultural backgrounds of the counselors were essential in providing credibility and expertise in Native American mental health programs.

Thus, in Thomason's study, the culture of the provider was highly crucial in determining provider credibility for more than half of the providers who work with Native American clients. The providers also emphasized that non-Native counselors should never lead or perform tribal spiritual methods or ceremonies, as these must be led by Native counselors only. They recommended that in order to increase expertise and credibility with Native clients, non-Native counselors should develop strong relationships with the Native community and Native elders. Other suggestions were made as to how non-Natives can develop cultural competency skills while not exceeding the boundaries of their competence. All of these recommendations reflect Indigenous characteristics that increase the credibility of the providers in the eyes of Native clients or Native mental health agencies, and these provider qualities differ significantly from Western psychological standards for clinical expertise (Thomason, 2011).

Emphasis on Treatment Manuals

Another hallmark of evidence-based practices is the recommendation for the development of standardized manuals for each evidence-based intervention. These manuals, according to evidence-based hallmarks, should have been subjected to rigorous Western scientific research protocols such as randomized clinical trials in order to evaluate the validity the treatment manual has for specific populations (Duncan & Miller, 2005; Goldfried & Wolfe, 1998). Chambless and Ollendick (2001) reviewed a number of research publications and reported that 108 manualized treatments had good empirical support. Duncan and Miller (2005) also acknowledged the positive roles that manuals have in enhancing internal validity, increasing treatment integrity, providing ways to improve supervision and training, and enhancing the technical competence of those who provide the intervention. Duncan and Miller (2005) did, however, also cite a number of studies that concluded that there was *no* significant relationship between the use of treatment manuals and the intervention's outcome. This calls into question the universal assumption that the evidence-based recommendation of having manuals for a specific intervention always increases the efficacy of that intervention.

Client Factors and Treatment Relationships

Duncan and Miller (2005) found that individual client factors as well as the quality of the treatment relationship were more powerful in contributing to positive clinical outcomes than were any particular types of intervention. They recommended that more research should be conducted in order to investigate the efficacy of evidence-based practices for underrepresented groups. As examples of the recommended type of research Duncan and Miller (2005) suggest are articles by Schaie (1993) and Grant (1996). Schaie (1993) focused on the difficulties of ageist language in research. Grant (1996) studied the impact of ageism on clinical interventions. Schaie (1993) and Grant (1996) addressed the roles that stereotypes about the young and the elderly play in increasing ageist biases in psychological research.

CONTRASTING MODELS: CULTURALLY SENSITIVE TREATMENTS AND BEST PRACTICES

The efficacy, relevance, and appropriateness of the use of evidence-based treatments with those who are not Caucasian, middle class, heterosexual—or who are otherwise different in some way from the mainstream—are controversial issues in psychology. To minimize the limitations of evidence-based practices, Roysicar (2009) proposed a model, termed "culturally sensitive treatment" (CST), as an alternative to evidence-based practices. Roysicar (2009) provided a general overview for enhancing cultural competency for different populations. *Cultural Adaptations: Tools for Evidence-Based Practice with Diverse Populations* (Bernal & Rodriguez, 2012) integrates multicultural concepts with evidence-based principles through reporting culturally adapted treatments that take into account the worldviews of a number of ethnocultural populations.

A cultural competency model for Indigenous peoples, developed by McNeil et al. (2006), includes a consideration of cultural history, the types of legal issues that occur between groups of a particular culture and the dominant culture, barriers to health care, ethical considerations, provider characteristics, and communication issues when developing, implementing, and researching treatment services for Indigenous peoples.

Backgrounds of the Authors, Researchers, and Theory Developers of Evidence-Based Practices

Critiques of evidence-based treatments are based on the fact that the treatments reflect the Euro-American worldviews of the individuals who conceptualize, develop, administer, and evaluate these treatments. In order to correct for a Euro-American bias, for example with Indigenous clients, all of the chapters in *Mental Health Care for Urban Indians: Clinical Insights from Native Practitioners* (Witco, 2006) are written from Native perspectives. The authors of *Cultural Adaptations: Tools for Evidence-Based Practice with Diverse Populations* (Bernal & Rodriguez, 2012) include a diversity of worldviews in their writing.

Historical Factors

Euro-American psychologists often underestimate the impact of historical factors that are crucial to understanding the current needs of vulnerable populations. In order to fill this informational gap for those who provide professional services to, or conduct research about, Indigenous clients, Witco's *Mental Health Care for Urban Indians: Clinical Insights from Native Practitioners* (Witco, 2006) provides Indigenous mental health providers' insights about, and extensive coverage of, the historical backgrounds of urban American-Indian clients. The book describes specific urban American-Indian treatment considerations and suggests new directions for working with urban American-Indians. Since all chapters are written by American-Indian scholars, researchers, and mental health practitioners working in Indian communities, the book is viewed as highly credible by both Indigenous clients and professionals working with Urban Indians. Although the book focuses on best practices for Native Americans, the principle of seeking clinical resources that have been developed, provided, and researched by individuals who hold the cultural worldviews of the population or group under study is applicable to other marginalized, underrepresented, or non-Euro-American populations.

One resource that offers insights to Euro-American psychologists regarding how non-Euro-American qualities and worldviews can provide the benchmarks for validity, reliability, and credibility in the eyes of the population being served is the set of principles developed for Indigenous peoples in the state of Oregon, termed *Tribal Best Practices* (Cruz, n.d.). Oregon's Department of Health Services has accepted these principles as an alternate set of standards to substitute for the requirements of evidence-based treatments for Native clients. These tribal best practices, however, are not widely known by Euro-American psychologists in Oregon (Duran, 2013). Because of this, traditional Native clients who are seen by Euro-American psychologists in Oregon may be given treatments that meet potentially biased Eurocentric evidence-based practice standards rather than tribal best practice standards. The services they receive still may reflect Euro-American biases that are potentially harmful.

Credibility and Client Trust Issues with Western Psychology

The cultural best practices for different populations may be unknown to dominant culture Western psychologists. Even when they attempt to integrate culture into their treatments, if they are not working with cultural experts to develop their programs, those attempts of Euro-American mental health providers may still result in harm to underserved populations.

Each culture has its own traditional healing practices that may have more credibility to many individuals from that culture than Euro-American Western psychological practices might have. It may be difficult for Euro-American psychologists to respect those alternate healing worldviews, and they may fail to understand that the contemporary mainstream Western psychological services they offer have less credibility with underserved populations than the services provided by that culture's traditional healers (Duran, 2000).

Psychologists must be aware of the pervasive, automatic imposition of evidence-based practices by Euro American providers onto people who hold other worldviews. While Native tribes are not against outcomes showing that some contemporary Western psychological programs are effective, due to specific Euro-American, government-issued policies, such as the Dawes Allotment Act, the Boarding School Systems, the Relocation Policy, and Termination Policy, and the sterilization of Native American women, concepts like Western "research," "science," and "studies" have produced resentment, fear, and distrust among the tribes (Cruz, n.d.).

One of the authors of *Radical Psychology* is a highly respected, Native American spiritual leader and visionary in Indian Country. When this elder was an adolescent, he visited with a counselor who attempted to conduct career counseling with him. The young man felt that the counselor's recommendations about his career options invalidated his own career interests through suggesting career goals that reflected Euro American stereotypes about Native Americans. After he heard about his grandson's visit with the White counselor, his grandfather suggested that he perform the Indigenous spiritual practice of smudging with sage to remove the negative energy of that career counseling session. This counselor probably had no conception of the harm that his biased career counseling recommendations had for this young Native man. His grandfather suggested that a spiritual cleansing would remove those harmful effects of "career-counseling-gone-wrong" on the young man.

PSYCHOLOGY'S RESPONSE TO PSYCHOLOGICAL COLONIZATION: THE ISSUE OF APOLOGIES

Australia

We have already stated that the current use of Euro-American treatments with individuals who hold other worldviews reflects a type of psychological colonization. Understanding that Indigenous peoples in Australia also experienced psychological colonization, the Australian Psychological Society recently printed a public apology to Indigenous peoples. The full apology is printed here because it captures the experience of populations in other countries that have also experienced European colonization.

Apology to Aboriginal and Torres Strait Islander People from the Australian Psychological Society

> Disparities between Aboriginal and Torres Strait Islander Australians and other Australians on a range of different factors are well documented. Aboriginal and Torres Strait Islander people experience much higher rates of psychological distress, chronic disease, and incarceration than other Australians. They manage many more stressors on a daily basis and, although suicide did not exist in their cultures prior to colonization it is now a tragically inflated statistic. The fact that these disparities exist and are long standing in a first world nation is deplorable and unacceptable.
>
> As we understand these challenging issues in relation to wellbeing and health, it is very important that we tell the stories of the strengths and resilience of Aboriginal and Torres Strait Islander peoples and communities.

> Aboriginal and Torres Strait Islander people are the proud custodians of the longest surviving cultures on our planet. With this in mind, Aboriginal and Torres Strait Islander peoples' resilience and resourcefulness could make a significant and positive impact on Australian society should they have the opportunity to contribute routinely in their areas of expertise. (Australian Psychology Society, 2016. Retrieved from public website)

The American Psychological Association

Recently, several individuals from the American Psychological Association (APA) made a formal statement at the 2017 National Multicultural Conference and Summit (Portland, Oregon), that included an apology that was made to representatives of the Society of Indian Psychologists. The apology was for the harm Western colonization psychological paradigms have imposed on Indigenous People in the United States. There has, however, been no formal apology offered by the APA for its history of colonization.

ONE PSYCHOLOGIST'S DECOLONIZING EFFORTS

Native American Postcolonial Psychology (Duran & Duran, 1995) is a classic in the field of Indigenous psychology. Its discussion of how psychology is still colonizing Indigenous people is highly relevant to both Native and non-Native populations. The book offers an alternate set of guidelines to help Euro-American psychologists understand how their current practices may reflect colonization. This book also discusses ethical principles that can also be applied to create culturally informed services for clients who hold other types of worldviews.

One of the authors of *Native American Postcolonial Psychology* (Duran & Duran, 1995), Eduardo Duran, is a Native American psychologist who was trained in a Euro-American Western institution. His later exposure to non-Western healing beliefs, tribal communities, the mentoring of an elder, and deep spiritual experiences dramatically changed his practice as a psychologist. One of Duran's books, *Buddha in Redface* (Duran, 2000) discusses that transition into cultural competency. The book includes cross-cultural dialogues that delve into topics that are sometimes ignored or disparaged by contemporary Western psychologists but are crucial elements of effective Native healing worldviews and practices. In this book, Duran discusses his frustration as an Indigenous psychologist by the limitations of the Eurocentric paradigms of the Western Euro American educational institution he attended. The principles Duran uses to evaluate Euro-American psychological practices can be considered for the evaluation of the relevance and efficacy of Western programs that are imposed on other minority, marginalized, or non-Anglo populations.

Duran's book, *Healing the Soul Wound: Counseling with American Indians and Other Native Peoples* (Duran, 2006), provides a model for the incorporation of the principles he writes about in *Native American Postcolonial Psychology* (Duran & Duran, 1995) and *Buddha in Redface* (Duran, 2000) into a comprehensive treatment for substance abuse. *Healing the Soul Would: Counseling with American Indians and Other Native Peoples* (Duran, 2006) is also highly relevant to psychologists who seek to develop non-Anglo treatment programs for psychological issues or concerns aside from substance abuse.

In their chapter, "Story Sciencing and Analyzing the Silent Narrative Between Words: Counseling Research from an Indigenous Perspective," Duran and Firehammer (2015) apply those same principles in proposing a research model that reflects cultural research practices that are relevant for those populations that do not hold Euro-American worldviews. While the principles that Duran and Firehammer (2015) propose are not yet widely used in research designs developed by contemporary Western psychological research scientists, the principles are consistent with Tribal Best Practices (Cruz, n.d.) and thus meet all of the Indigenous standards for research. This research design is also highly relevant to research about, and clinical services provided to non-Native populations.

Eduardo Duran's proposal for the greater use of narratives is a recommendation for the use of more qualitative measures in research. Qualitative methods can be used to "promote equity, access, participation and harmony for culturally diverse populations" (Lyons et al., 2013). Wendt and Gone (2016) report on a case study using a qualitative analysis that investigates the client's help-seeking behaviors, the incorporation of cultural perspectives and therapeutic agents that are incorporated into treatment, and the degree of willingness of the client and provider to discuss spiritual issues. This narrative clinical study exemplifies many of the principles that characterize culturally sensitive research at its best.

COMPETENCE ISSUES FOR PSYCHOLOGISTS

Supervision Issues and Boundaries of Competence

The APA's Ethical Code, Section 2.01, Boundaries of Competence (American Psychological Association, 2002, 2010, 2016), states: "Psychologists provide services, teach and conduct research with populations and in areas only within the boundaries of their competence, based on their education, training, supervised experience, consultation, study or professional experience." When diversity factors affect the efficacy of treatment or research, this standard states that psychologists "obtain the training, experience, consultation or supervision necessary to ensure the competence of their services."

Due to the increased diversity of psychology research and clinical practices, psychologists are likely to encounter clients who reflect many sources of intersecting diversity factors including culture, national origin, military status, geographic region, ethnicity, age, sexual orientation, socioeconomic status, physical ability, acquired disabilities, developmental disabilities, spirituality, religion, Indigenous heritage, national identity, primary language, gender expression, gender roles, gender expectations, gender relationships, race, ethnicity (Hays, 2008), and diversity associated with intersectionality (Collins & Bilge, 2016; Gallardo & McNeill, 2009). Obviously, it is impossible for any psychologist to become competent in providing cultural best practices for clients whose backgrounds reflect these many forms of diversity.

Inclusion Issues

It is our view that rather than seeking to develop all of the multicultural skills necessary for implementation of a particular cultural best practice—a goal that is impossible to fully meet due to the infinite nature of diversity elements—psychologists should instead apply the principle of inclusion in order to ensure that the developers, administrators, and researchers for those services will include members of the particular cultural group who have lived and been immersed in, those particular worldviews and cultures. It is crucial that these cultural elders have the power and respect equal to that of Euro American researchers, clinicians, and educators.

Limitations of Western Credentialing

One complication in following the principles of inclusion is that individuals who are seen by a particular cultural group as experts and as culturally competent may not have all of the Western credentials evidence-based practices require. In order to practice full inclusion, standards for hiring providers, researchers, and educators must be modified to reflect other forms of non-Western expertise. This requires that licensing agencies, educational institutions, federal and state institutions, and other Western credentialing agencies increase their multicultural competency through the inclusion of staff who hold non-Western credentials of expertise with underserved populations. This would counteract the Euro-American practice of developing research, practices, and theories about specific cultural groups without the direct involvement and participation of members of that group ("Nothing about us without us—nihil de nobis, sine nobis").

Again, Bias

As we have stated throughout the Preface and Introduction, biases are inherent in all cultures and worldviews. The unique biases of individual psychologists affect the quality of treatments offered to underserved populations. *Bias in Psychiatric Diagnosis,* (Caplan & Cosgrove, 2004) reviews Euro-American biases that are inherent in psychiatric diagnoses. Caplan and Cosgrove discuss the ways in which contemporary Western biases of psychiatric and psychological researchers and clinicians can lead to discrimination in academia, the health-care system, the legal system, and governmental agencies. Caplan and Cosgrove's book discusses some of the many forms that bias takes against the severely mentally ill, the elderly, the poor, children, individuals diagnosed with learning disabilities, women, rural women, those with an Axis II disorder such as histrionic personality disorder, people with posttraumatic stress disorder (PTSD), and individuals with eating disorders.

Non-Euro-American mental health professionals often see inherent, deep biases of the earlier *Diagnostic and Statistical Disorders Manual-IV-TR* (American Psychiatric Association, 2000), the "Bible" for diagnoses made by psychiatrists, psychologists, and other mental health professionals. Ali, Caplan, and Fagnant (2009) discuss the gender biases that characterize diagnostic criteria in psychiatric diagnoses. Assessment biases are discussed by Hill, Robbins, and Pace (2012), who discuss the ethical issues of using the Minnesota Multiphasic Personality Inventory-2 (MMPI-2; Butcher, Dahlstrom, Graham, Tellegen, & Kaemmer, 1989) with different cultural groups. They recommend additional empirical validation research for diverse groups in order to address test bias.

Inclusion and Collaboration

Gone and Calf Looking (2015) report on one model for interdisciplinary community-based collaboration between one investigator, who is an academic research psychologist, and another investigator, who has strong non-Western credentials as the director of a treatment center for a tribal nation. The article illustrates how psychologists can effectively collaborate with others who have different types of expertise when developing interventions for Native Peoples. The model is also relevant to working with those who do not hold contemporary Euro-American worldviews.

"Evidence-Based Practices with Ethnic Minorities: Strange Bedfellows No More" (Morales & Norcross, 2010), introduces six papers in the *Journal of Clinical Psychology in Session* that report on Euro-American Western research designs that have been modified using cultural best practices for African Americans, American-Indians, Alaska Natives, underserved populations experiencing poverty, Chinese immigrants, and an individual with intersecting identities: a gay Latino in a Spanish-speaking environment. Morales and Norcross (2010) include these studies in order to exemplify how cultural sensitivity and inclusiveness can be effectively implemented into clinical encounters with underserved populations.

Further Strengthening Cultural Competency

In addition to the mandate for Euro-American psychologists to practice inclusion by collaborating with colleagues who can challenge Euro-American evidence-based practice protocols, psychologists should continue to strengthen general cultural competency skills. Suggested resources for this purpose include *Counseling for Multiculturalism and Social Justice: Integration, Theory, and Application* (Ratts & Pedersen, 2014), *Internationalizing Multiculturalism: Expanding professional competencies in a globalized world* (Lowman, 2013), *Mental Health: Culture, Race, and Ethnicity—A Supplement to Mental Health: A Report of the Surgeon General* (U.S. Department of Health and Human Services, Substance Abuse and Mental Health Services Administration, Center for Mental Health Services, 2001), and for educators: *Meeting the psychoeducational needs of minority students: Evidence-Based guidelines for school psychologists and other school personnel* (Frisby, 2013). For researchers, *Foundations in Multicultural Psychology: Research to Inform Effective Practice* (Smith & Trimble, 2016) provides a synthesis of research findings that focus on culturally informed practices. Ratts (2011) discusses multicultural counseling as it interacts with social justice.

GENOCIDE AND CULTURAL COMPETENCY

It is well known that America has historically mistreated people who do not hold mainstream worldviews of those who are Christian, male, cis-gender, heterosexual, middle class, middle age, and able-bodied. Psychologists often ignore or minimize those historical factors of mistreatment. In the Preface and Introduction, we wrote about some of the ways that America has historically failed to protect, harmed, exploited, and/or committed genocide in its government policies toward people such as Native Americans, Alaska Natives, Hispanics, Latina/os, Asian Americans, Africans and African Americans, women, the queer community (LGBTQQIAAP—lesbian, gay, bisexual, transsexual, queer, questioning, intersex, asexual, allies, pansexual), refugees, those in poverty, the elderly, people with disabilities, non-Christians, and Holocaust survivors (including those who experienced the Native American Holocaust).

In understanding current psychological colonization issues, it is crucial for Euro-American research scientists, clinicians, and educators to be more acutely aware of how these harmful past traumas can still impact current relationships between the mainstream American dominant culture and other cultural groups.

History Through Many Cultural Lenses

Because Euro-American views of American history differ from the historical memories of underserved populations, there is a need for historical accounts to be written as seen through non-Euro-American lenses. Many authors have now provided those non-Euro-American perspectives of the history of the mistreatment by the U.S. government of such populations as Native Americans (Coyhis, Vergez, Farley, Frischmann, & White Bison, 2011; Dunbar-Ortiz, 2014), Alaska Natives (Williams, Kirk, & Starn, 2010), Jews (Michael, 2005; Schnall, 2006), those who endorse other forms of spiritual diversity (Ammerman, 2010), African Americans (Franklin & Higginbotham, 2010; Washington, 2006), Native Hawaiians (Silva, 2004), the elderly (Macnicol, 2006), women (Ruiz & DuBois, 2007), those in poverty (Isenberg, 2016), people with disabilities (Nielsen, 2012; Umansky, Bentall, & Longmore, 2001), the queer community (Bronski, 2012), Asian Americans (Lee, 2015), and individuals with overlapping or intersecting identities (intersectionality; Collins & Bilge, 2016).

Despite the prevalence of these non-Euro American historical perspectives, psychologists who strive to consider the impact of history on people from different cultures or worldviews often automatically rely on Euro-American historical perspectives rather than making an effort to seek out differing perspectives and historical accounts that are written by individuals who are not utilizing heterosexual, Caucasian, Euro-American, middle-class, male, healthy, Western-educated, Christian worldviews. By reviewing only literature with Euro American biases, this practice reflects a lack of inclusivity in information-gathering.

In learning about American history from other cultural or ethnic lenses, Euro-Americans are confronted with very different historical accounts due to specific differences in the content of the historical memories. In addition, there are differences that lie below the surface of our awareness. Donella Meadows, an American environmental scientist, teacher, and writer, wrote, "Your paradigm is so intrinsic to your mental process that you are hardly aware of its existence, until you try to communicate with someone with a different paradigm" (Meadows, n.d.). Thus, Euro-American psychologists who do not seek out other worldviews about the histories of a particular culture may remain unaware of their relevance on a particular paradigm, much less a Euro-American one (Boysen, 2000). Reading other cultural accounts of American history helps psychologists begin to understand more clearly how their powerful Euro-American worldviews reduce the quality of the services they offer to underserved populations.

Characteristics of Genocide

Reviewing history from the perspectives of other cultures is often painful to all, including those from the majority culture. Many of the traumatic experiences vulnerable populations have had with historical and current mainstream American policies and worldviews meet the U.S. criteria for genocide. The 1948 Convention on the Prevention and Punishment of the Crime of Genocide (CPPCG) (article 2) defines genocide as "any of the following acts committed with intent to destroy, in whole or in part, a national, ethnical, racial or religious group . . .," including the following:

- Killing members of the group;
- Causing serious bodily or mental harm to members of the group;
- Deliberately inflicting on the group conditions of life calculated to bring about its physical destruction in whole or in part;
- Imposing measures intended to prevent births within the group;
- Forcibly transferring children of the group to another group.

(Convention on the Prevention and Punishment of the Crime of Genocide, 1948)

Taking action to commit cultural genocide or ethnocide can include denying members of the group the right to speak their language, practice their religion, teach traditions and customs, create art, maintain social institutions, and preserve cultural memories.

The Convention states that genocide, whether committed in time of peace or war, is a crime under international law, and the primary responsibility to prevent and stop genocide lies with the country in which this international crime takes place (General Assembly of the Office of The Special Adviser on The Prevention of Genocide).

Examples of Genocide

Examples of genocide across the world include the Bosnian genocide (1992–1995), the Rwandan Massacre (1994), the Cambodian Genocide (1975–1978), the Holocaust (which began in 1933, when Adolf Hitler was appointed chancellor of Germany until 1945 when the war in Europe was officially ended), and the Soviet Ethnic cleansing (1920–1951). The Native

American Holocaust (Rodriguez, 2015), which began in 1492 when Christopher Columbus first arrived in America, is known as the "500 Year War" and the "World's Longest Holocaust in the History of Mankind and Loss of Human Lives" (Stannard, 2014).

Political scientist Joy James (2009) applied the term "genocide" to the racism, mass disenfranchisement, and genocide that has been historically directed at African Americans in America. "We Charge Genocide: The Crime of Government Against the Negro People" is a historic document that accuses the U.S. government of being complicit in a genocidal situation characterized by lynching, legal discrimination, disenfranchisement, police brutality, and health-care inequities (Civil Rights Congress, US, 1988). This document (United Nations General Assembly, 1948), first submitted to the United Nations Convention on the Prevention and Punishment of Genocide in 1951, is still cited by social justice activists. In 1996–97, the National United Front petitioned the United Nations, citing "We Charge Genocide" (Muhammad, 1997). The document was also recently cited by a group of Chicago activists who protested police violence against people of color in Chicago. This group, now named "We Charge Genocide" after the 1951 document by the same name, spoke with the United Nations Committee Against Torture in Geneva, Switzerland, to protest police brutality directed at Black Americans (We Charge Genocide: The Cry Rings True 52 Years Later [2003]).

Genocide and Racial-Based Traumatic Stress

Racial trauma, also called *racial-based traumatic stress*, has been shown to result from institutional racism, racial harassment, or witnessing racial violence. Symptoms of racial trauma include many symptoms characteristic of PTSD (Comas-Diaz, 2016). It is well known that African Americans were subjected without consent to many forms of medical experimentation such as occurred in the Tuskegee experiments, exposure to an untested smallpox vaccine, drug experiments, having their bodies used for anatomy classes, and other forms of scientific racism (Washington, 2006). The lasting impact of the trauma of slavery, termed *post traumatic slave syndrome* by DeGruy (2016), continues into the present. Kaelber (2014) writes about the history of sexual sterilization in North Carolina, which ranked third for the number of sterilizations in the United States between 1928 and 1983. Many of the sterilizations included women, African Americans, and those with psychological challenges.

Genocide and Cultural Losses

Genocide, colonization, exploitation, discrimination, and hate crimes toward minorities can result in many types of losses. For example, the American

Army took a cultural group's traditional means of subsistence and important resources away, as in the massive slaughter of the American Bison in the 1870s. The buffalo had supplied Native Americans with food, clothing, shelter, bedding, saddles, ropes, shields, and other articles used for ceremonial purposes. Colonel Richard Dodge stated, "Every buffalo dead is an Indian gone" (Jawort, 2011, May 9).

Forgotten Dead: Mob Violence Against Mexicans in the United States, 1848–1928 (Carrigan & Webb, 2013) covers eight decades in which lynch mobs murdered thousands (with 547 cases clearly documented) of Mexicans.

In acts of genocide, geographic isolation was often imposed through the forced evacuation, relocation, or internment of members of cultural groups, as happened to Japanese Americans during World War II (Takaki, 2008). German nationals and German-American citizens in the United States were detained during World War I and World War II. During World War II, the legal basis for internment was authorized under Presidential Proclamation 2526, made by President Franklin Delano Roosevelt under the authority of the Alien and Sedition Acts [Alien Enemies Act Presidential Proclamations (German American Internee Coalition, 1941/1978)].

Profound and systematic attempts were made to isolate members of these cultural groups through separation from the dominant culture, as in the segregation of facilities, services, housing, medical care, education, employment, and transportation.

Racist and discriminative economic losses occur during genocide as the result of actions such as these. Because of this, there may be reduced employment available through hiring discrimination, wage discrimination, higher prices for goods and services, and discrimination against workers, consumers, and minority-owned businesses (Brave Heart, 2013).

Other losses occur in response to colonization, genocide, and discrimination. Attempts made by the colonizing culture include efforts to destroy traditional family structures. *How Slavery Affected African American Families* (Williams, n.d.) recounts the devastating impacts slavery had on African American families. Before 1830 and to the end of slavery, enslaved people could not legally marry. Because of slavery, families with different owners were separated. Sometimes children were separated from their parents in order to prevent emotional ties (Williams, n.d.). More recently, in the 1950s, low-income African American mothers on welfare were told that they would have to agree to be sterilized or their welfare benefits would be cancelled (Hattery & Smith 2007). Sterilization increased from 23% in the 1930s to 64% in the 1960s.

Other colonization efforts included prohibiting use of Native language with Native Americans. In a documentary about the Native American Holocaust (*Journey of Forgiveness*, available from White Bison), an elder stated that when forced to live in an Indian Boarding school, one finger was amputated each time the child was heard to be speaking in the Native language.

When non-Euro-Americans use standard English, they often experience disparagement of the characteristics of their speech. "Linguistic discrimination" includes ridiculing an individual's vocabulary, accent, or syntax. Linguistic discrimination reflects unequal power between the colonizing agency and the non-dominant culture (Jaspal, 2009).

Other colonization acts include replacing traditional cultural educational formats with Euro-American educational systems. For example, Native American children were forcibly removed from their families and sent to Indian boarding schools. White administrators of Indian boarding schools told Native children that the "Indian in you shall die." Ann Piccard, a law professor at Stetson University College of Law, presents a legal argument for considering the use of Indian boarding schools as an act of genocide under international law (Piccard, 2013–2014). Whitt (2004) discusses biocolonialism and the commodification of knowledge, with illustrations of the differences in the views of what is "knowledge" across cultures.

Because cultural religious and spiritual beliefs are minimized or disparaged by the colonizing culture, cultural losses are another major result of genocide. The history of these experiences, as written by the mainstream culture minimizes or denies the degree of exploitation, genocide, or losses experienced by the colonized culture. As a result of the many losses resulting from colonization and genocide, racial and ethnic tension increases. Historical records and cultural artifacts are lost or destroyed. Information about spiritual laws, principles, and values of the colonized cultures are lost. Cultures are dismantled. Spirituality may be exploited by the colonizing culture (Takaki, 2008). Traditional geographic healing sites are lost. The impact of the loss of a spiritual geographic place is the focus of *Power and Place: Indian Education in America* (Deloria & Wildcat, 2001).

Why History Still Matters: Genocide and the Historic Trauma Response

Many historical losses that occur as the result of colonization continue to affect subsequent generations, including the present generation (Whitbeck, Adams, Hoyt, & Chen, 2004). The exposure of an earlier generation to traumatic events that continue to affect the subsequent generations produces symptoms that reflect *intergenerational trauma* (GreyWolf, 2011) and the *historic trauma response* (Brave Heart, 2013). GreyWolf and Brave Heart describe in depth the characteristics of these reactions to genocide, so readers are directed to their writing to fully understand what intergenerational trauma and historic trauma responses entail.

Two measures relating to historical trauma have been developed: The Historical Loss Scale and the Historical Loss Associated Symptoms Scale (Whitbeck, Adams, Hoyt, & Chen, 2004). The Trauma Symptom Inventory (Elhai, Gray, Kashdan, & Franklin, 2005) is also useful in assessing trauma. Familiarity with the intergenerational trauma responses that are experienced by marginalized populations helps psychologists recognize possible trauma symptoms that may occur across ethnicities and cultures. In addition, in looking at their own cultural competency skills and the influence of background factors, psychologists should conduct deep self-assessments regarding their own histories or their family's histories of historical loss and historical trauma. Psychologists themselves may have symptoms of historical loss and historical trauma.

Psychologists should also use the Cultural Formulation Interview in the DSM-5 (American Psychiatric Association, 2013) for self-assessment as well as for clinical service delivery.

EURO-AMERICAN RESISTANCE TO OPEN DISCUSSIONS OF GENOCIDE AND INTERGENERATIONAL TRAUMA

Affect-Laden Topics

Having participated in local, state, national, and international cultural competency presentations for more than two decades, we have observed that when the topics of cultural competency and social justice turn to colonization, genocide, and the potential harm of contemporary Western psychological treatments and research frameworks when applied to non-Euro American populations, the discussions become strongly affect-laden for many in the audience. Although some participants see these discussions of cultural competency and social justice as positive opportunities to present points of view that are not commonly endorsed by others in the mainstream culture, others, often from the dominant culture, resist or disagree with our assertions that by failing to fully develop cultural competence with their clients or populations under study and then taking action through social justice, they should no longer be considered to be showing general competence as psychologists, researchers, educators, or other mental health providers. It is not uncommon for us to hear statements of denial, confusion, resentment, feelings of being overwhelmed, and anger in our audiences, especially by those professionals who have Euro-American backgrounds.

Some participants—often the underrepresented or marginalized—are initially silent in responding to our presentations, confiding only privately to us that they fear speaking out in public due to potential retaliation by their agency, licensing boards, or other audience members.

These types of responses are some of the many signs of unhealthy dialogues about race (Sue, 1999, 2004, 2015). As our workshops progress, many of the initially silent participants begin to voice their perceptions about what it is like to work in institutions that deny equal access and opportunities. We then address negative responses that participants may have, such as denial, rejection, minimization, hostility, silence, aggression, arrogance, and/or anger.

Behavioral Characteristics of Resistance

In *Race Talk and the Conspiracy of Silence: Understanding and Facilitating Difficult Dialogues on Race*, Sue (2015) describes the characteristics, dynamics, and meaning of race talk, and he proposes solutions for having more honest racial dialogues between the dominant and nondominant culture. The succeeding chapters in *Radical Psychology* extend the principles in Sue's (2015) book and apply them to other forms of diversity beyond racial or ethnic variables.

Drawing on a list of different forms of the dissonance that both dominant and nondominant group members experience when they discuss multiculturalism and social justice, Ratts and Pedersen (2014, p. 118) describe a few negative responses to diversity discussions:

- Claims that the status quo is part of a "natural order,"
- Invalidation of targeted group members' experiences,
- Protection of [dominant] group members by targeted group members,
- [Dominant] group members' need to have own pain and hurt recognized,
- Invalidation [of the change agent],
- Anecdote raised to the status of generalized fact, and
- Hostile silence.

White Fragility

DiAngelo (2011) proposes the term *White fragility* to describe the negative feelings or responses that come from those in the dominant culture when issues of race are discussed. DiAngelo defines White fragility as a state in which even a minimum amount of racial stress becomes intolerable to those in the dominant culture, triggering a range of defensive moves. She states that this may occur in part because those in the dominant culture do not have to deal as often with daily microaggressions, and thus they have not developed the emotional competence skills to cope with discrimination. Examples of

White fragility include the outward display of emotions such as anger, fear, or guilt, and behaviors such as argumentation, silence, or exiting from the stress-inducing situation. DiAngelo states that these behaviors, in turn, often function to reinstate White racial dominance (DiAngelo, 2011).

At a university-mandated cultural competency workshop, we (SOG and MAP) noticed that an elderly White professor scowled, shook his head, and rolled his eyes during much of the presentation. Women of color sat on either side of him. Throughout the workshop, these two women sat quietly and looked down during many of what we felt were his passive-aggressive behaviors. In the anonymous workshop evaluations, a male stated, "This workshop was a waste of time. It should not have been required. I learned nothing. I have never, as a White man, ever committed any microaggressions, nor have I benefitted from White privilege. I didn't need this workshop." One of two other participants who wrote that they were women of color stated in evaluations, "There was a White man sitting between my friend and me. He was obnoxious. His behaviors made it difficult for us to focus on the presentation." The other woman expressed similar discomfort with the White male who sat between her and her friend: "We didn't say anything to him, as he is a professor with too many initials to his name. He really upset us."

It appears that the White male had no awareness of the ways in which he had hurt other participants, and his White privilege made it uncomfortable for others to confront him on these behaviors. Without inclusivity at that university, it was less likely that anyone in a position without power would be comfortable confronting this professor. This example of White fragility illustrates the concept of *blind spots* as discussed Johari's Window (Chandler & Munday, 2011).

Discussing White Privilege with Clients

Psychologists' willingness or disinclination to discuss the impact of White privilege with their clients has an impact on the effectiveness of their counseling. Miserocchi (2014) found that in complex ways, the three variables that influenced first counseling session outcome scores were White privilege remorse, a willingness to confront White privilege, and apprehension about addressing White privilege issues. They concluded that a therapist's awareness of White privilege has a complicated relationship with outcomes and with the therapeutic relationship.

Sue (2004) discusses the need for all psychologists to address the issues of whiteness and ethnocentric monoculturalism in order to make contemporary psychology relevant to all. Hall (1997) states that a failure to do so constitutes cultural malpractice.

Bias and High Self-Appraisal

As we have stated throughout the Preface and Introduction, psychologists are not immune to biases, and without conscious self-reflection, those biases are likely to affect the psychological research, educational, and clinical services that psychologists deliver. One of the factors that leads to bias is a high self-appraisal combined with a low appraisal of others (Pronin, Gilovich, & Ross, 2004). Markus, Kitayama, and Heiman (1996) write that this type of bias is especially prominent for Europeans and North Americans. The fact that Euro-Americans tend to see others as more susceptible to biases than themselves, and also their tendency to give greater credence to their own reflections, may reduce inclinations toward self-examination and self-questioning about biases.

This is complicated by the fact that some biases are known to the holder, while others are not, as discussed earlier. *Implicit biases* refer to attitudes that are unconscious and without intentional control. *Explicit biases*, in contrast, are conscious to the individual. Experimental studies of explicit and implicit bias among counselors report that counselors have many implicit biases that diverge from their self-reported attitudes (Boysen, 2009). Learning these biases can take place without a learner's awareness (Dovidio & Gaertner, 2005).

Wilson, Hugenberg, and Rule (2017) conducted seven experiments in which they examined bias associated with race. They showed their subjects photographs of Black and White faces. Although the people in the photographs were all equal in weight and height, non-White participants judged the Black men in the photographs to be stronger and "more capable of causing physical harm" compared with the White men in the photographs. They discuss the social justice implications stemming from this type of racial bias.

Western cognitive styles are biased in that they can lead to hierarchical, dichotomous, and linear thinking. This influences multicultural research, education, and clinical services. Hierarchical thinking occurs "when individuals put others or themselves into a superior or an inferior position" (Jun, 2010, p. 310). Attribution errors occur when "favoring the in-group over the outgroup to suggest positive behaviors as the internal traits of the in-group and negative behaviors as the internal traits of the outgroup" (Jun, 2010, p. 45). Inappropriate generalizations occur when one specific event or data point is used to make larger generalizations about characteristics such as intelligence (Jun, 2010). Dichotomous thinking is characterized by thinking that reflects only two extremes, which can lead to ethnocentric thinking (Jun, 2010). Jun provides numerous detailed examples of these characteristics of Western thinking, which differ from holistic thinking which reflects the ability to use multilayered or multidimensional thinking. Holistic thinking reflects multiplistic thinking that can be less linear, dichotomous, or stereotypical (Cordova, Moore, Peters, Jojola, & Lacy, 2007; Jun, 2010). Psychologists are not immune to the above biases, but they are rarely confronted about them by others due to White fragility (DiAngelo, 2011).

Psychological research has paid considerable attention to helping *clients* understand the impacts of the abovementioned types of cognitive factors in increasing anxiety and depression (Hoffmann, Asnanni, Vonk, Sawyer, & Fang, 2012). Less attention in the mainstream psychology literature has been given to examining how those same cognitive errors can increase the likelihood that a *clinician, educator, or researcher* will automatically utilize Euro-American Western psychological worldviews and thinking style.

Cultural Histories of Providers' Ancestors

The cultural background of the psychologist's ancestors shapes their worldview. In assessing their cultural backgrounds, psychologists might use the Cultural Formulation Interview of the DSM-5 (American Psychiatric Association, 2013) to frame their cultural self-assessment. David D. Moore discusses this in depth in chapter 3. In addition, psychologists should reflect on the historic traumas that were, or are still being, experienced by the cultural groups that reflect their own backgrounds.

Research shows that the descendants of Holocaust survivors experience symptoms of trauma (Rubenstein, Cutter, & Templer, 1989–1990). There is no reason to conclude that psychologists are immune to historical traumas in their own backgrounds. In addition to the cultural group's experience with trauma, the psychologist's family history may impact the psychologist's future interests and effectiveness in regards to certain multicultural and social justice topics (Briscoe & Khalifa, 2015).

Ethnocultural Transference and Countertransference

Students who are in training as mental health providers are taught early on about the concepts of transference and countertransference. They are trained to be on the alert for transference and countertransference issues in their clients and themselves (Barel, Van lizendoorn, Sagi-Schwartz, & Bakermans-Kranenburg, 2010). It is less common for the principles of transference and countertransference to be examined in regards to the counselor's multicultural counseling competence and social justice initiatives. This type of transference and countertransference is referred to as *ethnocultural transference* and *ethnocultural countertransference* (Comas-Diaz & Jacobsen, 1991). A question psychologists might ask themselves is, "How has my own cultural background influenced my skills, knowledge, professional abilities, and interests in working with this individual who holds different worldviews"? This question assists in the self-analysis of clinician transference and countertransference. The question "How does my client see me, given my cultural background?" can provide information about a type of cultural transference by the client. Those feelings, thoughts, reactions, and behaviors in both clinicians and clients reflect important transference and countertransference issues that must be openly acknowledged and addressed with clients in order to increase multicultural competency. Given White fragility (DiAngelo, 2011) about sensitive multicultural topics such as these, those topics may never be introduced by the provider or the client.

Psychologists have researched, studied, taught, and provided services in order to increase the interpersonal skills of their clients. Given the psychologist's own countertransference issues that relate to culture, however, it becomes imperative that mental health providers closely examine their own interpersonal skills in developing psychological services for underserved populations. In the Appndix, we provide a set of questions for provider self-assessment to exemplify how emotional competency skills can be assessed in regard to cultural competency and White fragility (DiAngelo, 2011).

There is considerable research that indicates that professionals can be affected by the same prejudices, stereotypes, or limited worldviews that may characterize their clients (Caplan & Cosgrove, 2004). Factors that may increase or decrease the likelihood that a mental health professional will hold a monocultural psychological worldview include some of the same elements that psychologists have often considered in developing research, education, and clinical services for their clients. These factors include the psychologist's own level of multicultural emotional competence, emotional resilience, multicultural interpersonal skills, stress management skills, overall communication skills, cultural humility, multicultural transference and countertransference factors, self-esteem as a multicultural counselor or social justice advocate, spiritual/religious beliefs, leadership skills in working with differences, teaching skills, goal-setting abilities, and issues linked to the individual's professional competence as a researcher, teacher, or clinician.

The National Center for Cultural Competence has published a self-assessment inventory, the Cultural Competence Health Practitioner Assessment (CCHPA). The fact that it and the above questions are self-assessments, however, poses limitations because of how attribution errors, cultural blind spots, and implicit biases can lead to faulty self-assessments (Smith & Trimble, 2016). In their meta-analyses of many studies on multicultural counseling and social justice, Smith and Trimble observed that many of the measures they studied were self-appraisals and should be replaced with more objective external evaluations.

INSTITUTIONAL CULTURAL FACTORS

Resiliency

In addition to conducting an individual self-assessment, psychologists must grapple with the fact that they work in clinical, research, or educational environments that may or may not promote cultural competence or social justice initiatives. In *Thinking in Systems*, Donella Meadows (Meadows & Wright, 2008) analyzes social systems and ecosystems. Sisodia (2011) summarizes Meadow's extensive coverage of the characteristics of systems that show resilience and have the ability to build complex structures (and smaller parts that can behave autonomously) and systems that fail in the face of change due to factors that include one or more of the following: a focus on events rather than system flows, inappropriate linear mind-sets, false boundaries, layers of limits, systems delays, resistance to new policies, a "new normal" of low performance, and following the letter, not the spirit, of the law. (S., 6/9/2011).

Covert Actions

The workplace climate is affected by the role that diversity plays in both the formal and informal policies of the institution or practice in which the psychologist is practicing. A book that was published some time ago but still holds true for one of the authors of this chapter (SOG) focuses on the differences between formal and informal agency policies *Working the Shadow Side: A Guide to Positive Behind-the-Scenes Management* (Eagan, 1994). This book discusses how to identify and respond to the covert, below-the-surface, shadow-side activities of an organization that may contradict institutional policies. The book's principles may be relevant to psychologists who find that Euro-American biases limit their agency's ability to practice the diversity and inclusiveness initiatives stated formally in mission statements. Eagan's book emphasizes that covert organizational activities are sometimes more powerful in shaping policies than are overt public goals.

Structural Violence

The term *structural violence* was introduced by John Galtung (1969) in an article entitled, "Violence: Reflections on a National Epidemic." Structural violence refers to any aspect of an institution that can be used to legitimize violence in its direct or structural form. Structural violence prevents people from meeting their basic needs and is related to direct violence such as racial violence, police violence, and state violence (Galtung, 1990; Gilligan, 1997). Structural violence in health care is related to inequalities related to economic, political, social factors, and human rights (Ho, 2007). When structural violence exists, there is an unequal distribution of resources, decided by the structural distribution of power (Ho, 2007).

One example of structural violence is described by Nagata (2017). Using a critical medical anthropology framework, Nagata (2017) writes that "anti-LGBT laws constitute structural violence and have many detrimental consequences including discrimination and violence; poorer mental and physical health outcomes; and risky sexual behaviors" (Nagata, 2017, p. 2).

"Structural violence" need not be physical, thus the term is relevant to institutions that practice Eurocentric psychology with people from other cultures or worldviews. Psychology research, teaching, and mental health institutions may have elements of structural violence due to Eurocentric policies.

The Organizational Climate and Diversity Assessment Tool

A recently developed tool, the Organizational Climate and Diversity Assessment (OCDA), could serve as a prototype for the study of the interactions between organizational climate, employee satisfaction, and client service. A multiyear research project at the University of Maryland was conducted to measure organizational climate and diversity. The OCDA was developed by the Association of Research Libraries, a division of the American Library Association. The research combined both qualitative and quantitative research methods that provided data for implementing organizational change. The workplace changes resulting from this research are expected to improve job satisfaction and commitment, decrease work conflict, increase employee empowerment, and ultimately improve customer service (Kyrillidou, Lowry, Hanges, Aiken, & Justin, 2009). The types of analyses conducted by the OCDA can be generalized to the study of the organizational climates of other types of organizations and institutions.

Institutional Change and Innovation Theory

In working toward institutional change, the authors of *Counseling for Multiculturalism and Social Justice: Integration, Theory, and Application* (Ratts & Pedersen, 2014) recommend the relevance of a theory of individual and organizational response to innovations, "diffusion of innovation theory" (Rogers, 2003). This theory incorporates findings of the research regarding the predictable processes that occur in the adoption of innovation, the roles people play in organizational change, and the decision-making process in response to innovation challenges.

Person-Environment Diversity Fit

Person-Environment Fit

"Person-environment fit" (Caplan, 1987) is a term that has been used to describe the impact of the degree of congruence between individuals and the environments in which they live and work. Congruence can be viewed in terms of person-job fit (Kristoff-Brown & Guay, 2011), person-person fit couplings such as supervisor-supervisee fit or person-mentor fit (Boon & Den Hartog, 2011), person-group fit, and the degree of match between the learning style of the learner and the teaching style of the teacher (Gilakjani, 2012). After decades of research on this subject, person-environment interactions are seen to be more complex than originally proposed, and there is disagreement about how to conceptualize person-environment fit, operationalize it, and research its outcomes (Edwards, 2008).

In general, good person-environment fits have historically been found to result in increased effectiveness and job satisfaction with employee work initiatives (Kristoff-Brown, Zimmerman, & Johnson, 2005). The attraction-selection-attrition (ASA) model (Schneider, 1987; Schneider, Goldstein, & Smith, 1995) further addresses the impact of the degree of person-environment fit on individuals and the organizations in which they work. Ostroff and Schulte (2007) also focus on person-situation fit, with a special emphasis on the importance of the individual's perception of the situation as it affects person-environment fit.

Person-Environment Mismatches

When there is a profound person-environment mismatch, the power dynamics of the community, state, or country in which social justice advocates work can lead to personal or professional retaliation. Ignacio Martin-Baró (Martin-Baró, Aron, Corne, & Mishler, 1996) was a social justice advocate, scholar, social psychologist, philosopher, and Jesuit priest. His work focused on the decolonization of psychology and politics during the Salvadoran Civil War. He wrote about a number of counselor assumptions that limit counselor effectiveness with marginalized client populations. The counselor assumptions that he felt reflected colonization included the high values ascribed by psychologists to individualism, hedonism, empirical research, and beliefs in the universal and impartial nature of psychology. Because of his social justice advocacy efforts, he faced severe persecution. He was aware that there was a grave danger in publishing controversial ideas, but he continued his efforts until a Salvadoran death squad assassinated him in 1989. His work led to the development of liberation psychology (Martin-Baró, Aron, Corne, & Mishler 1996) in Latin America. Martin-Baró's frameworks have been updated in order to expand the social consciousness of psychologists (Montero & Sonn, 2009).

In working toward social justice goals, there may be both personal and professional retaliation toward those who question the current power dynamics. Retaliation by mainstream Euro American agencies also occurs when prevailing paradigms are questioned. For example, when attempting to investigate the mistreatment and abusive medical experimentation on Black Americans, Washington (2006) was met with anger and denial by White academicians. Washington found that the documentation of these atrocities minimized, obfuscated, and hid the full nature of the abuse. Nagata (2017) wrote about the dilemmas of coming out as a gay health-care provider in Kenya, where LGBT rights were illegal. When Carl Jung broke with traditional psychoanalytic views, fearing retaliation, he insisted that his writing about spiritual, metaphysical, and other topics (*Memories, Dreams, Reflections*) not be published until after his death (Jung & Jaffee, 1963). Scott Peck, a noted psychiatrist and author who was educated at Harvard and Case Western Reserve, waited years before publishing two works that included a focus on the role of spirituality in mental diagnoses and treatment (Peck, 1998, 2005). Karen Horney was ridiculed because of her questioning of Freud's theories of penis envy. Caplan and Cosgrove (2004, p. xxvii) quoted Horney (1973, p. 13), writing, "Envy of or anger towards males came not from wishing to have a penis but from understanding that males had more power and influence in many realms and fewer restrictions than did females."

All of these individuals were presenting new psychological or psychiatric paradigms that challenged current thinking and were met with hostility, ridicule, criticism, personal and physical attacks, or assassination.

Person-Environment Fit and Multicultural Supervision

Person-environment theories can be applied to situations involving workplace discrimination (Velez & Moradi, 2012). One environmental factor in person-environment fit is the level of cultural competence of the multicultural supervisor, researcher, or administrator as perceived by the supervisee. Given that Euro American psychological services are often overseen by administrators and supervisors from the dominant culture, multicultural supervision of a minority staff member may be associated with many, often-unspoken, concerns of the supervisee. Issues may include fear of supervision due to the supervisee's previous traumatic experiences with the dominant culture; anxiety about how the supervisor might respond to differences in worldviews; the supervisor's level of credibility in the eyes of the supervisee; the possibility of frustration or anger due to covert or overt microaggressions by the supervisor; confusion about how to address different world paradigms with the supervisor; the level of perceived self-direction that the supervisee has in developing culturally informed treatment service; and the degree to which the supervisee views the supervisor as being a credible mentor. Given a fear of White fragility (DiAngelo, 2011), the supervisee may not feel comfortable in addressing these issues with the supervisor. Because of the supervisor's blind spots, those issues may be below the awareness of the supervisor.

Supervisory issues are complicated even more when a cultural expert with strong cultural credentials but without Euro-American credentials is brought into a leadership position in a Euro-American educational, clinical, or research program. If the Euro-American staff or administrators do not see the need to use differing provider credentials for individuals with different cultural backgrounds, the cultural expert may be hired under the auspices of having real power for change, while, in fact, the cultural expert may be constrained by the existing Euro-American institutional norms (Grayshield & Mihecoby, 2010).

Person-environment fit in multicultural supervision encompasses developmental factors for both the supervisor and supervisee (Stoltenberg, 2005). When inclusion is not practiced by the welcoming of colleagues with nontraditional cultural backgrounds, professional qualifications, and worldviews, the person-environment mismatches between the supervisor and supervisee may result in very difficult situations in which both parties feel misunderstood. Other dynamics occur with other types of person-environment supervisor-supervisee mismatches, such as when a cultural expert without Western credentials supervises an individual who lacks cultural competence but possesses all of the Western credentials. The result may be underperformance of the supervisee, feelings of frustration on both sides, and impaired supervision (Stoltenberg, 2005; Stoltenberg, McNeill, & Delworth, 1998).

MICROAGGRESSIONS COMMITTED BY PSYCHOLOGISTS: A FEW EXAMPLES

Inclusive supervision can help supervisees and supervisors be better educated about the microaggressions they may be committing in their social justice efforts. In an article entitled, "Evaluating the Ally Role: Contributions, Limitations, and the Activist Position in Counseling and Psychology," Mizock and Page (2016) provide an in-depth discussion of the potential limitations of allies acting as social justice advocates. As members of the dominant group, allies may easily overlook issues of intersectionality. In addition, by defining a group as *marginalized*, allies may "limit the empowerment of that group and reify dominant and subordinate statuses" (Mizock & Page, 2016, p. 22). A *hero-victim narrative* may be perpetuated by allies, "promoting a condescending narrative of allies as 'rescuers to the helplessly oppressed'" (Mizock & Page, 2016, p. 24). Allies may be "motivated by secondary gain and hidden agendas, such as acting out of guilt or expecting praise from the marginalized group" (Reason & Broido, 2005).

SOG: Microaggressions may only be clear to individuals from the non-dominant culture. One of my clients asked us what "microaggressions" meant. That client stated, "They shouldn't use the wordmicro' – there is nothing micro about microaggression. That 'micro' action is like a truck crashing by us. It is clearly seen, if not by you in the dominant culture, certainly by us!" He also suggested that the term itself may serve to underplay the psychological violence that such behaviors cause in others—in other words, it "whitewashes the offensive actions."

THE DEVELOPMENT OF SOCIAL JUSTICE INITIATIVES

Just as clients select a clinical focus for their personal growth based on their backgrounds, needs, experiences, and values, the process of developing social justice initiatives must take into account personal, group, and environmental factors. This may call into question many of the assumptions seasoned psychologists may make about themselves when immersed in Euro-American treatment paradigms.

Euro-American psychologists would do well to not assume that they will have strong emotional competence skills when working with individuals or groups who do not share similar worldviews. Due to blind spots, implicit biases, and unconsciously learned stereotypes that we all have, psychologists who do not work alongside traditional healers or other types of cultural experts may not be sufficiently challenged to address issues that clients or professionals from other cultures may have with them, such as concerns about credibility, secondary motives, transference and countertransference, ethnocultural issues, rescuer-victim dynamics, and other potentially harmful ways that Eurocentric psychologists may cause harm to others. It is important to go beyond consideration of the multicultural and social justice competencies such as those developed (Ratts, Singh, Nassar-McMillan, Butler, & McCullough, 2016).

In order to be able to receive feedback about these negative behaviors, Euro-American psychologists will need to develop many of the skills they ask their clients to develop in order to grow emotionally, behaviorally, intellectually, socially, and spiritually. In working with people from other cultures, ethnicities, races, or worldviews, psychologists must develop strong communications skills, assertiveness skills, resilience skills, emotional competence, stress tolerance, and rapport-developing, problem-solving, and interpersonal skills.

When increased accountability due to inclusivity becomes the norm, Euro-American psychologists will become more vigilant to avoid potentially harmful negative behaviors with nonmajority populations. This will create a greater potential for Euro-American psychologists to effectively move social justice initiatives forward. For example, allies from advantaged groups are able to mobilize institutional resources and increase the power that marginalized groups may lack. They can model privilege awareness and individual and organizational cultural competency assessments. Allies can speak up and challenge others to do the same (Mizock & Page, 2016).

A consideration of person-environment factors will help advocates develop initiatives that reflect their own social justice initiatives, whether they are individual goals, group-based initiatives, agency objectives, community goals, or national strategies. Developing objectives that are within the *zone of proximal development* (Kuusisaari, 2014) for advocates will lead to growth that is achievable, sustainable, and resilient. The zone of proximal development will include those goals that can be learned by individuals through the right balance of challenge and support by a teacher or mentor.

In considering an array of social justice topics for consideration, psychologists may refer to professional special interest organizations. For example, the organization Psychologists for Social Justice has committees that address social justice initiatives such as racial injustice, torture, the US Criminal justice system, the mistreatment of scholars, APA collusion with DoD on the psychological effects of solitary confinement, the force-feeding of hunger strikers in Guantanamo, budget cuts, the impact of climate change on psychological health, and support for same-sex marriage.

CONCLUSIONS

Earlier, we quoted Dr. Lisa Grayshield's (Grayshield & Mihecoby, 2010) disenchantment with the Eurocentric psychology paradigm she had been trained in and was now working in. We end this chapter with a quote by another individual, Anthony J. Marsella, professor emeritus at the University of Hawaii. He is an international leader in social justice and multicultural counseling. Here is his concern about the field of psychology:

> Psychology is neither the property, nor possession of the American Psychological Association (APA), or any of its related organizations! Psychology is not a "commodity" to be bought, owned, and/or distributed by any organization or institution, even as that organization or institution may seek to control its existence, definition, and standardization, or other uses through wealth, position, and person. Psychology is not to be used to establish "hegemony" by imposing

> an organization or institution's expressed purposes or empowering an organization or institution's implicit and explicit assumptions, goals, and intentions . . . Nor should psychology be driven in its purposes by political or ideological preferences, designed to favor one nation's pursuit of hegemonic control. (Marsella, 2015, p. 143)

Celebrating the goal of eliminating Eurocentric biases in social justice initiatives, the authors of *Radical Psychology* offer the chapters of this book to help readers understand the psychological dynamics behind the propulsion or hindrance of multicultural competence in psychological and social justice initiatives.

REFERENCES

Ali, A., Caplan, P. J., & Fagnant, R. (2009). Gender stereotypes in diagnostic criteria. In J. C. Chrisler & D. R. McCreary (Eds.), *Handbook of gender research in psychology* (pp. 91–109). New York: Springer-Verlag.

American Psychiatric Association. (2000). *Diagnostic and statistical manual of mental disorders –IV-TR*. Washington, DC: Author.

American Psychiatric Association. (2013). *Diagnostic and statistical manual of mental disorders* (5th ed.). Arlington, VA: Author.

American Psychological Association. (2002, Sept; 2010, June; 2016, June). Ethical principles of psychologists and code of conduct. *American Psychologist, 57*, 1060–1073. Note: amended on February 20, 2010, effective June 1, 2010; amended again on August 3, 2016, effective June 1, 2017 (APA website, APA.org). Washington, DC: Author.

American Psychological Association Task Force on Evidence-Based Practice. (2006, May-June). Evidence-based practice in psychology. *American Psychologist, 61*(4), 271–285. doi:10.1037/003-066X.61.4.271.

Ammerman, N. T. (2010, June). The challenges of pluralism: Locating religion in a world of diversity. *Social Compass, 57*(2), 154–167. doi: 10.1177/003776861036 2406.

Australian Psychology Society. (Read by Tim Carey, 2016, Sept. 13–16). *Apology to aboriginal and Torres Strait Islander Peoples*. Melbourne, Australia: Australian Psychological Society Congress Psychology.

Banaji, M. R., & Bhaskar, R. (2001). Implicit stereotypes and memory: The bounded rationality of social beliefs. In D. L. Schacter & E. Scarry (Eds.), *Memories, brain, and belief* (pp. 139–175). Cambridge, MA: Harvard University Press.

Banaji, M. R., & Greenwald, A. G. (2013). *Blindspot: Hidden biases of good people*. Unknown location: Delacorte Press.

Barel, E., Van ljzendoorn, M. H., Sagi-Schwartz, A., & Bakermans-Kranenburg, M. J. (2010, Sept.). Surviving the Holocaust: A meta-analysis of the long-term sequellae of a genocide. *Psychological Bulletin, 136*(5), 677–698.

Bemack, F., & Chung, R. C.-Y. (2008, Summer). A multicultural/social justice perspective to move beyond the nice counselor syndrome. *Journal of Counseling & Development, 86*, 372–381.

Bernal, G., & Rodriguez, M. M. D. (Eds.). (2012). *Cultural adaptations: Tools for evidence-based practice with diverse populations.* Washington, DC: American Psychological Association.

Boon, C., & Den Hartog, D. N. (2011). Human resource management, person-environment fit, and trust. [Monograph]. In R. H. Searle & D. Skinner (Eds.), *Trust and human resource management* (pp. 109–121). doi:10.4337/9780857932006.0013.

Boysen, G. A. (2009, October). A review of experimental studies of explicit and implicit bias among counselors. *Journal of Multicultural Counseling and Development, 37*(4), 240–249.

Brave Heart, M. Y. H. (2013, April 12). The historical trauma response and its relationship to alcohol and other drug use. [PPT]. Retrieved from: https://www.ihs.gov/.../historicaltrauma/htalcoholdrugabuse_041213.pdf.

Brave Heart, M. Y. H., Chase, J., Elkins, J., & Atschul, D. B. (2011). Historical trauma among Indigenous peoples of the Americas: Concepts, research, and clinical considerations. *Journal of Psychoactive Drugs, 43*(4), 282–290.

Briscoe, F. M., & Khalifa, M. A. (Eds.). (2015). *Becoming critical: The emergence of social justice scholars.* Albany, NY: SUNY Press.

Bronski, M. (2012). *A queer history of the United States (ReVisioning American history).* Boston, MA: Beacon Press.

Butcher, J. N., Dahlstrom, W. G., Graham, J. R., Tellegen, A., & Kaemmer, B. (1989). *Minnesota Multiphasic Personality Inventory (MMPI-2): Manual for administration and scoring.* Minneapolis, MN: University of Minnesota Press.

Caplan, R. D. (1987). Person-environment fit theory and organizations: Commensurate dimensions, time perspectives and mechanisms. *Journal of Vocational Behavior, 31*, 248–267.

Caplan, P. J., & Cosgrove, L. (Eds.). (2004). *Bias in psychiatric diagnosis.* New York: Jason Aronson (subsidiary of Rowman & Littlefield Publishing Group).

Carrigan, W. D., & Webb, C. (2013). *Forgotten dead: Mob violence against Mexicans in the United States, 1848–1928.* Oxford: Oxford University Press.

Chambless, D. L., & Ollendick, T. H. (2001). Empirically supported psychological interventions: Controversies and evidence. *Annual Review of Psychology, 52*, 685–716. doi:10.1146/annurev.psych.52.1.685.

Chandler, D., & Munday, R. (2011). *A dictionary of media and communication* (1st ed.). Oxford: Oxford University Press.

Civil Rights Congress. (1988). *We charge genocide: The historic petition to the United Nations for relief from a crime of the US government against the Negro People* (New ed.). New York: International.

Collins, P. H., & Bilge, S. (2016). *Intersectionality: Key concepts.* Cambridge: Polity Press.

Comas-Diaz, L. (2016). Racial trauma recovery: A race-informed therapeutic approach to racial wounds. In A. N. Alvarez, C. T. H. Liang, & H. A. Neville (Eds.), *The cost of racism for people of color: Contextualizing experiences of discrimination*. Cultural, racial, and ethnic psychology book series (pp. 249–272). Washington, DC: American Psychological Association.

Comas-Diaz, L., & Jacobsen, F. M. (1991, July). Ethnocultural transference and countertransference in the therapeutic dyad. *American Journal of Orthopsychiatry, 61*(3), 392–412.

Convention on the Prevention and Punishment of the Crime of Genocide. Adopted by the General Assembly of the United Nations on 9 December 1948 as General Assembly Resolution 260. Entered into force: 12 June, 1951 in accordance with Article XIII.

Cordova, V. F. (Author), Moore, K. D., Peters, K., Jojola, T., Lacy, A. (Eds.), & Hogan, L. (Forward). (2007). *How it is: The Native American philosophy of V. F. Cordova*. Tucson: The University of Arizona Press.

Coyhis, D., Vergez, K., Farley, M., Frischmann, L., & White Bison, Inc. (2011). *The Wellbriety movement: Journey of forgiveness*. [DVD]. Colorado Springs, CO: White Bison.

Cruz, C. M. (n.d.). *Many paths to follow: Tribal and minority best practices*. [PowerPoint]. Retrieved from npnconference.org or contact caroline.cruz@wstribes.org

DeGruy, J. A. (2016). *Post traumatic slave syndrome: America's legacy of enduring injury and healing* (Kindle ed.). Joy DeGruy Publications. Digital Download Only. joydegruy.com/product/post-traumatic-slave-syndrome-ebook-epub.

Deloria, Jr., V. (2003). *God is red: A Native view of religion* (30th anniversary edition). Golden, CO: Fulcrum Resources.

Deloria, Jr., V., & Wildcat, D. R. (2001). *Power and place: Indian education in America*. Golden CO: Fulcrum Resources.

DiAngelo, R. (2011). White fragility. *International Journal of Critical Pedagogy, 3*(3), 54–70.

Dovidio, J. F., & Gaertner, S. L. (2005). Understanding and addressing contemporary racism: From aversive racism to the common ingroup identity model. *Journal of Social Issues, 61*(3), 615–639. doi:10.1111/j:1540-4560.2005.00424.x.

Dunbar-Ortiz, R. (2014). *An Indigenous peoples' history of the United States*. Boston, MA: Beacon Press.

Duncan, B. L., & Miller, S. D. (2005). Treatment manuals do not improve outcomes. In J. Norcross, R. Levant, & L. Beutler (Eds.), *Evidenced-based practices in mental health: Debate and dialogue on the fundamental questions* (chapt. 3). Washington, DC: American Psychological Association Press.

Duran, E. (2000). *Buddha in redface*. Lincoln, NE: IUniverse.

Duran, E. (2006). *Healing the soul wound: Counseling with American Indians and other Native peoples*. New York: Columbia University, Teachers College Press. gaic.info/history/related-laws.

Duran, E. (2013, March). *Toward a new view of Intergenerational Trauma*. Symposium conducted at Portland Community College, Portland, OR.

Duran, E., & Duran, B. (1995). *Native American postcolonial psychology*. Albany, NY: State University of New York.

Duran, E., & Firehammer, J. (2015). Story sciencing and analyzing the silent narrative between words: Counseling research from an Indigenous perspective. In R. D.

Goodman & P. C. Gorski (Eds.), *Decolonizing "multicultural counseling" through social justice* (pp. 85–97). NY: Springer Science + Business Media.
Eagan, G. (1994, Oct.). *Working the shadow side: A guide to positive behind-the-scenes management.* San Francisco, CA: Jossey-Bass (a Wiley brand).
Edwards, J. R. (2008). Person-environment fit in organizations: An assessment of theoretical progress. *The Academy of Management Annals, 2*, 167–230. doi:10.1080/19416520802211503.
Elhai, J. D., Gray, M. J., Kashdan, T. B., & Franklin, C. L. (2005, Oct.). Trauma symptom inventory. *Journal of Traumatic Stress, 18*, 541–545. doi:10.1002/jts.20062.
Franklin, J. H., & Higginbotham, E. P. (2010). *From slavery to freedom: A history of African Americans*. New York: McGraw-Hill.
Frisby, C. L. (2013). *Meeting the psychoeducational needs of minority students: Evidence-Based guidelines for school psychologists and other school personnel.* Hoboken, NJ: Wiley.
Gallardo, M. E., & McNeill, B. W. (Eds.). (2009). *Intersections of multiple identities: A casebook of evidence-based practices with diverse populations (counseling and psychotherapy).* New York: Routledge.
Galtung, J. (1969). Violence, Peace, and Peace Research. *Journal of Peace Research, 6*(3), 167–191. doi:10.1177/002234336900600301.
Galtung, J. (1990, August). Cultural violence. *Journal of Peace Research, 27*(3), 291–305.
German American Internee Coalition. (1941/1978, December 7). *The Alien Enemies Act Presidential Proclamations*. German American Internee Coalition.
Gilakjani, A. P. (2012). A match or mismatch between learning styles of the learners and teaching styles of the teachers. *I. J. Modern Education and Computer Service, 11*, 51–60. doi:10.5815/ijmecs.2012.11.05.
Gilligan, J. (1997). *Violence: Reflections on a national epidemic*. New York: Vintage Books.
Goldfried, M. R., & Wolfe, B. E. (1998). Toward a more clinically valid approach to therapy. *Journal of Consulting andClinical Psychology, 66*(1), 145–150.
Gone, J. P., & Calf Looking, P. E. (2015). The Blackfeet Indian culture camp: Auditioning an alternative Indigenous treatment for substance use disorders. *Psychological Services, 12*(2), 83–91.
Goodman, R. D., & Gorski, P. C. (Eds.). (2015). *Decolonizing "multicultural" counseling through social justice*. New York: Springer.
Grant, L. D. (1996, Feb.). Effects of ageism on individual and health care providers' responses to healthy aging. *Health Social Work, 21*(1), 9–15.
Grayshield, L., & Mihecoby, A. (2010, Fall). Indigenous ways of knowing as a philosophical base for the promotion of peace and justice in counseling education and psychology. *Journal for Social Action in Counseling and Psychology, 2*(2), 1–16.
Greenwald, A. G., McGhee, D. E., & Schwartz, J. L. K. (1998). Measuring individual differences in implicit cognition: The implicit association test. *Journal of Personality and Social Psychology, 74*(6), 1464–1480.
GreyWolf, I. (2011, January). *Out of the darkness*. APA Division 35 Midwinter EC Meeting, Section 6 Presentation. Seattle, WA: Alaska Native/American Indian/Indigenous Women. doi:10.1037/e621012011-001.

Hall, C. C. (1997, July). Cultural malpractice: The growing obsolescence of psychology with the changing US population. *American Psychologist, 52,* 642–651. doi:10.1037/000-006X.52.6642.

Hattery, A. J., & Smith, E. (2007). *African American families*. Thousand Oaks, CA: Sage.

Hays, P. A. (2008). *Addressing cultural complexities in practice: Assessment, diagnosis, and therapy* (2nd ed.). Washington, DC: American Psychological Association.

Hayes, R. A. (2005). Evaluating readiness to implement evidence-based practice. In C. E. Stout & R. A. Hayes (Eds.), *The evidence-based practice: Methods, models, and tools for mental health professionals* (pp. 255–279). Hoboken, NJ: Wiley.

Henrich, J., Heine, S. J., & Norenzayan, A. (2010). The weirdest people in the world? *Behavioral and Brain Sciences, 33*(2/3), 1–75. doi:10.1017/S0140525X0999152X.

Hill, J. S., Robbins, R. R., & Pace, T. M. (2012, April). Cultural validity of the Minnesota Multiphasic Personality Inventory-2 empirical correlates: Is this the best we can do? *Journal of Multicultural Counseling and Development, 40*, 104–116. doi:10.1002/j.2161-1912.2012.00010.x.

Ho, K. (2007, September). Structural violence as a human rights violation. *Essex Human Rights Review 4*(2), 1–17.

Hoffman, S. G., Asnanni, A., Vonk, I. J. J., Sawyer, A. T., & Fang, A. (2012). The efficacy of cognitive behavioral therapy: A review of meta-analyses. *Cog TherRes, 36*(5), 427–440. doi:10.1007/s10608-012-9476-1.

Hook, J. N., Davis, D., Owen, J., & DeBlaere, C. (2017). *Cultural humility: Engaging diverse cultural identities in therapy.* Washington, DC: American Psychological Association.

Hooper, L., Stockton, P., Krupnick, J, & Green, B. (2011). Development, use and psychometric properties of the Trauma History Questionnaire. *Journal of Loss and Trauma, 16*(3), 258–283. doi:10.1080/15325024.2011.572035.

Horney, K. (1973). *Feminine psychology.* New York: Norton.

International Association of Genocide Scholars. (2016). *Arts & Culture.* Retrieved from http://www.genocidescholars.org/resources/arts-culture.

Isenberg, N. (2016). *White trash: The 400-year untold history of class in America.* Boston, MA: Cambridge University Press.

James, J. A. (2009, Summer). The dead zone: Stumbling at the crossroads of party politics, genocide and postracial racism. *Southern Atlantic Quarterly, 108*(3), 459–481. doi:10.1215/00382876-2009-003.

Jaspal, R. (2009, Sept.). Language and social identity: A psychosocial approach. *PsychTalk (British Psychological Society), 64*, 17–20.

Jawort, A. (2011, May 9). Genocide by other means: U.S. Army slaughtered buffalo in Plains Indian Wars. *Indian Country Today*. Retrieved from https://indiancountrymedianetwork.com/news/genocide-by-other-means-us-army-slaughtered-buffalo-in-plains-indian-wars/.

Jun, H. (2010). *Social justice, multicultural counseling, and practice: Beyond a conventional approach.* Thousand Oaks, CA: Sage.

Jung, C. G., & Jaffe, A. (Recorder and Ed.). (1963). *Memories, dreams, reflections.* New York: Vintage Books.

Kaelber, L. (2014). *Eugenics/sexual sterilizations in North Carolina.* University of Vermont College course study guide. Retrieved from www.mashpedia.com/Black_genocide_conspiracy_theory.

Kristof-Brown, A., & Guay, R. P. (2011). Person-environment fit. *APA handbook of Industrial and Organizational Psychology, 3*, 3–50. doi:10.1037/12171-001.

Kristof-Brown, A. L., Zimmerman, R. D., & Johnson, E. C. (2005). Consequences of individuals' fit at work: A meta-analysis of person-job, person-organization, person-group, and person-supervisor fit. *Personnel Psychology, 58,* 281–342.

Kuhn, T. S. (1962, 1970, 1996, 2012). *The structure of scientific revolutions.* Chicago, IL: University of Chicago Press.

Kuusisaari, H. (2014, Oct.). Teachers at the zone of proximal development: Collaboration promoting or hindering the developmental process. *Teachers and Teacher Education, 43,* 46–57. doi:10.1016/j.tate.2014.06.001.

Kyrillidou, M., Lowry, C., Hanges, P. J., & Aiken, J. R., & Justin, K. (2009, March 12–15). ClimateQUAL™: Organizational climate and diversity assessment. In D. M. Mueller (Ed.), *Pushing the edge: Explore, engage, extend* (pp. 150–164). Chicago: American Library Association.

Lee, E. (2015). *The making of Asian Americans: A history.* NY: Simon & Schuster.

Levant, R. F. (July 1, 2005). *Report of the 2005 Presidential Task Force on evidence-based practice.* Washington, DC: American Psychological Association.

Lowman, R. L. (2013). *Internationalizing multiculturalism: Expanding professional competencies in a globalized world.* Washington, DC: American Psychological Association.

Lyons, H. Z., Bike, D. H., Ojeda, L., Johnson, A., Rosales, R., & Flores, L. Y. (2013). Qualitative research as social justice practice with culturally diverse populations. *Journal for Social Action in Counseling and Psychology [Special Issue on Research and Social Justice], 5*(2), 10–25.

Macnicol, J. (2006). *Age discrimination: An historical and contemporary analysis.* Cambridge: Cambridge University Press.

Markus, H. R., Kitayama, S., & Heiman, R. J. (1996). Culture and "basic" psychological principles. In E. T. Higgins & A. W. Kruylanski (Eds.), *Social psychology: Handbook of basic principles* (pp. 857–913). New York: Guilford Press.

Marsella, A. J. (2015, summer). Trends, changes, challenges in North American (Eurocentric) psychology: Rethinking assumptions, practices, and organization in socio-political contexts. *Journal for Social Action in Counseling and Psychology, 7*(1), 143–152.

Martin-Baró, I. (Author), Aron, A. (Ed.), Corne, S. (Ed.), & Mishler, E. G. (Foreward). (1996, Sept.). *Writings for a liberation psychology* (Reprint ed.). Cambridge, MA: Harvard University Press.

McHugh, R. K., & Barlow, D. J. (2010, February-March). The dissemination and implementation of evidence-based psychological treatments: A review of current efforts. *American Psychologist, 65*(2), 73–84. doi:10.1037/a0018121.

McNeil, J. (Principal Investigator), Downer (Co-Principal Investigator), G. A., Daisy, F., Davis, Y. M., Duran, B., KualiI, C. M., Lambert, V., Lowe, J., Maresca, T. M., & Thomas, W. K. (2006). *Be safe: A cultural competency model for American Indians, Alaska Natives, and Native Hawaiians.* Washington, DC:

Howard University Medical School, National Minority AIDS Education and Training Center.

Meadows, D. (n.d.). Donella meadows quotes. BrainyQuote.com. Retrieved November 30, 2016, from BrainyQuote.com web site: https://www.brainyquote.com/quotes/quotes/d/donellamea394366.html.

Meadows, D. H. (Author), & Wright, D. (Ed.). (2008). *Thinking in systems – a primer*. White River Junction, VT: Chelsea Green Publishing.

Michael, R. (2005). *A concise history of American anti-Semitism*. Lanham, MD: Rowman & Littlefield Publishing Group.

Miserocchi, K. M. (2014). *The effect of therapist white privilege attitudes on client outcomes and the therapist-client relationship*. Theses and Dissertations-Educational, School, and Counseling Psychology. Paper 17. Retrieved from uknowledge.uky.edu/cgi/viewcontent.cgi?article=1022&context=edp_etds.

Mizock, L., & Page, K. V. (2016, Summer). Evaluating the ally role: Contributions, limitations, and the activist position in counseling and psychology. *Journal for Social Action in Counseling and Psychology, 8*(1), 17–33.

Montero, M., & Sonn, C. (2009). *The psychology of liberation. Theory and application*. NY: Springer-Verlag. doi:10.1007/978-0-387-85784-8.

Morales, E., & Norcross, J. C. (2010). Evidence-based practices with ethnic minorities: Strange bedfellows no more. *Journal of Clinical Psychology in Practice, 66*(8), 821–829. doi:10.1002/jclp.20712.

Muhammad, A. (1997, May 14). We charge genocide . . . again! *The Washington Informer*, accessed via ProQuest.

Nagata, J. M. (2017, January 6). *Challenges, health implications, and advocacy opportunities for lesbian, gay, bisexual, and transgender global health providers*. [Research Article]. Global Health Promotion (Sage). Retrieved from http:www.journals.sagepub.com. doi:10.1177/1757975916677504.

National Multicultural Conference and Summit. (2017, January 4–6). Portland, OR: Portland Marriott Downtown.

Nielsen, K. E. (2012, Oct.). *A disability history of the United States: Revisioning American history*. Boston: Beacon Press.

Norcross, J. C., Hogan, T. P., & Koocher, G. P. (2008, Fall). Evidence–based practice in psychology. *The Register Report*, p. 10–15.

Office of the Convention on the Prevention and Punishment of the Crime of Genocide. Office of the United Nations High Commissioner for Human Rights. (1951, January 12). Archived from the original on December 11, 2005.

Ostroff, C., & Schulte, M. (2007, January). Multiple perspectives of fit in organizations across levels of analysis. In C. Ostroff & T. A. Judge (Eds.), *Perspectives in organizational fit* (pp. 3–69). NY: Lawrence Erlbaum.

Peck, M. S. (1998). *People of the lie: The hope for healing human evil*. New York: Touchstone (Simon & Schuster).

Peck, M. S. (2005). *Glimpses of the devil*. New York: Free Press, Simon & Schuster.

Pew Research Center. (2011, November 17). *The global attitudes project*. Retrieved from www.pewglobal.org/files/2011/11/Pew-Global-Attitudes-Values-Report.

Piccard, A. (2013–2014). Death by boarding school: "The last acceptable racism" and the United States' genocide of Native Americans. *Gonzaga Law Review, 49*(1), 137–185.

Pronin, E., Gilovich, T., & Ross, L. (2004). Objectivity in the eye of the beholder: Divergent perceptions of bias in self versus others. *Psychological Review, 111*(3), 781–799. doi:10.1037/0033-295X.111.3.781.
Ratts, M. J. (2011, January). Multiculturalism and social justice: Two sides of the same coin. *Journal of Multicultural Counseling and Development, 39*(1), 24–37. doi:10.1002/j.2161-1912.2011.tb00137.x.
Ratts, M. J., & Pedersen, P. B. (2014, Dec.). *Counseling for multiculturalism and social justice: Integration, theory and application* (4th ed.). Alexandria, VA: American Counseling Association.
Ratts, M. J., Singh, A. A., Nassar-McMillan, S., Butler, S. K., & McCullough, J. R. (2016, January). Multicultural and social justice counseling competencies: Guidelines for the counseling profession. *Journal of Multicultural Counseling and Development, 44*(1), 28–48.
Reason, R. D., & Broido, E. M. (2005, Summer). Issues and strategies for social justice allies (and the student affairs professionals who hope to encourage them). *New Directions for Student Services, 110*, 81–89.
Rodriguez, T. (2015, March 1). Descendants of Holocaust survivors have altered stress hormones. *Scientific American.* Retrieved from https://www.scientificamerican.com/article/descendants-of.
Rogers, C. (1980). *A way of being.* New York: Houghton Mifflin.
Rogers, E. M. (2003). *Diffusion of innovations* (5th ed.). New York: Free Press.
Roysicar, G. (2009, April). Evidence-based practice and its implications for culturally sensitive treatment. *Journal of Multicultural Counseling and Development, 37*(2), 66–82. doi:10.1002/j.2161-1912.2009.tb00092.x.
Rubenstein, I., Cutter, F., & Templer, D. I. (1989–1990). Multigenerational occurrence of survivor syndrome symptoms in families of Holocaust survivors. *Omega: Journal of Death and Dying, 20*(3), 239–244. eric.ed.gov/Pid=EJ408232. doi:10.2190/ HX4R-N9QY-49B7-8UEM.
Ruiz, V. L., & DuBois, E. C. (Eds.). (2007, Nov). *Unequal sisters: An inclusive reader in U.S. women's history* (4th ed.). New York: Routledge Taylor & Francis Group.
Sisodia, Raj. (2011). Posting: Summary of thinking in systems by Donella Meadows. *Conscious Capitalism.* Website: consciouscapitalism.org
Schaie, K. W. (1993). Ageist language in psychological research. *American Psychologist, 48*(1), 49–51.
Schnall, E. (2006, Summer). Multicultural counseling and the Orthodox Jew. *Journal of Counseling & Development, 84*(3), 276–282.
Schneider, B. (1987). The people make the place. *Personnel Psychology, 40*, 437–453.
Schneider, B., Goldstein, H. W., & Smith, D. B. (1995). The ASA framework: An update. *Personnel Psychology, 48*, 747–779. doi:10.1089/tmj.2007.0077.
Silva, N. K. (2004). *Aloha betrayed: Native Hawaiian resistance to American Colonialism.* Durham, NC: Duke University Press.
Sloan, T., & Toporek, R. L. (2007, Spring). On social action in counseling and psychology: Visions for the journal. *Journal for Social Action in Counseling*

and Psychology, 1(1) (electronic version). Retrieved from http//www.psysr.org/about%20us.htm.

Smith, T. B., & Trimble, J. E. (2016). *Foundations of multicultural psychology: Research to inform effective practice.* Washington, DC: American Psychological Association.

Stannard, D. E. (2014). *American Holocaust: Columbus and the conquest of the New World* (Rev. ed.). Oxford: Oxford Press.

Stoltenberg, C. D. (2005, December). Enhancing professional competence though developmental approaches to supervision. *American Psychologist, 60*(8), 857–864. doi:10.1037/0003-066X.60.8.85.

Stoltenberg, D. C., McNeill, B., & Delworth, U. (1998). *IDM Supervision: An integrated developmental model of supervising counselors and therapists.* San Francisco: Jossey-Bass.

Stout, C. E., & Hayes, R. A. (2004). *The evidence-based practice: Methods models, and tools for mental health professionals.* Hoboken, NJ: John Wiley & Sons.

Sue, D. W. (1999). Creating conditions for a constructive dialogue on "race": Taking individual and institutional responsibility. In J. Q. Adams & J. R. Welsch (Eds.), *Cultural diversity: Curriculum, classroom, and climate* (pp. 15–20). Chicago: Illinois Staff and Curriculum Developers Association.

Sue, D. W. (2004, December). Whiteness and ethnocentric monoculturalism: Making the "invisible" visible. *American Psychologist, 59*(8), 761–769. doi:10.1037/0003-066X.59.8.761.

Sue, D. W. (2015). *Race talk and the conspiracy of silence: Understanding and facilitating difficult dialogues on race* (1st ed.). Indianapolis, IN: Wiley.

Takaki, R. (2008). *A different mirror: A history of multicultural America* (Rev. ed.). New York: Little, Brown, and Company.

Thomason, T. (2011). Best practices in counseling Native Americans. *Journal of Indigenous Research* [Special Issue], 1(1), article 3.

Umansky, L., Bentall, R., &, Longmore, P. K. (Eds.). (2001). *The new disability history: American perspectives.* New York: New York University Press.

United Nations General Assembly. (1948, Dec. 9). *General Assembly Resolution 260* (The Convention on the prevention and punishment of the crime of genocide). Entered into force on January 12, 1951.

United States Department of Health and Human Services. (2001). *Mental health: Culture, race, and ethnicity – A supplement to mental health: A report of the surgeon general.* Rockville, MD: U.S. Department of Health and Human Services, Substance Abuse and Mental Health Services Administration, Center for Mental Health Services.

Velez, B. L. & Moradi, B. (2012, May). Workplace support, discrimination, and person-organization fit: Tests of the theory of work adjustment with LGB individuals. *Journal of Counseling Psychology, 59*(3), 399–407. doi:10.1037/a0028326.

Washington, H. A. (2006). *Medical apartheid: The dark history of medical experimentation on Black Americans from colonial times to the present.* New York: Harlem Moon.

Wass, R., & Golding, C. (2014). Sharpening a tool for teaching: The zone of proximal development. *Teaching in Higher Education, 19*(6), 671–684. Retrieved from doi: 10.1080/13562517.2014.901958.

We charge genocide: The cry rings true 52 years later. (2003, Feb. 21). *Peoples World.* Retrieved 2016-12-20. http://peoplesworld.org/-we-charge-genocide-the-cry-rings-true-52-years-later/.

Wendt, D. C., & Gone, J. P. (2016, June). Integrating professional and Indigenous therapies: An urban American Indian narrative clinical case study. *The Counseling Psychologist, 44*(5), 695–729. doi:10.1177/0011000016638741.

Whitbeck, L. B., Adams, G. W., Hoyt, D. R., & Chen, X. (June, 2004). Conceptualizing and measuring historical trauma among American Indian people. *American Journal of Community Psychology, 33*(3–4), 119–130. doi:10.1023/B:AJCP.0000027000.77357.31.

Whitt, L. A. (2004). Biocolonialism and the commodification of knowledge. In A. Waters (Ed.), *American Indian thought* (pp. 188–213). Malden, MA: Blackwell.

Williams, H. A. (n.d.). *How slavery affected African American families. Freedom's Story*, TeacherServe. National Humanities Center. Retrieved from http://nationalhumanitiescenter.org/tserve/freedom/1609-1865/essays/aafamilies.htm.

Wilson, J. P., Hugenberg, K., & Rule, N. O. (2017, March 13). Racial bias in judgments of physical size and formidability: From size to threat. *Journal of Personality and Social Psychology, 113*(1), 59–80. doi:10.1037/pspi0000092.supp.

Witko, T. M. (Ed. and translator). (2006, April). *Mental health care for urban Indians: Clinical insights from native practitioners*. Washington, DC: American Psychological Association.

Chapter 2

The Existential Change in Perspective in the Diagnostic and Statistics Manual, Fifth Edition (DSM-5)

David D. Moore

EDITOR'S (SOG'S) INTRODUCTION

The *Diagnostic and Statistical Manual of Mental Disorders—Fifth Edition* (DSM-5) Cultural Formulation Interview (Fernández, Aggarwall, Hinton, Hinton, & Kirmayer, 2016) was developed to provide a standardized approach to cultural assessment, the results of which could then be integrated into contemporary Western clinical, teaching, and research practices that make use of the DSM-5 framework (American Psychiatric Association, 2013). The Cultural Formulation Interview covers four domains: individual cultural identity, the client's cultural explanations of illness, cultural factors related to the client's psychosocial environment and levels of functioning, and cultural factors relating to the client-clinician relationship.

The Cultural Formulation Interview does not provide specific guidelines to facilitate that self-assessment, nor does the assessment discuss in detail the many shapes that Euro-American psychology clinicians, educators, and researchers biases can take in the form of racism, ageism, ableism, classism, sexism, heteronormativity, and other biases against the young, those who face intellectual challenges, people in certain occupations, and individuals with mental disorders such as agoraphobia, depression, eating disorders, personality disorders, and posttraumatic stress disorder (PTSD) (Caplan & Cosgrove, 2004). In addition, mental health professionals attempting to use the Cultural Formulation Interview may experience confusion about how to integrate and apply the Cultural Formulation Interview or other cultural assessments to their own areas of professional interest such as research, clinical practice, and education.

David. D. Moore draws from his expertise in a number of areas: local, national, and international psychological research that has involved both Euro-American and Indigenous populations, international consulting with special populations, university graduate teaching, clinical practice with diverse populations, and credibility with both Euro-American and Indigenous populations. He demonstrates in-depth understandings of the diverse ethnocultural groups with whom he is interacting, a skilled understanding of the DSM-5, cultural humility, and a balanced approach in integrating best practices of Euro-American psychology with cultural state-of-the art best practices.

Combining the insights he has from those professional endeavors, he discusses both the strengths and limitations of DSM-5 conceptualizations in regard to the integration of culture into contemporary Western psychological research, teaching, and clinical practices. He clearly articulates ways that the DSM-5 can lead psychologists into greater cultural competency and social justice skills.

DSM-5: THE MAP TO POSTCOLONIAL PERSON-CENTERED PSYCHOLOGICAL SERVICES

This chapter began writing itself on May 30, 2013. Like many professionals in the behavioral health services, mine was among Amazon.com's first wave of preordered texts that showed up in mailboxes across the country announcing themselves to be the first printing of the DSM-5 (American Psychiatric Association, 2013). The DSM-5, its preordained nickname, arrived in all of the American Psychiatric Association's regal trappings of gold-embossed, deep-purple binding, which was to be expected from its predecessors of I (American Psychiatric Association, 1952), II (American Psychiatric Association, 1968), III (American Psychiatric Association, 1980), and various versions of IV (American Psychiatric Association, 1994, 2000). But outside of forsaking the Roman numerals in favor of the less-august simple number 5, this text offered a paradigm shift that could well prove to be of tectonic magnitude within the field of psychology—a full 180-degree shift of focus from the clinician to the consumer. While the publication of DSM-5 (American Psychiatric Association, 2013) can only point the direction, it is a clear map to diagnosis and treatment from an individual cultural case formulation based on the tenets of developmental psychology.

Gone is the primacy of group statistics and matching consumers to evidence-based treatment based on their "goodness of fit" to that standardization. It now becomes incumbent on the behavioral health service provider to consider the phenomenological perspectives of the consumer's unique developmental paths. Beyond that, as outlined in DSM-5 (American Psychiatric Association, 2013), a cultural case formulation comes from the client's own description of symptoms, personal health definitions, and desired service outcomes. Since this is a phenomenological model at its core, we can borrow from the descriptions of phenomenology that guided the original person-centered thinking of Carl Rogers (Farber, Brink, & Raskin, 1996; Rogers, 1942, 1951, 1961, 1986, 1995) and succeeding psychological trailblazers following his line of focus. A clear definition from Snygg and Combs (1940) is adapted for this chapter and text:

A phenomenological view of psychology emphasizes that the self is the true subject matter for psychology. Not the objective view of colonial psychology; with its attempt to fit each person to a group standardization process. The phenomenal field is how the subject, in this case the consumer of psychological services, sees their life path, how it intersects with seeking the clinician's services, and what they expect from the clinician. Each clinical dyad is a unique experience that must be formulated around the client's subjective view of the world. This is what is called the phenomenal field for diagnosis and treatment (Combs & Snygg, 1959; Snygg & Combs, 1949).

DSM-5 SECTIONS I AND II: REMOVING THE MULTIAXIAL STRUCTURE OF COLONIAL PSYCHOLOGY AND THE INSTITUTIONAL PRISON OF THE GLOBAL ASSESSMENT OF FUNCTIONING SCALE

"Dave: Blessings as you walk on the healing path. Prayers."

(E. Duran, personal communication, August, 2016)

The essence of this chapter and those that follow will introduce the reader to thinking from a phenomenological view of the authors. From different worlds of contemporary psychology, we are offering a new direction. There are many terms for the era we are leaving: "Western psychology," "European-American," or "clinical psychology"—just to name a few. The one truth that drives my own thinking has been coming to fully know that there were thriving nations in North America in the 1400s, just as there were in Europe. Those nations in North America drew what they needed from the world they inhabited to thrive and prosper across many generations. They expended a great deal of thought and energy to be a part of that world; allowing it to feed, clothe, celebrate, heal, and create an ever-refined narrative of a place-based culture. The nations of Europe were working in a different direction: to build machines that could change the land and its offerings as well as leave the place of their national origins to gain access to the materials and products of other centers of human existence. The nations of Europe colonized North America and subjugated the nations already there. In the early 1900s, they infused psychology into this colonization. I accept this as the most parsimonious definition of the era we are leaving behind and the basic attempt to, intentionally or not, use the external group view of cognitive behavioral and psychodynamic psychology in order to mold the individual to this world of standardization. The words at the beginning of this chapter were signed on the first page of my copy of the writings of Eduardo and Bonnie Duran on the Native American experiences with a call for postcolonial psychology (Duran & Duran, 1995)—almost two decades before some of its hope was ushered in by the DSM-5 of 2013.

How to make sense of the postcolonial world of DSM-5 (American Psychiatric Association, 2013)? What of the past is relevant for the future? Borrowing from the psychological theory behind the blossoming contemporary use of the word narrative to identify a person's unique developmental history, I would suggest that the task for each of us already in the service field, and those seeking a credentialed entry, is to understand that we each have our own narratives about what it means to be a psychologist (or other allied behavioral health services provider) and how people practice psychology. From there, you can review and deconstruct-reconstruct those meanings around those constructs.

If you remember back to your first "Psychology Practice Skills 101" or similar class, you likely took turns with a partner being the interviewer and the interviewee. I remember thinking I was awkward, not nearly as well prepared as my self-image led me to believe, but, above all, still maintaining an eagerness to be of service to others. When I began to read Section III (the Cultural Case Formulation) of DSM-5 (American Psychiatric Association, 2013), after almost two decades as a psychologist and three as a therapist, that entire experience came back to confront me. The Cultural Case Formulation model initially left me feeling adrift in the sea of traditional psychology.

In the short four years since the publication of the DSM-5 (American Psychiatric Association, 2013), I am realizing this to be a communal experience of the members' of psychology losing their anchors amidst the ocean of cognitive behavioral learning theory and the psychodynamic object relations training that permeated the clinical practice field and the research universities of the current era of learning, practice, research, and teaching. Certainly, some of us of that era had the person-centered interests of Carl Rogers or believed in the radical psychology of existentialists like R. D. Laing[1] (Burston, 2000; Laing, 1960). But with funding for practice oriented to standardization of measuring therapy against pre determined norms, or researchers chasing the holy grail of group norms and standard deviations—there was no real room for diagnosis and treatment based on a phenomenological, person-centered case formulation. Even after the Laing-inspired Rosenhan Experiments[2] were published in *Science* in 1973 (Rosenhan, 1973) and effectively destroyed the legitimacy of standardized diagnosis and treatment according to DSM-I (American Psychiatric Association, 1952) and DSM-II (American Psychiatric Association, 1968), the field of psychology (and its medical associates in psychiatry) simply continued to double down on the faulty premise of matching the individual to group norms.

Colonial psychology of standardization reached its apex in DSM-IV (American Psychiatric Association, 1994) and DSM-IV-TR (American Psychiatric Association, 2000), with the measuring and coding of each individual to the five domains of group expectations. Aptly termed "axes" for the way they chopped down individuals, with the release of DSM-5 (American Psychiatric Association, 2013) psychology and psychiatry did away with this colonial denial of the individual. Postcolonial psychology removed the multiaxial diagnosis and probably its most onerous axe—Axis V: Global Assessment of Functioning. Called the GAF, it measured each individual against the prevailing societal standards and expectations in the work place, the home, community laws, and procedures—even the colonial psychologist's perception of the person's judgment, decision-making, and mental state. In order to establish one's psychological health, a person needed to conform at ever-greater levels to this scale of 1–100. If anyone doubts how institutionalized the GAF is, there are countless examples in health-care funding, construction of community mental health systems to serve those in the range of 40–49, and institutionalization of persons based on their falling below a certain GAF level. In one of the states I practice in, Washington State, the GAF score of a consumer dictates whether or not a therapist with a particular type of credentialing may treat that client. The love of standardized measurement for the researcher at the universities producing the next generation of psychologists was fueled by this subjective measurement in the hands of those credentialed to wield Axis Number 5.

If a person currently in the field does not see the enormity of what lies ahead, she or he is still within the comfortable cocoon of denial constructed over 40 years since Rosenhan's experiments (Rosenhan, 1973). This experimental field research reality tested what was actually going on in our most preeminent training hospitals of psychology and psychiatry under the guidance of DSM-I (American Psychiatric Association, 1952) and DSM-II (American Psychiatric Association, 1968). This research clearly showed those emperors of colonial psychology continuing down the paths of the DSM with no clothes of logical health practices in subsequent editions of DSM-III (American Psychiatric Association, 1980) and -IV (American Psychiatric Association, 1994, 2000). This discredited process has been able to continue because it is abetted by the funding and credentialing foundation upon which our national psychological services system rests—at least until May 2013.

Before pointing a way forward, itself an individual task, let us look at what we are left with when psychological measurements of research and practice are banished from our everyday use. Professionals in the current mental health system will now have to diagnose and practice without measuring disability or service outcome by a GAF. All a person needs to do is to look to the common, phenomenologically driven World Health Organization Disability Assessment Schedule 2.03 (Gold, 2014). This is the suggested replacement for the GAF and has been published within DSM-5 to underscore that point. Consumers now identify their own difficulties in functioning within the communities they live in, including real issues of transportation, intra-household job sharing, and even the following 2 of the 36-item WHO DAS 2.0 from Section D6 (Gold, 2014) on assisting the consumer with "Participation in Society:"

D6.2. How much of a problem did you have because of barriers or hindrances in the world around you?
D6.3 How much of a problem did you have living with dignity because of the attitudes and actions of others?

If you hail from the networks of current psychology and its institutions, you should realize that this is not a task of simply changing the client's electronic health record dropdown menus of diagnosis, treatment, and billing for services. The local community psychological services facilities, which maintain the delusion that institutional bias and discrimination do not exist, need only look at the millions of dollars spent on its agency "information system" and the countless millions beyond that to the record-keeping that defines clients who have engaged their services. Beyond these standardized-based records—a foundational description of colonization—there are decades of policies and procedures to standardize the staff to the multiaxial system and GAF measurement driving it. Preservice and in-service training along with the weekly staff meeting to train to the policies and procedures have poured succeeding layers of cement on that foundation of clinical standardization. Psychologists, allied professionals, and those on a credentialing track, waiting for an institutional group-ordained path forward, are asking for a fix from the failed system that the DSM-5 (American Psychiatric Association, 2013) is designed to address. Why not follow the DSM-5's (American Psychiatric Association, 2013) set of individualized guidelines out of the quagmire of DSM I–IV (American Psychiatric Association, 1952, 1968, 1980, 1994, 2000) and their discredited foundation? Take yourself back to that first class on basic engagement with the client entering the space you would occupy as a psychologist. In this case, let DSM-5 (American Psychiatric Association, 2013) be the interviewer as you try to look through the new lens it has given you.

DSM-5, SECTION III: A PSYCHOLOGIST'S PATH FORWARD INTO CULTURAL CASE FORMULATION

Section 3 of DSM-5 (American Psychiatric Association, 2013) lays out the model for diagnosing and treating persons who engage the services of psychotherapists. It is fully described as a Cultural Case Formulation and includes questions for the clinician to pose to the client in order to ensure that the client's phenomenological views are heard and understood. I suggest that practitioners use those questions as guidelines in order to construct their own narratives about their fit in the world of psychology. Construct your own narratives and then be bold enough to deconstruct them after reading this book. Take what you find that is useful and leave the rest. Then reconstruct your destiny among the rest of us working to embrace postcolonial psychology. Perhaps my experience and the other authors in this text can inform your own journey.

The beginning of my deconstruction and reconstruction of 30 years in psychology and psychotherapy began with the DSM-5's (American Psychiatric Association, 2013) example of a Cultural Case Formulation that follows, not surprisingly, the use of the WHO DAS (World Health Organization, undated) as a replacement for the GAF. I simply took the role of the client in answering several of those questions, focusing on the fact that I had found myself struggling with the "problem" of the current European-American medical and colonial models of psychology. The questions are taken directly from DSM-5 (American Psychiatric Association, 2013), and my responses to those questions are based on my personal experiences since entering the profession of psychology. The first question is a classic example of the 180-degree change in focus ushered in by DSM-5 (American Psychiatric Association, 2013).

"People often understand their problems in their own way, which may be similar to or different from how doctors describe the problem. How would you describe your problem?"

My "psychological problem" began in 1987 on a journey from the University of Washington to a counseling psychology conference that was held in Atlanta, Georgia. Before beginning my psychology doctorate at the University of Washington, I had been a chemical dependency professional for six years. In the field of addictions, authenticity and one's own personal narratives are important to the professional base of the therapist. As I was introduced to the field of psychology, there was a profound difference between the clinical and counseling psychology divisions of the American Psychological Association—both were licensure tracks to becoming a licensed psychologist. I chose counseling psychology as my path to licensure and practice.

Within the clinical text of that era, Diagnostic and Statistics Manual, Fourth Edition—Text Revision (DSM IV-TR; American Psychiatric Association, 2000), the emphasis was on standards of behavior, averages, norms, and individual deviations from those norms. This was a world that rejected the transpersonal spaces and relationships between the therapists and clients in favor of external measurements and placing the client on a continuum of behavior. The personal narratives of the clinician or the existential phenomenological views of the client were nowhere to be seen in that text.

However, at that counseling psychology conference in 1987, I found that there was a world of psychology that lay just below that text which was largely the product of psychiatry, pharmaceutical research, and the clinical psychology division of the American Psychological Association. In that world of counseling psychology, I found the research in personality paradigms from Carl Rogers, R. D. Laing, Donald Super, and Irvin Yalom. My own travel partner, Dr. Larry Brammer, was president of Division 17, the Society of Counseling Psychology, that year. While not a solution for my psychological problem of the day, the seven days at that conference breathed life back into my quest to assist clients through the health services of a psychologist—a professional field of behavioral health that I felt I could find in the frameworks and teachings of humanists and existentialists within the counseling psychology world.

For you, what are the most important aspects of your background or identity? Are there any aspects of your background or identity that make a difference to your "psychological problem"?

Across the language of practitioners in psychology and psychiatry, the most oft-heard phrase is "evidence based practices." This phrase conjures up the notion that psychological practices being applied in any given situation are based on an empirical "best practice." This notion of best practice for the individual rests on research's having established that most people acquire the best behavioral health gains when using a standard prescription of treatment interventions—which is synonymous with "truth." Therefore, what is "a best practice" for everyone is the same practice that should be applied to every person across from the clinician. And there lies the dilemma—the clinician "is doing something to" the client, who has come seeking improvement in his or her individual behavioral health. But where is the individual's truth about what will work best in her or his life, supportive community, and integration with past developmental experiences? In other words, how can one arrive at an individualized case formulation by trying to fit each client into the squares and circles of DSM-IV (American Psychiatric Association, 1994, 2000)?

The entire existing paradigm is washed away with the loss of the GAF scale, multiaxial research outcomes, and the associated structure that represents the foundations of colonial psychology.

Fortunately for those seeking licensure as a psychologist, individuals must include the education and knowledge of the field of psychology as part of their educational endeavors. As I wrote before, I had arrived at this venture of psychological licensure from a previous field of credentialing as a chemical dependency professional. In that field, the individual's life experiences, the defenses that barricaded them from others, and their loss of reality testing were starting points in chemical dependency services of the 1980s. That field was fairly impervious to the notion of standardized evidenced-based practices.

The field of the chemical dependency professionals had been well established in the work of Vernon Johnson that laid out the parameters of addiction treatment in 1970 (Johnson, 1973). Having had the good fortune to be appointed the director of the last treatment facility designed by Vernon Johnson, Scripps Memorial Hospital and its McDonald Center in La Jolla, California, I can attest that in the year 2000 nothing had truly changed from that core text. That text, which the American Medical Association used as a defining guide to declaring alcoholism a disease in 1970, was often called the Minnesota Model due to its initial use in the hospitals and residential facilities of the Twin Cities in Minnesota. Diagnosis and treatment were based on two principles that remain unchanged today: (1) that addiction therapists need to facilitate addicts' discovery of themselves as feeling persons among their fellows and (2) that therapists and consumers needed to work together to identify the individual defenses that block that discovery. This was very much a phenomenological, and individualized, process of assessment and treatment. Today, even with the chemical dependency field having been diluted by the world of DSM-IV (American Psychiatric Association, 1994, 2000) psychology—which has close to swallowed the separate professional field of addiction counselor and treatment facility licensure—addiction psychologists and allied counseling staff will tell you that a diagnosis of abuse or dependency is worth very little unless it is a phenomenological self-diagnosis.

For me and for others in that field over the past 35 years, there was no supposition on the part of clinicians that we knew in advance what lie behind the defenses of each person entering their care or how those individuals would reach a self-assessment of their behavioral health problems. The idea that a standardized, evidenced-based practice could be applied to each alcoholic or addict who came into the clinical world of the chemical dependency professional would have been foolhardy. Clinicians had to join with that client and assist with his or her individual journey by modeling themselves as an authentic, genuine, and unconditionally caring professionals.

In 1985, as I moved into the world of research and inquiry around the field of psychology and its medical cousin of psychiatry, the first concept I ran into was research targeting the fundamental question of behavioral health: "Does psychotherapy work?" I found that question had been answered in the affirmative decades before by Dr. Carl Rogers, a humanist who believed that each person's psychological difficulties could only be defined by herself or himself in a phenomenological way. Psychotherapy had been proven to work as a health practice based on research derived from Rogers' findings that it was the therapeutic dyad that made the difference in psychotherapy. What clinicians needed to bring to the dyad, as they joined with their clients, were the fundamentals of being genuine, unconditionally accepting, and congruent in words and the nonverbal manner in which that clinician entered into the partnership. Although mired in the world of DSM-IV (American Psychiatric Association, 1994) and DSM-IV-TR (American Psychiatric Association, 2000) from 1987 to 2014, I was able to hold on to the truths I had found as an early clinician in the chemical dependency profession: knowing that within the world of psychology and psychiatry the validation that psychotherapy, or psychology if you will, worked was solidly founded on what existentialist R. D. Laing called, almost reverently, the transpersonal space: a space that worked to produce positive change if the practitioner could bring to the consumer the Rogerian capacities of genuineness, consistency, congruence with the client, and unconditional positive regard (Laing, 1960).

DECONSTRUCTING THIRTY YEARS OF PRACTICE, RESEARCH, AND TEACHING IN THE WORLD OF DSM-IV

Answering the questions from the DSM-5 (American Psychiatric Association, 2013), Cultural Case Formulation creates a personal narrative that is rich in the experiences of living a life—both the Rogerian Peak Experiences and the low valleys of failure, probably better seen as many of the mentors who helped me out of the crevasses would say, "Another opportunity for personal growth." As one of the authors of this text, I hope the reader experiences some of that kind of reflection that I found in the 208 pages of the Durans' writing on what the era of postcolonial psychology could be (Duran & Duran, 1995). Their basic truths resonated with me as the best fit as a Prologue to DSM-5 (American Psychiatric Association, 2013). There was no reason that the psychologist of today cannot first deconstruct the whole into the mountains and valleys, with the subsequent reconstruction of a new sense of self and purpose.

I like to think that this constructionist psychological approach would resonate with several of the members of the Wednesday Psychological Society of 1901, which is seen as the caldron that produced what we think of as Modern European-American Psychology. Meeting in Sigmund Freud's home, this "Baker's Dozen" of theoreticians included Carl Jung and Erik Erikson. Jung, Freud's heir apparent, was cast out to his worldwide study of psychological truth among Indigenous peoples. He looked for the core of psychology, psychic DNA, in the archetypes of tribes of people across the world. Jung sought common truths in the place-based populations who found their goodness-of-fit with the world that sustained them over generations.

When Erik Erikson took leave of this group, it was then called the Viennese Psychoanalytic Society in honor of the group's developmental stage theory of Oedipal and Electra lust, with the destructive passion of Thantos thrown in for good measure. Erikson did not journey to the European universities of his day to further reality test this Greco-Roman tale of how a child matures into the adult. As he came across the Atlantic Ocean in search of the refinements he would bring to the tale of child-to-adult, he did not seek the cognitive behaviorists of Columbia and Harvard universities or their preeminent thinkers represented by Thorndike, Watson, and Skinner. He went to the Lakota Sioux Nation and its Seven Councils rather than to the colleges of the 45 colonized United States of the time. He passed on these teachings as a full cycle of life known as Erikson's Stage Theory—from the clan trust learned by the newborn to the integrity of life experiences that are passed on in teachings from the elders. Erikson's teachings would blossom into some of the most successful psychological endeavors during the colonial era, including the Head Start program with its echoes of clan support to the tribe's children. This is my truth as well. There is much to learn from colonial psychology, whether by maintaining an experience that was stronger than the foundation that brought it forth—or for that most sacred of experiences—that which represents the wrong fork taken in pursuit of something good and which clearly lights the way back to a newly clarified truth.

For my colleagues and fellow field researchers at the University of Washington, Johns Hopkins, and Argosy University, DSM-5 (American Psychiatric Association, 2013) has offered me a way to index two cycles of national research: 1987–1996 and 2001–2012. Both cycles are closely aligned with the practitioner focus of chapter 3 of this book. The first cycle represents a strengthening of a national movement to stop the twin threats faced by our children in their pursuit of adulthood—substance abuse and violence. As this movement largely collapsed during the second cycle of research, that which remained allows for a transitional view from the research-driven DSM-IV (American Psychiatric Association, 1994, 2000) to the client-centered view of DSM-5 (American Psychiatric Association, 2013).

Many Research 101 courses teach the perspective that field research which fails to show the expected success often has as strong a value as that which succeeds in meeting outcome expectations. After almost 30 years of field research, I wish I could return to my Program Evaluation or Quasi-Experimental Design courses of the mid-1980s and rewrite the syllabi around the theme of "They DO shoot the messenger." Whether it was the community parents refusing to accept the rising rate of teenage depression or their daytime surrogates of the school districts deciding to ignore their alternative high school population as having rates of substance abuse well above two-thirds of the student body—the Drug-Free Schools and Communities Act of 1986 initiated 25 years of funding to implement the now 300+ "evidence-based" prevention programs listed on the National Registry of Evidence-Based Programs. The untold tens of billions of dollars that were spent to impact the behavioral health of our children using the psychological standards of group statistics and "evidence of effectiveness" in the era of DSM-IV's (American Psychiatric Association, 1994, 2000) colonial psychology were a resounding failure—even though I never saw any program evaluations that noted a failure of outcomes that pointed the next round of programming on a different pathway.

The lack of "evidence of ineffectiveness" to learn from, in retrospection, seems incredible to me looking at the end of the Office of Safe and Drug-Free Schools in 2012—under a Democratic Presidency and Democratic Congress. What little funding remained looks nothing like the Grand Experiment in social engineering that was kicked off with such fanfare in 1986. Having been the program evaluator for much of the Safe and Drug Free Schools research grants within the University of Washington's Center for the Study and Teaching of At-Risk Students from 1987 to 1995, I fully acknowledge being part of the published research that institutionalized a system built upon group standardization, using the National Registry of Evidence Based Programs and Practices (NREPP) registry that measured "evidence" by those tests of significance (Moore, 1993; Moore & Forster, 1993). Significance being changes of a very small percentage of behavior in a teenage population under the siege of substance-use disorders since the 1970s. Binge drinking would go up as the "illicit" use of pot was trending downward. The suppression of pot another year would see a rise of methamphetamine—as if outcomes were the Pillsbury Doughboy of ripple effects. But showing some evidence, in the group data of choice, won another round of funding. As we assemble this text among the rising tide of opiate addiction, there is simply no credible evidence that a massively funded effort to change the behavioral health of our youth, using an evidence-based registry of over 300 "Effective Programs" born in the era of DSM-IV (American Psychiatric Association, 1994, 2000) colonial research and practice has been anything but marginally successful.

THE C-STARS DEVELOPMENTAL RESEARCH ARCHIVES TO THE FIRESTARTER MOVEMENT

It is extremely difficult to write about the second research cycle of 2001–2012 and avoid sweeping individuals into the massive institutional failures of that era, but my perspective remains that this was a national case example of colonial psychology social engineering. I served as program evaluator for four Safe and Drug Free Communities national grants from the Substance Abuse and Mental Health Services (SAMHSA). Each grant received $500,000 in federal funds matched to a similar amount of local contributions.

These DFC Grants, as they were called, continued at the University of Washington's Center for the Study and Teaching of At-Risk Students (UW C-STARS), where I was the associate director for these grants and the much larger Safe Schools and Healthy Students grants. UW C-STARS closed its doors in 2004, and I concluded this research cycle as a research assistant faculty member at Johns Hopkins' Bloomberg School of Public Health from 2004 to 2007. During the same period, I served as a program evaluator for two of the oversized Safe Schools Healthy Students grants: one had a three-year grant of $3 million in federal funds and the other had a three-year grant of $9 million.

The goal of this chapter is to use those many national research endeavors at the end of the DSM-IV era to establish a transition point into the postcolonial world of DSM-5. It also allows the reader to cross-reference real-life experiences in which communities attempted to approach behavioral health strategies in order to reduce problems in the children and youth populations, most notably: (1) those disorders that emanate from, or are associated with, substance use disorders; (2) school dropout learning difficulties, often related to ADHD or associated oppositional and conduct disorders; (3) behavioral health disorders that caused aggression toward self or others; and (4) the range of stressors that created an array of adjustment disorders with associated problems of anxiety, depression, and disordered conduct.

In the first research cycle of 1987–1996, when the University of Washington housed the C-STARS, the field research was based on the Student Assistance Program model. Early research on stopping the youth substance-use epidemic relied on the adult model of Employee Assistance. Instead of connecting behavioral health services to the adult's employer, the behavioral health services for children and youth were connected to the school district. After the first decade of Student Assistance Program field research, a replication of the Special Education Team emerged within local school structures. The Drug Free Schools and Communities Act of 1986 partially funded and directed the schools to house behavioral health policies and procedures in order to identify students who showed symptoms of substance-use difficulties and related behavioral health problems.

Since this was somewhat similar to the Special Education "Focus of Concern" (PL 94–142) used to identify students with significant learning problems, it was not surprising to see the emergence of (1) a Student Assistance Team (SAT) similar to the Special Education Team, with a (2) community behavioral health professional conducting consultations and evaluation for the SAT that mirrored the role of the school psychologist, and (3) community behavioral health therapy similar to a school's special education services (Moore and Forster, 1993). In some of the more successful models, the clinical services were housed in the schools, which today live on in the integration of community behavioral therapy in the Special Education Programs for students who meet both the school district functional learning definition of Severely Emotionally Disturbed (SED) and the community mental health agencies diagnostic definition of SED. What is important to understand is that whether using the school SED or the mental health SED classifications, the funding attached to these children is on a case rate basis. In other words, schools or agencies receive weekly funding for each case and are allowed wide latitude to spend those funds particularly in terms of the credentialing of staff and use of para-professionals, as well as having great leeway in creating service models in which the absence at therapeutic activities (no-show rates) does not harm reimbursement rates at nearly the level as having reimbursement tied directly to attended services (called fee-for-service).

Unfortunately, when considering the overall prevalence rates of 13–20% of children and youth who suffer mental health problems, the remaining 9–16% of children do not qualify for case rates and, under fee-for-service, the credentialing and no-show costs have been far too prohibitive to maintain the school-based services for identifying students outside of traditional special education.

As for additional funding, Drug Free Communities was expanded to Safe and Drug Free Communities in order to include the on-campus violence following the Columbine High School shootings in Littleton, Colorado, on April 20, 1999. This also moved from the lower level of community-based funding in the Safe and Drug Free Communities mobilization dollars ($100–150,000 annually in matching) to the over-sized school-based mobilization dollars ($1–3 million) under Safe and Healthy Schools. Today, the DFC program continues in a greatly reduced level of funds based on the finding that communities that stay mobilized at the level of $200–250,00 a year have lower rates of substance use than those that don't. The meta-analysis researchers who wish to determine whether the change is meaningful in an overall behavioral health perspective or whether it can be sustained after federal dollars are gone can do their own evaluations.

As for my experience, except for the Juneau DFC grant and local funds that allowed us to transition into the sustainable prevention model that still exists in that community (2007–2011), the DFC grants and larger Safe and Healthy Schools grants have little to commend them. At one of my SSHS sites, the community coalition and evaluators were removed and replaced with a group of local social service providers in order to use the funding to buy services instead of engaging in systems change. No systems change occurred, and services ended with the grant. At one DFC site, the school board stopped participating in the national biennial survey of student health behaviors. This effectively erected a barrier to most grants that would address their high rates of substance use that were identified in the era of DSM-IV but remain unknown for the past decade. This is in sharp contrast to the other 22 school districts in their area where all, or certainly an overwhelming majority, continue to monitor their student health behaviors.

This text is meant to be a guide into the new postcolonial psychological world, with the DSM-5 (American Psychiatric Association, 2013) being the gateway into seeing the world as a phenomenological construct based on the person before the behavioral health practitioner, whether that person be a psychologist, social worker, chemical dependency professional, mental health professional, marriage or family therapist, or any of the other titles that denote a certain level of education and experience provided by universities or other groups that hold the knowledge necessary to assist the person along their behavioral health path to credentialing. These diverse behavioral health practitioners of the post-DSM-IV and postcolonial era of psychology are now joining with consumers as people acting in service to other people by engaging with them for their behavioral or social service knowledge. This means that the titles or diplomas after one's name are offered to the consumer as a starting point in a new era of "Informed Consent."

As the author of this chapter describing a new behavioral health paradigm, it is important to provide the reader with the materials written in the language of the developmental research that largely influenced this chapter. Rest assured, as best we could, those of us implementing DSM-5 philosophy, strategies, and methodology (often well before publication of DSM-5 (American Psychiatric Association, 2013) were required to write down "the path less traveled" for the funding bodies and other researchers in the language of that era.

In the next chapter, Don Coyhis (White Bison, 2006) and I will introduce you to what we have reconstructed from the learnings of the two field research cycles, particularly in Juneau, Alaska, where there was only one path of prevention leadership left after the inability of local behavioral health systems and the school district to engage in systemic change—the network of Pediatric Primary Care; the Juneau United Medical Practices and Parents (JUMPP) was born out of the last DFC Grant in 2008—developing a system of integrated Psychological and Primary Care Services a full two years before that philosophy was included in the Affordable Care Act of 2010 (Moore & Coyhis, 2010).

NOTES

1. http://www.psychologistanywhereanytime.com/famous_psychologist_and_psychologists/psychologist_famous_r_d_lang.htm.
2. https://en.wikipedia.org/wiki/Rosenhan_experiment.

REFERENCES

American Psychiatric Association. (1952). *Diagnostic and statistical manual of mental disorders*. Washington, DC: Author.

American Psychiatric Association. (1968). *Diagnostic and statistical manual of mental disorders* (2nd ed., text rev.). Washington, DC: Author.

American Psychiatric Association. (1980). *Diagnostic and statistical manual of mental disorders* (3rd ed., text rev.). Washington, DC: Author.

American Psychiatric Association. (1994). *Diagnostic and statistical manual of mental disorders* (4th ed.). Washington, DC: Author.

American Psychiatric Association. (2000). *Diagnostic and statistical manual of mental disorders* (4th ed., Text Revision). Washington, DC: Author.

American Psychiatric Association. (2013). *Diagnostic and statistical manual of mental disorders* (5th ed.). Arlington, VA: Author.

Burston, D. (2000). *The crucible of experience: R. D. Laing and the crisis of psychotherapy*. Cambridge, MA: Harvard University Press.

Caplan, P. J., & Cosgrove, L. (Eds.). (2004). *Bias in psychiatric diagnosis* (A project of the Association on for Women in Psychology). New York: Jason Aronson.

Combs, A. W., & Snygg, D. (1959). *Individual behavior: A perceptual approach to behavior*. New York: Harper.

Duran, E., & Duran, B. (1995). *Native American postcolonial psychology*. Albany, NY: State University of New York.

Farber, B. A., Brink, D. C., & Raskin, P. M. (Eds.). (1996). *The psychotherapy of Carl Rogers: Cases and commentary*. New York: Guilford Press.

Fernández, R. L., Aggarwall, N. K., Hinton, L., Hinton, D. E., & Kirmayer, L. J. (2016). *DSM-5 handbook on the cultural formulation interview*. Washington, DC: American Psychiatric Publishing.

Gold, L. H. (June, 2014). Assessment Schedule 2.0 (WHODAS 2.0). Journal of the American Academy of Psychiatry and the Law Online, 42(2), 173–181.

Johnson, V. (1973). *I'll quit tomorrow*. New York: Harper & Row.

Laing, R. D. (1960). *The divided self: An existential study in sanity and madness*. London: Penguin.

Moore, D. D. (1993). New directions in working with at-risk children. *Journal of Emotional and Behavioral Problems*, 2(3), 28–32.

Moore, D., & Coyhis, D. (2010, July). The multicultural Wellbriety peer recovery support program: Two decades of community-based recovery. *Alcoholism Treatment Quarterly*, 28(3), 273–292. doi:10.1080/07347324.2010.488530.

Moore, D. D., & Forster, G. (1993). Student assistance programs: New approaches for reducing adolescent substance abuse. *Journal of Counseling and Development*, 71(3), 259–261. doi:10.1002/j.1556-6676.1993.tb02221.x.

Rogers, C. (1942). *Counseling and psychotherapy*. Boston, MA: Houghton Mifflin Company.

Rogers, C. (1951). *Client-centered therapy*. Boston, MA: Houghton Mifflin Company.

Rogers, C. (1961). *On becoming a person: A therapist's view of psychotherapy*. Boston, MA: Houghton Mifflin.

Rogers, C. (1986). Carl Rogers on the development of the person-centered approach. *Person-Centered Review*, 1(3), 257–259.

Rogers, C. (1995). *On becoming a person: A therapist's view of psychotherapy* (2nd ed.). Wilmington, MA: Mariner Books (Houghton Mifflin Harcourt Imprint).

Rosenhan, D. (1973, January). On being sane in insane places. *Science*, 179 (4070), 250–258. doi:10.1126/science.179.4070.250.

Snygg, D., & Combs, A. W. (1949). *Individual behavior: A new frame of reference for psychology*. New York: Harper.

White Bison, Inc. (2006). *The red road to wellbriety: In the native American way, 1st edition*. Colorado Springs, CO: Author.

World Health Organization (undated). WHO disability assessment schedule (WHODAS 2.0). Retrieved from http://www.who.int/classifications/icf/more_whodas/en/.

Chapter 3

The Psychologist and Allied Behavioral Health Facilitators Retrained as Humanistic Firestarters

David D. Moore and Don Coyhis

If you are a psychologist or other allied professional, the issuance of DSM-5 (American Psychiatric Association, 2013) calls for you to rethink your entire vocational life and your plans for living in a healthy way among clients, colleagues, patients, peers, and the broader community. This chapter introduces a way of reeducation (or continuing education if you wish a slower path of challenging professional denial) by using the framework of Wellbriety to shape yourself into a Firestarter Psychologist or Firestarter of any other behavioral health field. This approach is broader than the phenomenological tectonic shift begun by DSM-5 (American Psychiatric Association, 2013) and allows for placing your vocational identity on the right side of a fundamental commitment to humanity in relation to the peoples of North America.

The Wellbriety movement has been passed down from the Hoop Journeys of 1999–2003, the Fifth Hoop Journey of Forgiveness[1] that took place in 2009—beginning at the Museum of the American Indian in Washington D.C. and ending in Salem Oregon at the Chemawa Indian School—and the many smaller journeys of Don Coyhis and members of the White Bison organization.

THE ARCHIVES OF WELLBRIETY

The knowledge that comprises Wellbriety comes from the Hoop Journeys among the over 500 Indian Nations within the United States, the tribes of Canada and Mexico, as well as some of the Indigenous peoples of the Pacific Rim. A person who learns how to develop a personal and professional life in Wellbriety is a person who lives life as a Firestarter. A Firestarter builds a behavioral health world in the spirit of DSM-5 and an even larger commitment to honoring the sanctity of each individual life and its fulfillment.

The first part of this chapter comes from over 300 oral teachings of Don Coyhis that can be found online at White Bison's website (www.whitebison.org) or in YouTube videos under his name or under "Wellbriety." As the coauthor of this chapter, I will borrow from Don's teachings, which he credits as coming from the elders he listened to on the four Hoop Journeys that gave birth to his teachings under the way of life called *Wellbriety*. The Fifth Hoop Journey of Forgiveness in 2009 outlines how Wellbriety has gone far beyond alcoholism and addiction, expanding along its wider behavioral health structure into problems in functioning and achieving a fulfilled life that are passed across generations (Coyhis & White, 2011). This developmental, cross-generational, view of the individual's well-being is explicit in the DSM-5 Cultural Case Formulation (Radhakrishnam, 2016).

Although Don Coyhis has authored several written texts about Wellbriety and other Native teachings from the elders of the Hoop Journeys (Coyhis, 2007), this introduction is primarily excerpted from his traditional oral teachings. In the second half of this chapter, I write as person who goes on to describe his postcolonial path as a psychologist, reeducated as a Firestarter. I am sure that if other Firestarters described their paths, they would draw from different oral teachings. In the era of the Internet and videotaping, searching these oral histories for what will have meaning for everyone is not nearly as quick and tidy as PsycINFO, EBSCO, or any of the other print databases. But how can one ask a search engine to return information for a database that comes from outside one's own research and inquiry world of training anyway?

This chapter offers some of the more completely transcribed oral histories of Wellbriety. Many peoples' favorites come from the hand-recorded conference presentations or early Hoop Journey recordings. For me, a psychologist who began a journey in Wellbriety and became a Firestarter in 2002, preparing for this chapter was often overwhelming and powerful. It was like sitting next to Don as I watched home movies that brought back memories of an education vastly different and more rewarding than my doctoral and psychological residency education. Ten years after reading the written words and then traveling off into the oral histories of Wellbriety, the hope of all the authors in this text is that you experience the same feelings.

POSTCOLONIAL PSYCHOLOGY AND WELLBRIETY

A psychologist or allied behavioral health professional considering the paradigm shift called for in DSM-5 (American Psychiatric Association, 2013) would be best advised to come to grips with the term *post-colonial psychology*. The idea of "gripping" this historical understanding is an apt metaphor. Unless you, the reader, come from an Indian Nation of North America, you will assuredly have to wrestle with the role psychology and the other sciences of the United States have played in building the institutions of this country (Duran, 2013). Ours is a nation that currently sits among the remnants of a genocide so sweeping and complete (and largely unacknowledged) that only 1% of the Indian Nations that predate any of the first 13 and subsequent colonial statehoods were left alive by 1920.

How have we in the field of psychology avoided that fundamental and far-reaching understanding? This denial comes despite an ethics code (American Psychiatric Association, 2010) that issues a wide-sweeping mandate to promote human welfare and basic rights in the face of modern-day torture, abuse, neglect, and emotional harm to others. One reason is that the Indian Nations' archival knowledge[2] has largely been in oral histories not found in our revered written journals, precisely sculpted and bound dissertations, as well as texts like the one in your hand or on your computer screen at this very moment.

Coming to learn about history from this colonial view of our nation's institutions will begin the reeducation of the psychologist as the phenomenological clinician called for in DSM-5 Part III—to encounter each person as a new individual and to understand her or him phenomenologically within a unique Cultural Case Formulation (American Psychiatric Association, 2013). It is unlikely that anyone except a fully informed Native descendent of the precolonial Indian Nations can understand the roots of Wellbriety without making a commitment to a phenomenological understanding unlike any in their previous learning.

It is important to understand the difference between these Indian Nations and their counterparts across the Atlantic Ocean in the European Continent. It is not anywhere near an easy task to grasp the reality that the Nations of Europe conquered and colonized the Nations of North America.

Understanding the archival nature of Wellbriety is one thing, opening one's learning to the knowledge contained in the Fifth Hoop Journey as a path to the entirety of its potential for human behavioral health is quite another. The initial Hoop Journeys brought forward the first teachings of Wellbriety and how they could be used for recovering from personal or family addictions.[3] The more encompassing nature of Wellbriety is as a comprehensive set of learnings that describe a personality theory of behavioral health that is documented and has been researched over generations.

As with other personality theories that have been field-tested in profound human suffering, such as Viktor Frankl's Existential Theory (Frankl, 1984) born in the Concentration Camp at Auschwitz, to understand Wellbriety is to understand the Fifth Hoop Journey of Forgiveness and the very nature of colonial psychology. This is an understanding which must precede a phenomenological understanding that comes from descendants of the Indian Nations that existed prior to their conquest and colonization. A summary of what is found in that reeducation into a postcolonial worldview can be found in the documentary of the Fifth Hoop Journey.[4] This is an undeniable phenomenological account of genocide that compares the cross-cultural definition of genocide and then lists the existing, and overwhelming, evidence that this took place against the Indian Nations by colonizing nations of Europe. Underlying that genocide which took place in direct policy choices across the terms of 34 presidents and reduced the Native population by 99% was the colonizing European immigrants' belief that this conquest was their Manifest Destiny

"Manifest Destiny" is a term that was coined in 1839 that summarized the "why" of the preceding century of colonization. It was revised in 1845 to sanction the colonization of North America by the European colonists of the Eastern Seaboard. Manifest Destiny was used to designate the belief that these United States were destined, even divinely ordained, to expand across the North American continent. This allowed them to marginalize the Indian Nations they had already pushed away from the Eastern Seaboard and forced to resettle westward, with this doctrine now also allowing them to claim the remaining geographical expanse of countless Indian Nations between the Atlantic and Pacific coasts. By 1920, 99% of the Indian Nations' population had been wiped out in what was perhaps the greatest act of genocide in the nineteenth and twentieth centuries.

Prior to the release of this documentary, White Bison explained how healing could, and had, taken place through the tenets of Wellbriety. This included describing the cycle of life that occurs within a Wellbriety Forest[5] using the place-based knowledge familiar to many Indian Nations. The familiar nature of the Medicine Wheel[6], visually reflected in the Wellbriety Hoop of 100 Eagle Feathers, serves as a backdrop to much more than a transformed 12 steps—with a harmonizing view of four races of skin color (what Don calls our "Earth Suits") made stronger by a coming together. An archive of the Wellbriety teachings that are brought together with both formal and informal Firestarter Trainings can be found at the White Bison YouTube Channel, which, at this writing, included 37 videos of oral teachings.[7]

A PSYCHOLOGIST'S VIEW OF THE FIRST FIRESTARTER

Wellbriety comes from an entire understanding of knowledge, intergenerationally handed down by word of mouth. This is dramatically different than the path I followed in 1991 upon the completion of my own dissertation, as well as those dissertations I subsequently helped compile with my doctoral students. This important first understanding is the concept that the Indian Nations' source of knowledge is almost completely outside this countries' research universities and training institutions of "higher" education.

Even when found in written form, it is a knowledge that is most often *place-based*, which means there is a primary imperative to find harmony with the two-legged, four-legged, winged, and water-bound living things that inhabit a unique geography. In the introductory chapter of the text, *The Red Road to Wellbriety: In the Native American Way* (White Bison, 2002), White Bison describes the unique intelligence of the Indian peoples using many examples, including the construction of a canoe without a written design. Yet this same canoe has a lightness to allow it to be carried around waterfalls and the strength of materials bound together without soldering to carry the weight of many persons and belongings. Other examples, like local medicines and gaining information from other living creatures and that geography, all speak to finding harmony with the place-based natural order to things.

On April 6, 2011, Don Coyhis[8] provided an hour-long talk on the Wellbriety movement. In this talk, he focuses on the place-based nature of his views. This talk begins by anchoring who he is to his Indian Nation, the Mohican, his clan (the Turtle Clan on his mother's side) and how his identity (his Mohican Nation name) was given to him by the elders of his community. He seamlessly moves from introducing himself in the Native way into talking about where he is now and that he is a guest of the land, a land that is owned by the aboriginal people of that area. He then asks, with their permission, if he can pass on some of his own ancestral teachings. If you watch that opening before his passing on of the Wellbriety message, you may find yourself thinking he is an interesting man to listen to and categorizing his remarks as a wonderful display of Native culture. You would not be alone in that thought, for it is the first impression that passed through my own mind when I first met Don Coyhis at Hugo, Oklahoma, in 2001. What I later realized was that I was witnessing not a professional trainer or teacher, but, rather, the First Firestarter passing along the ancestral knowledge of Wellbriety given to him by the elders and the Hoop Journeys.

Partway through my own Firestarter training in 2002, I realized the power and force behind the ancestral knowledge that fueled Don Coyhis and his approach to psychological well-being. Instead of talking from an observer's view, Don and I spoke of two very vivid Firestarter experiences. As with all things phenomenological, I am sure he would share the amazing nature of our shared story at those points in time differently.

Wellbriety and the First Firestarter Engage in Community Healing

My first shared experience with the power of Wellbriety was where the humility of the First Firestarter and Wellbriety changed the course of development for an entire community of over 1,000 high school students on March 29, 2004 (Moore, 2004). Juneau Douglas High School (Juneau, Alaska) had just been splintered by a teenage racist group calling itself KAN (Kill All Natives). Although probably a small group of students, the spray-painted symbols and words led to a communitywide fracturing based on smoldering racial tensions. This included members of the Tlingit and Haida tribes, dressed in full native regalia, confronting the Juneau School Board. This Board meeting and newspaper coverage occurred during a school recess. Upon returning to the first day of classes, the entire student body was ushered into the auditorium.

While the school principal did not attend the first day of classes, the superintendent walked out to the middle of the auditorium and said, "We're here for a day of listening. I would like to introduce you to my new friend, Don Coyhis." With that, she left the entire basketball court empty except for a lone member of the Mohican Tribe who briefly centered himself as a guest of that place and asked if the leader of the students was there for him to meet. Although surprised, the student body president (at the urging of his fellow students) made a long walk down from the top of the bleachers to meet Don Coyhis for the first time. They had a brief and sincere conversation, heard by all, where he asked in a clearly genuine manner if he could speak to the students in that room.

After replying affirmatively to his direct request from the students to speak with them, the students listened as he asked them to set aside the pain that he believed they had inherited from previous generations who had walked through the halls of the same school and had not been capable of finding a way out in earlier eras. It was only much later that I realized he had passed along the Wellbriety message of healing from intergenerational trauma.[9]

He told them they no longer needed to bear the burden of the pain from past generations, who had done nothing to deal with the clash of cultures. Today, he said, they now had a rare opportunity to solve many of the problems for the generations of students that would come after them. We had randomly selected 200 students to participate in Wellbriety Talking Circles to elicit the individual phenomenological views of those students. Each person in those talking circles was heard, orally or in writing if they preferred, and we transcribed those thoughts into a document called "The Day of Listening."[10] The president of the Central Council of Tlingit and Haida Indian Tribes of Alaska (CCTHITA) and the Juneau school superintendent presented those findings directly to the students who worked within that framework to truly begin to solve many intergenerational problems of the high school community. Ironically, a Firestarter helped the students themselves put out a centuries-old firestorm that had threatened to consume the community. There has not been a racially charged incident since that time.

The use of the term *institutional racism* emerged through that experience to describe intergenerational trauma that was handed down without obligating the current generation to simply bear the burden. This allowed the adult community to have multiple meetings with the Casey Foundation, and a Second Day of Listening included the adult school staff. While this part was not transcribed for publication, there was a parallel student experience that was published (Moore & James, 2006). The ability of students to openly talk about the facets of institutional racism and intergenerational pain was remarkable. Both of the Days of Listening were phenomenological experiences with large samples of individual students selected by stratified (across grades) random sampling. There were 204 students in 12 Talking Circle Focus Groups which generated 798 unique beliefs that could be analyzed in the Day of Listening of 2004. By 2006, the "no talk rule" about intergenerational pain had succumbed to such a level that 139 students in 14 Talking Circle Focus Groups had generated 1,738 unique beliefs about community safety and thoughts about what could be done about it. This time, the students went far beyond racism and into money, neighborhoods, and school activities that separated students. In Juneau, the phenomenological process from Wellbriety had transformed a community.

One of Many Private Examples of the First Firestarter Bringing the Healing of Wellbriety

The second shared experience with Wellbriety came when I accompanied Don Coyhis as we followed an invitation by the Red Lake Tribe of Indians (Red Lake, Minnesota) to help them find a way out of the pain of the country's second deadliest school shooting. While most people remember Columbine's or Santee High School's (San Diego)[11] deadly student shooting sprees, they don't recall the shooting of high school students on the campus connected to the Red Lake Reservation of the Ojibway Indian Nation. The Red Lake shooting incidents of spree killing, on March 21, 2005, occurred in two places on the Red Lake Indian Reservation—primarily at Red Lake High School. When it was over, there were ten dead, including the student perpetrator—at Columbine, 13 had died, and at Santee there had been two deaths. In all three shootings, many others were wounded, and, particularly at Santee, most of the student body had seen and witnessed the traumatic deaths.

The trauma rippled out into the entire community as the FBI took friends of the shooter to question at great length, including the son of the tribal chairman—who was charged with conspiracy. The feelings of the community were summarized by a member of the local university—which has a large enrollment of students of the Ojibway Nations in Northern Minnesota—Anton Treuer, executive director of the Bemidji State University American Indian Resource Center, who called the investigation a witch hunt: "When there was a shooting at Sandy Hook or Columbine," he said, "they weren't shaking down everybody's third cousin" (Enger, 2015). The Red Lake Band of the Ojibway Nation has a small population that is deeply connected to a place-based way of life, as noted by their Department of Natural Resources:

> Red Lake retains the only contiguous, un-allotted reservation in the state, and the Tribe is one of only a few in the United States, which resisted allotment. The Tribe holds all land in common for the benefit of all its members: 840,000 acres of land and water across nine northern Minnesota counties.
>
> The land provides a means to hunt, fish and gather natural resources for harvesting purposes. Throughout the history of the Tribe, natural resources have factored into their survival and continue to provide a source of income through commercial fishing and logging, among others. Both industries are important to the economic welfare of the Tribe and affect all members.[12]

The loss of life had a devastating effect on this closed reservation with a population of only 5,162 residents,[13] with Ojibway as the official language, and very much run on the system of wisdom of the elders. In the aftermath, the community got pulled into the larger national arguments about gun control, the Goth culture, and even conspiracy theorists.[14] While trying to mourn their loss and find a personal Native meaning from the tragedy, their community was contaminated by others trying to pull them into external forces of "national politics" which had little to do with the phenomenological belief systems of their own nation.

By January of 2006, the community was still wrestling with a lack of closure. Don and I received a letter from the tribal chairman. The tribal chairman was clear that he wished us to explain Wellbriety and the Day of Listening to the community, then the tribe would carry their version of those approaches forward. When we walked into the meeting room as guests on their land, I could offer little but nodding support when Don explained things that happened to heal in other communities with large numbers of tribal families and different Wellbriety messages. It would be hard, and inappropriate, to talk much about the eight hours of a Firestarter-led Talking Circle at Red Lake. But I am comfortable in speaking to one central part of the experience. The room was filled with many elders—some of the most listened-to had not spoken of the event. or if they had, it was not in a public forum like this. After about an hour, they began to take over facilitating the conversation of "what to do." They spoke of what The Lake knew, how she had been hurt, and what their ancestral beliefs indicated should come next. Readers, having reached this point, will understand the phenomenological power of community health initiated in that meeting. The principles of Wellbriety simply started the fire within the tribe and its elders—to accomplishing what countless federal teams of trained crisis responders had not been able to do with their standardized evidence-based programs of healing. I have rarely liked what I often feel is a canned goodbye in the world of behavioral health, but that day I truly "felt honored and thankful" for being in the home of the Red Lake Tribe of the Ojibway Nation. I doubt I will feel the fullness of that again in my lifetime. It was also my introduction to Wellbriety's principles of *Warrior Down*,[15] which can be used for supporting community safety or offering community support for prison or juvenile justice reentry. Three years later, a Firestarter training was held at the Red Lake Reservation (Figure 3.1).

THE POST-COLONIAL REEDUCATION PROCESS: BECOMING A FIRESTARTER IN WELLBRIETY

Regardless of a professional title or credentialing as a behavioral health practitioner, there is nothing in current licensure that says explicitly that a health facilitator can engage the consumer with a client-centered practice capability.

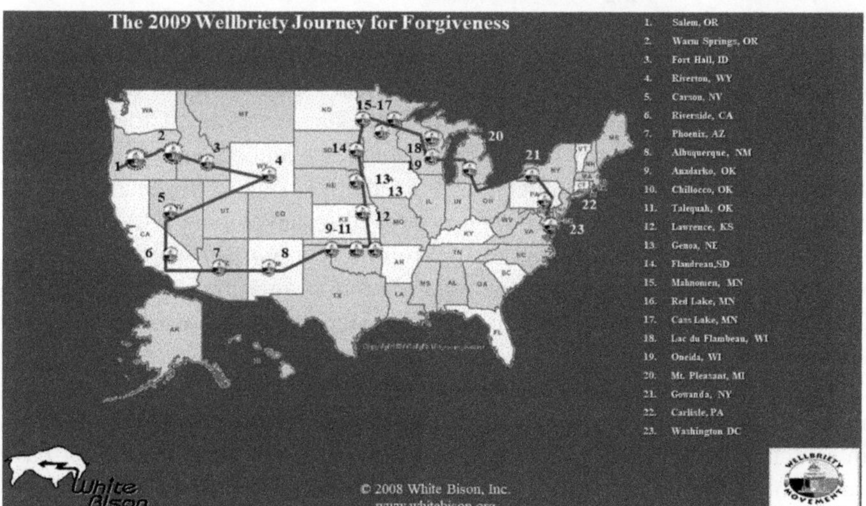

Figure 3.1 The 2009 Wellbriety Journey of Forgiveness. *Reprinted with permission from Don Coyhis, White Bison, Inc.*

In fact, in the post-colonial world of DSM-5; it is more likely that current license-holders will need re-training to overcome their institutionalized practice bias. The humanistic nature of counseling psychology training, a professional clan that credentialed me, espouses the principles of client-centered therapy described by Dr. Carl Rogers (Rogers, 1958) and its strong research base (Rogers, 1985). However, in the postlicensure practice environment of DSM-IV, the cognitive behavioral reimbursement models and journals devoted to standardized evidence-based methods created pragmatic blocks to follow a consumer's phenomenological perspective.

The reorientation process that I have seen work across a study of 388 diverse behavioral health facilitators was their training in Wellbriety (Moore & Coyhis, 2010) and its approach to clients from a peer perspective. This trained the facilitators as Firestarters and acknowledged that they could create a transpersonal therapeutic space (Laing, 1982) of Wellbriety and engage with their clients as peers who also practiced the Wellbriety principles. Much like the true-informed consent of outlining to the client how the facilitative process will work in advance, it is acknowledged that the transpersonal environment of Wellbriety may not fit the needs of every consumer. However, I have found that the peer approach of living the principles of the change environment oneself is a powerful force for trust and engagement. Intuitively, to most clients, it also gets rid of the parent-child medical model ("Here is what you should do") in favor of the adult-adult peer model ("I have some learning and practice information you may find helpful" (Berne, 1961). In my work educating graduate-level counseling psychology students on how to set up an existential transpersonal space, there is no better example than R. D. Laing's 1985 videotape[16] at the Pioneers of Psychotherapy conference that drew 7,200 participants to listen to pioneers such as Aaron Beck, Albert Ellis, Zerka Moreno, Carl Rogers, Carl Whitaker, Jay Haley, Cloe Madanes, and Rollo May. The postdemonstration arguments among audience members are microcosms of the conflict that played itself out in the changes from DSM-IV and DSM-5. Is becoming reoriented to developing a transpersonal therapy space using the principles of Wellbriety a journey worth the effort? Let me turn to the deciding points that led me to an affirmative response in 2002, and my subsequent role as a psychologist who has also been a Firestarter since that time.

The introduction to this chapter acquainted the reader to Don Coyhis, a modern-era Carl Jung who traveled the Indian Nations of North America in search of common cross-cultural truths about behavioral health that have come to be known as Wellbriety (White Bison, 2006). Since the first edition of the Wellbriety teachings in 2006, this model of behavioral health has often been cited as a recovery path for alcoholism and addiction (Galanter & Kaskutas, 2008). However, Wellbriety is much more than a treatment for the addicted person or family. It can be viewed as a basic personality theory for healthy living, one that was gathered from four Hoop Journeys among the Indian Nations of North America and the Pacific Islander regions. Unlike many personality theories which are clearly linked to biases and individual lives of their authors (Sollad, Monte, & Wilson, 2008), Wellbriety claims more of a kinship with Carl Jung's approach to his searches for a common "psychic DNA" that might be shared cross-culturally in his personality theory of archetypes.[17] Jung is most well known for his own journeys across national borders in search of common transnational truths, similar in nature to the Wellbriety Hoop Journeys. Jung himself began traveling among the North American Indian Nations, most notably the Taos Pueblo Tribe (McGuire, 1995), followed by his "Bugishu Psychological Expedition" to East Africa (Dohe, 2016), and his final journey to the Indian Subcontinent (Lachman, 2010).

There were initially seven different Firestarter Trainings, based on the type of health practice focus of the person (gender, age, individual, or family); but they all included the core components of Wellbriety gathered from the Hoop Journeys: the Four Principles of Change, a place-based model of harmony called the Wellbriety Forest, and the Wellbriety Medicine Wheel with four quadrants that connect to teachings of Jung, Erik Erikson, and the modern era-range of 12-step programs. There was also a strong emphasis on learning interpersonal skills and using community connection tools that are less amenable to therapy dyads. To advance these objectives, the Wellbriety Talking Circles are emphasized as adjunctive to individual or family therapy. Our Center for the Study and Teaching of At-Risk Students (C-STARS) clinics have offered these groups every week since 2004.

Becoming a Firestarter: One Psychologist's Journey in Wellbriety

I met Don Coyhis in 2001, which was in the middle of his four Hoop Journeys of 1999, 2000, 2002, and 2003 (Coyhis & White, 2002). At that time, our research group at the University of Washington had just begun the second cycle of field research in 2001. The weakness of the school-centered model of Student Assistance and the SAMHSA National Registry of Prevention Programs, described in the preceding chapter, had not yet emerged into the light of published field research results. However, it was becoming clear that in the community we designated for a full environmental prevention model (Juneau Alaska),[18] there were insurmountable obstacles. Even though dropout, substance abuse and the other traditional mental health markers all showed a glaring disproportionality between the 20% Native population (19% Alaskan Native, 1% Native American) and the rest of the 4,736 students in the Juneau

School District[19], the School Board and other community political entities refused to acknowledge that there was institutional bias in how the developmental resources of the community were organized—until after the Days of Listening (2004–2006) had showed how a Wellbriety process of phenomenologically based community health practices could confront institutional racism and begin to reverse intergenerational emotional pain and trauma.

One benefit from the initial community denial of inequity in resources was that this conflict of institutional racism had not yet permeated the discussion of school-community change. Both tribal and non-tribal representatives cooperated in recruiting the University of Washington's C-STARS to bring federal research dollars to their community and embark on an environmental approach to prevention (Gruenewald, Holder, & Treno, 2003), rather than trying to stack categorical programs together from the National Registry of Evidence Based Programs and Practices (NREPP) menu.

On C-STARS's side of the collaboration equation was a desire to facilitate change where it was truly needed. The community's youth behavioral health markers were staggering: Juneau's rate of teen suicide, like Alaska, was twice the national average[20]; 27% of enrolled students of 9th–12th grade were abusing alcohol and 11% were abusing marijuana, as well as that "within the last 30 days" statistic 12 % had brought a weapon to school. Students under the age of 13 had already used alcohol (23%) and marijuana (13%) at alarming levels.[21] The Juneau project included a full design of youth treatment systems (2001–2003), with C-STARS providing the procedures and, including my project director role, also assuming the dual hat as the program's treatment director to gain state licensure.

As part of the prevention and treatment process, Don Coyhis and the Wellbriety dissemination organization, White Bison, came to Juneau to infuse Wellbriety into the systems building that was to form the community prevention and early intervention environment. This was when I was exposed to the entire movement to change behavioral health services by focusing on the environment and stakeholders ahead of any attempt to simply resort to one or two limited "evidence-based" programs. The Wellbriety infusion was comprised of "The Seven Trainings" that aimed to create a Wellbriety Forest of wellness, where the individual was supported to reach a healthy adulthood (prevention) or regain health (recovery or treatment; Moore & Coyhis, 2010).

While there are many principles involved in Wellbriety, the one that is most descriptive of the post-colonial service provider is the First Law of Individual Change—before providing services to other community members, the Firestarter undertakes the same personal health journey. As described earlier, it is a type of individual narrative therapy that employs the 12 steps familiar to members of the vast array of those fellowships—from the completely non-spiritual versions (e.g., Secular Organizations for Recovery) to the religious in nature (e.g., Celebrate Recovery), as well as the family versions that are preventative in nature (e.g,. Alanon, Naranon, Alateen, and Codependents Anonymous). Arranged in a Medicine Wheel structure with four groups of three activities, Wellbriety sets aside the sequential ladder approach up to the usual seeming finale of "practicing these principles in all our affairs." Without contradicting any of the traditional or revised 12-step communities, Wellbriety simply says the person can employ the four approaches as the day or experience warrants: finding one's harmony with the world, it's living inhabitants, and a personal understanding of a creator (Steps 1–3)[22]; finding oneself (Steps 4–6); finding relationships with others (Steps 7–9); and finding one's place in the community (Steps 10–12).

Tracing the 12 steps back to its actual roots, one finds the founders of AA giving credit for the principles to Carl Jung (Alcoholics Anonymous, 1984)—an understanding that has grown richer as historians have continued to look back into this connection (McCabe, 2015). Unlike the other founding mothers and fathers of psychology; Carl Jung sought the optimum environment to teach an individual to engage in self-analysis and focus on a unique individuation. Today's Firestarter can look to Jung's travels among Indigenous communities or the White Bison Hoop Journeys among the Indian Nations of North America. For the 326 collected stories of these individual Firestarters preparing to facilitate the mental health of persons seeking their services, I would refer you to "The Multicultural Wellbriety Peer Recovery Support Program: Two Decades of Community-Based Recovery" (Moore & Coyhis, 2010), which is included in a special edition of Alcoholism Treatment Quarterly that is devoted to Peer Recovery Support Programs.[23]

The door has been thrown open by DSM-5 to the next generation of behavioral health facilitators. It is a challenge to support the consumer in a phenomenological way that has many connections to the SAMHSA Peer Recovery Support Programs. The practice material in the text appendix to this chapter has its roots in my journey as a Firestarter in keeping faith with the Cultural Case Formulation guidelines of DSM-5.

Firestarters in the Field of Psychological Research

In coauthoring this chapter, I am a Firestarter who also happens to be a licensed psychologist affiliated with a range of universities. This includes conducting field research under the traditional umbrellas of the University of Puget Sound, University of Washington University of California at San Diego Extension, the Department of Mental Health in Johns Hopkins Bloomberg School of Public Health, and Argosy University-Seattle. The 1987–2004 archives of this journey are warehoused within the University of Washington's C-STARS national research funded by the United States Department of Education, the United States Department of Justice, the United States Department of Health and Human Services, and their state counterparts in Washington, Alaska, Hawaii, and California.

Program Evaluation Model in the Era of DSM-IV

The 2004–2012 archives of this practice and research journey are warehoused in a new C-STARS[24], which is community based in Federal Way, Washington, and Juneau, Alaska. This second set of archives, while funded under federal and state auspices, was largely financed and influenced by the United States Department of Education's Safe and Healthy Schools research initiative and the Center for Substance Abuse Prevention's Drug Free Communities initiative, as well as SAMHSA efforts to make programming both more peer led and driven by a community coalition.

These two very different research initiatives can be compared very easily to the ending era of DSM-IV (Safe and Healthy Schools) and the new era of DSM-V (Drug Free Communities and Peer Recovery Support Programs). There are contrasts in terms of funding, with Safe and Healthy Schools providing the $1 million annually that was completely controlled by the Juneau Alaska School District. Contrast that to the $100,000–$150,000 annually that was completely controlled by a community coalition that was required to have representation from eight distinctly separate stakeholders. After what could be best described as eight years of systems failures in the school district and different configurations of community behavioral health and social services, we had reached the end of what existing mental health models could provide, particularly in an already-overburdened school system now grappling with the mandates of No Child Left Behind Act.[25]

Through program evaluation that had showed what would not work, by default we arrived at the only viable community-wide network that could lead the environmental prevention initiative forward. This network was the Pediatric and Family Practice Clinics under an Integrative Physical and Psychological Services approach. This was a true innovative solution based on allowing our failures to guide us, as well as our rare successes to nudge us to consider a solution not being tried anywhere else among the over 720 Drug Free Communities' grants in 2006.

Primary Care was an environment in which a genuine listening to the family in a phenomenological way was institutionalized. An irony of primary care diagnosis and treatment is that the DSM-5 has now done away with the unwieldy multiaxial approach—in favor of what has been in the primary practice medical files for the last 25 years of DSM-IV: (1) a list of disorders and stressors; (2) a personalized note relating health to the individual person, akin to a mini Cultural Case Formulation; and (3) targeted health objectives the person wants to meet. I have honestly never seen a Global Assessment of Functioning number to describe the health of a patient.

It would be counterproductive to outline the deep disappointments that occurred in Juneau as standardized Colonial practice grants of the U.S. government came unraveled, since those failures have been replicated across the country. Field research, by its very nature, relies on the Program Evaluation model of analysis. Interestingly, at the 1987 Georgia Conference on counseling psychology, a fellow student representative from Iowa and I, assisted by some old hands on the research committee, developed standards to formally adopt program evaluation as a legitimate form of research and inquiry. This became the research I was devoted to from that day onward.

Unfortunately, unless standards are scrupulously upheld, the evaluator "cherry picks" from descriptive statistics to "prove" the program is successful (Wheeler, 1976). There were four national indicators that have been embedded in the national substance-use prevention program funding since shortly after the enactment of the Government Performance and Results Act (GPRA).[26] Those four measures were largely ignored in Juneau and many other communities mainly because in over 12 years of biennial measurement the only indicator that went in a consistently positive direction was the steady rise in age of first use. As the population, aged 0–11, dramatically decreased the use of tobacco, alcohol, and marijuana, it became easier to draw the prevention line in the sand with the pediatric services. In 2007, we formed that partnership and asked them to lead us forward into an Integrative Model of Care—based on the emerging model of a "Medical Home" centered on the primary care practice.[27]

NEW RESEARCH METHODS IN THE ERA OF DSM-5

Looking past just the program evaluation model of genuine community phenomenological health services, what is the research methodology that can be most relevant in the postcolonial era of psychological research and inquiry? Here again, the DSM-5 offers an entirely new array of diagnostic tests and underlying psychometrics. Having done away with trying to compartmentalize each stressor or disorder so that it becomes as close to a sterile microscope slide as possible, DSM-5 (American Psychiatric Association, 2013) notes that there are no clear dividing lines in some disorders, in particular using the disorders found in depressive and anxiety domains. So how shall we discuss diagnostic reliability?

There is a great deal of emerging discussion about using the interrater reliability statistic known as Kappa to describe the reliability of a diagnostic process. This description of interrater reliability has great utilitarian value—a statistic gleaned from comparing the actual use of diagnostic processes across clinicians and patients. It can be considered a real-life data point over a group of N=1 case studies. It will illuminate areas of needed caution as the Kappa dips—indicating difficulties among clinicians and individual clients within the development of Cultural Case Formulations.

Developmental psychology is not the clean multiaxial measurement that tried to use group standardization scores and coefficient Alpha, test-retest, and split-half reliability of the colonial researcher. This reflects a research paradigm, when used in the DSM "diagnosis and statistics" model, that has been largely debunked since the Rosenhan field experiments in the early 1970s (Rosenhan, 1993). The emerging use of Kappa (and explanations found behind a dip in the coefficient) can provide real utilitarian value for the postcolonial psychologist working with the individual and their phenomenological view.

Having given in to the understanding that client-based psychology will yield variations, DSM-5 (American Psychiatric Association, 2013) now proposes that, at the beginning of client assessment processes, the clinicians use the 23-item Level One Self-Rated Cross-Cutting Symptom Measure, which has 23 items for adults and 25 for adolescents. Like the WHODAS 2.0 areas of functional problems, these instruments have 13 areas of functioning that often *cut across* diagnoses.

There are Level Two instruments that can explore these dimensions further. Clarke and Kuhl (2014) describe how the instruments allow the client to characterize life difficulties over the preceding two weeks in language that is meaningful to the client and helps the psychologist to understand the phenomenological view of the individual:

> The items on the DSM-5 CC Symptom measures do not relate to any specific disorder and as such are not intended to be diagnostic or to serve as screening measures for any disorder (8). Instead, the measures were developed to be used as adjunct tools "to give clinicians quantitative ratings that characterize patients in a way that is simple, useful, and clinically meaningful" (8). It is hoped that the information from these measures will inform clinical decision-making and treatment. For instance, the ability to characterize patients has the potential to lead to customizable treatment plans and improvement in treatment outcomes.

These cross-cutting measures and new reliability methodologies, such as Kappa, have been discussed in relation to diagnosis and treatment research. What about the validity models favored by the group norm-driven cognitive behavioral world of psychology?

During the last several decades of DSM-IV (American Psychiatric Association, 1994, 2000), when psychologists stated their theoretical orientation, over 45% declared that they worked from the cognitive and/or behavioral viewpoint that rests on colonial group norms and client comparisons based on deviating or conforming to those norms. As for the phenomenological era ushered in with DSM-5 (American Psychiatric Association, 2013), in these past studies, only 1.7% declared that their work fell in the developmental psychology area and just 4.1% declared an affiliation with the phenomenological paradigm of the humanist/existential perspective.[28] While acknowledging there have been N=1 single-case study research models that will return to prominence, there are also new research methods that focus more on validity models that are not bound to the characteristics of the normative group.

We are still talking about gathering research data to analyze in large populations of people, often an N=250 or more. Research results done with group methods of analysis, but not relying on group composition except to a general attempt to sample with a generic width of population, have been available since the 1960s (Rasch, 1960b). It was not until the end of the DSM-IV era that they have become more widely used in place of concurrent, divergent, and all the other traditional "validities." This methodology is called *latent trait evaluation* as developed under item response theory (IRT).

The psychometric instruments prepared for use in DSM-5, both in the text and online, largely use instruments built through IRT (Gelhorn et al., 2008; Kendel et al., 2010). Beyond simply developing screening instruments, IRT can be used for broader latent trait research such as that being used to redevelop the new model of personality disorders (Hopwood et al., 2012).

While it is beyond the scope of this chapter to do more than introduce the postcolonial methodology that is available to the Firestarters' path of humanistic phenomenology, Cohen et al. (2013) offers a text that describes classic test construction psychometrics in comparison to IRT (Cohen, Swerdlik, & Sturman, 2013). It is a text that recently walked one of my doctoral students in counseling psychology through a postcolonial research study that defined the latent trait of *pansexuality*, using IRT, in support of efforts to bring that sexual orientation (Callis, 2014) under antidiscrimination statutes (e.g., Los Angeles Bisexual Task Force, 2015). The resulting 41-item instrument (Parks, 2017) describes a latent trait in which each item is located on a continuum based on the level of pansexuality it represents.

In IRT, each item is validated, which allows for individual responses to have meaning in the assessment and treatment environment. In classic test theory, the strength is in the total number of "yes" (or variation) responses that a person gives related to a construct. Each item has little meaning beyond its relation to the group. Latent Trait Theory and its statistical underpinnings, such as the most common model of Rasch Scaling (Rasch, 1960a, 1960b, 1961), largely does away with the characteristics of a research population. Items that are not stable in relation to the trait they are describing are not validated when analyzed through Rasch Scaling. For instance, in my own development of an instrument that described the latent trait of adolescent substance abuse (Moore, 1991), the typical, "Have you ever been arrested for something you did while intoxicated?" was unstable. This item, or a variation, is found in virtually all tests that identify the level of a teen's substance abuse. A closer look at this item, through IRT, shows that youth from the communities of color answer "yes" to this item at low levels of substance abuse, while European-American teens answer "yes" at higher levels of substance abuse. In other words, when we were doing research in the late 1980s—this item was filled with too much error and said more about community policing than a measurable problem with substances.

Instability, or lack of validity when using Rasch Scaling, is not always so clear. However, unless each item is consistently validated at a specific level of the trait, it is not included in a final psychometric description of the construct under study. Like short instruments in the DSM-5 (American Psychiatric Association, 2013) measures, the items in the instrument I validated in my 1991 study were used in short (4-item) screening by pediatricians in Washington State (Moore, 1984) and a short (20-item) form developed by the National Center for Juvenile Justice (Thomas, Moore, Mullen, Murakawa, Willett, & Winters, 1993) for use by juvenile justice facilities around the country.

A FIRESTARTER'S PATH IN WELLBRIETY'S HEALING FOREST

The interview laid out in DSM-5's (American Psychiatric Association, 2013) steps toward a phenomenological Cultural Case Formulation is a beginning point. But the next generations of psychologists and other behavioral health facilitators need a way to engage in a collaborative process forward from that beginning.

The Psychologist as Speaking a Foreign Language as a Traveler in the Uncharted Territory that is the Life Path of the Client

I usually introduce myself to the client as a person who understands a language like French and they speak Italian. I go on to explain that I must learn Italian before my knowledge and training in French will be of much good to them at all. I will go on to illustrate this by way of a one-page form I use called a Histogram (we can put a one-third-page example here). This is akin to what a traveler might have as a one-page sheet of commonly used phrases in the foreign country he or she was visiting. This is an easy-to-use sheet that allows me to track people, places, and developmental milestones that are important to that client. Beginning from birth to the present day, it can take anywhere from one to two 50-minute sessions to complete. Many of my students have made these cheat sheets in the form most comfortable to them; with a nod to a very abbreviated genogram from family therapy and intergenerational influences.

The Introduction of Developmental Psychology to the Client

My underlying paradigm to understanding the client's phenomenological view comes from the Wellbriety developmental stages like the Erikson stages, but more related to the environment and learning process support that takes place. A nonpathological and utilitarian learning model of how children respond to stress as they grow into adults dates to 1967 and the work of Holmes and Rahe (1967).

This historical learning paradigm is that the individual is exposed to stress with two potential outcomes—*eustress* that is effectively handled and the *distress* that causes challenges to behavioral health. Borrowing from Sarason and Sarason's (2004) three learning challenges to describe stress-inducing situation, the existential questions that appear to cover most of an individual's experiences are as follows:

1. What is that? Defining new people, places, and things in the environment.
2. How do these things work? Both individual and interactive behavior outcomes.
3. How can I control the outcomes in my world? Strategies for favorable outcomes?

As in any paradigm held by the facilitator or helper, no matter how cross-cultural it may be, it may still not fit the client's worldview. The entire ethical principle of informed consent is far more encompassing than HIPPA mandates or third-party payer requirements—it is finding a common understanding of how the facilitator has arranged the information gained through education and experiences. After more than 15 years of serving others as a Firestarter, this model has evolved out of countless revisions in search of common ground. Many different professions conceptualize the individual from different-depth models of biology, sociology, psychology, or learning. Most conceptualizations have two parts (depths) and have accommodated well to this paradigm. As we integrated these different social and health services around the pediatric offices, the final model for understanding the individual within the clan and community is outlined in Figure 3.2.

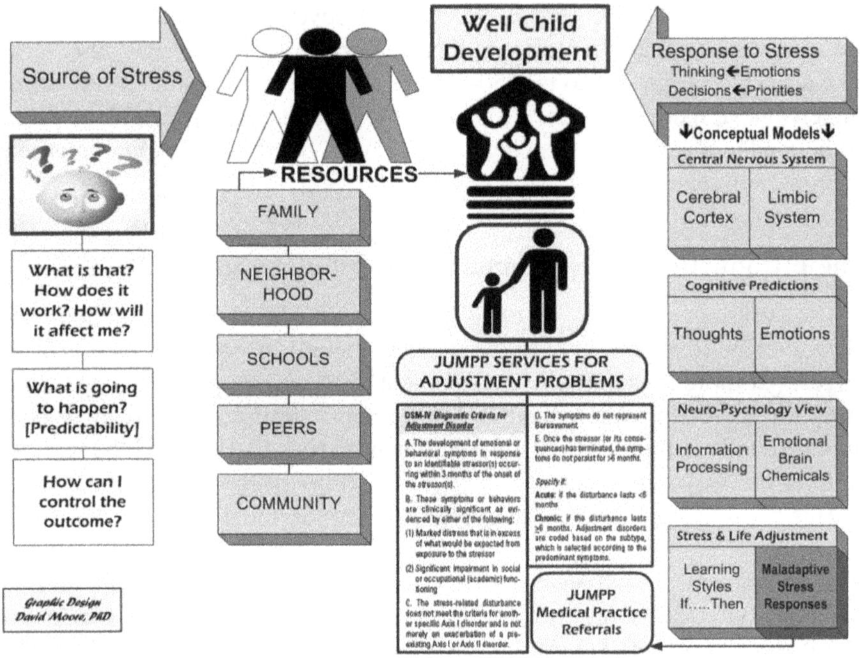

Figure 3.2 Juneau United Medical Practices and Parents Model. *Figure created by David D. Moore Ph.D., C-STARS.*

A Firestarter-Led Integrated Pediatric Medicine System

The Juneau United Medical Practices and Parents (JUMPP) is now well past the field research that developed it from 2001 to 2013. It is has gone from a coalition, to a limited liability endeavor to a 501c3 nonprofit organization—controlled and answerable to the local pediatric clinics. It is safe to say that it offers services not found elsewhere in the country—unless the reader knows where any pediatrician can order up a full neurodevelopmental baseline assessment[29] and annual follow-up testing to baseline to see the impact of family strategies, therapy, and/or medication management. As noted earlier, pediatric primary care is a unique system of phenomenological service delivery between family and clinician. Looking at the suggested Cultural Case formulation interview in DSM-5 (American Psychiatric Association, 2013) for the first time, the questions and dialogues are no different than what we hear every day in discussions between pediatric clinicians and parents. Without that phenomenological view, a pediatrician could never engage adolescents effectively. Psychology and pediatrics are an integration long overdue.

Stressors and Problems with Adjustment

The developmental model fits well into early interventions in which the client is struggling with environmental stressors that rise to the level of an adjustment disorder. In the DSM-5's (American Psychiatric Association, 2013) developmental perspective, adjustment disorders with depression, anxiety, and/or conduct problems can easily be viewed as preceding more categorical problems than are defined by those three areas. This etiological view across time and disorders also opens the door to the intergenerational model of health in the Wellbriety Forest. The DSM-5 (American Psychiatric Association, 2013) categories of *Stressors* have been greatly amplified, particularly in the area of childhood barriers to development described in the next section.

The Nonpathological Measurement of a Child's Response to Distress and its Utilitarian Cross-Cultural Use

C-STARS programs, including JUMPP, owe a debt of gratitude to the University of Pittsburgh's Emeritus Professor Louis Chandler from the School of Education and his applied work in developmental psychology that preceded DSM 5 (American Psychiatric Association, 2013). We have adopted Chandler's model of Maladaptive Stress Responses (Chandler, Shermis, & Marsch, 1985) to stressors that precede an adjustment disorder. This allows for a non-pathological diagnostic process and Cultural Case Formulation that is keyed to a specific stressor(s) (Moore, 1993) in the child's or teen's life. In 1995, when his instrument went off the market (Chandler, 1985), he was gracious enough to send C-STARS the templates for the Stress Response Scales (SRS) and allow us to continue its use.

After over 20 years of SRS use by C-STARS in many cultures and settings, this model has been shown to have great utilitarian value because it describes common behaviors that parents understand. In addition, it suggests a wealth of formal and informal strategies, involving written and oral histories, of how to approach each maladaptive response style. Consistent with the model, children may be seen to respond in five common patterns: Impulsive (acting out), passive-aggressive, impusive (overactive), repressed, and dependent. These have their counterparts in family systems (e.g., the parentalized child = repressed child and identified patient = acting-out child), and whole texts have been written about counterparts in children from chemically dependent or unstable families (Wegscheider-Cruse, 1988; for example, family hero = repressed child and family scapegoat = acting out child). In 2014, we initiated its use in the Juneau Integrated Pediatric Medicine system.

Of utilitarian importance, is the ability to use environmental stressors (Z codes) to describe the developmental impacts of a variety of external experiences or conditions, such as low income or poverty, that are causative to a disorder. In particular, the adjustment disorders have become extremely important as a way to translate the DSM-5 into the clients' language and understandings. This includes being able to assign depression, anxiety, or anger (conduct) as an adjustment to an environmental or institutional cause. This includes discriminatory behavior, unavailability of resources, and conflict with others in a way that the client perceives that conflict. This also includes providing a range of childhood abuse or neglect events, which is important since most people see a large importance in the developmental influences of the childhood and teen years, a time when families and communities should be protecting and nurturing healthy behavioral growth

Describing the Value of the Humanistic-Existential (Cain & Seeman, 2002; Thorne, 2007) Model to the Client

Juneau created a Wellbriety Forest using a developmental model that is consistent with the model of persons responding to stressors in their environment after introducing the client to the model of the psychologist as having a foreign language.

In making a histogram, I will draw a circle on the back of the piece of paper I'm using as my graphic for a child, teen, or adult. Then will come the drawing of hashmarks to create many boxes within that circle. Then, I will randomly fill in some of the boxes around developmental parts that are important to the client themselves—calling out the areas represented by a variety of the boxes. Examples of this would be: a client's understanding of what a father is, how a client visualizes things or uses other senses, what the client learned in different cities she or he has lived in, important representatives of the maternal figure, a client's unique sense of neighborhood or other dwelling areas, the high school social experiences, and many similar areas.

I will then go on to tell the client that I'm not going to learn the entire dictionary of Italian (in Juneau, I might use a language like Tlingit or Haida as a language I haven't mastered) representing the client's phenomenological knowledge, but I will zero in on specific areas in that life sphere of the client. I will go on to say that the client is probably waking up in the morning with difficulties in finding solutions to problems from different areas of this prior learning—and trying these past personal strategies on for effectiveness has not been successful. Thus, the client has ended up in the psychologist's office largely because this random search through the large archives of personal learning has been ineffective. They have come to use my understanding of the broad nature of human development to focus in on those parts of the client's life in which the answers most likely will be found. The clients themselves can expect, by this focused experience, to become more alert and attuned to the areas of their own knowledge that will solve their life questions for them.

In turn, I become a mentor who is merely moving information in their own language over to their world;, where they will be able to grow in their own life experiences and find new answers. This is the core of the Rogerian (Rogers, 1958) experience that is my way of beginning a Firestarter dialogue with a new person.

Having introduced the client to the idea that (1) I had to learn their language and (2) I was limited in areas of my own knowledge of diagnosis and treatment, I show a great deal of enthusiasm in becoming the researcher for a client's options for behavioral change. I always take notes during a client session, writing down things that I know are both important to the client and me, which makes the client understand that this is a collaborative venture we are embarking upon together.

CONCLUSION

Just as at C-STARS, where each of our clients is on a new journey, in this chapter, you have been introduced to the journeys of two close friends in Wellbriety as we face the post-colonial era of psychology that has just begun under DSM-5 and the Fifth Hoop Journey of Forgiveness. May what we have learned enable you to more effectively continue on your own social justice journeys.

NOTES

1. Like much of the knowledge of the Indian nations, this archival knowledge has been passed down in oral tradition and is housed on the White Bison website for future scholars: http://www.whitebison.org/Archives/NewsStories.aspx.
2. A talk at the Tulalip Tribe, March 10, 2011, on the oral archives of Native knowledge by Don Coyhis. https://www.youtube.com/watch?v=lxnfAEottcU.
3. Don Coyhis' Medicine Wheel 12 Steps, five example tapes from the early years of Wellbriety, like the second author's memories of his beginning Firestarter education in Juneau, Alaska, published in December of 2013; by Margo Vaughn. https://www.youtube.com/watch?v=vFjbPKa2KYQ, https://www.youtube.com/watch?v=0UcOrbBPp0g, https://www.youtube.com/watch?v=IZC9tjuxC08, https://www.youtube.com/watch?v=h33qQQIey-A, https://www.youtube.com/watch?v=sUAcmfghPaE.
4. Published on Mar 1, 2011, Documentary on the Abuses of the Indian Boarding Schools. Discusses the intergenerational trauma in native communities. The "Wellbriety Movement: Journey of Forgiveness" is now available on YouTube, www.whitebison.org, or free on DVD. Email info@whitebison.org for DVD, include mailing address.

5. The Wellbriety Movement and Intergenerational Trauma; published by White Bison on the Internet on April 6, 2011. https://www.youtube.com/watch?v=BqAqsrr9AnU&t=1271s.

6. Medicine Wheel teachings of the Lakota Sioux; White Bison often points to the knowledge base of this Indian Nation. The same nation was the place of healing and transformation for Psychologist Erik Erikson and 26th President Teddy Roosevelt; https://www.youtube.com/watch?v=fIGrFHy463g&list=PLmb1vJ9P2g72rQQBsM3ENhEIsxHlXPdOx.

7. https://www.youtube.com/user/WBDonC.

8. The Wellbriety Movement and Intergenerational Trauma; https://www.youtube.com/watch?v=BqAqsrr9AnU.

9. Healing from Intergenerational Trauma Program Description; Don Coyhis. Published December 22, 2011. https://www.youtube.com/watch?v=XIe45StCUhk.

10. Available from C-STARS.

11. Where I served as part of the team putting that campus together in four weeks of 2000; Aftermath of Santee School Shootings Becomes a Testing Time for Counselors; Los Angeles Times; March 20, 2001.

12. http://www.redlakenation.org/tribal-programs/infrastructure/dnr.

13. The 22nd United States Census, known as Census 2000 and conducted by the Census Bureau; retrieved on July 25, 2017 from https://en.wikipedia.org/wiki/2000_United_States_Census.

14. March 30, 2005 CBS News: Red Lake Shooting Conspiracy; http://www.cbsnews.com/news/red-lake-shooting-conspiracy/.

15. Frankie Feather's Warrior Down Group Song, one of many oral histories he has brought to the internet. https://www.youtube.com/watch?v=0L7Nmdm6f2o&list=PLF8AB847CE41660F4&index=6.

16. https://catalog.erickson-foundation.org/item/the-evolution-psychotherapy-1985-classics-cd.

17. Jung, C.G. (1947/1954/1960), Collected Works vol. 8, The Structure and Dynamics of the Psyche, pp. 187, 211–216 (384, 414–420). "Just as the 'psychic infra-red,' the biological instinctual psyche, gradually passes over into the physiology of the organism and thus merges with its chemical and physical conditions, so the "psychic ultra-violet," the archetype, describes a field which exhibits none of the peculiarities of the physiological and yet, in the last analysis, can no longer be regarded as psychic, although it manifests itself psychically."

18. Moore, D., & Tonsmeire, K. (2006). Wellbriety drug-free communities strategic plans (DFC Grant SP 12110, 2001–2006) including Safe Schools/Healthy Students grant (2006 SAMHSA/Department of Education Cohort). Juneau: Alaska Staff Development Network.

19. 2015 Facts and Figures; Juneau School District, "About our District" http://www.juneauschools.org/.

20. Alaska Bureau of Vital Statistics, 1994–2000; http://dhss.alaska.gov/SuicidePrevention/Pages/Statistics/aksuiciderate_national_sr.aspx.

21. Juneau School District, Safe Schools and Healthy Students Grant Application (2004); U.S. Department of Education.

22. The reader should remember that the Indian Nations have a very place-based connection with spirituality and the creation of the living things and geography they seek harmony with.

23. Journal *Alcoholism Treatment Quarterly*, Volume 28, 2010 - Issue 3: Recovery Community Services Programs.

24. Center for Systematic Therapy and Research Services.

25. The No Child Left Behind Act of 2001 (NCLB) was a U.S. Act of Congress that reauthorized the Elementary and Secondary Education Act.

26. Public Law 103-62-August 3, 1993. An act to provide for the establishment of strategic planning and performance measurement in the Federal Government and for other purposes.

27. American Academy of Pediatrics. The National Center for Medical Home Implementation is supported by the Health Resources and Services Administration (HRSA) of the U.S. Department of Health and Human Services (HHS) under grant number U43MC09134. https://medicalhomeinfo.aap.org/Pages/default.aspx.

28. Source: 2008 APA Survey of Psychology Health Service Providers, American Psychological Association, Center for Workforce Studies, October 2009. Table 15 N=5,051.

29. Wechsler age-appropriate IQ battery (Preschool and Primary, Intelligence Scales for Children, Adolescent/Adult Intelligence Scales) and corresponding Memory Scale Battery (Children's Memory Scales, Wechsler Memory Scales).

REFERENCES

Alcoholics Anonymous. (1984). *Pass it on: The story of Bill Wilson and how the A. A. message reached the world.* New York: Alcoholics Anonymous World Services.

American Psychiatric Association. (2013). *Diagnostic and statistical manual of mental disorders* (Fifth ed.). Arlington, VA: American Psychiatric Publishing. ISBN 978-0-89042-555-8.

American Psychological Association. (2010). *Ethical principles of psychologists and code of conduct* (PDF). Washington, DC: Author. Retrieved August 11, 2015. Adopted August 21, 2002. Effective June 1, 2003. With the 2010 Amendments. Adopted February 20, 2010. Effective June 1, 2010.

Berne, E. (1961). *Transactional analysis in psychotherapy*. New York: Grove Press.

Cain, D. J., & Seeman, J. (2002). *Humanistic psychotherapies: Handbook of research and practice*. Washington, DC: American Psychological Association.

Callis, S. (2014). Bisexual, pansexual, queer: Non-binary identities and the sexual borderlands. *Sexualities, 17*(1), 63–80.

Chandler, L. A. (1985). *Assessing stress in children.* New York: Praeger Press.

Chandler, L. A., Shermis, M. K., & Marsh, J. (1985, March 1). The use of the stress response scale in diagnostic assessment with children. *Journal of Psychoeducational Assessment, 3*(1), 15–29.

Clark, D. E., & Kuhl, E. A. (2014). DSM-5 cross-cutting symptom measures: A step towards the future of psychiatric care? *World Psychiatry, 13*(3), 314–316. doi:10.1002/wps.202154.

Cohen, R. J., Swerdlik, M., & Sturman, D. E. (2013). *Psychological testing and assessment: An introduction to tests and measurement.* New York: McGraw-Hill.

Coyhis, D. (2007). *Meditations with Native American elders: The four seasons.* Colorado Springs: Coyhis Publishing & Consulting.

Coyhis, D. & White, W. L. (2006). *Alcohol problems in Native Americans: The untold story of resistance and recovery: The truth about the lie.* Aurora, CO: Coyhis Publishing.

Coyhis, D., Moore, D. D., & White, W. (preface). (2011). *The Wellbriety movement comes of age: The fulfillment of prophecy.* Aurora, CO: Coyhis Publishing.

Coyhis, D., & White, W. L. (2002). Addiction and recovery in Native America: Lost history, enduring lessons. *Counselor, 3,* 16–20.

DeMaria, R., Weeks, G. R., & Twist, M. L. C. (2017). *Focused genograms: Intergenerational assessment of individuals, couples, and families* (2nd ed.). Abingdon-on-Thames: Routledge.

Dohe, C. B. (2016). *Jung's wandering archetype: Race and religion in analytic psychology* (pp. xi + 26.). London and New York: Routlege.

Duran, E. (2013, April 4). Wellbriety recording of clinical psychologist speaking at the beginning of the Fifth Hoop Journey of Forgiveness in 2009, published to the Internet on April 4, 2013. https://www.youtube.com/watch?v=D4d2Y3PHJfo.

Enger, J. (2015, March 19). *The shooting at Red Lake: What happened.* St Paul: Minnesota Public Radio (MPR) News.

Frankl, V. E. (1984). *Man's search for meaning: An introduction to logotherapy.* New York: Simon & Schuster.

Galanter, M., & Kaskutas, L. A. (Eds.). (2008). *Alcoholism research: Alcoholics anonymous and spirituality. Recent developments in alcoholism* (Vol. 18). New York: Springer Publishing.

Gelhorn, H., Hartman, C., Sakai, J., Stallings, M., Young, S., Rhee, S., Corley R, Hewitt J, Hopfer C., & Crowley, T. (2008). Toward DSM-V: An item response theory analysis of the diagnostic process for DSM-IV alcohol abuse and dependence in adolescents. *Journal of the American Academy of Child and Adolescent Psychiatry, 47*(11), 1329–1339.

Gruenewald, P. J., Holder, H. D., & Treno, A. J. (2003). Environmental approaches to prevention. In A. W. Graham, T. K. Schultz, M. F. Mayo-Smith, R. K. Ries, & B. B. Welford (Eds.), *Principles of addiction medicine* (3rd ed.). Chevy Chase, MD: American Society of Addiction Medicine.

Holmes, T. H., & Rahe, R. H. (1967). The social readjustment rating scale. *Journal of Psychosometric Research, 11*(2), 213–218.

Hopwood, C. J., Thomas, K. M., Markon, K. E., Wright, A. G. C., & Krueger, R. F. (2012). DSM-5 personality traits and DSM-IV personality disorders. *Journal of Abnormal Psychology, 121*(2), 424–432.

Kendel, F., Wirtz, M., Dunkel, A., Lehmkuhl, E., Hetzer, R., & Regitz-Zagrosek, V. (2010). Screening for depression: Rasch analysis of the dimensional structure of the PHQ-9 and the HADS-D. *Journal of Affective Disorders, 122*(3), 241–246.

Lachman, G. (2010). *Jung the mystic: The esoteric dimensions of Carl Jung's life and teachings: A new bibliography*. New York: Jeremy P. Tarcher/Penguin.

Laing, R. D. (1982). *The voice of experience: Experience, science, and psychiatry*. Harmondsworth: Penguin.

Los Angeles Bisexual Task Force. (2015). Welcome to the LA bi task force. Retrieved from: http://labicenter.org/.

McCabe, I. (2015). *Carl Jung and Alcoholics Anonymous: The twelve steps as a spiritual journey of individuation*. London: Karnac Books.

McGuire, W. (1995). Firm affinities: Jung's relations with Britain and the United States. *Journal of Analytical Psychology, 40*(3), 301–326.

Moore, D. D. (1984). *The client substance index*. Olympia, WA: Department of Health and Social Services/Department of Juvenile Rehabilitation.

Moore, D. D. (1991). *Doctoral dissertation: The psychometric measurement of adolescent substance abuse*. Seattle: University of WA, Educational Psychology.

Moore, D. D. (1993). New directions in working with at-risk children. *Journal of Emotional and Behavioral Problems, 2*(3), 28–32.

Moore, D. D. (2004). *A day of listening: Unifying and dividing forces among students of Juneau Douglas High School*. Seattle, WA: Center for the Study and Teaching of At-Risk Students, College of Education. Now available from C-STARS of Washington and Alaska (information.CSTARS@gmail.com).

Moore, D. D., & Coyhis, D. (2010). The multicultural wellbriety peer recovery support program: Two decades of community-based recovery. *Alcoholism Treatment Quarterly, 28*(3), 273–292.

Moore, D. D., & James, C. (2006). *Day of Listening 2006: Enhancing student connections and school safety*. Johns Hopkins University. The Bloomberg School of Public Health, Center for Youth Violence Prevention. Retrieved from C-STARS (information.CSTARS@gmail.com).

Parks, A. (2017). *The personality trait of pansexuality: Defining and validating the psychological construct*. Argosy University, Seattle. Dissertation.

Radhakrishnan, R. (2016, Feb.). DSM-5® handbook on the cultural formulation interview. *American Journal of Psychiatry, 173*(2), 196–197.

Rasch, G. (1960a). *Probabilistic models for some intelligence and attainment tests*. Chicago, IL: MESA Press.

Rash, G. (1960b). On general laws and the meaning of measurement in psychology. Paper at the Fourth Berkley Symposium on Mathematical Statistics and Probability, Statistical Laboratory, University of CA, June 20-July 30.

Rasch, G. (1961). On general laws and the meaning of measurement in psychology. In J. Neyman (Ed.), *Proceedings of the Fourth Berkley Symposium on Mathematical Statistics and Probability: Vol IV: Contributions to Biology and Problems of Medicine* (pp. 321–333). Berkley, CA: University of California Press.

Rogers, C. (1951). *Client-centered therapy: Its current practice, implications, and theory*. London: Constable. ISBN 1-84119-84004.

Rogers, C. R. (1958). The characteristics of a helping relationship. *The Personnel and Guidance Journal, 37*, 6–16. doi:10.1002/j.21641-4918.1958.tb01147.x

Rogers, C. R. (1985). The necessary and sufficient conditions of therapeutic personality change. *Journal of Consulting Psychology, 21*(2), 95–203.

Rosenhan, D. (1973, January). On being sane in insane places. *Sciences, 179*(4070), 250–258. doi:10.1126/science.179.4070.250.

Sarason, I. G., & Sarason, B. R. (2004). *Abnormal psychology: The problem of maladaptive behavior.* Princeton, NJ: Pearson.

Sollad, R. N. (Author), Monte, C. F. (Author), & Wilson, J. P. (Editor). (2008). *Beneath the mask: An introduction to theories of Personality* (8th ed.). Hoboken, NJ: Wiley.

Thomas, D., Moore, D. D., Mullen, R., Murakawa, Y., Willett, R., & Winters, K. (1993). *Manual for developing a substance abuse screening protocol for the juvenile court and implementing the client substance index-short form (CSI-SF).* Alexandria, VA: National Center for Juvenile Justice under a grant (# Sil-91-1U-E-035) from the State Justice Institute.

Thorne, B. (2007). Person-centered therapy. In W. Dryden (Ed.), *Dryden's handbook of individual therapy* (5th ed.). London: Sage.

Wegscheider-Cruse, S. (1988). *Another chance: Hope and health for the alcoholic family* (2nd revised ed.). East York, Ontario: Hushion House.

Wheeler, M. (1976). *Lies, damn lies, and statistics: The manipulation of public opinion in America.* New York: Liveright.

White Bison, Inc. (2002, 2006). *The Red Road to wellbriety: In the Native American way.* Center City, MN: Hazelden Publishing & Educational Services.

Chapter 4

Treatment Interventions for Intimate Partner Violence in the Lives of African American Women

A Social Justice Approach

Carolyn M. West

EDITOR'S (SG) INTRODUCTION

Dr. Carolyn M. West is Professor of Psychology and the Division Chair of Social, Behavioral, and Human Sciences in the School of Interdisciplinary Arts and Sciences at the University of Washington in Tacoma, where she teaches courses on family violence, sexual violence and sex crimes, and the psychology of Black women. With more than two decades of teaching experience, she writes, trains, consults, and lectures internationally on intimate partner violence (IPV) and sexual assault, with a special focus on violence in the lives of women of color. Dr. West is the editor/contributor of the award-winning book *Violence in the Lives of Black Women: Battered, Black, and Blue* (2003), which was published by Routledge. She has written more than 50 journal articles and book chapters and has produced the documentary *Let Me Tell y'all 'bout Black Chicks: Images of Black Women in Pornography*. In recognition of her scholarship, teaching, and service, the University of Washington has honored her with the 2016 Distinguished Research Award, the first Bartley Dobb Professorship for the Study and Prevention of Violence (2005–2008), and the 2013 Distinguished Teaching Award.

> while understanding links between racism and domestic violence is an important component of any effective intervention strategy, it is also clear that women of color need not await the ultimate triumph over racism before they can expect to live violence-free lives. (Crenshaw, 1994, p. 104)

MY PATH TO A SOCIAL JUSTICE APPROACH

According to a national study, 45.1% of Black[1] women experienced sexual violence, physical violence, and/or stalking by an intimate partner in their lifetimes. This prevalence rate translates into an estimated 6,349,000 survivors (Smith et al., 2017). United Methodist clergyperson, Traci West (1999), wrote: "There is no more compelling societal problem in need of redress than black women's experience of male violence" (p. 1). I agree. Accordingly, I have dedicated my personal and professional life to understanding this pervasive social and public health problem.

Three pivotal life experiences set me on the path to articulating a social justice treatment approach to addressing IPV in the lives African American women. At age 13, I borrowed the book *Scream Quietly or the Neighbors will Hear* (Pizzey, 1974), which was one of the early academic efforts to investigate wife battering. I became passionate about using research to eradicate all forms of family violence and sexual assault. Around the same time, I discovered the "Clinical Psychologist" entry in the *World Book Encyclopedia* and intuitively knew that this would be my future career.

The second major event that shaped my professional life happened ten years later. It was February 1987, and I was a precocious, idealistic 23-year-old graduate student who was fulfilling my childhood dream of becoming a psychologist. For about three years, I experienced academic sexual harassment. After filing an Equal Employment Opportunity Complaint (EEOC) and a successful sexual harassment lawsuit against the University of Missouri, I earned my doctoral degree in Clinical Psychology in 1994. Along the way, I learned how to craft a resistance strategy using the media and the legal system, and I learned that activists of all backgrounds can collaborate and agitate to force institutional changes within universities. Equally as important, I learned that culturally aware psychologists can facilitate the healing process. With the help of these mental health professionals, loving family members, and supportive friends, as well as my teaching, writing, community activism, and strong faith, I labeled my victimization, which enabled me to evolve into an empowered survivor and activist-scholar (West, 2010).

The third important life-changing event happened during my postdoctoral research fellowship at the University of New Hampshire's Family Research Laboratory. During spirited scholarly debates and research meetings with my mentors and peers, I grew frustrated with the scarcity of literature on IPV in marginalized populations. For that reason, I made a personal promise to accomplish two career goals. One, I would become a productive scholar by conducting large systematic literature reviews, which I hoped would make the research more accessible to scholars and service providers (West, 2012, 2016b, 2016c).

The second promise: In the process of my writing, I vowed to amplify my radical voice and challenge all forms of oppression. As a self-identified Black feminist scholar living in rural New England at the time, I found solace in quotes by Audre Lorde (1982), a self-proclaimed Black feminist, poet, activist, teacher, and warrior: "For the master's tools will never dismantle the master's house. They may allow us temporarily to beat him at his own game, but they will never enable us to bring about genuine change" (p. 112). Having the "master's tools" in my toolbox meant producing rigorous scholarship, which was practical and accessible enough to be used by mental health professionals who, in turn, could make real social change. This strong desire and the sage advice of Toni Morrison, "If there is a book you want to read, but it hasn't been written yet, then you must write it," led me to collaborate with advocates and activists to edit the book *Violence in the Lives of Black Women: Battered, Black, and Blue* (West, 2003).

Today, I write, train, consult, and lecture internationally on interpersonal violence and sexual assault, with a special focus on violence among African American women. I am deeply devoted to creating inspirational material to empower domestic violence/sexual assault survivors during their healing journey, delivering keynote addresses, conducting workshops, and customizing innovative training material to educate and equip professionals with the skills to provide culturally sensitive services. In that spirit, I will provide a brief overview of IPV in the lives of African American women, discuss what social justice looks like in theory, and end with practical applications for treatment interventions.

INTIMATE PARTNER VIOLENCE AND AFRICAN AMERICAN WOMEN: AN OVERVIEW

Despite their vulnerability, the interpersonal violence that African American women experience in their homes, communities, and workplaces remains "hidden in plain sight." That is, their victimization is so hypervisible and pervasive that the violence against them appears to be normal and routine, which renders their violation as invisible in the larger culture. Paradoxically, Black women are perceived as *not* at risk for—and simultaneously to blame for—the violence that has been perpetrated against them (West, 2016b).

At the same time, the physical injuries (Anderson, Stockman, Sabri, Campbell, & Campbell, 2015) and mental health problems (Lacey, Sears, Matusko, & Jackson, 2015) that are associated with the IPV in their lives is very visible. Yet, when compared to survivors of other ethnic groups, Black battered women frequently underutilize traditional therapeutic mental health services, such as counselors, therapists, and support groups (Nnawulezi & Murphy,

2017). In this section I will define IPV, briefly discuss the prevalence rates and the mental and physical health consequences associated with this form of victimization, and end with a discussion of Black women's help-seeking behavior.

Defining what constitutes IPV is challenging and complex; however, a comprehensive definition includes *physical aggression*, ranging from less injurious violence, such as slapping and shoving, to more lethal forms of violence, including beatings and assaults with weapons. *Rape* can take the form of completed or attempted alcohol- or drug-facilitated forced anal, oral, or digital penetration. Other forms of sexual violence include *reproductive coercion* (e.g., pressuring a woman to become pregnant against her wishes and preventing her from using birth control), *sexual coercion* (e.g., unwanted penetration obtained through nonphysical pressure), and *unwanted sexual contact* (e.g., kissing and fondling). Examples of *psychological aggression* include name-calling, insulting, and humiliating and those of *coercive control* include behaviors that are intended to monitor, control, or threaten an intimate partner. Finally, *stalking* encompasses being the recipient of unwanted communication via email or through social media, or being watched or followed at home, work, or school. These forms of violence can occur in any intimate partnership and can be perpetrated by legal or common-law spouses, boyfriends/girlfriends, cohabitating, dating, or casual sexual partners (Smith et al., 2017).

When compared to their White and Latino/a counterparts, African Americans, whether as individuals or couples, consistently reported higher rates of overall, severe, mutual, and recurrent past-year and lifetime physical IPV victimization and perpetration in general population, community, and university samples (West, 2012, 2016c). According to the National Intimate Partner and Sexual Violence Survey (NISVS), Black women reported a broad range of IPV: 41.2% had been physically abused, 9.5% had been stalked, and 8.8% had been raped by an intimate partner during their lifetime (Breiding, Chen, & Black, 2014). Moreover, between 2003 and 2014, Black women experienced the highest rates of homicides (4.4 per 100,000), which were primarily committed by former or current intimate partners (Petrosky et al., 2017).

In a national sample of Black battered women, severe physical IPV was associated with an increased risk of suicide attempts and suicidal ideation as well as lifetime mental health problems, including mood disorders (dysthymia, major depression disorder, and bipolar disorder), anxiety disorders (panic disorder, agoraphobia, generalized disorder, obsessive disorder, and posttraumatic stress disorder [PTSD]), substance disorders (alcohol or drug use and abuse/dependence), and eating disorders (bulimia and binge eating) (Lacey et al., 2015). In addition, when compared to survivors who had experienced one or two forms of victimization, Black women who sustained cumulative violence (physical, sexual, and emotional abuse) reported higher rates of clinically significant depressive symptoms, PTSD, self-mutilation, suicidal thoughts and attempts, drug problems, and eating disorders in the past year (Sabri et al., 2016).

The physical health of African American battered women also is compromised by IPV. When compared to their nonvictimized counterparts, survivors of recent assaults sustained bruises and facial, dental, and head injuries, which often required stitches and surgeries, broken bones and dislocated jaws, and a loss of consciousness. Furthermore, in the year prior to the study, recent victims were hospitalized or sought treatment in the emergency room more frequently (Anderson et al., 2015). In addition to their immediate medical trauma, Black victims reported a range of health concerns in the past year, including problems with their central nervous system (headaches, fainting, back pain, and seizures), gynecological/reproductive health problems (abnormal vaginal bleeding, vaginal infection, pelvic pain, painful intercourse, fibroids, urinary tract infection, and sexually transmitted infections, including HIV/AIDS), and gastrointestinal problems (loss of appetite, digestive problems, and abdominal problems) (Schollenberger et al., 2003). African American women who reported more frequent partner violence, particularly if it was accompanied by PTSD symptoms (Iverson et al., 2013), cumulative violence exposure (Sabri et al., 2016), and recent violence exposure (past-year compared to lifetime exposure to IPV) (Schollenberger et al., 2003) were more likely to self-rate their overall physical health as "fair," "poor," or "very poor."

On one hand, African American women are active help-seekers who utilized internal sources of strength, such as their spirituality and self-reliance. They physically fought back to defend themselves and their children and they terminated their abusive relationships. Moreover, they sought help from informal sources of support, such as family members and friends, and formal help sources, including the police and courts (Sabri et al., 2016; St. Vil, Sabri, Nwokolo, Alexander, & Campbell, 2017).

On the other hand, African American women underutilized other services. For example, despite potentially lethal, severe physical victimization, which co-occurred with PTSD and depression, 66% of low-income Black battered women who lived in Baltimore and the U.S. Virgin Island did not use the services of mental health providers (counselors, therapists, and caseworkers) (Sabri et al., 2013). In fact, many survivors had limited knowledge or lacked access to these forms of help. To illustrate, 37% did not know about domestic violence services (domestic violence hotlines/advocates or shelters) and 82.8% did not have access to mental health counselors or therapists (Sabri et al., 2015).

To conclude, African American women have high prevalence rates of IPV, experience serious mental and physical health consequences that are associated with this form of victimization, and typically lacked the knowledge and access to mental health services to enable themselves to heal. At the same time, they are resilient survivors. In recognition of this complexity, Traci West (1999) prefers the term "victim-survivor":

> I do so to rhetorically remind us of the dual status of women who have been both victimized by violent assault and have survived it. Black women are sometimes denied an opportunity to have their victimization recognized. The strength of their coping and survival abilities is commonly emphasized at the expense of an appreciation of their injury and anguish. (p. 5)

SOCIAL JUSTICE IN THEORY

A social justice approach, I believe, requires a theoretical understanding of an ecological model of IPV, an understanding of intersectionality, which is the recognition of the multiple identities possessed by Black victim-survivors; and a fearless commitment to addressing our unconscious biases based on race and other forms of oppression.

Ecological Model

No single factor can explain why some people or groups are at higher risk for interpersonal violence; rather, violence is an outcome of a complex interaction among many factors, which can occur at four levels (Centers for Disease Control and Prevention [CDC], 2009). Accordingly, an ecological model can be beneficial to help us understand IPV in the lives of African American women. At the *individual level*, we should consider how a person's sociodemographic characteristics, such as social class or gender, and formative history, such as exposure to child abuse and substance use, increase their risk of IPV. The *relationship level* considers the interactions between the survivor and her partner, family members, and peers, whereas the *community level* considers the environment in which the person lives, for example exposure to neighborhood crime. Finally, the ecological model includes larger societal factors, such as norms, policies, and structural inequalities, including racism and sexism (West, 2016c).

There are several benefits of using an ecological model. Researchers have persuasively argued that when individuals live with multiple community disadvantages, which have their foundations in historical and structural racism, their frustration and anger can spill over into intimate relationships and culminate in interpersonal violence, including homicide (Cheng & Lo, 2016). Thus, an ecological model moves us beyond viewing victimization as an abnormality or personal defect that resides within the individual survivor or within the relationship. Instead, an ecological model compels us to consider the structural inequalities and the context in which the survivor and the couple exist. Thereby, the web of trauma and the barriers to help-seeking in the lives of Black victim-survivors become more visible (West, 2016c).

At the same time, poverty as the sole explanation for IPV is too simplistic. We risk implying that IPV is "natural" or "normal" among Black women because it occurs all too frequently. Moreover, it is perilous to attribute male-perpetrated violence to an amorphous, impersonal factor identified as "poverty" (West, 1999). From a social justice perspective, it is important to remember that "while understanding links between racism and domestic violence is an important component of any effective intervention strategy, it is also clear that women of color need not await the ultimate triumph over racism before they can expect live violence-free lives" (Crenshaw, 1994, p. 104).

Intersectionality

"Intersectionality" is a term coined by Kimberle Crenshaw (1994) to describe overlapping or intersecting social identities and related systems of oppression, domination, or discrimination as well as privilege and power. The premise is simple: "It is fallacious to suppose that one experiences abuse first as a human being, then as a woman, then as a Black person, then as a lesbian, and so forth. A woman's responses cannot be correlated to aspects of her social identity on a neat flowchart" (West, 1999, p. 56). Conwill (2010) concluded that "from a social justice perspective and in the context of the U.S. and the Americas intersectionality is an excellent tool for examining both the interpersonal and institutional dimensions of domestic violence in lower-class Black communities" (p. 36).

To illustrate, by understanding the social location in which low-income Black women reside, intersectionality can help us to understand how and why they experience IPV in the context of high rates of poverty, mass incarceration, housing instability, and community violence, which, in turn, elevates their risk for a host of physical and mental health problems—HIV, substance abuse, and anxiety (O'Leary & Frew, 2017). The combination of poverty and IPV can also predispose African American women who live in economically distressed, urban communities to mental health problems, such as depression (Mugoya et al., 2017).

Unconscious Biases

Biases can be triggered based on a client's race/ethnicity, age, gender or gender identity, sexual orientation, religious affiliation, and physical disabilities, to name a few. Our biases can be conscious (explicit) or unconscious (implicit) (Cuellar, 2017). Honestly, what do you see when you sit with a Black victim-survivor: "An angry woman who solicited violence due to her hostile behavior, a seductive temptress who liked or enjoyed violent interactions, a stoic matriarch preferring to stay with an abusive partner or a host of other possible configurations" (Ashley, 2017). These (mis)perceptions, when acted out verbally or nonverbally, can be perceived as *racial microaggression*, subtle forms of racism that deter battered women from seeking our services (Nnawulezi & Sullivan, 2014). Even positive stereotypes, such as the super strong resilient Black woman, can present a barrier to service provision and reduce intervention effectiveness (Davis et al., 2009). It is incumbent upon mental health providers to explore the origin of these beliefs and to challenge ourselves and others to become more aware of them (Danzer, Rieger, Schubmehl, & Cort, 2016).

To conclude, using an ecological model, being aware of intersectionality, and becoming aware of our unconscious biases are a good step toward social justice. However, it is not enough. We need to move from theory to practice.

SOCIAL JUSTICE IN PRACTICE

To practice cultural competency, mental health providers should strive to become more culturally sensitive and aware, which "is more than being politically correct or tolerating diversity, it is a sincere commitment, active engagement in, and dedication to a lifelong learning process to enrich the delivery of services to domestic violence survivors and other persons seeking the services of helping professionals" (Lockhart & Mitchell, 2010, p. 6). In fact, if we listen carefully, Black victim-survivors have clearly and eloquently articulated the organizational policies and structures that are embraced by culturally responsive agencies and service providers. Specifically, Black victim-survivors wanted mental health providers who were welcoming to African Americans, sensitive to the process of leaving abusive relationships, and supportive of their unique needs (Gillum, 2009). Based on a growing body of research, practicing cultural awareness is an effective way to help victim-survivors. Low-income and suicidal African American abused women who participated in a culturally sensitive 10-week psychoeducational intervention program, which was conducted by a multiracial team of therapists, reported lower levels of depressive symptoms and general distress (Kaslow et al., 2010). Next, I will discuss how to put social justice in practice by conducting culturally responsive assessments and using a strength-based approach that honors how Black women have historically healed themselves from all forms of trauma.

Culturally Responsive Assessments

Even for the most seasoned professional, assessing for possible interpersonal violence can be intimidating. However, knowing what questions to ask and when can make the difference in providing the best care for victim-survivors (for a review of assessment tools, see Carney, 2015; Mortiere, 2015). In this section I will discuss how to consider intersecting identities of Black victim-survivors in our assessments, recommend a range of types violence exposure to explore with our clients, discuss respectful ways to explore mental and physical health problems, and investigate cultural barriers to help-seeking.

Intersecting Identities

A social justice approach requires us to be mindful of the intersecting identities of our clients. Focusing on the commonality of women's experience of abuse, rather than recognizing the multiple identities of women and the cultural context in which they exist, the domestic violence movement has created yet another structural barrier to equitable service delivery. For example, Sarita, an impoverished, urban-dwelling, battered Black lesbian with mental health problems explained the challenges of accessing services:

> You offer me this place over here for mental illness. Then I go to this domestic violence shelter . . . that's not helping me with my mental illness . . . So, I go back over here [mental health agency] so at least they can monitor my meds. (Simpson & Helfrich, 2014, p. 455)

We should avoid asking our clients to fragment themselves and to present one identity when they seek help, while neglecting other important parts of themselves. Instead, a social justice, culturally responsive comprehensive service, would welcome her to bring all aspects of her identity into treatment. It is simple; what Sarita and most of our clients want is: "the opportunity to define for themselves who they are and what aspects of their identities are most important or relevant to their situations at a particular point in time" (Simpson & Helfrich, 2014, p. 459).

Therefore, incorporating intersectionality into our assessments and practice can help us to think differently about the multilayered intersection of identity, power, and privilege (for a visual representation of an intersectionality of cultural diversity among IPV survivors, see Lockhart & Mitchell, 2010, p. 21). For example, we should consider asking how some of the following identities influence the victim-survivor's experience with violence and her help-seeking efforts:

- *Age*. Special attention should be paid to unique forms of violence and challenges that victim-survivors experience across the age spectrum. Black adolescents, particularly those who are poor, are at risk for dating violence in their intimate relationships, family violence in their homes, and sexual harassment in their neighborhoods and schools (Miller, 2008). At the other end of the age continuum, older African American women may be financially abused by their adult children and physically and emotionally abused by their spouses. In addition, older victims often lack resources for independent living, including stable housing, personal income, and good physical health (Lichtenstein & Johnson, 2009).

- *Ethnicity*. The abuse experience can vary based on the ethnicity of the victim-survivor. For example, African immigrant battered women face unique challenges around language barriers, immigration status, religion, and gender roles (West, 2016a). Compared to their African American counterparts, severely abused Black Caribbean women reported higher rates of eating disorder (Lacey et al., 2015). Consequently, mental health providers should consider ethnicity and immigration status and avoid the assumption that every phenotypically Black woman identifies as African American and traces her roots to the transatlantic slave trade.
- *Social class*. In addition, the abuse experience can vary across social class. African American women who live in economically distressed, urban communities are predisposed to mental health problems, such as depression (Mugoya et al., 2017). Yet, middle-class Black women face challenges as well. Revealing their victimization could jeopardize their professional status or the reputation of their partners. Moreover, their disclosure of abuse or request for services may be met with skepticism because they appear to be financially secure and successful (West, 2016b).
- *Sexual orientation/gender identity*. Transgender Black women and Black lesbians face barriers that prevent them from freely and safely accessing services, such as heterosexism, discrimination, and stigma. They also encounter institutional and agency-specific barriers, homophobia and transphobia in the Black community, and racism in the LGBTQ community (Simpson & Helfrich, 2014).

Mental health providers can use the Multicultural Power and Control Wheel as a visual representation to help themselves and their clients grasp how various systems of oppression (e.g., ageism, heterosexism, ableism, racism, and classism) shape their experiences as victim-survivors (Chavis & Hill, 2009). As we put intersectionality into practice, it is important that we remember that many diverse factors that correlate with privilege (such as sex, race, and socioeconomic status) are based on visible traits or observable characteristics. However, numerous identity factors, including gender identity, immigration status, dis/ability challenges, religion, sexual orientation, and education are sometimes ambiguous or invisible. Therefore, we have to listen to victim-survivors tell their stories and describe their identities.

To conclude, a social justice approach requires us to recognize and acknowledge the multiple identities of our clients. An intersectional analysis is crucial because "continuing to offer fragment services, wherein issues are individually treated and not considered within the context of their intersections, is an inefficient, and ultimately *ineffective*, means of providing services" (Bent-Goodley, Chase, Circo, & Rodgers, 2010, p. 74).

RANGE OF VIOLENCE EXPOSURE

After more than three decades of working as a professor, therapist, researcher, and expert witness in domestic violence homicide cases, I continue to be deeply disturbed by the range of violence and brutality in the lives of African American women. To strive for social justice, we should make all forms of violence more visible, both to ourselves as mental health professionals and our clients. Again, the Multicultural Power and Control Wheel can be used to illustrate how perpetrators' coercive control tactics are shaped by intersecting identities (e.g., race, social class, and sexual orientation) and varying systems of oppression (e.g., racism, classism, and heterosexism). These forms of abuse include isolation, emotional abuse, sexual abuse, using children to control and harass the victim, intimidation, and physical violence (Chavis & Hill, 2009). However, service professionals need to be aware of several neglected forms of violence that disproportionately impact Black victim-survivors. They are specific types of interpersonal violence (women's use of aggression, reproductive coercion, nonfatal strangulation, and intimate partner homicide) as well as historical trauma, structural violence and inequalities, and community violence.

Women's Use of Aggression

African American women sometimes use aggression as a form of self-defense, in retaliation for past abuse, or to preempt future abuse. However, the use of aggression may not serve them well. Direct confrontation may not stop the primary aggressor over the long term; in fact, the violence may escalate. Black women who used this strategy seldom felt a sense of control, independence, or power within their relationships; rather, they reported symptoms of depression, anxiety, and PTSD (West, 2007, 2016b). Moreover, Black victim-survivors become victim-defendants when they are arrested. The social and legal consequences can be devastating and include the problems that are associated with a felony conviction: unemployment or possible eviction from public housing. Although they are not the primary perpetrator, victim-survivors also may be court mandated to participate in batterer's treatment program (West, 2007).

Mental health providers can discuss the advantages and disadvantages of using aggression and strategize about more appropriate tactics to end the violence. They may also educate clients about arrest policies and the legal consequences associated with their use of violence (St. Vil et al., 2017). Remembering that their use of aggression often occurs in the context of their victimization can help us to avoid the unconscious bias and stereotype of the inherently angry and hyper-violent Black woman (West, 2007).

Reproductive Coercion

A frequently overlooked form of sexual violence that impacts Black victim-survivors is reproductive coercion, such as birth control sabotage (removing the condom during intercourse, destroying a woman's contraceptive device or birth control pills) and pregnancy pressure (verbal or emotional pressure to get pregnant or to terminate a pregnancy). This form of victimization has often resulted in high rates of unintended pregnancies among African American women (Nikolajski et al., 2015). Accordingly, mental health providers should become familiar with all forms reproductive coercion and be prepared to conduct a culturally sensitive assessment with their clients (for a toolkit on reproductive coercion, see Cappelletti, Gatimu, & Shaw, 2014).

Strangulation

It is important to ask our clients about strangulation, a unique form of physical aggression, which can be used, sometimes just once, to immobilize and terrorize the victim. It is a potentially lethal but invisible form of violence, in that there is seldom immediate external evidence. Bruising and swelling may not appear until days later, especially on women of darker complexions. Immediate and lasting fear are the primary postevent reactions to strangulation (Thomas, Joshi, & Sorenson, 2014).

Domestic Homicide

When compared to victim-survivors of other ethnic backgrounds, Black women are murdered at higher rates by their intimate partners, often with a handgun during the course of an argument. Therefore, it is imperative that mental health providers use a lethality screening tool, such as the Danger Assessment, which considers nonfatal strangulation to determine a client's risk for intimate partner homicide (Campbell et al., 2003).

Historical Trauma

During 250 years of slavery, followed by 90 years of *de facto* and *de jure* segregation in the form of Jim Crow laws, and the shameful incompletion of the modern civil rights movement, one thing remained constant in the lives of African Americans: high rates of violence in the form of beatings, rapes, and lynching. Historical trauma has been defined as "the collective spiritual, psychological, emotional and cognitive distress perpetuated intergenerationally deriving from multiple denigrating experiences originating with slavery and continuing with patterns forms of racism and discrimination to the present day" (Williams-Washington, 2010, p. 32). Marriage and family therapists and other mental health professionals should strive to educate themselves about the impact that historical trauma of slavery has had on African Americans and the clinical implications of this trauma (Danzer et al., 2016; Dixon, 2017; Wilkins, Whiting, Watson, Russon, & Moncrief, 2013).

Structural Violence and Inequalities

In order to capture the full range of violence that is experienced by Black women, we need to have a discussion about *institutional racism*, which are unfair policies and discriminatory practices of particular institutions that have a disparate impact on people of color. Relatedly, *structural racism* is the cumulative and compounding effects of an array of societal factors including the history, cultural, ideology, and interactions of institutions and policies that systematically privilege White people and disadvantage people of color (West, 2016b).

Although they seem to be invisible, these forms of inequalities are very real in the lives of our clients. For example, among low-income Black women (Stueve & O'Donnell, 2008) and Black men (Reed et al., 2010), IPV perpetration and victimization have been linked to microaggressions in the form of perceived racial discrimination in the community (e.g., being unfairly stopped and frisked by police or followed by store clerks and called insulting names or physically attacked because of skin color and race). Furthermore, Black women who reported both a history of racial discrimination and IPV experienced a higher prevalence of anxiety and nonspecific physical health symptoms compared to Black women who reported either or neither of these forms of trauma (Waltermaurer, Watson, & McNutt, 2006). In our efforts to use a social justice perspective, a more comprehensive medical and mental health assessment could include a measure of "structural vulnerability" to help providers to think more clearly, critically, and practically about the ways in which social structures and inequalities result in health disparities (Bourgois, Holmes, Sue, & Quesada, 2017).

Community Violence

A form of trauma that disproportionately impacts Black women is community violence. It may involve experiencing or witnessing homicide, gun violence, assaults, robberies, or exposure to drug markets. The combination of interpersonal violence within the home and violence in the neighborhood means that safety is illusive for many Black victim-survivors, which further compromises their physical and emotional health. Therefore, our assessments should ask survivors about the communities that they call home (Stueve & O'Donnell, 2008; Violence Policy Center, 2017).

Mental and Physical Health Problems

As previously discussed, IPV has been associated with physical injuries and a broad range of mental health problems, including mood disorders, anxiety disorders, and eating disorders (Anderson et al., 2015; Lacey et al., 2015). We can assess for mental health problems without seeing our clients as personifying a diagnosis. Instead, we can ask them how they cope with symptoms of depression or PTSD (e.g., intrusive recollections, distressing dreams, flashbacks, and emotional numbing). While keeping in mind that they may have experienced IPV in conjunction with multiple types of violence (structural inequalities, historical trauma, and community violence), have they adopted healthy or unhealthy coping strategies (Sullivan, Weiss, Price, Pugh, & Hansen, 2017)?

It is especially important that we include an assessment of suicidal behavior and substance abuse. A history of partner violence, more than doubles the risk of suicide attempts among African American battered women. Negative life events, childhood maltreatment, distress and depression, feelings of hopelessness, lower levels of spiritual well-being, and substance use increased their risk of suicidal behavior (Davis et al., 2009). Black women also may self-medicate with drugs and alcohol to cope with childhood abuse and IPV. Substance using Black women wanted counselors who could "keep it real," which meant being honest, making them feel like they mattered as a client, and allowing them to make informed decisions (Blakey & Grocher, 2017). In addition, for Black victim-survivors, particularly those who are low-income, the following techniques are helpful: mindfulness-based stress reduction (Dutton, Bermudez, Matas, Majid, & Myers, 2013), motivational interviewing (Wahab et al., 2014), and culturally sensitive psychoeducational programs focused on reducing depression (Davis et al., 2009).

Cultural Barriers to Help-Seeking

Therapists need to be attentive to structural barriers to help-seeking, for example racist policies and procedures in shelters (Nnawulezi & Sullivan,

2014) and homophobic practices that deny services to Black lesbians and transgender survivors (Simpson & Helfrich, 2014). In addition, they should attend to cultural barriers that hinder Black women's ability to get help. For instance, the "Strong Black Women" mandate is "the notion of indefatigable strength can obstruct black women's acknowledgement of the ways that they have been emotionally hurt by black male violence" (West, 1999, p. 78). More specifically, they may avoid reporting their partners' abuse or they may use physical aggression in self-defense, which can increase their risk of injury, because they perceived themselves as being resilient enough to handle the situation alone (Anyikwa, 2015).

To summarize, in order to implement a culturally competent, social justice–based intervention, mental health professional might do the following: consider the multiple identities of Black victim-survivors in their assessments, ask about a broad range of violence exposure (interpersonal violence, such as women's use of aggression, reproductive coercion, nonfatal strangulation, risk of intimate partner homicide; historical trauma, structural violence, and community violence), respectfully discuss mental and physical health problems, and investigate cultural barriers to help-seeking. To conclude, "African American women's voices are a non-negotiable source for developing an ethical assessment of, and response to, violence" (West, 1999, p. 182). This requires us to listen, not in a passive way, but in a politically engaged way with active expressions of empathy.

STRENGTH-BASED APPROACH

Rather than seeing Black victim-survivors as deficient and their relationships as defective, a social justice perspective encourages us to adopt a strength-based approach that acknowledges the healing strategies that have been successfully used by African American women. This entails encouraging internal strength and empowerment, fostering the victim-survivors' social support system, and participating in activism to combat IPV and other forms of oppression.

Encourage Internal Strength and Empowerment

Many Black victim-survivors rely on their internal strength, in the form of self-reliance, self-esteem, prayer, and spirituality to cope and heal in the aftermath of IPV (Sabri et al., 2016). Among the central characteristics of the "Strong Black Woman" image is the notion that African American women are inherently strong, resilient, and capable of surviving significant adversity. Up to a point, this image can help mitigate some of the negative mental and physical health consequences of IPV. However, the protective effects are reduced as the abuse becomes more severe (Iverson et al., 2013). At the same time, the image of the strong Black woman was identified as a barrier to both recognizing depression and substance abuse among battered Black women (Nicolaidis et al., 2010). Hence, as therapists we should consider discussing the psychological advantages and disadvantages of this (mis)representation and often unrealistic expectation of Black women's strength and resilience.

Using a strength-based approach, mental health professionals can strive to help African American survivors to simultaneously express their vulnerability and celebrate their resilience. Storytelling, journal writing, creating and listening to music, and reading books and poetry produced by African American survivors are all artistic forms of expression that can help survivors to heal themselves (Evans, Bell, Burton, & Blount, 2017).

In addition, from a social justice perspective we can conceptualize new models for empowering Black victim-survivors, and indeed all women, who have experienced IPV. For women with access to certain kinds of economic or emotional resources, such as money, housing, and social support, taking control over one's situation can be effective and energizing. In contrast, for those without means, attempting to "take control" or "solve" the problem of abuse can be met with failure and magnify existing power inequalities, resulting in further distress. Accordingly, we should reconceptualize our notion of empowerment. Cattaneo and Goodman (2015) defined empowerment as "a meaningful shift in the experience of power attained through interaction in the social world" (p. 84). Specifically, a more sensitive empowerment model

> describes the process of building empowerment as an iterative one, in which a person who lacks power sets a personally meaningful goal oriented toward increasing power, takes action, and makes progress toward that goal, drawing on his or her evolving self-efficacy, knowledge, skills, and community resources, and support, and observes and reflects on the impact of his or her actions. (p. 84)

Applying this empowerment model means that we are working to understand the victim-survivor's goals, helping her to articulate her aims, acknowledging the structural barriers to achieving those objectives, and working with her to craft a strategy to overcome the challenges that she faces. Her unique circumstances and hopes for the future are moved to the forefront. This is preferable to offering her options for assistance that are based on the availability of services or the mission of a domestic violence organization.

Foster the Survivor's Social Support System

A strength-based approach might routinely include inquiries into the availability and nature of the victim-survivor's support system and service providers can incorporate women's social support networks into their programs, policies, and practices. For example, higher levels of social support from relatives and friends were associated with better mental health status among abused Black women. Therapists can educate the victim-survivor's informal social support network about dynamics of domestic violence. Social support also can happen in the form of group therapy, which promotes healthy relationships and builds effective coping and problem-solving skills (Davis et al., 2009). When compared to women from other ethnic groups, Black victim-survivors are more likely to rely on their clergy, spirituality, and religion to cope with IPV (Nnawulezi & Murphy, 2017). Dyer (2016) recommends that social workers and mental health workers develop partnerships with clergy members. For instance, they can discuss with faith leaders how the clinical interventions and faith interventions complement, at times overlap, and possibly diverts from each other.

Finally, service providers should strive to create a broad range of services to help victim-survivors, their children, and the larger community to combat IPV:

> From the standpoint of social justice, helping to empower poor black communities to develop culturally competent domestic violence shelters—prevention, neighborhood-based crisis intervention, shelters for women and children, counseling, and economic assistance—to promote families and households in their struggle against domestic violence is a salient ethical issue for counselors (Conwill, 2010, p. 42).

CONCLUSION

In this chapter, I provided a brief overview of IPV in the lives of African American women, discussed what social justice looks like in theory, and ended with some practical applications for treatment interventions. My personal and professional vision is simple: To educate empower, and inspire a multicultural alliance of survivors and professionals to prevent all forms of violence and to help survivors to heal themselves. From a social justice perspective, mental health professions, in collaboration with victim-survivors, should strive to commit to activism at the local, state, and national levels. As advocates for victim-survivors of abuse, it is imperative that this awareness is reinforced by deliberate engagement in efforts to reduce the impact of these oppressions within society. This will not only result in successful and individualized treatment of survivors, it will address prevention of violence in all forms.

NOTE

1. The terms *Black* and *African American* will be used interchangeably in this chapter.

REFERENCES

Anderson, J. C., Stockman, J. K., Sabri, B., Campbell, D. W., & Campbell, J. C. (2015). Injury outcomes in African American and African Caribbean women: The role of intimate partner violence. *Journal of Emergency Nursing, 41,* 36–42.

Anyikwa, V. A. (2015). The intersections of race and gender in help-seeking strategies among a battered sample of low-income African American women. *Journal of Human Behavior in the Social Environment, 25*, 948–959.

Ashley, W. (2017). Black eyes matter: Nuances of intersectionality and their impact on inclusion and support. *Sociology and Criminology, 5,* 1–5.

Bent-Goodley, T. B., Chase, L., Circo, E. A., & Rodgers, S. T. (2010). Our survival, our strengths: Understanding the experiences of African American women in abusive relationships. In L. L. Lockhart & Fran S. Danis (Eds.), *Domestic violence: Intersectionality and cultural competent practice* (pp. 67–99). New York: Columbia University Press.

Blakey, J. M., & Grocher, K. B. (Article first published online: May 19, 2017). "Keeping it real": The relational effects of trauma among African American women and their substance abuse treatment counselors. *Journal of Interpersonal Violence*. doi:10.1177/0886260517708403.

Bourgois, P., Holmes, S. M., Sue, K., & Quesada, J. (2017). Structural vulnerability: Operationalizing the concept to address health disparities in clinical care. *Academic Medicine, 92,* 299–307.

Breiding, M. J., Chen, J., & Black, M. C. (2014). *Intimate partner violence in the United States—2010.* Atlanta, GA: National Center for Injury Prevention and Control, Centers for Disease Control and Prevention. Retrieved on July 26, 2017 from https://www.cdc.gov/violenceprevention/pdf/cdc_nisvs_ipv_report_2013_v17_single_a.pdf.

Campbell, J. C., Webster, D., Koziol-McLain, J., Block, C., Campbell, D., Curry, M. A., et al. (2003). Risk factors for femicide in abusive relationships: Results from a multisite case control study. *American Journal of Public Health, 93*, 1089–1097.

Cappelletti, M. M., Gatimu, J. K., & Shaw, G. (2014). *Exposing reproductive coercion: A toolkit for awareness raising, assessment, and intervention.* The Feminist Women's Health Center (FWHC) and The National Coalition Against Domestic Violence (NCADV). Retrieved on July 26, 2017 from https://www.ncadv.org/files/RCtoolkit.pdf.

Carney, A. (2015). Assessing for intimate partner violence. In P. T. Clements, J. Pierce-Weeks, K. E. Holt, A. P. Giardino, S. Seedat, & C. M. Mortiere (Eds.), *Violence against women: Contemporary examination of intimate partner violence* (pp. 17–31). Saint Louis, MO: STM Learning, Inc.

Cattaneo, L. B., & Goodman, L. A. (2015). What is empowerment anyway? A model for domestic violence practice, research, and evaluation. *Psychology of Violence, 5*, 84–94.

Centers for Disease Control and Prevention. (2009). *The socialecological model: A framework for prevention.* Retrieved on July 26, 2017 from https://www.cdc.gov/violenceprevention/overview/social-.

Chavis A. Z., & Hill, M. S. (2009). Integrating multiple intersecting identities: A multicultural conceptualization of the Power and Control Wheel. *Women & Therapy, 32*, 121–149.

Cheng, T. C., & Lo, C. C. (2015). Racial disparities in intimate partner violence examine through the multiple disadvantage model. *Journal of Interpersonal Violence, 31*, 2026–2051.

Conwill, W. L. (2010). Domestic violence among the Black poor: Intersectionality and social justice. *International Journal of Advancement Counselling, 32*, 31–45.

Crenshaw, K. W. (1994). Mapping the margins: Intersectionality, identity politics, and violence against women of color. In M. A. Fineman & R. Mykitiuk (Eds.), *The public nature of private violence: The discovery of domestic abuse* (pp. 93–117). New York: Routledge.

Cuellar, N. G. (2017). Unconscious bias: What is yours? *Journal of Transcultural Nursing, 28*, 333.

Danzer, G., Rieger, S. M., Schubmehl, S., & Cort, D. (2016). White psychologists and African Americans' historical trauma: Implications for practice. *Journal of Aggression, Maltreatment, and Trauma, 25*, 351–370.

Davis, S. P., Arnette, N. C., Bethea, K. S., Graves, K. N., Rhodes, M. N., Harp, S. E., et al. (2009). The Grady Nia Project: A culturally competent intervention for low income, abuse, and suicidal African American women. *Professional Psychology: Research and Practice, 40*, 141–147.

DiAngelo, R. (2011). White fragility. *International Journal of Critical Pedagogy, 3*(3), 54–70.

Dixon, P. (2017). *African American relationships, marriages, and families: An Introduction*. New York: Routledge.

Dutton, M. A., Bermudez, D., Matas, A., Majid, H., & Myers, N. L. (2013). Mindfulness-based stress reduction for low-income, predominantly African American women with PTSD and a history of intimate partner violence. *Cognitive and Behavioral Practice, 20*, 23–32.

Dyer, J. T. (2016). Just social work? Collaborating with African American clergy to address intimate partner violence in churches. *Social Work & Christianity, 43*, 33–54.

Evans, S. Y., Bell, K., Burton, N. K., & Blount, L. G. (2017). *Black women's mental health: Balancing strength and vulnerability*. New York: State University of New York Press.

Gillum, T. L. (2009). Improving services to African American survivors of IPV: From the voices of recipients of culturally specific services. *Violence Against Women, 15*, 57–80.

Iverson, K. M., Bauer, M. R., Shipherd, J. C., Pineles, S. L., Harrington, E. F., & Resick, P. A. (2013). Differential associations between partner violence and physical health symptoms among Caucasian and African American help-seeking women. *Psychological Trauma: Theory, Research, Practice, and Policy, 5*(2), 158–166.

Kaslow, N. J., Leiner, A. S., Reviere, S., Jackson, E., Bethea, K., Bhaju, J., et al. (2010). Suicidal, abused African American women's response to a culturally informed intervention. *Journal of Consulting and Clinical Psychology, 78*, 449–458.

Lacey, K. K., Sears, K. P., Matusko, N., & Jackson, J. S. (2015). Severe physical violence and Black women's health and well-being. *American Journal of Public Health, 105*, 719–724.

Lichtenstein, B., & Johnson, I. M. (2009). Older African American women and barriers to reporting domestic violence to law enforcement in the rural deep South. *Women & Criminal* Justice, 19, 286–305.

Lockhart, L. L., & Mitchell, J. (2010). Cultural competence and intersectionality: Emerging frameworks and practical approaches. In L. L. Lockhart & Fran S. Danis (Eds.), *Domestic violence: Intersectionality and cultural competent practice* (pp. 1–28). New York: Columbia University Press.

Lorde, A. (1982). *Sister outsider: Essays and speeches.* New York: The Crossing Press.

Miller, J. (2008). *Getting played: African American girls, urban inequality, and gendered violence.* New York: New York University Press.

Mortiere, C. (2015). Risk assessment in intimate partner violence. In P. T. Clements, J. Pierce-Weeks, K. E. Holt, A. P. Giardino, S. Seedat, & C. M. Mortiere (Eds.), *Violence against women: Contemporary examination of intimate partner violence* (pp. 33–47). Saint Louis, MO: STM Learning, Inc.

Mugoya, G. C., Witte, T., Bolland, A., Tomek, S., Hooper, L. M., Bolland, J., & Dalmida, S. G. (Article first published online: February 13, 2017). Depression intimate partner violence among African American women living in impoverished inner-city neighborhoods. *Journal of Interpersonal Violence.* doi:10.1177/0886260517691519.

Nicolaidis, C., Timmons, V., Thomas, M. J., Waters, A. S., Wahab, S., Mejia, A., et al. (2010). "You don't go tell white people nothing": African American women's perspective on the influence of violence and race on depression and depression care. *American Journal of Public Health, 100*, 1470–1476.

Nikolajski, C., Miller, E., McCauley, H. L., Akers, A., Schwarz, E. B., & Freedman, L., et al. (2015). Race and reproductive coercion: A qualitative assessment. *Women's Health Issues, 25*, 216–223.

Nnawulezi, N., & Murphy, C. (in press). Understanding formal help-seeking among women whose partners are in abuser intervention programs. *Psychology of Violence.*

Nnawulezi, N. A., & Sullivan, C. M. (2014). Oppression within safe spaces: Exploring racial microaggressions within domestic violence shelters. *Journal of Black Psychology, 40*, 563–591.

O'Leary, A., & Frew, P. M. (2017). *Poverty in the United States: Women's voices.* New York: Springer.

Petrosky, E., Blair, J. M., Betz, C. J., Fowler, K. A., Jack, S., & Lyons, B. H. (2017). Racial and ethnic differences in homicides of adult women and the role of intimate partner violence-United States, 2003–2004. *Morbidity Mortality Weekly Report, 66*, 741–746.

Pizzey, E. (1974). *Scream quietly or the neighbors will hear.* New York: Penguin.

Reed, E., Silverman, J. G., Ickovics, J. R., Gupta, J., Welles, S. L., Santana, M. C., & Raj, A. (2010). Experiences of racial discrimination and relation to violence perpetration and gang involvement among a sample of urban African American men. *Journal of Immigrant Minority Health, 12*, 319–326.

Sabri, B., Bolyard, R., McFadgion, A. L., Stockman, J. K., Lucea, M. B., et al. (2013). Intimate partner violence, depression, PTSD, and use of mental health resources among ethnically diverse Black women. *Social Work in Healthcare, 52*, 351–369.

Sabri, B., Holliday, C. N., Alexander, K. A., Huerta, J., Cimino, A., Callwood, G. B., et al. (2016). Cumulative violence exposures: Black women's responses and sources of strength. *Social Work in Public Health, 31*, 127–139.

Sabri, B., Huerta, J., Alexander, K. A., St. Vil, N. M., Campbell, J. C., & Callwood, G. B. (2015). Multiple intimate partner violence experiences: Knowledge, access, utilization and barriers to utilization of resources by women of the African Diaspora. *Journal of Health for the Poor and Underserved, 26*, 1286–1303.

Schollenberger, J., Campbell, J., Sharps, P. W., O'Campo, P., Gielen, A. C., Dinemann, J., et al. (2003). African American HMO enrollees: Their experiences with partner abuse and its effects on their health and use of medical services. *Violence Against Women, 9*, 599–618.

Simpson, E. K., & Helfrich, C. A. (2014). Oppression and barriers to service for Black, lesbian survivors of intimate partner violence. *Journal of Gay & Lesbian Social Services, 26*, 441–464.

Smith, S. G., Chen, J., Basile, K. C., Gilbert, L. K., Merrick, M. T., Patel, N., Walling, M., & Jain, A. (2017). *The National Intimate Partner and Sexual Violence Survey (NISVS): 2010–2012 state report.* Atlanta, GA: National Center for Injury Prevention and Control Centers for Disease Control and Prevention. Retrieved on July 26, 2017 from https://www.cdc.gov/violenceprevention/pdf/NISVS-StateReportBook.pdf.

St. Vil, N., Sabri, B., Nwokolo, V., Alexander, K. A., & Campbell, J. C. (2017). A qualitative study of survival strategies used by low-income Black women who experience intimate partner violence. *Social Work, 62*, 63–71.

Stueve, A., & O'Donnell, L. (2008). Urban young women's experiences of discrimination and community violence and intimate partner violence. *Journal of Urban Health, 85,* 386–401.

Sullivan, T. P., Weiss, N. H., Price, C., Pugh, N., & Hansen, N. B. (in press). Strategies for coping with individual PTSD symptoms: Experiences of African American victims of intimate partner violence. *Psychological Trauma: Theory, Research, Practice, and Policy.*

Thomas, K. A., Joshi, M., & Sorenson, S. B. (2014). Do you know what it feels like to drown? Strangulation as coercive control in intimate relationships. *Psychology of Women Quarterly, 38*, 124–137.

Violence Policy Center. (2017). *The relationship between community violence and trauma: How violence affects learning, health, and behavior*. Retrieved on July 26, 2017 from http://www.vpc.org/studies/trauma17.pdf.

Wahab, S., Trimble, J., Mejia, A., Mitchell, S. R., Thomas, M. J., Timmons, V., et al. (2014). Motivational interviewing at the intersections of depression and intimate partner violence among African American women. *Journal of Evidence-Based Social Work, 11*, 291–303.

Waltermaurer, E., Watson, C. A., & McNutt, L. A. (2006). Black women's health: The effect of perceived racism and intimate partner violence. *Violence Against Women, 12*, 1214–1222.

West, C. M. (Ed.). (2003). *Violence in the lives of Black women: Battered, black, and blue*. New York: Routledge.

West, C. M. (2007). "Sorry, we have to take you in:" Black battered women arrested for intimate partner violence. *Journal of Aggression, Maltreatment & Trauma, 15*, 95–121.

West, C. M. (2010). Resistance as recovery: Winning a sexual harassment complaint. In A. White (Ed.), *African Americans doing feminism: Putting theory into everyday practice* (pp. 175–188). New York: State University of New York Press.

West, C. M. (2012). Partner abuse in ethnic minority and gay, lesbian, bisexual, and transgender populations. *Partner Abuse, 3*(3), 336–357.

West, C. M. (2016a). African immigrant women and intimate partner violence: A systematic review. *Journal of Aggression Maltreatment and Trauma*, *25*, 4–17.

West, C. M. (2016b). Hidden in plain sight: Structural inequalities and (In)visible violence in the lives of African American women. In L. Wilton & E. Short (Eds.), *Talking about structural inequalities in everyday life: New politics of race in groups, organizations, and social systems* (pp. 85–102). Charlotte, NC: Information Age Publishing.

West, C. M. (2016c). Living in a web of trauma: An ecological examination of violence among African Americans. In C. C. Cuevas & C. M. Rennison (Eds.), *The Wiley-Blackwell handbook on the psychology of violence* (pp. 649–665). Oxford: John Wiley & Sons.

West, T. C. (1999). *Wounds of the spirit: Black women, violence, and resistance ethics.* New York: University of New York University Press.

Wilkins, E. J., Whiting, J. B., Watson, M. F., Russon, J. M., & Moncrief A. M. (2013). Residual effects of slavery: What clinicians need to know. *Contemporary Family Therapy, 35*, 14–28.

Williams-Washington, K. N. (2010). Historical trauma. In R. L. Hampton, T. P. Gullotta, & R. L. Crowel (Eds.), *Handbook of African American health* (pp. 31–49). New York: Guilford Press.

Chapter 5

Immigration and Social Justice

Alfonso Mercado and Amanda C. Venta

IMMIGRATION

Many individuals and families migrate to the United States for an array of reasons. Many immigrant groups are escaping violence or poverty. Many are reuniting with family members who have been living in the United States for a long time or are seeking educational and economic opportunities. The United States is currently home to approximately 40.4 million immigrants (U.S. Census Bureau, 2011) of which one-third are from Mexico and 55% originate from Latin America (U.S. Census Bureau, 2011). There has also been an increase in immigrants and refugees from the Middle East given the unrest in that part of the world (Kiely, Farley, & Gore, 2015). One in five individuals living in the United States is a first- or a second-generation immigrant, and almost a quarter of children under the age of 18 have an immigrant parent (Mather, 2009). One current estimate of America's undocumented immigrants is 11.7 million (Passel, Cohn, & Gonzalez-Barrera, 2013). Immigrant youth, documented and undocumented, are the fastest-growing child population in the United States. Today, approximately 16 million children have at least one parent who is an immigrant, and nearly 23% of the youth under the age of 18 have immigrant parents; this population is expected to grow 30% by 2030 (Casas, 2017).

These numbers represent millions of lives who are disenfranchised in various ways. Therefore, it is imperative to understand the importance of the connection between immigration and social justice. As the children of immigrant parents and bilingual psychologists who provide psychological services to the immigrant population in a border community and conducts research on Latina(o)'s and immigrant groups, we find it imperative to be voices of advocacy for this population—a population that is part of the United States' rich history and strengthens our nation on many fronts.

PSYCHOLOGY AND SOCIAL JUSTICE

Social Justice has been defined as "fairness" and "equality," and its theories highlight human rights including basic needs, education, and medical attention for all (Kitchener & Anderson, 2011). In Melba Vasquez's (2012) *American Psychologist* article, *Why We Do What We Do*, she postulated that psychological science is significantly related to social justice in its goal to "decrease human suffering and promote human values of equality and justice" (p. 338). A commitment to social justice in psychology has evolved in the last few years and most recently in this current political climate. Vasquez (2013) emphasizes that the American Psychological Association's (APA) mission, vision, goals, and ethics code provide a rationale for psychologists' involvement in social issues. However, regardless of the science that informs us on psychological perspectives on social issues, there are some individuals who are in disagreement when associations address controversial issues through policies and public statements (Vasquez, 2013).

The social justice perspective in psychological treatment is rooted in the belief that psychological treatment should be available to all people—all of whom have the right to equitable treatment and fair allocation of societal resources (Crethar, Rivera, & Nash, 2008). Professionals that are committed to social justice must challenge systemic inequalities thus requiring a paradigm shift (Corey, Corey, & Callanan, 1998). Casas (2017) recommends that clinicians conceptualize clients via an ecological framework that includes consideration of all contributing factors when serving immigrant groups, as this will allow for a comprehensive assessment needed in order to develop and identify effective interventions.

When conceptualizing social justice and immigration, it is important to understand that social justice goes beyond providing effective and culturally appropriate interventions to these populations, as will be later discussed in this chapter. Rather, it involves motivating change at a systemic level, engaging in acts that ameliorate the inequality and unfairness that currently exist for immigrant groups. For example, social justice helps ensure the protection of educational rights and opportunities for all children, addresses culturally responsive practices, promotes nondiscriminatory practices, and encourages advocating for/with individuals or groups of individuals who may not be able to advocate for themselves. Social justice may also entail providing information on medical resources available at low cost or no cost in respective communities, immigrant support groups, or legal organizations, or advocating for them in community, state, or national levels.

SOCIAL JUSTICE AT THE TEXAS-MEXICO BORDER

Practicing in a border community, we have seen a rise in unaccompanied minors and immigrant mothers, fathers, and children from Latin America and beyond crossing the Rio Grande River, which borders Northern Mexico and Texas. This is a distinct region in the United States. It is a predominantly Latino community and is a meeting point for many immigrants groups and cultures (Mercado, Rogers, Villarreal, Colunga-Rodriguez, Terracciano, & Finn-Nguyen, 2016). South Texas is considered an underserved community with regard to health care and where approximately 90% of the population is of Latino descent (Mercado et al., 2016). The community is also in a geographically distinct area of the United States where the highest rates of obesity and diabetes occur (U.S. Health News and World Reports, 2012).

There was a 131% increase in the number of children and families crossing the Southwestern border of the United States between 2015 and 2016 (U.S. Customs and Border Patrol, Southwest Border Sectors, 2016). Approximately 52,000 minors of ages five and older—mostly from Honduras, Guatemala, and El Salvador—crossed the U.S./Mexico border in 2015. Additionally, it should be noted that migration from Mexico to the United States accounts for 28% of the U.S. foreign-born population, with 21% of Mexican immigrants ultimately settling in Texas. The undocumented and unaccompanied youth entering the United States have significantly increased during the last two years, something that is evident in the border community where we practice and conduct research. Due to these diverse demographics, psychologists and mental health professionals are increasingly serving immigrant children and adults, both documented and undocumented, who present with a multitude of problems across settings including schools, clinics, hospitals, and prisons (Casas, 2017). Thus, clinicians should be aware of this important population as practitioners and researchers in an ever-growing multicultural society.

As psychologists conducting research and clinical work with recently immigrated individuals, we provide the following examples of our work to illustrate our operationalization of social justice in our professional lives.

CLINICAL INTERVENTION

Culturally diverse individuals face an array of obstacles when seeking mental health treatment. A literature review of the last 15 years noted that ethnic minorities face a number of barriers to mental health care such as, accessibility, availability, and appropriateness (Turner et al., 2016), which may include communication issues, lack of trust, therapist bias, and no insurance coverage of treatment. At the most basic level, if a clinician does not speak Spanish and is working with a monolingual Spanish speaker, the language barrier could hamper the relationship with the client and contribute to patient dropout (Turner et al., 2016). Beyond these barriers, there is a well-documented lack of culturally and linguistically sensitive mental health treatments for Latinos (Turner et al., 2016). To abate this problem in mental health treatment, it is essential to provide culturally sensitive evidenced-based interventions to ethnically diverse clients. It is critical that clinicians and students begin to utilize cultural psychotherapy frameworks (La Roche, 2013) to effectively deliver evidenced-based interventions. Miranda et al. (2005) highlighted that culturally adapted interventions are shown to be effective; however, efficacy studies have not identified to what extent an intervention needs to be adapted to ethnic minorities and guide treatment. Mercado and Hinojosa (2017) have attempted to fill the gap in specialized treatment modalities with Latino and immigrant groups. For example, dialectical behavior therapy (DBT) has proven to be effective across clinical groups as an empirically supported treatment, but it has yet to be studied in ethnic minority groups. Mercado and Hinojosa (2017) offered a culturally adapted DBT modality with Latino clients in South Texas and noted that, when delivered in a culturally responsive manner, a reduction in mental health symptoms and improved interpersonal functioning occurs. The authors incorporated Latino cultural values in DBT's skills and interventions with a Latina adult client diagnosed with anxiety and depression. This study offers new knowledge to other health-care providers and contributes to the reduction of health-care disparities in Latino groups.

RESEARCH WITH IMMIGRANT GROUPS

A second initiative that surrounds social justice is the study of the Hispanic Health Paradox with recently arrived immigrant groups and refugees at a local Humanitarian Respite Center in McAllen, Texas. The *Hispanic Health Paradox* refers to an existing literature base showing that, despite elevated health risk (e.g., low socioeconomic status[SES], limited access to health care, and insurance), Hispanics in the United States generally report better health than non-Hispanic Whites (Ruiz, Hamann, Mehl, & O'Connor, 2016). This Hispanic health advantage is evident in life expectancy (Heron, 2016), infant mortality (Collins, Soskolne, Rankin, & Bennett, 2013), cardiovascular disease (Mozaffarian et al., 2015), and cancer (Ruiz, Campos, & Garcia, 2016). The advantage is most pronounced among Hispanic immigrants (i.e., foreign born; Singh, Rodriguez-Lainz, & Kogan, 2013) and erodes with increasing time and generations in the United States, as Hispanic acculturation to U.S. culture increases (Kondo, Rossi, Schwartz, Zamboanga, & Scalf, 2016). The Hispanic health advantage was initially identified three decades ago (Markides & Coreil, 1986), and much of the health data collected predates unprecedented increases in violence in Central America—particularly El Salvador, Guatemala, and Honduras. This shift is recent, with Honduras reporting the highest homicide rate globally in 2011; 2013 marked the end of a truce between major gang powers in El Salvador; and crime victimization was cited as a major reason for Central American migration in 2014 (Hiskey, Cordova, Orces, & Malone, 2016). As the sociopolitical climate of Central America has changed, so have patterns of Hispanic immigration to the United States. Between 2015 and 2016 alone, there was a 131% increase in the number of children and families crossing the Southwestern border of the United States, reflecting large numbers of families seeking "humanitarian protection" (U.S. Border Patrol, Southwest Border Sectors, 2016). The unprecedented danger in Central America has been cited as a "humanitarian emergency" by former president Obama, with children and families needing "special attention" (Declaration by the Government Of The United States Of America and the Government Of The United Mexican States Concerning Twenty-First Century Border Management, 2010) and "particular focus" (Federal Strategic Action Plan on Services for Victims of Human Trafficking in the United States, 2014). Dramatic increases in rates of violence in Central America correspond to dramatic increases in reports of trauma and posttraumatic symptoms among recent waves of Hispanic immigrants (U.S. Conference on Catholic Bishops, 2014). No prior research has considered the impact of trauma on the Hispanic health advantage.

The authors are collaborating with a Humanitarian Respite Center in a Texas-Mexico border community addressing trauma and cultural values on the Hispanic health advantage. Several hypotheses regarding the mechanisms underlying the *Hispanic Health Paradox* have been theorized. The conceptual model utilized is one of sociocultural resilience put forth by Ruiz et al. (2016). This model posits that the Hispanic health advantage (including decreased susceptibility to disease and increased survival) is driven by sociocultural resilience factors that promote positive health—specifically, collectivist values including "family (*familismo*), interpersonal harmony (*simpatía*), and valuing of elder community members (*respeto*)" (Ruiz et al., 2016, p. 467). The possible protective role of these sociocultural values has been widely conjectured as an explanation for the *Hispanic Health Paradox*, and its erosion as acculturation to U.S. culture increases. However, empirical support for this model is limited by a research base that rarely assesses these sociocultural values directly. Instead, studies have linked "proxies of Latino culture" (Ruiz, Campos, & Garcia, 2016) like higher neighborhood ethnic density (Shaw & Pickett, 2013), foreign nativity (Holmes, Driscoll, & Heron, 2015), and low U.S. acculturation (Kondo, Rossi, Schwartz, Zamboanga, & Scalf, 2016) to positive health, and assumed that increased endorsement of Hispanic cultural values drives the observed relations. A need to directly assess relations between proposed sociocultural resilience factors and health remains and has dominated recent calls for research (e.g., Ruiz et al., 2016). Moreover, examinations of this conceptual model have not considered the role of trauma exposure or symptoms—despite high rates of trauma in modern waves of Hispanic immigrants and evidence that trauma has a deleterious effect on health in other groups.

Therefore, our research examines Ruiz and colleagues' (2016) sociocultural model of Hispanic health resilience by specifically assessing trauma (exposure and symptoms) and Hispanic cultural values in relation to the physical health of Central American immigrant mothers, fathers, and their children within 24 hours of arrival in the United States. Critically, this provides the first direct exploration of this sociocultural resilience model in recently immigrated mothers and children. Moreover, this study seeks to examine the role of trauma, a psychosocial experience of increasing prevalence in Central America, in relation to the physical health of mothers, fathers, and children. These findings will serve to develop the first integrated model of Hispanic health that includes both sociocultural resilience factors and trauma-related risk factors in recently immigrated families from Central America. This is an ongoing study that addresses important variables surrounding social justice in psychological science that are critical to a population that is understudied, specifically, newly arrived immigrant groups from Latin America and beyond.

COMMUNITY INVOLVEMENT

The Hispanic Health Paradox with immigrant groups is currently being investigated at a Humanitarian Respite Center in South Texas. An average of 150 families have historically arrived daily, but these numbers have significantly decreased due, apparently, to the recent U.S. political climate surrounding immigration. This is the first time the Catholic Charities of South Texas have opened their doors to a university to conduct research that carries immense potential benefits for immigrant health and psychological well-being. This center is located in a border community in South Texas.

The Humanitarian Respite Center works diligently to restore humanity to a marginalized group by offering food, shelter, showers, and hygienic items, courtesy calls to their relatives, a safe space to spend the night, and assistance with travel and immigration paperwork to incoming immigrants from Central and South America, and beyond. Many immigrants arrive at the local bus station after having been detained and processed at local Immigration and Custom Enforcement facilities; they are welcomed at the Respite Center with applause and embracing smiles. Children and women make up the majority of this marginalized population, but fathers and their children are also seen. Even though migrants may have differing destinations, they all share a common vision of the American Dream. After they have had a warm meal, a shower, and a change of clothes, immigrants are transported in a van to the local bus station at various times throughout the day. Occasionally, they depart to their destination a day after their arrival, staying the night in tents (which are cleaned daily by volunteers) at the Respite Center. Finally, they are driven back to McAllen's Central Bus Station where the next bus awaits their traveling, hope-filled souls.

TEACHING SOCIAL JUSTICE IN PSYCHOLOGY

The established partnership between the Humanitarian Center and the University of Texas-Rio Grande Valley allows students to obtain a firsthand experience of the arising immigration phenomena. In this enriching project, they learn to better understand human behavior and psychological processes beyond the classroom lectures or textbook readings. The integration of social justice into college courses provides an opportunity to engage students in social justice scholarship and research; faculty and students are acting in concert with their core values and ethical standards for the purpose of improving the lives of others in real-world settings. In addition, they engage in dialogue related to why this content is important and develop mission statements/core training goals related to social justice. Students are exposed to meaningful experiences that help make 'social justice' a real thing, not simply a theoretical construct or aspiration. Lastly, providing a safe and supportive forum for eliciting voice and constructive dialogue aids in the effective teaching of social justice in psychology courses.

The American Psychological Association (APA) also has Guidelines on Multicultural Education, Training, Research, Practice, and Organizational Change that reflect knowledge and skills needed for the profession in the midst of dramatic historic sociopolitical changes in U.S. society, as well as needs from new constituencies, markets, and clients (APA, 2002). One specific goal of these guidelines is to provide psychologists with "the rationale and needs for addressing multiculturalism and diversity in education, training, research, practice, and organizational change" (APA, 2002).

SOCIAL JUSTICE IN LOCAL PSYCHOLOGICAL ASSOCIATIONS

National, state, and local psychological associations have mission and vision statements that include social justice. For example, the APA emphasizes social justice in its Ethical Codes of Conduct, General Principle D. Justice, and existing Bylaws 1.1, noting: "The objects of the American Psychological Association shall be to advance psychology as a science, a profession, and as a means of promoting health, education and human welfare" (APA, 2008a). In addition, APA's mission is "to advance the creation, communication and application of psychological knowledge to benefit society and improve people's lives" (APA, 2008b, para 2).

Similarly, the mission of the Texas Psychological Association (TPA) is to represent and enhance the profession of psychology in Texas, promoting human health and welfare through education, science, and practice. Its purpose is to advance psychology as a scientific profession and as a means of promoting human welfare

(a) by the promotion of research in psychology and the improvement of research methods and conditions;
(b) by the improvement of qualifications and usefulness of psychologists through high standards of professional ethics, conduct, education, training, and achievement;
(c) by the increase and diffusion of psychological knowledge through meetings, professional contacts, reports, papers, discussions, and publications, thereby to advance scientific interest and inquiry and to foster the application of psychology in the promotion of the public welfare.

Within its efforts to protect, promote, and defend the professional practice of psychology in Texas, TPA may from time to time choose to take a public position on a variety of issues, including matters of social justice and public interest. In an effort to engage in an appropriate level and degree of discernment when considering what may be controversial issues, the Association developed a communication process policy that considers social justice issues on a case-by-case basis, recognizing that psychologists may have valuable input to further the public discourse. Public positions are informed by careful analysis of the ethics and potential ethical imperatives, research, and the general domain of psychological knowledge. This policy helps guide the TPA Board of Trustees in their efforts to determine prudent and professionally responsible means of addressing potentially controversial public interest or social responsibility issues.

SOCIAL JUSTICE IN NATIONAL ORGANIZATIONS: APA'S CROSSROADS REPORT

In 2013, the APA Presidential Task Force on Immigration published *Crossroads: The Psychology of Immigration in the New Century*, "an evidence-based report on the psychological factors related to the immigration experience . . . focusing on factors that impede and facilitate adjustment" (APA, 2013). The report was also intended to facilitate decision-making in regards to immigration, which has become a societal, political, and legal issue in contemporary America.

The report outlines three guiding principles: (1) immigrants are resilient and resourceful, (2) immigrants are influenced by their social contexts and, thus, ecological circumstances should be considered when framing their experiences, and (3) it is essential to use cultural lenses with the diverse immigrant-origin population (APA Guidelines on Multicultural Education, Training, Research, Practice, and Organizational Change for Psychologists, 2013). The report indicates that first-generation immigrants often display better physical and behavioral health than subsequent generations, despite having to face many challenges such as language barriers, racial discrimination, poverty, occupational disappointments, social isolation, and educational difficulties (APA, 2013). Racial discrimination is one of the most difficult stressors that newly arrived immigrants are faced with, and it is also one of the most researched. Discrimination is experienced in the workplace, neighborhood, schools, and even service agencies. For many immigrants, immigration to the United States provides their first encounters with racial discrimination (APA, 2013). Even without the undue experiences of racial discrimination, acculturation is not without its own challenges. Age is a factor in how well immigrants acculturate to their new environment; younger immigrants generally acculturate faster and with greater ease than their older counterparts (APA, 2013). Although immigrants may come to adopt many of the values and behavioral practices of the new culture, the values and practices of the country of origin are rarely abandoned entirely (APA, 2013). The process of acculturation has the potential to strain the dynamics of the parent-child relationship. Children may begin to lose faith in their parent's ability to understand and help them cope with the challenges they face in the new culture (APA, 2013).

Immigrants are often disadvantaged and perform below their actual competencies when tested with clinical and educational assessments that may not be sufficiently attuned to their cultural background, or frame of reference (APA, 2013). In the clinical realm, immigrants are particularly disadvantaged when administered ability, aptitude, and achievement tests. Although many first-generation immigrants are less adapted to the language of their new country, they often display certain advantages in educational contexts such as optimism, high aspirations, dedication to hard work, positive attitudes towards school, and family support (APA, 2013). However, they tend to perform poorly at "high-stakes testing," according to the report. The needs of immigrant students are often inadequately addressed within the educational systems, and they are often at a significant disadvantage.

The report states that immigrants have not been shown to suffer from mental illnesses more frequently than nonimmigrants, with the exception of refugees (APA, 2013). However, when such illnesses do occur within this population, they are frequently a product of the immigration process—loss of and separation from [the] country of origin, family members, and familiar customs and traditions; changes in social class and/or socioeconomic status; exposure to a new physical environment; and the need to navigate unfamiliar cultural contexts" (APA, 2013). The issues of immigrants can often be classified according to three categories: (1) acculturation-based problems, (2) trauma-based presenting problems, and (3) discrimination-, racism-, and xenophobia-based problems (APA, 2013). The report highlights that the recognition and appropriate utilization of culture-specific coping should be promoted within the clinical context. The report identifies three kinds of barriers to culturally sensitive treatment with immigrants: (1) social-cultural barriers, such as differences in frame of reference regarding the causes and treatments of mental illness, (2) contextual-structural barriers, which included lack of access or knowledge of culturally sensitive mental health services, and (3) clinical-procedural barriers, which may be described as "clinical bias" due to lack of cultural sensitivity, language barriers, misdiagnosis, and lack of recognition of culture-specific forms of coping and resiliency (APA, 2013).

Overall, the field of psychology, particularly in the context of immigration, was enhanced by this important report that former APA president, Dr. Melba Vasquez, initiated during her presidency at APA. Members of the task force compiled pertinent data and reviewed critical literature to set forth these important guiding principles and frameworks when working with immigrant groups.

ACCULTURATION, RESILIENCY, AND COUNSELING PERSPECTIVES WORKING WITH IMMIGRANT GROUPS

It is therefore important to consider critical factors when working with immigrant groups in the clinical setting. These include acculturation, resiliency, and counseling perspectives that can aid in the effective delivery of mental health treatment.

Acculturation

Acculturation is an important concept when examining ethnic minority groups. Organista, Chun, and Marin (1998, p. 77) defined acculturation within an ethnic group as the "process of changes that occur within the context of cultural attitudes, values, and behaviors when coming in contact with another, more dominant culture." Acculturation refers to a bidimensional process in which an individual will range from high to low on affiliation with their host (postmigration) culture and, on a separate axis, from high to low on affiliation with their culture of origin (Sam & Berry, 2010). Individuals high in affiliation with their host culture and low in affiliation with their culture of origin, for instance, are described as "assimilated," whereas individuals high on both axes are referred to as "bicultural/integrated." Individuals low in both metrics are described as "marginalized," and individuals with high affiliation with their culture of origin only are referred to as "traditional/separated." Overall, acculturation among immigrants is conceptualized as a change in cultural identity that includes shifts in various cultural dimensions including typical practices, values, and identifications (Schwarz, Unger, Zamboanga, & Szapocznik, 2010).

Literature regarding the link between acculturation and mental health is mixed, with some studies of the *Immigrant Paradox* reporting that lower acculturation with the host country accounts for health benefits (e.g., Kaplan & Marks, 1990) and others showing that low acculturation among immigrants is risk factor for negative mental health outcomes (e.g., Hwang & Ting, 2008). Indeed, the aforementioned *Immigrant* and *Hispanic Paradox* literatures cite that individuals with lower acculturation to the United States experience greater benefits (Teruya & Bazargan-Hejazi, 2013). Some of the identified health benefits noted in *Paradox* research erode with increasing time and generations in the United States as both Hispanic acculturation to U.S. culture and damaging health behaviors (e.g., smoking) increase (Kondo et al., 2016). Numerous theories have been put forth to explain these inconsistent findings, including heterogeneity within and across immigrant groups, inconsistent measurement of acculturation, and lack of measurement of related variables regarding ethnic identity (Bulut & Gayman, 2015). In studies that have endeavored to address these limitations, acculturation emerges as a complex construct without simple relations to mental health. Indeed, findings do not link simple conceptualizations of high or low acculturation to mental health, but rather identify risk in specific interactions between both axes put forth by Sam and Berry (2010). Specifically, marginalization appears to be relatively consistently associated with negative mental health outcomes, whereas integration is associated with positive mental health outcomes (Yoon et al., 2013). Support for this conclusion has been documented with regard to both Latino and Asian immigrants (Bulut & Gayman, 2015), and the worst outcomes have been noted among recently arrived immigrants.

Critiques of existing literature on acculturation in the context of mental health, however, have cited inconsistent measurement and definition of acculturation across studies (Bulut & Gayman, 2015; Teruya & Bazargan-Hejazi, 2013). Acculturation is often treated as though it is synonymous with acculturative stress—self-reported distress during the acculturation process (e.g., distress associated with speaking with an accent). Literature regarding acculturative stress is relatively consistent across immigrant groups, suggesting that distress while adjusting to acculturation has a negative impact on all ethnic groups' mental health (Caplan, 2007; Teruya & Bazargan-Hejazi, 2013; Turner, Lloyd, & Taylor, 2006) with particularly profound impacts on substance use of Hispanics in the United States (Turner et al., 2006). Relatedly, perceived racism and discrimination have been linked to negative mental health and academic outcomes in immigrant youth in the United States (Smokowski & Bacallao, 2006; Suárez-Orozco, Rhodes, & Milburn, 2009). In studies that account for both acculturation level and acculturative stress, the latter emerges as the significant risk factor for psychopathology (Hwang & Ting, 2008), indicating that experiences of perceived discrimination and related distress are more relevant to mental health in immigrant groups than cultural identification alone.

Resiliency

Another important characteristic that is apparent when working with immigrant groups in clinical and research settings is in the level of resiliency. Many researchers have highlighted the role of the Latino culture in how it positively affects health outcomes. For example, Gallo, Penedo, de los Monteros, and Arguelles (2009) conceptualize the Reserve Capacity Model, which helps explain how multiple types of psychosocial factors might contribute to the disparities related to SES. Individuals with less reserve capacity may have fewer social factors to help deal with stress. These factors can include interpersonal (support, relationships, social roles), intrapersonal (perception of control, future, optimistic views), and tangible factors as well (transportation, saving, day care). To be able to have a better chance of being resilient, the more reserve capacity, the higher is the probability for overcoming obstacles. Reserve capacity may be a protective factor that enhances resiliency in individuals who maintain high levels of reserve capacity even in the context of adverse circumstances. Latino cultural values can play a significant role in resiliency. Some important values include allocentrism, familismo, and simpatia. Allocentrism and familismo focus on the idea that the group or family needs come before individual needs. This allows for individuals to have stronger social networks and support. Simpatia reflects a drive towards nonconfrontational social interactions.

Another prominent model discussed previously, The *Hispanic Health Paradox,* includes the aforementioned sociocultural resilience factors put forth by Ruiz et al. (2016). This model posits that the Hispanic health advantage is driven by sociocultural resilience factors that promote positive health—specifically, collectivist values including "family (*familismo*), interpersonal harmony (*simpatía*), and the valuing of elder community members (*respeto*)" (Ruiz et al., 2016, p. 467).

Counseling Perspectives

In order to provide the most effective mental health interventions to immigrant groups, several guiding principles have been proposed by La Roche et al. (2017) and Casas (2017). One important movement in psychotherapy has been the development of cultural evidenced-based psychotherapies (CEBPs). CEBPs refer to evidenced-based counseling interventions that emphasize race, and ethnicity, but also integrate cultural proximal variables, such as socioeconomic status, neighborhood violence, and religion (La Roche et al., 2017). By integrating cultural and proximal factors, clinicians can have a better understanding of the psychotherapeutic process. One important consideration La Roche and colleagues (2017) highlight is the importance of operationally defining race, ethnicity, and culture and examining the effects of cultural variables as each impacts the psychotherapeutic process. Doing so can further enhance the efficacy of cultural competency recommendations.

Casas (2017) also postulates imperative guiding principles for clinicians to work effectively with culturally diverse groups while specifically identifying the immigrant population. First, the author suggests using an ecological framework proposed by Brofenbrenner and Morris (2006) to guide interventions. This perspective highlights the human experience as a result of reciprocal interactions between people and the environment and focuses on how it varies from individuals, contexts, culture, and time (Casas, 2017). This allows clinicians to better understand the immigrant experience and thus develop appropriate interventions. A second guiding principle includes the necessity of integrating evidenced-based practice with practice based interventions (Casas, 2017; La Roche, 2017). The third guiding principle supports the APA Presidential Task Force on Immigration (2012) report, which postulates the importance of cultural competency, which includes cultural knowledge, therapist's attitudes, beliefs, and the skills needed for the effective delivery of culturally appropriate interventions. A fourth guiding principle includes the significance of utilizing comprehensive community-based interventions. This allows the clinician to collaborate with the various systems that are part of the client's life, such as primary care, mental health, social, legal, and educational resources. Collaborating with various social service entities allows the client to be validated and empowered (Casas, 2017). The fifth and final guiding principle used in the effective delivery of clinical interventions with immigrant groups includes the importance of using a social justice perspective as a driving force for all services (Casas, 2017). We have found this to be a vital factor in the implementation of effective treatment delivery. The belief that all people have the right for equitable treatment and fair allocation of societal resources is critical and is a paradigm shift among mental health providers. There are obstacles that some may face, and playing an active role in advocacy and policymaking for humane treatment of all persons including immigrant groups is of outmost importance. Advocacy in local, state, and national platforms is critical in order to advance social justice and mental health.

SUMMARY AND CONCLUSION

The broad aim of this chapter was to discuss the intersection of social justice, psychological science and practice, and recent immigration trends. Psychologists have a long history of engagement with social justice through multiple professional roles. Within the broader context of immigrant mental health, delivering and researching culturally- and linguistically sensitive interventions is an immediate application of social justice principles to psychological practice. Likewise, the authors' current research studies are described, not with the pretense of suggesting excellence, but rather with the aim of documenting how research can combine both scientific pursuits and social justice concern. Finally, psychologists are able to organize at local, state, and national levels and can, therefore, as a group organize in support of social justice concerns—particularly those most relevant to the profession (e.g., mental health-care availability). The topics outlined in this chapter should not be thought of as unique to the immigration context, rather, this context is one that serves to illustrate how we, as psychologists, have integrated our professional identities as practitioners, researchers, teachers, and advocates behind shared social justice goals.

REFERENCES

American Psychological Association. (2002). *APA guidelines on multicultural education, training, research, practice, and organizational change for psychologists*. Retrieved from http://www.apa.org/pi/oema/resources/policy/multicultural-guidelines.aspx.

American Psychological Association. (2008a). *Bylaws of the American Psychological Association.* Retrieved from http://www.apa.org/about/governance/bylaws/article-1.aspx.

American Psychological Association. (2008b). *Mission statement for APA*. Retrieved from http://www.apa.org/about/policy/chapter-6.aspx.

American Psychological Association Presidential Task Force on Immigration. (2013). *Crossroads: The psychology of immigration in the new century*. Retrieved from http://www.apa.org/topics/immigration/executive-summary.pdf.

Brofenbrenner, U., & Morris, P. A. (2006). The bio-ecological model of human development. In W. Damon & R. M. Lerner (Eds.), *Handbook of child psychology: Vol. 1. Theoretical models of human development* (6th ed., pp. 793–828). Hoboken, NJ: Wiley.

Bulut, E., & Gayman, M. D. (2015). Acculturation and self-rated mental health among Latino and Asian immigrants in the United States: A latent class analysis. *Journal of Immigrant and Minority Health, 18*(4), 836–849.

Casas, M. J. (2017). Caution: Immigration maybe harmful to your mental health. In J. M. Casas, L. A. Suzuki, C. M. Alexander, & M. A. Jackson (Eds.), *Handbook of Multicultural Counseling*. Thousand Oaks, CA: Sage Publications.

Caplan, S. (2007). Latinos, acculturation, and acculturative stress: A dimensional concept analysis. *Policy, Politics, & Nursing Practice*, *8*(2), 93–106.

Crethar, H. C., Rivera, E. T., & Nash, S. (2008). In search of common threads: Linking multicultural, feminist, and social justice counseling paradigms. *Journal of Counseling & Development*, *86*(3), 269–278. doi:10.1002/j.1556-6678.2008.tb00509.x.

Collins, J. W., Soskolne, G. R., Rankin, K. M., & Bennett, A. C. (2013). Differing first year mortality rates of term births to white, African American, and Mexican-American US-born and foreign-born mothers. *Maternal and Child Health Journal*, *17*(10), 1776–1783. doi:10.1007/s10995-012-1197-2.

Corey, G., Corey, M. S., & Callanan, P. (1998). *Issues and ethics in the helping professions* (5th ed.). Pacific Grove, CA: Brooks/Cole Publishing.

Declaration by The Government of the United States of America and The Government Of The United Mexican States concerning twenty-first century border management. (2010). Retrieved from https://www.whitehouse.gov/the-press-office/declaration-government-united-states-america-and-government-united-mexican-states-c.

Federal strategic action plan on services for victims of human trafficking in the United States. (2014). Retrieved from http://www.ovc.gov/pubs/FederalHumanTraffickingStrategicPlan.pdf.

Gallo, L. C., Penedo, F. J., de los Monteros, K. E., & Arguelles, W. (2009). Resiliency in the face of disadvantage: Do Hispanic cultural characteristics protect health outcomes? *Journal of Personality*, *77*(6), 1707–1746. doi:10.1111/j.1467-6494.2009.00598.x.

Heron, M. (2016). Deaths: Leading causes for 2013. *National Vital Statistics Report: From the Centers for Disease Control and Prevention, National Center for Health Statistics, National Vital Statistics System*, *65*(2), 1.

Hiskey, J., Cordova, A., Orces, D., & Malone, M. (2016). Understanding the Central American refugee crisis: Why they are fleeing and how U.S. policies are failing to deter them. *American Immigration Council Special Report.* Washington, DC. Retrieved from: http://immigrationpolicy.org/sites/default/files/docs/understanding_the_central_american_refugee_crisis.pdf.

Holmes, J. S., Driscoll, A. K., & Heron, M. (2015). Mortality among US-born and immigrant hispanics in the US: Effects of nativity, duration of residence, and age at immigration. *International Journal of Public Health, 60*(5), 609–617. doi:10.1007/s00038-015-0686-7.

Hwang, W. C., & Ting, J. Y. (2008). Disaggregating the effects of acculturation and acculturative stress on the mental health of Asian Americans. *Cultural Diversity and Ethnic Minority Psychology, 14*(2), 147.

Kaplan, M. S., & Marks, G. (1990). Adverse effects of acculturation: Psychological distress among Mexican American young adults. *Social Science & Medicine, 31*(12), 1313–1319.

Kiely E., Farley, R., & Gore, D. (2015). *Facts about the Syrian refugees.* Retrieved from www.factcheck.org/2015/facts-about-the-syrian-refugees/.

Kitchener, K. S., & Anderson, S. K. (2011). *Foundations of ethical practice, research, and teaching in psychology and counseling* (2nd ed.). New York: Routledge.

Kondo, K. K., Rossi, J. S., Schwartz, S. J., Zamboanga, B. L., & Scalf, C. D. (2016). Acculturation and cigarette smoking in Hispanic women: A meta-analysis. *Journal of Ethnicity in Substance Abuse, 15*(1), 46–72.

La Roche, M. (2013). *Cultural psychotherapy: Theory, methods, and practice.* Thousand Oaks: SAGE Publications.

La Roche, M., Christopher, M. S., & West, L. M. (2017). Toward a cultural evidenced-based psychotherapy. In J. M. Casas, L. A. Suzuki, C. M. Alexander, & M. A. Jackson (Eds.), *Handbook of Multicultural Counseling.* Thousand Oaks, CA: Sage Publications.

Markides, K. S., & Coreil, J. (1986). The health of Hispanics in the southwestern United States: An epidemiologic paradox. *Public Health Reports (1974-), 101*(3), 253–265.

Mather, M. (2009). *Children in immigrant families chart new path.* Washington, DC: Population Reference Bureau. Retrieved from www/prb.org/pdf09/immigrantchildren.pdf.

Mercado, A., & Hinojosa, Y. (2017). Culturally-adapted dialectical behavior therapy in an underserved community mental health setting: A Latina adult case study. *Practice Innovations, 2*, 80–93.

Mercado, A., Rogers, D., Villarreal, D., Colunga-Rodriguez, C., Terracciano, A., & Finn-Nguyen, K. (2016). Personality and substance use in Mexicans and Mexican Americans. *International Journal of Mental Health and Addiction*, 14, 907–920.

Miranda, J., Bernal, G., Lau, A., Kohn, L., Hwang, W., & LaFromboise, T. (2005). State of the science on psychosocial interventions for ethnic minorities. *Annual Review of Clinical Psychology, 1*, 113.

Mozaffarian, D., Benjamin, E. J., Go, A. S., Arnett, D. K., Blaha, M. J., Cushman, M., . . . on behalf of the American Heart Association Statistics Committee and Stroke Statistics Subcommittee. (2015). Heart disease and stroke Statistics-2015 update:

A report from the American Heart Association. *Circulation, 131*(4), e29–e39. doi:10.1161/CIR.0000000000000152.

Organista, P. B., Chun, K. M., & Marin, G. (1998). *Readings in ethnic psychology*. New York: Routledge.

Passel, J. S., Cohn, D., & Gonzalez-Barrera, A. (2013). *Population decline of unauthorized immigrant's stalls, may have reversed. Pew Research Hispanic trends project*. Washington, DC: Pew Research Center. Retrieved from www.pew-hispanic .org/2013/09/23/population-decline-of-unauthorized-immigrants-stalls-may-have-reversed/.

Ruiz, J. M., Campos, B., & Garcia, J. J. (2016). Special issue on latino physical health: Disparities, paradoxes, and future directions. *Journal of Latina/o Psychology, 4*(2), 61–66. doi:10.1037/lat0000065.

Ruiz, J. M., Hamann, H. A., Mehl, M. R., & O'Connor, M. F. (2016). The Hispanic health paradox: From epidemiological phenomenon to contribution opportunities for psychological science. *Group Processes & Intergroup Relations, 19*(4), 462–476.

Sam, D. L., & Berry, J. W. (2010). Acculturation when individuals and groups of different cultural backgrounds meet. *Perspectives on Psychological Science, 5*(4), 472–481.

Schwartz, S. J., Unger, J. B., Zamboanga, B. L., & Szapocznik, J. (2010). Rethinking the concept of acculturation: Implications for theory and research. *American Psychologist, 65*, 237–251.

Shaw, R. J., & Pickett, K. E. (2013). The health benefits of Hispanic communities for non-Hispanic mothers and infants: Another Hispanic paradox. *American Journal of Public Health, 103*(6), 1052–1057. doi:10.2105/AJPH.2012.300985.

Singh, G. K., Rodriguez-Lainz, A., & Kogan, M. D. (2013). Immigrant health inequalities in the United States: Use of eight major national data systems. *The Scientific World Journal, 2013,* 1–21.

Smokowski, P. R., & Bacallao, M. L. (2006). Acculturation and aggression in Latino adolescents: A structural model focusing on cultural risk factors and assets. *Journal of Abnormal Child Psychology, 34*(5), 657–671.

Suárez-Orozco, C., Rhodes, J., & Milburn, M. (2009). Unraveling the immigrant paradox academic engagement and disengagement among recently arrived immigrant youth. *Youth & Society, 41*(2), 151–185.

Suzuki, L., & Wilton, L. (2015). Assessment with racial and ethnic minorities and special populations. In J. C. Norcross, G. R. VandenBos, D. K. Freedheim, & R. Krishnamurthy (Eds.), *APA Handbook of clinical psychology. Vol 3, Applications and methods* (pp. 251–266). Washington, DC: American Psychological Association.

Teruya, S. A., & Bazargan-Hejazi, S. (2013). The immigrant and hispanic paradoxes a systematic review of their predictions and effects. *Hispanic Journal of Behavioral Sciences, 35*(4), 486–509.

Turner, E. A., Cheng, H. S., Llamas, J., Tran, A., Hill, K., Loung-Tran, C., Fretts, J. M., & Mercado, A. (2016). Factors impacting the current trends in the use of outpatient psychiatric treatment among diverse ethnic groups. *Current Psychiatric Reviews, 12,* 199–220.

Turner, R. J., Lloyd, D. A., & Taylor, J. (2006). Stress burden, drug dependence and the nativity paradox among US Hispanics. *Drug and Alcohol Dependence*, *83*(1), 79–89.

U.S. Census Bureau. (2011). *Selected Population profile in the United States: Selected characteristics of native and foreign-born populations.* 2010 American Community Survey 1-year estimates. Retrieved from www.factfinder.census.gov/faces/tableservices/jsf/pages/productiview.xhtml?src=bkmk.

U.S. Conference on Catholic Bishops. (2014). *Testimony of most reverend mark Seitz . . . On unaccompanied children house judiciary committee.* Retrieved from http://www.usccb.org/about/migration-policy/upload/BSeitzfinaltest.pdf.

U.S. Customs and Border Patrol. (2016). *Southwest border unaccompanied alien children (FY2016).* Retrieved from https://www.cbp.gov/newsroom/stats/southwest-border-unaccompanied-children/fy-2016.

U.S. Health News and World Reports. (2012). Obesity in America: 10 fattest cities. Retrieved from http://health.usnews.com/health-news/articles/2012/03/13/obesity-in-america-10-fattest-cities.

Vasquez, M. J. T. (2012). Psychology and social justice: Why we do what we do. *American Psychologist*, *67*(5), 337–346. doi:10.1037/a0029232.

Yoon, E., Chang, C. T., Kim, S., Clawson, A., Cleary, S. E., Hansen, M., . . . & Gomes, A. M. (2013). A meta-analysis of acculturation/enculturation and mental health. *Journal of counseling psychology*, *60*(1), 15.

Chapter 6

Moving Beyond Culturally Competent Services for Vietnamese Americans

Working Toward Social Justice

Kim Nguyen-Finn and Jerome Fischer

Cross-cultural competency is essential for providing quality mental health services. The focus in the literature is on the need for culturally competent services for Asian Americans, as well as delineations of what those services might entail. Cultural competency is also a foundation of social justice work in mental health care, in that it seeks to challenge systemic inequities in treatment provision and view presenting problems within an ecological framework. Client problems, in a social justice framework, are not viewed in isolation but instead are conceptualized through the intersectionality of accessibility, stigma, cultural values, clinician cultural competency, traditional cultural healing paradigms, and contemporary Western psychology or medicine. Multiculturalism is an integral component of social justice work, and a greater understanding of Vietnamese Americans can help counselors address inequities in mental health service provision.

Social justice, according to Marsella (2015), should also work toward decolonization, or liberation, of the client's mind and behaviors from historical contexts and imposed cultural traditions and socializations. Similar to the political meaning of the term, decolonization seeks to free clients from abuses of power, not only in the counseling office, but in society at large. Social justice counselors recognize how they are in a position of power, and actively work to redistribute power to clients. Clients, through the course of therapy, raise awareness of social, political, and other sources of oppression and how they contribute to their difficulties, learn how they can challenge existing systems, and gain more of a sense of internal locus of control.

Political colonization occurred in Vietnam for nearly 100 years. France ruled Vietnam as French Indochina until 1954. In its long history, Vietnam also experienced four periods of Chinese domination prior to French colonization. After French withdrawal from Indochina, Vietnam found itself a battleground of the Cold War between the United States and the Soviet Union for 21 years. This resulted in historical trauma for the people of Vietnam. Historical trauma refers to a people's repeated experiences of traumatic events across generations, which may negatively affect an individual's emotional and psychological health. Postcolonial psychology and liberation psychology look beyond the borders of individual disciplines to recognize the intersectionality of culture, history, economic inequities, and sociopolitical oppression and their effects on mental health.

Colonization in psychological treatment manifests through the minimization of clients' cultural values and practices or the denial of culture, including the assertion of color-blindness (Tate, Rivera, & Edwards, 2015). To better serve Vietnamese American clients in a social justice framework, mental health practitioners must first have an understanding of the history of the Vietnamese people and the cultural identity of their clients.

ASIAN AMERICANS

The term "Asian American" encompasses more than 20 ethnic subgroups, each of which is unique and separate. According to the 2010 United States Census, approximately 5.7 percent of the population identify as being at least part Asian. The seven main census response categories for Asian Americans are Asian Indian, Chinese, Filipino, Japanese, Korean, Vietnamese, and Other Asian. Examples of "Other Asian" are Cambodian, Pakistani, Malaysian, and Thai. In addition, census data indicates that the Asian population increased in the United States at a faster rate than any other race or ethnic group.

While each group is unique, Asians share several common characteristics. Kim, Atkinson, and Yang (1999) describe six grouping factors of cultural norms in their study on the psychometric properties of the Asian Values Scale. These are as follows:

Conformity to norms. This includes the adherence to familial and social norms, the development of consensus, and the assuming of a middle position. An old Japanese saying, "The nail that sticks out is the one that will be hammered" ("*deru kugi ha utareru*" [Watanabe, 2012]), highlights the importance of group cohesion and the sense of belongingness over individualism.

Family recognition through achievement. Occupational and educational achievements are emphasized as avenues to bring pride and honor to one's family.

Emotional self-control. Self-control requires modesty in behavior, humbleness in expectations, and appropriate hesitation even when a person highly desires something. It also connotes an unwillingness to intrude on other's time, energy, or resources. Emotional self-control also translates to stoicism and an uncomplaining attitude in the face of adversity, a high tolerance for pain both physical and emotional, and an implied rather than expressed show of parental love.

Collectivism. Awareness of the social milieu and sensitivity to the opinions and feelings of others are important Asian values. Individuals are expected to subordinate their feelings in the interest of social solidarity. In addition, the achievements of the individual are recognized as the family's achievements.

Humility. Individuals are expected to be self-effacing and attribute accomplishments to the help received from others.

Filial piety. This translates to respect for, and obedience to, parents. Asian children are expected to comply with the wishes of their elders, even to the point of sacrificing personal desires and ambitions. Asian families being patriarchal in nature, primary deference is given to male family members, and wives respect the authority of not only their husband but the husband's parents. Family is expected to be an individual's main source of dependence.

DIVERSITY WITHIN ASIAN AMERICAN

While the abovementioned cultural norms are viewed as shared traditional cultural values of Asians, there are differences within the population based on factors such as acculturation, immigration history, and generation. According to Choi (2001), the myriad ethnicities, languages, religions, immigration histories, and other demographic factors make Asian Americans one of the most heterogeneous groups in the United States. These differences may account for variations in the expression of intrapsychic symptoms. As an example, Chung (2001) studied 320 Asian American college students and found that Southeast Asian American (which includes Vietnamese and Korean American) students scored significantly higher on the Family Expectations subscale of the Intergenerational Conflict Inventory than Japanese Americans. Items in this subscale include pressure to learn their own language, following cultural traditions, helping family, and meeting gender role expectations.

Immigration status accounts for some differences among Asian Americans. In their study of 177 university students of Chinese heritage, 53% of whom were foreign-born (recent immigrants residing in the United States for less than six years and early immigrants residing for six or more years), and the remainder born in America (second- to fourth-generation American), Sue and Zane (1985) found that recent immigrants were significantly less happy and satisfied in general than their counterparts who were early immigrants or American born. Recent immigrants also scored significantly higher on anxiety measures than the other students studied. Westermeyer, Neider, and Vang's (1984) earlier study of Hmong immigrants had similar results. The authors examined the psychological symptoms of those who had lived in the United States for 1.5 and 3.5 years, including measures of somatization, obsessive-compulsiveness, anxiety, feelings of inadequacy, and depression. Findings indicated that those who lived in the United States longer reported less symptomology, and the authors posited that acculturation contributed to these reductions.

Acculturation to the dominant culture may also affect the degree to which Asian Americans adhere to traditional Asian values. Some believe that the more acculturated one is, the fewer traditional cultural values retained. Yoon, Langrehr, and Ong (2011), in their extensive review of acculturation research, described a bilinear model of acculturation that postulates that one does not necessarily become disenculturated from one's own culture as she/he/zie becomes more acculturated to the dominate culture. The bilinear model assumes that enculturation and acculturation are independent variables that may occur simultaneously.

How one expresses acculturation behaviorally is important. Kim, Atkinson, and Yang (1999) found that while generational factors (being second-, third-, or fourth-generation American) are not important indicators of acceptance of the values of the dominant culture, they do explain 30.4% of the variance in the acculturation of common behaviors related to those values. Acculturation can also be an important factor to consider when assessing Asian American clients. Chung's (2001) research found that the levels of intergenerational conflict between adolescent and young adult Asian Americans and their parents were significantly lower for the acculturated group than the low-acculturated and bicultural groups.

VIETNAMESE AMERICANS AS A UNIQUE POPULATION

Multiple studies have examined the internal heterogeneity of Asian Americans (Chung, 2001; Chung & Bemak, 2002; Ho, 1990). Approximately 10% of Asian Americans are Vietnamese, either alone or in combination with other races or ethnicities (U. S. Census, 2010). This population size, and differences with other Asian American ethnicities, warrant separate examination of Vietnamese Americans.

When examining the characteristics of Vietnamese Americans, considerations should be given to gender, generation, and immigration. It should also be remembered that Vietnamese Americans as are Asian Americans as a whole are a heterogeneous population. Within-group differences must therefore be recognized. Colorism, for example, is a factor that may influence a Vietnamese American's experiences and self-concept. Colorism is the stratification of individuals based on skin tone. Jones (2013) asserted that for many Asian Americans, skin color is used to denote levels of class and beauty. The author noted that she observed Vietnamese women shielding themselves from the sun, and was told this was to avoid getting tanned. Being tanned, she was told, is a sign an individual is of a more impoverished laborer class. Being fair skinned was an indication that the individual was privileged and could afford to avoid difficult work outdoors. However, the avoidance of getting tanned, Jones (2013) observed, seemed to occur more often among women than men. Other authors have also observed how skin color is associated with socioeconomic class for many Asian groups, including Vietnamese Americans (Hunter, 2007; Jones, 2004; Rondilla & Spickard, 2007).

Immigration History

Having been a refugee is a special consideration. After the end of the Vietnam War in 1975 the United States saw a huge wave of immigration from Vietnam. Initially, many immigrants were those formerly in political or military positions in South Vietnam and others who worked closely with the Americans during the war. As such, these immigrants tended to be educated, partially "Americanized," and familiar with American culture. There were also a large number of "war brides": Vietnamese women who married American servicemen and arrived into the United States with their husbands. These women often share similar stories of leaving their families and homeland for an unfamiliar, lonely place and not having a firm grasp of the language or culture.

(The following anecdote and others throughout this chapter are from personal conversations the first author had with various individuals who shared their stories. Names have been changed to protect the identities of the individuals in these narratives.)

Thu Le arrived in America in 1971 with her new husband, a noncommissioned officer in the U.S. Army. She experienced multiple traumas and close-calls with death before she met the man who would be her husband in a G.I. bar in which she worked selling watered-down drinks and dances to American servicemen. Thu Le's younger brother, who served in the North Vietnamese Army, was adamantly opposed to her marrying an American, his enemy. Her sisters simply did not want her to leave for another country, fearing they would never see her again. If her parents were still alive or her brother was older than her, she would not have made the decision to marry the American and leave Vietnam. America was a strange and confusing place, but she was more confused about the people. Often while out, she felt stares and dirty looks. While she was in labor with her second child, a delivery nurse, apparently thinking she would not understand, commented in a tone of disgust to another nurse, "These people keep having babies. Don't they know how to keep their legs shut?" In the years that passed, she never came to feel American or felt fully accepted as American, despite years of living in the country and gaining American citizenship. After 22 years in the United States, Thu Le was finally able to visit her family in Vietnam. While the reunion was joyous, she faced a harsh truth. Thu Le no longer felt or was accepted as fully Vietnamese, either.

After the initial wave of immigration, the focus became one of reunification of families. From the late 1970s to the early 1990s, more immigrants would arrive as "boat people," named as such because they fled Vietnam crammed onto boats. The waves of boat people left Vietnam largely due to extreme economic hardships and oppressive government policies, and they tended to be less educated and less familiar with American culture. The journey out of Vietnam was perilous and traumatizing, and their experiences in the refugee camps that were scattered in various countries prior to their reunification with relatives in the United States were often also traumatizing.

Cho was 17 years old when he decided to leave Vietnam alone. It was 13 years since the Liberation of Saigon as the North called it, and he had been saving money and planning his escape in secret. Not even his mother, with whom he was very close, knew of his plans. His mother's sister lived in America, and Cho hoped that once he arrived at a refugee camp, she would sponsor him to join her. Every night, he recited his American aunt's address and phone number so that he would not forget in case he lost his papers on his journey. In the middle of the night, Cho snuck out of the home he shared with his parents and two siblings and headed to the beach. There, a fishing boat was expected to be at the designated location for him and others. Their goal was to get to Thailand, one of the nearby countries to which others before him had fled. The waters were rough, and there were stories of pirates who intercepted boats to rob, rape, and murder those trying to emigrate from Vietnam. Once he arrived at the beach, Cho steeled himself. Another group of people had attempted to leave that night, but their bodies were strewn about on the beach. He assumed the group was spotted by government forces and their boat attacked. Cho quickly darted over and around the bodies to get to the boat. He was lucky, and he thanks Buddha and his ancestors every day for his good fortune. His boat was not intercepted by pirates but by a German oil tanker which picked up his group and took them to a refugee detainment center in what was then West Germany.

Oan's cousin was already in America as the bride of a U.S. serviceman. Seven years after the war ended, the situation in Vietnam continued to be difficult. Pregnant and desperate, Oan left on an overcrowded, old fishing boat with her husband, two young sons, and 16-year-old brother. The boat captain aimed to travel to the Philippines to avoid the ruthless pirates infesting the sea in the opposite direction. Halfway through their journey, the boat ran out of fuel and eventually also fresh water. Stranded for days, they drank their own urine to quench their thirst. She recalled the irony of their situation—being surrounded by water and dying from the lack of it. Their relief at being rescued by the Philippine military was soon replaced by fear once they arrived at the refugee camp. Food and supplies were scarce, and gangs of young thugs would often harass the camp's occupants. Her husband and brother were both skilled in martial arts and frequently fought with others in the camp. Hunger was a constant staple at the camp, and occupants were convinced that camp officials were hoarding supplies. Oan recalled one night that some of the men in the camp, including her husband and brother, went to break into the storage area for food. She feared for their safety during the raid, and they all feared reprisals from camp officials.

The influx of boat people ended in the early 1990s. After that, Vietnamese continued to immigrate, but mainly on educational or occupational visas. As reported by the Migration Policy Institute, Vietnamese were the sixth-largest group immigrating into the United States (Zong & Batalova, 2016). Vietnamese immigrants report lower English proficiency than other immigrant groups (67% Vietnamese immigrants had lower English proficiency compared to 44% for other groups) and have lower educational attainment (25%:29%). Overall 3 however, they have a higher income level than both other immigrant groups and Native-born populations (Vietnamese immigrants: $59,933; Other immigrants: $49,487; Native-born: $54,565).

Migration Trauma

How long ago and by what means one immigrated into the United States may be significant factors in counseling Vietnamese Americans. These factors impact how individuals conceptualize their problems and, in fact, may be the source of the difficulties they face. Refugees may have experienced multiple traumas, which increases the likelihood of developing a trauma-related disorder or a mood disorder. In a study of 261 Vietnamese American adults, Ngo, Tran, Gibbons, and Oliver (2001) found that those with lower levels of acculturation experienced stronger effects of premigration trauma on symptoms of depression compared to those who scored higher on an acculturation scale, identifying acculturation as a moderator variable. The results confirmed the findings of an earlier study by Chung, Bemak, and Wong (2000), who found that first-wave Vietnamese immigrants, who are generally more educated, financially stable, and exposed to American culture, experienced significantly lower levels of distress than second-wave immigrants, who had higher levels of premigration trauma, less education, fewer financial resources, and less prior exposure to American culture.

Female refugees are especially at risk for psychological distress. Chung and Bemak (2002) surveyed 2180 Laotian, Cambodian, and Vietnamese refugees and found that women experienced psychological distress at a significantly higher rate than men. The authors also reported that among their 359 female Vietnamese participants, financial difficulties were a significant distress predictor, indicating the difficulty the women had in gaining financial autonomy while in the United States. Vietnamese women also often reported in this study that the decision to flee Vietnam was not made by them. Those who reported not participating in the decision-making process to leave Vietnam frequently reported psychological distress. Age of arrival in the United States and English-language proficiency may also impact level of distress. Brown, Schale, and Nilsson (2010) surveyed 83 Vietnamese women who are immigrants or refugees and found that older age of arrival in the United States and less-proficient English-language skills were strongly associated with greater somatic distress. The latter was also reported to have a significant negative correlation with general distress.

Women and Domestic Violence

Linda, who adopted her "American" name approximately ten years after she arrived in the United States from a refugee camp in the Philippines in the 1980s, recalled the time she discovered her husband's infidelity in Vietnam. She had known that her husband was unfaithful for months, but she never confronted him out of deference. A husband's infidelity was something Linda was taught to ignore. To compound this, her husband, Vinh, was a harsh man who often belittled and sometimes struck Linda. One day while shopping in the market, Linda spotted a woman wearing Vinh's jacket. This public disrespect was something Linda could not ignore, and she physically attacked the woman at the market and took the jacket back. When her husband spotted the jacket at home, he became enraged and severely beat Linda. The public embarrassment to the family and the severity of the physical abuse by Vinh were not tolerated by the family. Linda's mother demanded and received the apology of Vinh's mother and older brother, who participated in place of his deceased father. Linda recalled that Vinh's mother and brother had to enter her mother's home on their knees before being able to ask for forgiveness. Linda added that his brother and mother were so furious at Vinh for his public indiscretion and the resulting humiliation of the apology that his brother beat Vinh in retribution. Vinh's mother took it a step further and threw a knife at her son, missing Vinh's head by inches.

In many ways, Vietnamese culture may discourage domestic violence victims from seeking outside help. Asian values of respect for patriarchal authority, keeping problems within the family, not drawing attention to oneself or the family, and sublimating one's feelings or wishes for the good of the family, while helpful to the individual and community in many ways, may also serve to keep women in abusive relationships.

People often seek comfort and guidance in their religious institutions. However, as Bui and Morash (2007) found from their interviews with 62 Vietnamese American women with a history of domestic violence victimization, churches may encourage victims to avoid the legal system and to submit to their spouses for the sake of family harmony. Involving the criminal justice system brings outsiders into the community, which may bring shame onto the family and community. Shiu-Thornton, Senturia, and Sullivan (2005) and Ho (1990) postulated that traditional Asian values may minimize and encourage the hiding of domestic violence. Ho (1990) asserted that fatalism and emotional restraint are additional values that serve to perpetuate abuse against women. A history of discrimination may also lead to a distrust of authority, further reducing contacting law enforcement as a viable option to assist Asian American women to leave abusive situations. Friends and family are often a strong source of support. However, Bui and Morash (2007) reported that many Vietnamese American victims said that the disparate messages received from friends and family ran the spectrum from being supportive of the women to being angry at them for contacting the police. Vietnamese women often view marital strife as normal, and incidences of domestic violence are viewed as personal, family matters (Shiu-Thornton, Senturia, & Sullivan, 2005). When Vietnamese Americans witness spousal abuse in their communities, they often look the other way, considering it a private matter.

Traditional Vietnamese American women often feel required to give deference to their mothers-in-law, who may share responsibility for the perpetration of abuse. When women get married in traditional Vietnamese society, they are often perceived as leaving their family to join that of their husband. The couple may live with the husband's parents, as living with extended family is not unusual. Mothers-in-law may watch their daughters-in-law closely, reporting perceived indiscretions to their sons, encouraging physical punishment for misbehavior, and, in some cases, beating the daughters-in-law themselves.

Vietnamese American women who came as brides of U.S. servicemen during the Vietnam War were especially at risk for spousal abuse due to their lack of financial resources and social support (Ho, 1990). They are generally not living in a Vietnamese community, but are more isolated in a military installation. Prejudice against interracial and possibly interreligious marriages may further isolate Vietnamese American women married to servicemen, making them even more vulnerable to abuse.

Mental Health Help-Seeking Behaviors

Asian Americans utilize mental health services at a lower rate than many other groups (Kim & Omizo, 2003; Phan, 2000; Turner et al., 2016). There are a variety of factors that affect willingness to use mental health services, especially adherence to cultural values. Luu, Leung, and Nash (2009) found in their study of help-seeking attitudes that the more acculturated Vietnamese Americans were, the more favorably they viewed seeking psychological assistance. This is consistent with earlier research on Asian American usage of Western health-care services (Chung & Lin, 1994; Kim & Omizo, 2003; Phan, 2000). Fung and Wong (2007), in their study of 1,000 Asian female immigrants or refugees, found that those who adhered to a Western stress model of illness had a significantly more positive view of seeking professional mental health care than those who did not.

Nguyen and Anderson (2005) conducted a study of 148 U.S. residents and American citizens of Vietnamese heritage to identify variables that affected their attitude toward seeking mental health services and found that most participants tended to focus more on their physical rather than mental health issues. While psychological problems may exist, they may be minimized or ignored because priority is placed on physical problems. Psychological problems may be viewed as having a physical origin. The traditional Vietnamese belief of mental illness is that there is either an organic cause or supernatural origin for symptoms (Nguyen & Anderson, 2005). If a physical origin of symptoms of mental illness is suspected, then medical assistance would be likely sought. Psychological problems that are believed to be caused by supernatural entities such as spirits and demons as retribution for offenses committed by one's ancestor, curses, or mind-body-spirit imbalances may be addressed through prayer and other rituals. Adherence to spiritual beliefs was found to affect help-seeking attitudes. Luu, Leung, and Nash (2009), in their study of 210 Vietnamese Americans, concluded that lower levels of belief in spiritual origins of mental health issues were associated with more favorable attitudes toward help-seeking.

When Loan was five years old, her family lived in housing for enlisted families on a U.S. Army base in Germany that she and her mother believed was haunted. Every night, Loan would wake up screaming, telling her parents that she saw things in her bedroom that her parents could not. Sleeping in her parents' bedroom gave no relief as the nightly fits of screaming continued. Her father, an American, insisted that Loan needed to see a psychiatrist. Her Vietnamese mother believed the cause was evil spirits. Embarrassed and afraid that Loan's father would leave her if he found out, Loan's mother decided to conduct an exorcism after he left for work one morning. Flagrantly brandishing a long chef's knife, Loan's mother walked through their home loudly threatening and cursing at the evil spirits to leave her family alone. Her mother then left the knife standing on its point and leaning against the wall under Loan's bed. After this ritual was completed, Loan slept through the night for the first time in weeks.

Stigma Against Mental Health Care

There is typically a cultural stigma against mental illness, for many Vietnamese, which makes help-seeking behaviors difficult (Fancher, Ton, Meyer, Ho, & Paterniti, 2010; Nguyen & Anderson, 2005). Mental illness is not considered solely an individual problem, but brings about familial shame, perhaps even shame on one's ancestors, due to its perceived origins. Mental illness is often viewed in traditional Vietnamese culture as being caused by moral deficiency, bad parenting, black magic, or punishment by spirits (Nguyen & Anderson, 2005).

Nguyen and Anderson (2005) posited that traditional Vietnamese culture dictates that problems are to be solved first within the family. Outside assistance is sought only if the problem is not manageable by the family, and the preference then is for priests, Buddhist monks, or traditional healers to be consulted. Seeking outside assistance is often perceived as a sign of weakness and is frowned upon by less acculturated Vietnamese Americans. This resistance to seeking assistance outside of the immediate family was also found in a qualitative study by Fancher et al. (2010). In that study, 11 Vietnamese Americans were interviewed to gain understanding of the subjects' views on depression and help develop more culturally informed mental health-care interventions. The researchers found four themes in participant responses: social functioning and the role of the family (keeping problems within the family), stigma and "face," traditional healing and beliefs about medications, and language and culture. Due to the stigma against mental illness, the authors stated that "depression" was viewed by participants as too harsh a word, and another, "softer" word should be used with Vietnamese American patients. A concern about a lack of sensitivity to cultural differences was also a barrier for providing services for the participants. Participants frequently noted that even when they believed they needed to seek mental health assistance, they did not think "American" doctors would be able to help them. Aside from the language difference, the Vietnamese American participants stated that they believed Western providers would not understand Vietnamese culture, thereby not only limiting their ability to help clients, but potentially expecting clients to adhere to goals that were unknowingly in opposition with Vietnamese cultural values.

IMPLICATIONS FOR COUNSELING

Consideration of cultural factors should be made by mental health clinicians when providing services to Vietnamese Americans, and clinicians should be prepared to address clients' concerns directly or through appropriate referrals. The incorporation of multicultural practices into the counseling process is not only a requirement of the various mental health professions' code of professional ethics, but therapist multicultural competency is also shown to increase client outcomes (Tao, Owen, Pace, & Imel, 2015). Additionally, given that Asian American clients have historically underutilized mental health services for the reasons stated earlier, taking care to demonstrate cross-cultural competencies may mitigate the effects of traditional Asian-values against seeking Western health-care services. Incorporating multicultural competencies may also improve client perceptions of counseling, thereby increasing the likelihood that clients will continue with therapy. Wang and Kim (2010) showed sample counseling session videos to 113 Asian American college students, one of which incorporated multicultural core competencies including communication skills (verbal and nonverbal), language, intervention strategies, and client advocacy skills. They found that participants rated the counseling sessions that utilized multicultural skills significantly higher than the session that did not.

Traditional Euro-American counseling values such as independence, self-disclosure, active participation, and autonomy in decision-making may not work well with Vietnamese clients. Patience is a skill that counselors should especially utilize. It may have been extremely difficult for Vietnamese clients to seek counseling services, and they may feel ashamed to have done so, having already exhausted other options. Due to the stigma against mental illness and the pressure Vietnamese culture places on practicing emotional restraint and solving problems within the family, the disclosure of emotions and personal problems is difficult for many Vietnamese Americans. Clients may enter counseling feeling a "loss of face" at needing to talk with a stranger about their issues and feeling unable to successfully address them on their own. For this reason, group counseling may be an even more difficult undertaking for Vietnamese American clients.

Lan, a second-generation Vietnamese American, had difficulty relating to her traditional parents. Born and raised in America, she was more acculturated and struggled with her parents' expectations and discipline. Lan found herself increasingly angry, depressed, and withdrawn, but her parents interpreted her actions as rebelliousness. A friend of her parents suggested they seek family counseling, but Lan recalled that her parents were embarrassed by the suggestion and insisted the family was not in need of repair. The problem, as her parents saw it, was that Lan was raised too leniently in American culture and needed to be more strictly disciplined.

Lan's story is consistent with the findings of Chang, Natsuaki, and Chen (2013). Their research on generational status and other variables related to Asian Americans and mental health service use found that family cultural conflict is an important determiner for help-seeking behaviors. The U.S. Census Bureau in 2000 reported that Vietnamese American youth were the most recent second-generation Asian group in which the parents displayed the unique immigration pattern of fleeing ones' homeland without sufficient time or assistance to prepare. In addition, the U.S. Census Bureau reported that almost 79% of Vietnamese youth are second-generation. Asian Americans, especially those who are second-generation, report less family cohesion and have more conflicts with their family regarding cultural issues, which may give these individuals more impetus to seek professional mental health services.

Ample time should be spent patiently building trust and comfort with the counseling process to allow for such disclosure. Mental health clinicians can also assist clients in recognizing the possible relationship between their emotional and mental health and other difficulties they may be facing. Due to the priority Vietnamese Americans may place on physical health concerns over mental health issues, clients may be referred to a mental health clinician by a medical provider. Clinicians should be prepared to work collaboratively with clients' health providers. Counselors should also avoid minimizing or discrediting client priorities. Therapists should be willing to allow the use of traditional healers as collaterals in treatment. Cross-cultural work recognizes and respects clients' belief in Indigenous healing practices and traditions. Clients may believe that mental illness has a supernatural cause, and may wish to consult a herbalist, spiritual healer, or folk healer.

Immigration history is another important consideration for counseling. Clients may likely enter counseling for an issue that arose postmigration, but psychological distress may be impacted by events that occurred preimmigration. Chung, Bemak, and Wong (2000) underscored the importance of exploring premigration trauma and adjustment issues when addressing the distress levels of Vietnamese refugees. The authors noted that this is especially important when working with female refugees, as women reported significantly higher levels of distress than male refugees. This disparity could be accounted for, not only by traumatic experiences, but also by changes in gender roles, family dynamics, and employment opportunities.

MICRO CONSIDERATIONS OF CROSS-CULTURAL COUNSELING

Aside from the considerations addressed earlier, mental health professionals should keep other, finer points in mind while providing services to

Vietnamese Americans. Micro skills are the basic counseling attending skills and include competencies in observation, questioning, body language, reflection, focusing, and confrontation. Another consideration is how providers show respect to their clients. Respect is especially important in traditional Asian culture. Punctuality is critical as a form of showing respect to the client. Clinicians should be sure to schedule and start sessions on time. Asian culture also demonstrates much respect to one's elders. It is therefore also good practice to give a slight bow at the beginning and end of the counseling session, particularly when working with elderly Vietnamese Americans. In a group meeting, providers should strive to acknowledge the older individuals first.

Due to social stigma, group counseling may be particularly difficult for some Vietnamese American clients. They might be reluctant to share emotions and thoughts in a group forum. Shiu-Thornton et al. (2005) cautioned that Vietnamese American women who are victims of domestic violence may be hesitant to disclose the abuse they are experiencing due to the cultural normalization of abuse and the stigma against accepting outside assistance. Care should be taken to patiently build trust with Vietnamese American clients to allow for disclosure.

Nonverbal Communication

Nonverbal communication is also important. Eye contact may be viewed as hostility. It is important for clinicians to avoid excessive eye contact for this reason. During case conceptualizations, mental health clinicians often view lack of eye contact as a sign of client deception. Clinicians may perceive that clients are attempting to hide something or are uncomfortable in session. However, traditional Vietnamese American values dictate that looking directly in the eyes for an extended period of time with someone they are speaking with is disrespectful, especially if that individual is someone in authority. Females may especially avoid prolonged eye contact.

Smiling is another culturally dictated behavior that may impact counseling. Smiling can signify not only happiness, but also anger, embarrassment, discomfort, or rejection. This is especially true with Asian Americans. Clinicians should be cognizant of this when conceptualizing a case or completing a mental status examination. Vietnamese American clients may not be smiling inappropriately if they are doing so to cover hostility or anger, or to be stoic in the face of adversity, as these behaviors are cultural expectations.

When asking questions, clinicians should allow time for Vietnamese American clients to answer. Clients may not understand questions due to limited English proficiency or they may be taking their time to phrase an answer. Additionally, a "yes" or nod of the head may mean "maybe" or

"I understand." Clinicians should clarify the meaning behind the response so that there is no misunderstanding of assent by the client. "Maybe" may actually mean "no," as Vietnamese American clients may attempt to avoid blunt honesty and rudeness. A negative response by clients is sometimes offered through a squint of the eyes or tipping back of the head while inhaling, then waiting for the other person to speak. Counselors should also be mindful of proxemics or personal space. A forward lean, commonly performed by clinicians to signal interest in what the client is saying, may be interpreted by Vietnamese American clients as aggressive or intrusive.

In terms of body contact, clinicians should be cognizant of cultural rules on social touching. Social physical contact with the opposite sex is generally not done in traditional Vietnamese culture, including male-to-female handshakes, and may be perceived as offensive or threatening. In addition, clinicians should avoid touching a child on the head or touching anyone's hair as it is considered offensive. It is not uncommon for very young children to be patted on the head in Western culture. However, traditional Vietnamese Americans view the head as being the home of the spirit and it is considered impolite to touch it.

Clinicians as Authority Figures

Traditional Asian culture has a strong respect for authority. Mental health clinicians may be viewed as authority figures and may be expected to act in an authoritative manner. This means that, although client autonomy is an important ethical principle, clinicians may want to consider being more directive with Vietnamese American clients. In addition, Ho (1990) asserted that Asians tend to stay in counseling for a brief time. For these reasons, clinicians should consider the use of solution-focused or problem-solving approaches. Clinicians should also practice flexibility and be more directive when they deem it beneficial.

Clinicians should also act in the manner expected of those in authority by traditional Vietnamese Americans. A hearty salutation in a loud voice is perceived by the general American population as a warm greeting. However, for traditional Vietnamese Americans, that may be undignified and even rude. A restrained voice and manner will help clinicians be accepted by traditional Vietnamese American clients.

"Saving Face"

Because of the difficulty in entering counseling and the need for traditional Vietnamese Americans to "save face," Kim Berg and Miller (1992) suggested that Asian clients be asked to identify exceptions to the presenting problem, which may help the client "save face" by the recognition that the clients are in control of their issues. As examples, if a client enters counseling due to depression, clinicians can ask the client when she/he/zie does not feel depressed. If a couple reports marital difficulties, the clinician can ask them to identify times when they feel secure and content in their relationship. Through these questions, clinicians empower their clients and reassure them of their strengths and coping skills. Asking traditional Vietnamese American clients the miracle question is also recommended. The miracle question may be phrased as: "If you woke up tomorrow and everything was exactly the way you would wish it, how would you know? What would be different?" This question can not only serve as a framework for goal-setting, but it can also help the clinician and client generate solutions that are consistent with the client's traditional values. The exercise is also future-focused; it allows the clients to maintain integrity by avoiding the assignment of blame through focusing on past mistakes or difficulties.

Self-Care for the Clinician

Finally, it is important for mental health professionals, to be most effective with clients, to take care of themselves first. Self-care is crucial to prevent burnout and compassion fatigue. As Kitano and Maki (1996) pointed out, there is a potential for the professional to invest far more time and energy into a counseling case when both the client and the mental health clinician are Asian American. Counselors from every background are at risk, but Asian American providers are especially at risk when their clients also have an Asian heritage.

COUNSELING VIETNAMESE AMERICANS AS SOCIAL JUSTICE WORK

The adaptation of Western counseling techniques for Vietnamese Americans serves to provide quality treatment to this underserved population. The intersectionality of factors related to accessibility, or lack thereof, of treatment resources, stigma against mental health services, language and cultural barriers, traditional Asian beliefs about medicine and mental health, perceived discrimination from American society, and multicultural competencies of helping professionals serve to perpetuate the lack of quality care for Vietnamese Americans. Understanding these factors helps mental health providers identify methods of countering their effects, thereby assisting clients to change the conditions that negatively impact their psychological health.

Above all, counselors working with Vietnamese Americans should strive to value the individual voices of their clients. By examining their own biases about Asians, Vietnamese Americans, and mental health issues (such as abuse, disability, and depression), counselors increase their self-awareness of how those biases may impact their work. Clinicians who also have a Vietnamese background, should be especially cognizant of their own explicit and implicit biases, as their work may be more susceptible to transference issues. In addition, counselors should also challenge if necessary, not only themselves, but other counselors and agencies when potentially harmful or culturally insensitive practices are being utilized.

SOCIAL JUSTICE PROGRAMMING IN COUNSELOR PREPARATION

Counselor educators are in a unique position to further weave social justice work into counseling practice. Counselor preparation programs may play an important role in addressing and promoting social justice by training emerging counselors how to be conscious to social justice issues and tailor their practice to integrate a social justice framework.

Delgado-Romero and Wu (2010) described a social justice group intervention they conducted for international counseling students from Asia. The group was formed after some informal conversations revealed that the students were experiencing common difficulties. The issues faced were of a social justice nature—there were no overt incidents of racism described, but dichotomous feelings of being both privileged and marginalized, acculturative stress, systemic inequities, and institutional barriers were discussed. Initially, the students deferred to the group leader for guidance, which the authors noted was typical of the Asian cultural deference to authority. Through the course of the group, the students learned about sociopolitical inequities and system challenges, came to feel a sense of power over their environment and situations, and actively worked toward positive change. While engaging in group counseling that focused on social justice advocacy during their training, the counseling students learned firsthand how to integrate social justice into psychological practice.

Glosoff and Durham (2010) also espouse the integration of social justice orientation into counselor preparation programs and counseling supervision. They assert that counselors should address not only cultural issues affecting client needs, but also broader concerns related to systemic oppression and inequities. This, the authors state, better addresses client needs by improving equitable access to services. In addition, as multicultural counseling requires clinician self-awareness of their own cultural background, Glosoff and Durham (2010) stated that counseling supervisors who operate in a social justice framework need to be aware of how their understanding of issues of privilege, class, oppression, and ability affect supervision.

Counseling supervision presents the opportunity for the supervisee to engage in parallel processing, whereby supervisees present the cases of their clients, supervisors act as therapists, and supervisees take on the role of client to assist the supervisees in conceptualizing and approaching cases. In addition, parallel processing can take the form of drawing similarities or parallels of the supervisor-supervisee relationship and the therapist-client relationship, presenting a way for the trainee to reflect upon and improve their work as clinicians. In discussing the literature, Glosoff and Durham (2010) note the importance of supervisors and supervisees to address issues related to cultural diversity early in the supervision process, which includes a discussion of their respective ethnicities and culture. The authors believe that addressing issues related to culture, power, privilege, and oppression with supervisees will assist them in their competencies for doing that with their clients. As Estrada, Frame, and Williams (2004) assert, failing to address such issues with supervisees may lead to the use of ineffective and even harmful counseling interventions. While the authors strongly suggest discussing social justice issues with counselor trainees, many supervisors are not engaging readily in conversations with supervisees regarding the subject. Durham and Glosoff (2010) cite several reasons why supervisors do not generally discuss social justice issues with their supervisees. These include (1) the false belief that supervisees are better trained and prepared to address diversity and social justice issues than they truly are, (2) some supervisors do not believe social justice is a relevant issue to address, (3) some stated they fear others' possible perception that they are "too concerned" with social justice issues, and (4) some may feel they lack the competence to adequately address social justice issues with supervisees. However, bringing up the issues of cultural similarities and differences with supervisees can assist emerging counselors to feel more comfortable addressing the topic with clients (Glosoff & Durham, 2010). In this regard, seasoned counselors continue making systemic changes through their work guiding a new generation of clinicians.

REFERENCES

Brown, C., Schale, C. L., & Nilsson, J. E. (2010). Vietnamese immigrant and refugee women's mental health: An examination of age of arrival, length of stay, income, and English language proficiency. *Journal of Multicultural Counseling and Development, 38*(2), 66–76.

Bui, H. N., & Morash, M. (2007). Social capital, human capital, and reaching out for help with domestic violence: A case study of women in a Vietnamese-American community. *Criminal Justice Studies, 20*(4), 375–390. doi: 10.1080/14786010701758146.

Chang, J., Natsuaki, M. N., & Chen, C. N. (2013, July). The importance of family factors and generation status: Mental health service use among Latino and Asian Americans. *Cultural Diversity and Ethnic Minority Psychology, 19*(3), 236–47. doi: 10.1037/a0032901.

Choi, N. G. (2001). Diversity within diversity: Research and social work practice issues with Asian American elders. *Journal of Human Behavior in the Social Environment, 3*(3/4), 301–319.

Chung, R. H. G. (2001). Gender, ethnicity, and acculturation in intergenerational conflict of Asian American college students. *Cultural Diversity and Ethnic Minority Psychology, 7*(4), 376–386. doi: 10.1037//1099-9809.7.4.376.

Chung, R. C. Y., & Bemak, F. (2002). Revisiting the California southeast Asian mental health needs assessment data: An examination of refugee ethnic and gender differences. *Journal of Counseling & Development, 80*(1), 111–119. doi: 10.1002/j.1556-6678.2002.tb00173.x.

Chung, R. C. Y., & Lin, L. (1994). Help-seeking behavior among Southeast Asian refugees. *Journal of Community Psychology, 22*(2), 109–120.

Chung, R. C. Y., Bemak, F., & Wong, S. (2000). Vietnamese refugees' level of distress, social support, and acculturation: Implications for mental health counseling. *Journal of Mental Health Counseling, 22*(2), 150–161.

Delgado-Romero, E. A., & Wu, Y. (2010). Asian international students in group programs: A group intervention to promote social justice. *The Journal for Specialists in Group Work, 35*(3), 290–298. doi: 10.1080/01933922.2010.492896.

Durham, J. C., & Glosoff, H. L. (2010). From passion to action: Integrating the advocacy competencies and social justice into counselor education and supervision. In M. J. Ratts, J. A. Lewis, & R. L. Toporek (Eds.), *ACA advocacy competencies: A social justice framework for counselors* (pp. 139–150). Alexandria, VA: American Counseling Association.

Estrada, D., Frame, M. W., & Williams, C. B. (2004). Cross-cultural supervision: Guiding the conversation toward race and ethnicity. *Journal of Multicultural Counseling & Development, 32*, 307–319.

Fancher, T. L., Ton, H., Meyer, O. L., Ho, T., & Paterniti, D. A. (2010). Discussing depression with Vietnamese American patients. *Journal of Immigrant Minority Health, 12*(2), 263–266. doi: 10.1007-s10903-009-9234-y.

Fung, K., & Wong, Y. R. (2007). Factors influencing attitudes toward seeking professional help among East and Southeast Asian immigrant and refugee women. *International Journal of Social Psychiatry, 53*(3), 216–231. doi: 10.1177/0020764006074541.

Glosoff, H. J., & Durham, J. C. (2010). Using supervision to prepare social justice counseling advocates. *Counselor Education & Supervision, 50*, 116–129.

Ho, C. K. (1990). An analysis of domestic violence in Asian American communities: A multicultural approach to counseling. *Women & Therapy, 9*(1–2), 129–150. doi: 10.1300/J015v09n01_08.

Hunter, M. (2007). The persistent problem of colorism: Skin tone, status, and inequality. *Social Compass, 1*(1), 237–254. doi: 10.1111/j.1751-9020.2007.00006.x.

Jones, V. (2004, August 19). Pride or prejudice? A formally taboo topic among Asian Americans and Latinos comes out into the open as skin tone consciousness sparks a backlash. *Boston Globe.* Retrieved from http://archive.boston.com/yourlife/articles/2004/08/19/pride_or_prejudice/.

Jones, T. (2013). The significance of skin color in Asian and Asian American communities: Initial reflections. *U.C. Irvine Law Review, 3*(4), 1105–1123.

Kim Berg, I., & Miller, S. (1992). Working with Asian American clients: One person at a time. *Families in Society: The Journal of Contemporary Human Services, 73*, 356–363.

Kim, B. S. K., & Omizo, M. M. (2003). Asian cultural values, attitudes toward seeking professional psychological help, and willingness to see a counselor. *The Counseling Psychologist, 31*(3), 343–361. doi: 10.1177/0011000003252268.

Kim, B. S. K., Atkinson, D. R., & Yang, P. H. (1999). The Asian values scale: Development, factor analysis, validation, and reliability. *Journal of Counseling Psychology, 46*(3), 342–352.

Kitano, H. H. L., & Maki, M. T. (1996). Continuity, change, and diversity: Counseling Asian Americans. In P. B. Pedersen, J. G. Draguns, W. L. Lonner, & J. E. Trimble (Eds.) (4th ed.), *Counseling across cultures* (pp. 124–145). Thousand Oaks, CA: SAGE Publications.

Luu, T. D., Leung, L. P., & Nash, S. G. (2009). Help-seeking attitudes among Vietnamese Americans: The impact of acculturation, cultural barriers, and spiritual beliefs. *Social Work in Mental Health,* 7(5), 476–493. doi: 10.1080/15332980802467456.

Marsella, A. J. (2015). Decolonization of mind and behavior: A responsibility of professional counselors. In R. D. Goodman & P. C. Gorski (Eds.), *Decolonizing "multicultural" counseling through social justice* (pp. 41–54). New York: Springer.

Ngo, D., Tran, T. V., Gibbons, J. L., & Oliver, J. M. (2001). Acculturation, premigration traumatic experiences, and depression among Vietnamese Americans. *Journal of Human Behavior in the Social Environment, 3*(3/4), 225–242.

Nguyen, Q. C. X., & Anderson, L. P. (2005). Vietnamese Americans' attitudes toward seeking mental health services: Relation to cultural variables. *Journal of Community Psychology, 33*(2), 213–231. doi: 10.1002/jcop.20039.

Phan, T. (2000). Investigating the use of services for Vietnamese with mental illness. *Journal of Community Health, 25*(5), 411–425.

Rondilla, J., & Spickard, P. (2007). *Is lighter better?: Skin-tone discrimination among Asian Americans.* Lanham, MD: Rowman & Littlefield.

Shiu-Thornton, S., Senturia, K., & Sullivan, M. (2005). "Like a bird in a cage": Vietnamese women survivors talk about domestic violence. *Journal of Interpersonal Violence, 20*(8), 959–976. doi: 10.1177/0886260505277677.

Sue, S., & Zane, N. W. S. (1985). Academic achievement and socioemotional adjustment among Chinese university students. *Journal of Counseling Psychology, 32*(4), 570–579. doi: 2048/10.1037/0022-0167.32.4.570.

Tao, K. W., Owen, J., Pace, B. T., & Imel, Z. E. (2015). A meta-analysis of multicultural competencies and psychotherapy process, and outcome. *Journal of Counseling Psychology, 62*(3), 337–350. doi: 10.1037/cou0000086.

Tate, K. A., Rivera, E. T., & Edwards, L. M. (2015). Colonialism and multicultural counseling competence research: A liberatory analysis. In R. D. Goodman & P. C. Gorski (Eds.), *Decolonizing "multicultural" counseling through social justice* (pp. 41–54). New York: Springer.

Turner, E. A., Cheng, H., Llamas, J. D., Tran, A. G. G. T., Hill, K. X., Fretts, J. M., & Mercado, A. (2016). Factors impacting the current trends in the use of outpatient psychiatric treatment among diverse ethnic groups. *Current Psychiatry Review, 12*, 199–220. doi: 10. 2174/1573400512666160216234524.

United States Census Bureau. (2000). *Statistical abstract of the United States: 2000.* Washington, DC: U.S. Government Printing Office.

United States Census Bureau. (2012). *2010 Census Briefs: The Asian population: 2010.* Washington, DC: U.S. Government Printing Office. Retrieved from https://www.census.gov/prod/cen2010/briefs/c2010br-11.pdf.

Wang, S., & Kim, B. S. K. (2010). Therapist multicultural competence, Asian American participants' cultural values, and counseling process. *Journal of Counseling Psychology, 57*(4), 394–401. doi: 10.1037/a0020359.

Watanabe, A. (2012, July 17). 'The nail that sticks out gets hammered down': Bullying in Japan. *Asian Correspondent.* Retrieved from https://asiancorrespondent.com/2012/07/the-nail-that-sticks-out-gets-hammered-down-bullying-in-japan/#bbHqCq6yrDMDHPxM.97.

Westermeyer, J., Neider, J., & Vang, T. F. (1984). Acculturation and mental health: A study of Hmong refugees at 1.5 and 3.5 years postmigration. *Social Science &Medicine, 18*(1), 87–91.

Yoon, E., Langrehr, K., & Ong, L. Z. (2011). Content analysis of acculturation research in counseling and counseling psychology: A 22-year review. *Journal of Counseling Psychology, 58*(1), 83–96. doi: 10.1037/a0021128.

Zong, J. & Batalova, J. (2016, June 8). Vietnamese immigrants in the United States. *Migration Immigration Source: The Online Journal of the Migration Policy Institute.* Retrieved from http://www.migrationpolicy.org/article/vietnamese-immigrants-united-states.

Chapter 7

Adventures in Intersectionality

The Journey of an Early Career Psychologist

Jessica L. Binkley

EDITOR'S (SOG) INTRODUCTION

As the psychological profession seeks to integrate differing cultural and ethnic worldviews into contemporary Western psychology theory, research, and praxis, questions arise about the role cultural factors play in shaping beliefs about which specific research practices and professional writing styles are acceptable according to Euro-American research protocols. Euro-American research psychologists strive to meet very specific, standard protocols for conducting and reporting the results of quantitative and qualitative research (American Psychological Association, 2003). There are now more and more calls for more flexibility in research design, however, especially when conducting research with those who do not endorse Euro-American worldviews. Cross-cultural researchers are increasingly integrating cultural factors into quantitative and qualitative research designs (e.g., Ponterotto, 2010, Zane, Bernal & Leong, 2016). Lyons, Bike, Ojeda, Johnson, Rosales, and Flores (2013) discuss the importance of considering social justice interfaces with qualitative research designs for culturally diverse populations.

For many cross-cultural researchers, narrative storytelling is a time-honored form of research (Duran & Firehammer, 2015, p. 124). Stake and Hoffman (2000) write that personal history should be a valid source of knowledge when evaluating pedagogical methodologies. Multicultural researchers stress the importance of personal—including ethical—reflexivity (the study of how a person's values, beliefs, acquaintances, and interests influence one's work) and epistemological reflexivity [a process aimed at identifying the foundations of knowledge and the implications of those findings in order to more fully reveal the cultural aspects of social justice activities (Teo, Gao, & Sheivari, 2014)]. Self-examination is a hallmark of social justice activities

(Goodman, Liang, Helms, & Weintraub, 2004). Thus, multicultural researchers view introspective personal narratives as valid research methodologies in furthering knowledge about cross-cultural populations.

The first page of *Radical Psychology* includes a quotation (Grayshield & Mihecoby, 2010) in which Dr. Grayshield uses a narrative style to write about her responses to learning and working within environments that reflect contemporary Western psychology in light of her Indigenous heritage. Chapter 2 of *Radical Psychology* includes a discussion of Eduardo Duran's (2000) narrative reactions to being trained in Euro-American psychological paradigms given his Native heritage. Both Dr. Grayshield's article and Dr. Duran's book include first-person narrative accounts that bring the conflicts they experienced to life. Their writing emphasizes self-examination (Goodman, Liang, Helms, & Weintraub, 2004), reflexivity, the narrative processes (Mitchell & Egudo, 2003), and the inclusion of a "thick" description of their work within the context of cultural factors (Goodall, 2001).

Using a similar approach in this chapter, Jessica L. Binkley has woven first-person narratives into relevant Western research findings to illustrate her professional development as a social justice advocate. Similar to Grayshield and Duran, the author makes use of the processes of reflexivity. Her personal reflections examine how her values and beliefs influence her work. She reflects on the role of identity intersectionality as it affects White privilege, implicit and explicit biases, elements of her own White privilege (Miserocchi, 2014), cultural humility (Shaw, 2017), her role as an ally (Mizock & Page, 2016), the "nice counselor syndrome" (Bemak & Chung, 2008), and the interpersonal skills she seeks to develop to strengthen her rapport with diverse clients. Finally, she discusses the importance of mentoring when engaging in personal reflexivity. Her chapter illustrates the many internal processes that social justice activists must engage in to address their own cultural biases before planning social justice initiatives. She also integrates research findings and theoretical formulations that are relevant to the topics she discusses.

OVERVIEW

Some of the most memorable experiences I have had during my graduate training and early career have involved opportunities to explore the intersections between my own cultural identities and those of my colleagues, patients, students, and supervisees. I was fortunate to attend a graduate program in which I had professors and mentors who encouraged and valued social justice and diversity and thus believed that going into internship (and later, postdoc and professional practice) I might be more prepared to explore and identify how my own cultural identities impacted my clinical work. Like many psychologists, I believed that I was active in exploring how my experiences of privilege and marginalization impacted work with patients and was hopeful that my clinical work was benefitting both patients and the larger community. However, as Pierce (1995) reminds us, "Almost all oppressors are unmindful of the withering effects of cumulative, individual, and collective microaggressions toward victims, even honestly believing that they themselves have inflicted no damage upon socially devalued persons" [p. 277]. Consider the following example:

One day on internship, in my early work with a Black family of Honduran descent, I was working with the mother to create a cultural genogram (Hardy & Laszloffy, 1995). After describing and creating spaces for her family and ancestors, she turned to me and remarked, "I want to know where you come from." After providing what I thought were "professional" responses (e.g., reviewing my status as a trainee, where I was doing my internship) and attempting to mask my rising anxiety, her facial expression communicated that this was not the question she was asking. She then specified that she was curious about my racial and ethnic background, adding that we had been exploring her racial, ethnic, and cultural background without any mention or reciprocity from me about my own identities. I felt ill-prepared to answer concisely and appropriately *who* I was as a racial, ethnic, or cultural being in a way that did not dismiss her question, while also adding to the work we were doing. Additionally, I had never before had a patient ask me outright about my racial or ethnic background (this likely is a result of White privilege, which I will address later). I found (and still find) myself wondering why it was so difficult for me to answer this patient's question, and I felt a surge of worry about how my response would impact our work, as well as how my disclosures would be received by my supervisors. My face flushed, and I eventually acknowledged that I was from a family of both White and Native American descent from the Southeastern region of the United States. The patient smiled and commented that she had suspected that I was "mixed," and that this made her feel relieved; her response also generated a series of emotional reactions related to my own ethnic identity development, which I later processed in supervision and with supportive mentors.

As the abovementioned example demonstrates, for many clinicians navigating issues of personal and cultural identity in clinical work can be challenging, particularly when issues such as White fragility and privilege are unrecognized. However, taking an attitude of cultural humility and engaging in culturally affirming supervision and consultation may support clinicians from all backgrounds in more effectively navigating personal and clinical interactions. In addition to supervision, consultation, and personal study, our profession's ethical standards and aspirational principles (APA Ethics Code,

2012) can also serve as tools in sound decision-making and the provision of culturally responsive care. For instance, psychologists are ethically obligated to (1) examine their ability to competently serve members of marginalized groups (APA Ethics Code 2.01 Boundaries of Competence), (2) refrain from discriminatory or harassing practices on the basis of factors such as "age, gender, gender identity, race, ethnicity, culture, national origin, religion, sexual orientation, disability, socioeconomic status, or any basis proscribed by law" (APA Ethics Code 3.01 Unfair Discrimination, p. 5; 3.03 Other Harassment), and (3) consider the impact of culture, language, and other identity variables when selecting and interpreting assessments (APA Ethics Code 9.02 Use of Assessments and 9.06 Interpreting Assessment Results). Additionally, our aspirational principles encourage psychologists to examine the extent to which biases as well as cultural, individual, and role differences (e.g., race, age, gender, gender identity, culture, national origin, sexual orientation, disability, language, and class) may impact clinical work (APA Ethics Code Principle D: Justice; Principle E: Respect for People's Rights and Dignity; APA Ethics Code, 2012).

In this chapter, I will describe how a focus on intersectionality and cultural humility as a foundational layer of clinical practice may support clinicians in providing optimal patient care while also encouraging an attitude of lifelong learning in regard to social justice, diversity, and cultural identities. I will differentiate the concepts of cultural humility (Tervalon & Murray-Garcia, 1998) and cultural competence, as well as describe the concept of White fragility (DiAngelo, 2011). Additionally, I will describe a visual teaching tool created by Kliman (2010) and discuss how this social matrix may aid clinicians in attending to intersecting identities in clinical practice, including teaching, supervision, and patient care. Further, I will provide examples from my professional work and discuss how my own intersecting identities highlight the aforementioned concepts. I will also describe the role of elders and mentors in my development as an early career psychologist. Finally, I will describe early advocacy efforts and some of the professional hurdles I have encountered in striving to become more active in the field of social justice.

EARLY EXPERIENCES WITH INTERSECTIONALITY

My early academic experiences relating to cultural diversity and multicultural psychology were primarily focused on learning about the Other (Canales, 2000), that is, having a limited focus on my own cultural identities and more of an emphasis on exploring the client's cultural backgrounds. However, I was fortunate in graduate school to have several mentors and professors who encouraged me and other students to consider how our own backgrounds influenced clinical work. One of the most surprising and formative experiences I had during graduate school was during our school's diversity lab, in which our class engaged in an exercise focused on social class. Magnusson (2011) defines *social class* as a system of hierarchies between societal groups based on economic resources, positions of status or power, political or economic interests, and/or a sense of belonging to a particular social group (e.g., sharing attributes, practices, and standards of living).

During this exercise, about 40 of my cohort peers and I participated in a "privilege walk"; this exercise required students start by standing all together in a line facing the front of the class. We were then asked to take a step forward or backward on the basis of whether a particular experience applied to us before the age of 18. We explored issues such as food and housing insecurity, access to transportation, medical care, and extracurricular activities. For example, we were asked about being on food stamps (step back), participating in sports or other after-school activities (step forward), taking family vacations (step forward), having a family vehicle (step forward), and having a parent or guardian able to stay home with us if we were sick (step forward). We were also asked to examine our class-based expectations in a variety of settings (e.g., expectation of being treated fairly in banks, stores, school situations; cf., Liu, Pickett, and Ivey [2007]).

I remember feeling shocked to discover, about halfway through the exercise, that I was so far toward the front of the class that I had reached the wall and could no longer move forward. I felt uncomfortable about the many class-related privileges I had experienced that my peers had not, and in particular, I felt ashamed that I had never before considered many of these experiences as reflections of privilege (e.g., access to medical care if sick). I also recall being so focused on my own experiences and feelings during the exercise that I was unable to consider how my peers—particularly those on the other end of the class—may have been feeling. It was later brought to my attention by a friend that my defensive reaction to class privilege (guilt, defensive silence, mentally distancing from the stress-inducing situation, and focus on self) paralleled what many White people demonstrate when exposed to even mild levels of racial stress—what DiAngelo (2011) describes as *White fragility.*

DiAngelo (2011) discusses a variety of triggers to behaviors reflective of White fragility. For example, she describes triggers including the suggestion that a White person's viewpoint stems from a racialized frame of reference ("challenge to objectivity," p. 57) and people of Color choosing not to protect the racial feelings of white people regarding race ("challenge to white racial expectations and the need/entitlement to racial comfort," p. 57). During our class exercise and the ensuing discussions, I remember feeling surprised with the (belated) revelation that much of my worldview and expectations in a variety of settings were not only reflective of my racial privilege, but also from a framework of significant class privilege. I also recall bristling at my friend's suggestion that I possessed (and was unaware of) class privilege, and felt tempted to engage in what we later referred to as "Diversity Olympics" (a form of one-upping and defensive deflection) by pointing out areas in which he, too, was privileged. As DiAngelo notes (p. 57), I was unable to respond to his kindly delivered feedback in a constructive way, as I did not possess the skills or the stamina to manage even a mild confrontation of my privileged statuses. In other words, I was used to expecting both racial and class-based comfort.

Later in my internship, I was introduced to the concept of *intersectionality*, which broadened my ability to consider multiple aspects of identities (rather than just one or two), as well as how these identities impact each other (Crenshaw, 1993). As Magnusson notes (2011, p. 94), "No single identity category or social category can satisfactorily account for the meanings a person places on his or her social relations, life events and social surroundings, nor for how he or she is responded to by these surroundings." Early in my internship, my cohort had the opportunity to learn and participate in an exercise focusing on intersectionality with a guest lecturer (Dr. Jodie Kliman). Dr. Kliman introduced our cohort to a graphic model for understanding and examining intersecting identity variables in clinical work and supervision. This model, known as the *social matrix*, can be used to explore assumptions, clarify misunderstandings, identify points of shared experience or connection, and limit performances of privilege within family systems, clinical relationships (e.g., clinician-patient), and supervision (Kliman, 2010).

Kliman (2010) describes the social matrix as having five specific functions: (1) depicting the multiplicity and salience of intersecting social identities and relationships, (2) increasing curiosity within relationships (e.g., family, supervision, and clinical) about the meanings of various social locations within their unique contexts, (3) highlighting the combined influence of identity variables (e.g., the impact of race on class privilege), (4) portraying each identity domain or axis of social membership as a continuum from power/privilege to subjugation/marginalization, and (5) providing a general sense of a person's overall relative privilege or marginalization (Kliman, 2010, p. 41). On the social matrix graphic, points of privilege are plotted at the center, whereas points of marginalization are plotted at the outside of the graphic (see Figure 7.1).

In completing our social matrices, our cohort was asked to examine each domain of identity on the social matrix (e.g., ethnicity, household income, and age) in terms of our perceived privilege or marginalization for each variable, and then plot each domain on the social matrix. As each domain was examined, by connecting the dots between the axes, each of us was able to create a polygon depicting not only our overall relative privilege or

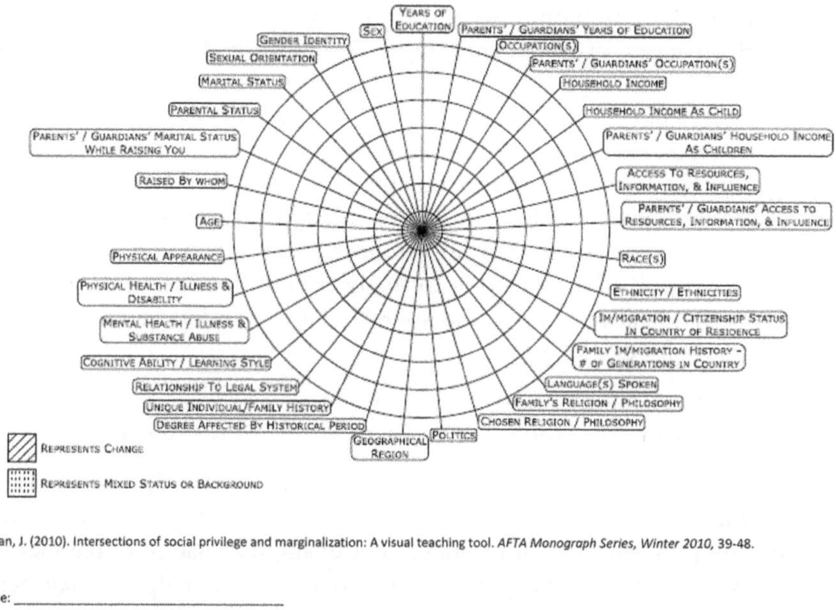

Figure 7.1 Blank Template for the Social Matrix. *Reprinted from "Intersections of social privilege and marginalization: A visual teaching tool," by J. Kliman (2010). AFTA Monograph Series, Winter 2010, 39–48. Reprinted with permission.*

marginalization, but also any areas of change over time and mixed statuses/backgrounds. Dr. Kliman then led our group in a discussion about our social matrices and reactions to the exercise.

One of the most salient aspects of the social matrix exercise for me was examining the impact of having a mixed ethnic background on other identity variables. At the time of the exercise, I had not disclosed to our larger intern group that my family is of both White and Native American descent, in great part due to the conflict I was feeling about my own racial identity and its development. I had been exploring and was curious about my family's Indigenous background since childhood, but felt concerned that others would not accept me in my cohort or internship. I wondered: Was I "Native enough"? Would other Native interns and faculty accept me? Worse, would I be seen as a White woman attempting to downplay her racial privilege? Early experiences of silencing and shame about my Native heritage had taught me to keep hidden this aspect of my identity and to hold tightly onto any and all White privilege I was afforded. I had also learned and seen directly that, particularly in the South, being seen as non-White could be dangerous. Further, I questioned my own motivations to disclose this aspect of my identity—especially if in disclosing I would then be less subject to scrutiny about my White privilege, or hold myself less accountable for my own performances of White privilege. As Townsend, Fryberg, Wilkins, and Markus (2012) suggest, I was also in a privileged position to be able to choose between disclosing or not. Not only was I an intern at one of the few APA-approved internship sites focusing solely on multicultural issues (an opportunity not afforded to most students or applicants), but because of my class and White privilege I would not be likely to experience serious social or economic consequences due to disclosing. As Townsend et al. further highlight, I was also in a position to likely benefit both personally (i.e., by being seen or considering myself as somehow more "unique" or distinct) and professionally by disclosing.

Positive Benefits of Mentorship; Repairing Relationships

I was very fortunate to have several mentors at my internship that supported me in exploring my racial identities while also encouraging me to be accountable for my performances of privilege. For example, I had multiple mentors who empowered me to give voice to the conflict I was feeling about being "Native enough" through their patience and sharing of their own experiences. I felt tremendously relieved to have the support of faculty who had been through similar internal conflicts, felt confident in their identities, and were also able to be accountable for their own biases and privileged statuses. Other mentors empowered me by providing language to describe my identities and better understand my responsibilities related to using specific language or identifying in specific ways. For instance, before internship I had never before heard the term "Two Spirit" (a pan-Indian term used to describe gender and sexual identities with specific social and/or spiritual roles in Native populations; Adams & Phillips, 2009; Balsam, Huang, Fieland, Simoni, & Walters, 2004). Still others challenged me to examine my personal prejudices and stereotypes about Native and mixed peoples; for instance, was my "Native enough" questioning related to how I did or did not match phenotypic stereotypes about Indigenous peoples—especially those presuming a lack of heterogeneity in appearance, dress, and behaviors? These mentors also invited me to openly discuss my hesitations, prejudices, and personal reactions; at times, my efforts to put words to my experiences resulted in harmful performances of privilege, such as rambling and emotional monologues that silenced the voices of others.

Fortunately, through the guidance of mentors and willingness of peers to call out my harmful actions, I was also introduced to valuable tools to reshape monologues into dialogues (Kamya & Trimble, 2002)—such as Hardy and Laszloffy's (2002) acknowledgment, validation, apology, and forgiveness

(AVAF) model. This model proposes a four-step process in healing relational injuries caused by power and privilege. In her article about developing a culturally respectful clinical stance, Kliman (2005) applies the AVAF model to family therapy and other clinical settings. As she discusses, the first step, *acknowledgement*, involves (1) an acceptance that regardless of intent one has caused injury and (2) communicating their awareness of the injury to the other party. The second and third steps, *validation* and *apology*, respectively, involve (1) accepting and acknowledging the injured party's feelings about the injury and (2) accepting responsibility for the harm done. The fourth step, *forgiveness*, occurs only if and when the injured party is ready; as Kliman notes, the party which has caused the injury is responsible for validation and being accountable for the injury even in the event that forgiveness is not forthcoming.

In the AVAF model, Hardy and Laszloffy (2002) stress that the privileged party is more responsible for healing in their respective domains of privilege; that is, even if both parties are accountable to each other on some level, each are responsible for healing injuries caused by their own displays of privilege or power. Hardy and Laszloffy propose six tasks for each party (i.e., privileged and subjugated/marginalized). More specifically, as Kliman (2005) notes, the privileged party is responsible for the following:

a. Resisting the temptation to engage in a competition over victim status (see my earlier-mentioned story about "Diversity Olympics"),
b. Acknowledging the injury caused (regardless of intention!),
c. Resisting the temptation to tell the injured party the meaning of their experiences,
d. Developing the stamina needed to respond compassionately despite one's own feelings of injury,
e. Allowing feelings of remorse, rather than guilt, to increase accountability and corrective actions, and
f. Staying in the relationship even if one does not receive appreciation or "kudos" (Kliman, 2005, p. 54).

In addition to tasks of the privileged party, Hardy and Laszloffy also define six tasks of the injured (subjugated/marginalized) party. These include the following:

a. Resisting internalized oppression and self-shaming,
b. Resisting any pulls by the privileged party to educate them,
c. Resisting any pulls by the privileged party to take care of/comfort them because of their actions,

d. Resisting silencing by being the author of your own story (Kliman, 2005),
e. Channeling rage to constructive paths,
f. Resisting the temptation to allow acquired privilege in one realm to detract from your ability to participate in the struggle against marginalization.

On the whole, in my personal and professional life, there have been many instances where I have been in the role of the privileged party and have caused injury to another person or group. As reflected in the earlier stories about the privilege walk and ethnic identity monologues, one of the challenges that I have experienced to engaging more meaningfully in cross-cultural dialogues has been my own feelings of guilt and shame (the fifth task of the privileged party in the AVAF model). One specific component that has contributed to feelings of guilt and shame has been a sense that missteps, lack of knowledge/language, or mistakes may be reflective of some type of moral failing—likely a reflection of both educational and racial privilege, as well as my own internalized Eurocentric contemporary values focusing on knowledge (see White Bison [2002] table).

As previously mentioned, DiAngelo (2011) notes that, when exposed to mild levels of racial stress, Whites may use many strategies to attempt to restore a sense of their moral standing and deflect feelings of guilt. These strategies may include silences, shutting down, exiting the stressful situation, or engaging in a "discourse of victimization" (p. 64) by portraying themselves as being blamed, attacked, or unfairly targeted during conversations about race. This type of attitude may also result in behaviors such as avoiding conversations about race and/or denial of personal racism, both types of microaggressions that have been commonly reported by patients (Hook et al., 2016).

Cultural Humility: Creating a Cultural Genogram

One strategy that has allowed me to utilize feelings of guilt to empower meaningful behavioral change has been to embrace a perspective of cultural humility in which attaining knowledge, skills, and awareness regarding cultural variables is an ongoing journey, rather than a target that can be achieved (as is the case in approaches focusing on cultural competency). Briefly, *cultural humility* involves continual self-reflection and self-critique, a commitment to patient-centered care, maintaining an awareness of power imbalances in patient-provider communication, and a dedication to developing and maintaining respectful partnerships with patients and communities (Tervalon & Murray-Garcia, 1998). As Tervalon and Murray-Garcia (1998) note, cultural humility involves taking an attitude of curiosity and flexibility when assessing and inviting the cultural experiences of each patient. This includes the ability to "say that they do not know when they truly do not know" (p. 119) and to take responsibility for exploring resources and information that could better serve patients. Hook, Davis, Owen, Worthington, and Utsey (2013) describe cultural humility as an interpersonal stance that involves respectful openness to others' cultural experiences, including intersections of identities that may impact the therapeutic and/or supervisory relationship (Hook, Watkins, Davis, Owen, Van Tongeren, & Ramos, 2016). Emerging research (cf., Hook et al., 2013; Owen et al., 2016) suggests that patients who rate their clinicians as more culturally humble report better therapy outcomes, including a stronger working alliance.

An important step in taking a stance of cultural humility is to continually engage in self-reflection and self-critique (Tervalon & Murray-Garcia, 1998). Creating a *cultural genogram* (Hardy & Laszloffy, 1995) is one way that clinicians and/or supervisees can explore the cultural backgrounds, beliefs, and values of their family of origin. Much like a traditional genogram, in a cultural genogram the first step is to write down the names of family members going back two or three generations. The next step is to define each family member's culture(s) of origin (i.e., the major group(s) from which a person has descended, which were the first generation to come to the United States (except for Native Americans); Hardy & Laszloffy, 1995). Next, it is important to identify the *organizing principles* of each group comprising the culture(s) of origin; organizing principles are basic constructs shaping the perceptions, beliefs, and behaviors of a group. For example, in White culture, an expectation of being treated "fairly" (often an unconscious, unspoken expectation reflective of racial privilege) may be an organizing principle.

Organizing principles also serve to identify aspects of a culture that are deemed positive or negative—Hardy and Laszloffy (1995) refer to these aspects as *pride/shame issues*. For example, the degree to which one's behavior is in line with the Protestant Work Ethic—a value system with religious underpinnings emphasizing hard work, personal obligation, and individual responsibility to succeed financially—may be a pride/shame for some White communities (Cokley, Komarraju, Pickett, Shen, Patel, Belur, & Rosales, 2007). In their article about the cultural genogram, Hardy and Laszloffy provide a series of guiding questions and additional instructions for the preparation and review of cultural genograms within various dyads which further allow for exploration of the impact of values, prejudices and stereotypes, experiences of oppression, within-group differences, and other variables on beliefs and behaviors.

Through the use of a cultural genogram (Hardy & Laszloffy, 1995) as well as the social matrix (Kliman, 2010), I have been able to continue exploring with peers and colleagues aspects of my own intersecting identities which may influence my personal and professional behaviors. These tools have been helpful for me in uncovering unconscious biases and shedding light on some of my personal reactions to clinical and supervisory encounters. For example, two topics that were frequently brought "to the table" during my internship training were religion and spirituality. Consistent with findings by Crook-Lyon et al. (2012) that many mental health professionals express a lack of preparation to address religious and spiritual issues in therapy, my exposure to the topics of religion and spirituality as diversity issues during graduate school was limited.

When I expressed a sense of discomfort and surprise about the frequency with which clients and faculty brought spirituality and religion into our work, a mentor challenged me to consider why I had not personally sought out additional training and self-reflection on this topic. This mentor's feedback was a gift; their modeling, encouragement, and support in exploring the ethics surrounding incorporation of spirituality into clinical work felt like an expression of permission as well as an invitation to explore spirituality, dreams, and religious worldviews in a respectful and responsible fashion (cf., Eason & Robbins, 2012). This feedback allowed me to identify the intersections of religion and spirituality as an area of needed personal reflection, particularly given my upcoming transition into residency.

EARLY ADVOCACY EFFORTS AND STRUGGLES

The transition into my early career as a psychologist began with my return to the Pacific Northwest for a postdoctoral residency with a Latino/bilingual focus at a student training clinic. In addition to patient hours, part of my responsibility as a resident was to provide mentorship and cultural consultation to first-year student clinicians. I was also asked to organize, review, and teach courses and trainings explicitly focused on culturally informed mental health services, as part of the training program's mission statement was a focus on social justice.

During internship, I had been introduced to a variety of strategies and activities to promote change in organizational cultures aiming to provide more culturally responsive services. For example, Miller and Garran (2008) provide a list of several guidelines ("activities toward becoming an anti-racism organization," p. 295) for organizations to explore the kinds of activities their agency may consider in their commitment to anti-racism. These authors discuss the value of increasing staff training/seminars focusing on culturally informed service delivery, holding ongoing discussions on racism and race, exploring worldviews, biases, and assumptions of staff, and creating opportunities/structures to address and resolve problematic policies and practices related to race. I was excited about going into a residency that encouraged and offered opportunities for these kinds of activities.

As I transitioned from student to doctor during residency, however, one of the biggest barriers I encountered to becoming more active in the field of social justice was my own anxiety and pride. I felt grateful to have mentors and supervisors who allowed me to be autonomous in my clinical work, provided guidance in responding to microaggressions, and encouraged me to be creative and inventive when providing trainings and courses focusing on social justice. I was also privileged not to encounter much resistance from those in higher positions of power, a position that I recognized that other young professionals—particularly those of color—may not receive. Further, I was fortunate to be in a position of racial, educational, and institutional privilege where I could assertively respond to microaggressions I experienced regarding my perceived ethnic background and sexual orientation without risking my standing in the program or fearing a lack of support from supervisors.

Despite the great amount of support I received, I still felt worried and anxious about how students would respond to me. I had read the research on how teaching antiracism can often have a deleterious impact on one's career and interpersonal relationships with students (cf., Boatright-Horowitz & Soeung, 2009), and had seen some of the behaviors described in this research (e.g., White students gathering to complain or commiserate after discussions of racism [the "resistance perspective" (Bowman, 2009, p. 184)], White students feeling as though discussions of racism or privilege are personal attacks on them or their family, and student projection of frustration or other emotions onto the instructor). I was also aware of research that students in more privileged positions may be more likely to show improvements in knowledge and awareness in diversity classes or trainings because the information is more novel to them—what Bowman (2009) describes as the "exploration perspective" (p. 183).

I noticed in teaching my first few courses that while many students seemed to benefit, others met the material with a great deal of resistance and reactivity, much of which was manifested in behaviors such as refusal to participate, expressions of anger toward me as the instructor, or extended monologues during discussion time (Cole, Case, Rios, & Curtin, 2011). Though I wanted the students to benefit from the classes and trainings, and to challenge their own biases and beliefs, I was also acutely aware of the desire to be liked and seen as competent, and struggled with how to respond to student resistance. On the whole, in considering how to respond to student resistance, I was again confronted with my own lack of racial and emotional stamina to tolerate mild levels of even perceived or threatened conflict. I was also aware of my responsibility, as Hardy and Bobes (2016, p. 11) highlight, to be a "broker of permission" to give voice to previously silenced topics by initiating difficult dialogues and modeling a tolerance of discomfort and intensity. After all, how could I expect students to confront their own anxieties, insecurities, and biases if I was unwilling to do so?

Integrating Intersectionality into Professional Work

One particularly memorable experience I had in confronting my own biases and anxieties came when I was asked to teach a course focusing on LGBTQ+ populations. Over the course of the term, it became clear that one group which had been given less attention in both the syllabus and in my lecture material were those who identify as bisexual. Students shared that this microinvalidation sent the message that, consistent with other messages they had received within the LGBTQ community, there was a "hierarchy of queerness"—with bisexual people in a position of reduced power. Notably, this type of bisexual erasure is consistent with research highlighting the frequency of invisibility, avoidance, and/or minimization of sexual orientation in clinical work (Shelton & Delgado-Romero, 2011). Although I was initially embarrassed, I invited the class to openly discuss the impact of bisexual erasure on our classroom dynamic. Some students were brave enough to share feelings of disappointment that I, as a member of the queer community, would reproduce a hurtful dynamic they had experienced outside the classroom. Others expressed surprise when I acknowledged that my own personal stereotypes and biases had impacted why I had not invited this group "to the table." Fortunately, acknowledging, validating, apologizing, and requesting the students' forgiveness (Hardy & Laszloffy, 2002) allowed for a reparative experience within our classroom, as well as corrective action (e.g., altering the syllabus for next year's class).

Another memorable experience in my early journey toward taking a perspective of cultural humility came while I was teaching the LGBTQ+ class mentioned earlier. Midway through our term, a gunman shot and killed 49 people at Pulse, a gay nightclub in Orlando, Florida. I found out about the shooting on Monday morning, when members of my family sent me texts to affirm their love and support and inquire about my welfare. I remember feeling nauseated, shocked, and at a loss as to how to process my fear and grief while still being able to go to work, see patients, and teach later that week. I was frightened and worried for the Latinx and Puerto Rican people I knew and loved, and unsure of how to support them. Further, I felt troubled by the massacre being described as the deadliest mass shooting in U.S. history, as this erased Wounded Knee and countless other massacres of Indigenous peoples, including those of Latinx descent. I questioned how to support the class in processing and grieving the Pulse shootings, while also making space to bring other voices to the table. In preparing for class, I recalled the words of one of my mentors and elders, who shared:

> It is probably one of the most common Native American experiences; that is, to find ourselves left out and confronted with the responsibility to speak forthrightly and honestly to our comrades for forgetting us . . . to leave us out of dialogues, to forget us, is to lose profound and vital psycho-spiritual perspectives that have emerged from a near genocidal oppression. We deserve a voice. I had to speak. (Robbins, 2012, p. 98)

As our class processed the events at Pulse, I felt both empowered and privileged to be in a position to support the students in expressing their fear and grief while also allowing my own reactions to be present. I believe this opportunity allowed our class to begin the process of collective healing by acknowledging and honoring those whose voices had been silenced, and, using our relative privilege (e.g., in participating in a graduate education course), to explore the juxtaposition of being allies and/or members of a marginalized community with our role as supporters to others (e.g., to provide therapy to clients). It was humbling to be in a position to teach this kind of class and honor individuals (e.g., early leaders and advocates of LGBTQ+ rights, mentors, and elders) whose sacrifices and work had paved the way for powerful institutions, such as graduate schools, to recognize the need for LGBTQ+ affirmative mental health care.

CONCLUSIONS AND RECOMMENDATIONS

In my experiences as a trainee and early career psychologist, I have encountered both benefits and barriers in taking a perspective of intersectionality and cultural humility in my professional and personal work. Three main themes have emerged over the course of my early journey in exploring cultural humility and intersectionality: (1) the importance of personal awareness and knowledge about intersecting identities, (2) the value of mentors and elders in strengthening a culturally humble stance, and (3) the importance of practice in developing stamina to initiate and remain engaged in conversations about cultural identity.

The use of various teaching tools, such as Kliman's (2010) social matrix, Hardy and Laszloffy's (1995) cultural genogram, and Hardy and Laszloffy's (2002) AVAF model, have served as valuable models to guide my intellectual and cognitive understanding of intersectionality. These models have also provided me with language to identify and explore how my own culture, background, and biases impact my behavior in relationships (e.g., supervision, teaching, and clinical work). Many authors (cf., BICAP, 2016; Hook et al., 2016) have also offered organizational case studies which can support mental health professionals and students and help them gain greater awareness of their intersecting identities as well as develop skills to identify how these identities impact relationships. For instance, Hook et al. (2016) discuss an *initiate-invite-instill* approach to supervision in which supervisors initiate conversations about culture, invite supervisees to consider and participate in these dialogues, and instill the value of cultural humility through modeling of respectful and culturally sensitive behaviors. I believe that in addition to utilizing the initiate-invite-instill approach in supervision, it is possible to adapt this approach to clinical work, teaching, mentoring, and personal conversations.

More valuable than having an intellectual and cognitive awareness of intersectionality, however, has been mentorship and guidance from colleagues and elders who have been able to model cultural humility and accountability. These individuals have provided encouragement and support, and they have challenged me to recognize the ways in which my privileged statuses may impact my approach to teaching and clinical work. Their support has allowed me to recognize how performances of White fragility and/or withdrawing from advocacy roles due to anxiety can cause harm to my relationships with others or detract from the quality of my teaching activities. Research suggests that mentoring relationships can support organizations in recruiting and retaining diverse trainees and faculty, improving these individuals' teaching abilities, as well as increasing trainee's and faculty members' sense of confidence (Chan, Yeh, & Krumboltz, 2015; O'Neil et al., 2015; Rogers & Molina, 2006; Troisi, Leder, Stiegler-Balfour, Fleck, & Good, 2015). Thus, students and professionals desiring to enhance their ability to take a culturally humble stance may benefit from engaging in mentorship activities in their training institutions and organizations.

Lastly, in order to "stay the course" in developing cultural humility and an intersectional lens, it is important to examine factors that may make it difficult to remain engaged and open during conversations about race and culture. As Kliman notes (2005), "It is never productive to ask someone to care about your oppression while you are contributing to theirs (p. 45)." Consistent with my earlier discussion of the deleterious impact of anxiety with respect to practicing and remaining engaged during difficult dialogues about race, research (cf., Sue, Torino, Capodilupo, Rivera, & Lin, 2009) suggests that White trainees and professionals express concerns that engaging in racial dialogues may result in a perceived loss of control and/or create an emotionally overwhelming experience. As Sue et al. (2009b) note, responding with avoidance strategies, such as withdrawing, leaving the situation, and avoiding conversations altogether, only further heightens distress and sends a message to students and faculty in marginalized positions that such conversations are unwelcome. These authors suggest that individuals in privileged positions consider acknowledging the intensity of feelings in the moment, demonstrate a willingness to continually circle back and revisit difficult dialogues, and model the ability to both recognize and tolerate uncomfortable situations through appropriate self-disclosure of personal challenges, fears, and biases.

Clinicians, supervisors, professors, and other mental health providers are in a unique position to model the ability to initiate and invite dialogues about culture as well as address and repair ruptures in relationships—both themes consistent with a social justice perspective. I believe that in addition to utilizing an intersectional lens and taking an attitude of cultural humility during professional contacts, it can be beneficial to adapt these approaches to personal conversations and relationships. As the aforementioned examples suggest, continued practice exploring and dialoguing about race and culture can enhance one's own awareness as well as facilitate compassion, reduce prejudice, dispel stereotypes, and increase mutual respect and understanding across both personal and professional contexts (Sue, Lin, Torino, Capodilupo, & Rivera, 2009; Willow, 2008).

REFERENCES

Adams, H. L., & Phillips, L. (2009). Ethnic related variations from the Cass model of homosexual identity formation: The experiences of two-spirit, lesbian, and gay Native Americans. *Journal of Homosexuality, 56*(7), 959–976. doi: 10.1080/00918360903187895.

American Psychological Association (APA). (2003). Guidelines on multicultural education, training, research, practice, and organizational change for psychologists. *American Psychologist, 58*(5), 37–402. doi: 10.1037/0003-066X.58.5.377.

American Psychological Association. (2012). *Ethical principles of psychologists and code of conduct.* Retrieved from: http://www.apa.org/ethics/code/.

Balsam, K. F., Huang, B., Fieland, K. C., Simoni, J. M., & Walters, K. L. (2004). Culture, trauma, and wellness: A comparison of heterosexual and lesbian, gay, bisexual, and two-spirit Native Americans. *Cultural Diversity and Ethnic Minority Psychology, 10*(3), 287–301. doi: 10.1037/1099-9809.10.3.287.

Bemak, F., & Chung, R. C.-Y. (2008). New professional roles and advocacy strategies for school counselors: A multicultural/social justice perspective to move beyond the nice counselor syndrome. *Journal of Counseling & Development, 86*, 372–381. doi: 10.1002/j.1556-6678.2008.tb00522.x.

Boatright-Horowitz, S. L., & Soeung, S. (2009, September). Teaching white privilege to white students can mean saying good-bye to positive student evaluations. *American Psychologist, 64*(6), 574–575. doi: 10.1037/a0016593.

Boston Institute for Culturally Affirming Practices (BICAP). (2016). Deconstructing power to build connection: The importance of dialogue. In E. Pinderhughes, V. Jackson, & P. A. Romney (Eds.), *Understanding Power: An imperative for Human Services* (pp. 195–218). Washington, DC: NASW Press.

Bowman, N. (2009). College diversity courses and cognitive development among students from privileged and marginalized groups. *Journal of Diversity in Higher Education, 2*, 182–194. doi: 10.1037/a0016639.

Canales, M. K. (2000). Othering: Toward an understanding of difference. *Advances in Nursing Science, 22*(4), 16–31. doi: 10.1097/00012272-200006000-00003.

Chan, A. W., Yeh, C. J., & Krumboltz, J. D. (2015). Mentoring ethnic minority counseling and clinical psychology students: A multicultural, ecological, and relational model. *Journal of Counseling Psychology, 62*(4), 592–607. doi: 10.1017/cou0000079.

Cokley, K., Komarraju, M., Pickett, R., Shen, F., Patel, N., Belur, V., & Rosales, R. (2007). Ethnic differences in endorsement of the Protestant Work Ethic: The role of ethnic identity and perceptions on social class. *The Journal of Social Psychology, 147*(1), 75–89. doi: 10.3200/socp.147.1.75-89.

Cole, E. R., Case, K. A., Rios, D., & Curtin, N. (2011). Understanding what students bring to the classroom: Moderators of the effects of diversity courses on student attitudes. *Cultural Diversity and Ethnic Minority Psychology, 17*(4), 397–405. doi: 10.1037/a0025433.

Crenshaw, K. (1993). Mapping the margins: Intersectionality, identity politics, and violence against women of color. *Stanford Law Review, 43*, 1241–1299. doi: 10.2307/1229039.

Crook-Lyon, R. E., O'Grady, K. A., Smith, T. B., Jensen, D. R., Golightly, T., & Potkar, K. A. (2012). Addressing religious and spiritual diversity in graduate training and multicultural education for professional psychologists. *Psychology of Religion and Spirituality, 4*(3), 169–181. doi: 10.1037/a0026403.

Duran, E. (2000). *Buddha in redface*. Lincoln, NE: IUniverse.

DiAngelo, R. (2011). White fragility. *International Journal of Critical Pedagogy, 3*(3), 54–70.

Eason, E. A., & Robbins, R. R. (2012). Walking in beauty: An American Indian perspective on social justice. *Counseling and Values, 57*, 18–23. doi: 10.1002/j.2161-007x.2012.00003.x.

Geertz, C. (1973). Thick description: Toward an interpretive theory of culture. In C. Gertz (Ed.), *The interpretation of cultures: Selected essays* (pp. 3–30). New York: Basic Books.

Goodall, B. H. K. (2001). *Writing the new ethnography*. Walnut Creek, CA: AltaMira.

Goodman, L. A., Liang, B., Helms, J. E., & Weintraub, S. R. (2004, January). Training counseling psychologists as social justice agents. *Counseling Psychologist, 32*(6), 793–836. doi: 10.1177/0011000004268802.

Hardy, K. V., & Bobes, T. (2016). Core competencies for executing culturally sensitive supervision and training. In K. V. Hardy & T. Bobes (Eds.), *Culturally sensitive supervision and training* (pp. 11–15). New York: Routledge.

Hardy, K. V., & Laszloffy, T. A. (1995). The cultural genogram: Key to training culturally competent family therapists. *Journal of Marital and Family Therapy, 21*(3), 227–337. doi: 10.1111/j.1752-0606.1995.tb00158.x.

Hardy, K. V., & Laszloffy, T. A. (2002). Couple therapy using a multicultural perspective. In A. S. Gurman & N. S. Jacobson (Eds.), *Clinical handbook of couple therapy* (3rd ed., pp. 569–593). New York: Guilford Press.

Hook, J. N., Davis, D. E., Owen, J. Worthington, E. L, Jr., & Utsey, S. O. (2013). Cultural humility: Measuring openness to culturally diverse clients. *Journal of Counseling Psychology, 60,* 353–366. doi: 10.1037/a003295.

Hook, J. N., Farrell, J. E., Davis, D. E., DeBlaere, C., Van Tongeren, D. R., & Utsey, S. O. (2016). Cultural humility and racial microaggressions in counseling. *Journal of Counseling Psychology, 63*(3), 269–277. doi: 10.1037/cou0000114.

Hook, J. N., Watkins, C. E., Davis, D. E., Van Tongeren, D. R., & Ramos, M. (2016). Cultural humility in psychotherapy supervision. *American Journal of Psychotherapy, 70*(2), 149–166.

Kamya, H., & Trimble, D. (2002). Response to injury: Toward ethical construction of the other. *Journal of Systemic Therapies, 21,* 19–29. doi: 10.1521/jsyt.21.3.19.23338.

Kliman, J. (2005). Many differences, many voices: Toward social justice in family therapy. In M. P. Mirkin, K. Suyemoto, & B. Okun (Eds.), *Women in psychotherapy: Exploring diverse contexts and identities* (pp. 42–63). New York: Guilford.

Kliman, J. (2010). Intersections of social privilege and marginalization: A visual teaching tool. *AFTA Monograph Series, Winter 2010,* 39–48.

Liu, W. M., Pickett, T., & Ivey, A. E. (2007). White middle-class privilege: Social class bias and implications for training and practice. *Journal of Multicultural Counseling and Development, 35*(4), 194–206. doi: 10.1002/j.2161-1912.2007.tb00060.x.

Lyons, H. Z., Bike, D. H., Ojeda, L., Johnson, R., & Flores, L. Y. (2013). Qualitative research as social justice practice with culturally diverse populations. *Journal for Social Action in Counseling and Psychology, 5*(2), 10–25. Reviews best practices in socially justice qualitative research processes.

Magnusson, E. (2011). Women, men, and all the other categories: Psychologies for theorizing human diversity. *Nordic Psychology, 63*(2), 88–114. doi: 10.1027/1901-2276/a000034.

Miller, J., & Garran, A. M. (2008). *Racism in the United States: Implications for the Helping Professions.* Belmont, CA: Thomson Brooks/Cole.

Mitchell, M., & Egudo, M. (2003, November). *A review of narrative methodology.* Edinburgh, South Australia 5111, Australia: DSTO Systems Sciences Laboratory.

Mitzock, L., & Page, K. V. (2016, Summer). Evaluating the ally role: Contributions, limitations, and the activist position in counseling and psychology. *Journal for Social Action in Counseling and Psychology, 8*(1), 17–33.

O'Neil, J., Chaison, A. D., Cuellar, A. K., Nguyen, Q. X., Brown, W. L., & Teng, E. J. (2015). Development and implementation of a mentoring program for Veterans Affairs psychology trainees. *Training an Education in Professional Psychology, 9*(2), 113–120. doi: 10.1037/tep0000065.

Owen, J., Tao, K. W., Drinane, J. M., Hook, J., Davis, D. E., & Kune, N. F. (2016). Client perceptions of therapists' multicultural orientation: Cultural (missed) opportunities and cultural humility. *Professional Psychology: Research and Practice, 47*(1), 30–37. doi: 10.1037/pro0000046.

Pierce, C. (1995). Stress analogs of racism and sexism: Terrorism, torture, and disaster. In C. Willie, P. Reiker, B. Kramer, & P. Brown (Eds.), *Mental health, racism, and sexism* (pp. 277–293). Pittsburgh, PA: University of Pittsburgh Press.

Ponterotto, J. G. (2010). Qualitative research in multicultural psychology: Philosophical underpinnings, popular approaches, ad ethical considerations. *Cultural Diversity and Ethic Minority Psychology, 16*(4), 581–589. doi: 10.1037/a0012051.

Robbins, R. R. (2012). A Native American voice in multicultural psychology: Finding healing in an interpersonal tapestry. *Journal of Multicultural Counseling and Development, 40*, 93–103. doi: 10.1002/j.2161-1912.2012.00009.x.

Rogers, M. R., & Molina, L. E. (2006). Exemplary efforts in psychology to recruit and retain graduate students of color. *American Psychologist, 61*, 143–156. doi: 10.1037/003-066X.61.2.143.

Shaw, S. (2017, January). Practicing humility. *Counseling Today*, 41–45.

Shelton, K., & Delgado-Romero, E. A. (2011). Sexual orientation microaggressions: The experience of lesbian, gay, bisexual, and queer clients in psychotherapy. *Journal of Counseling Psychology, 58*, 210–221. doi: 10.1037/a0022251.

Stake, J. E., & Hoffman, F. L. (2000). Putting feminist psychology to the test: The experience of women's studies from the student and teacher perspectives. *Psychology of Women Quarterly, 24*(1), 30–38.

Sue, D. W., Capodilupo, C. M., Torino, G. C., Bucceri, J. M., Holder, A. M. B., Nadal, K. L., & Esquili, M. (2007). Racial microaggressions in everyday life: Implications for clinical practice. *American Psychologist, 62,* 271–286. doi: 10.1037/0003-066X.62.4.271.

Sue, D. W., Lin, A. I., Torino, G. C., Capodilupo, C. M., & Rivera, D. P. (2009). Racial microaggressions and difficult dialogues on race in the classroom. *Cultural Diversity and Ethnic Minority Psychology, 15*(2), 183–190. doi: 10.1037/a0014191.

Sue, D. W., Torino, G. C., Capodilupo, C. M., Rivera, D. P., & Lin, A. I. (2009b). How White faculty perceive and react to difficult dialogues on race: Implications for education and training. *The Counseling Psychologist, 37*(8), 1090–1115. doi: 10.1177/0011000009340443.

Teo, T., Gao, Z., & Sheivari, R. (2014). Philosophical reflexivity in social justice work. In C. V. Johnson & H. Friedman (Eds.), *The Praeger handbook of social justice and psychology* (pp. 65–78). Santa Barbara, CA: Praeger.

Tervalon, M., & Murray-Garcia, J. (1998). Cultural humility versus cultural competence: A critical distinction in defining physician training outcomes in multicultural education. *Journal of Health Care for the Poor and Underserved, 9*(2), 117–125. doi: 10.1353/hpu.2010.0233.

Townsend, S. J., Fryberg, S. A., Wilkins, C. L., & Markus, H. R. (2012). Being mixed: Who claims a Biracial identity? *Cultural Diversity and Ethnic Minority Psychology, 18*(1), 91–96. doi: 10.1037/a0026845.

Troisi, J. D., Leder, S., Stiegler-Balfour, J. J., Fleck, B. K. B., & Good, J. J. (2015). Effective teaching outcomes associated with the mentorship of early career psychologists. *Society for the Teaching of Psychology, 42*(3), 242–247. doi: 10.1177/0098628315587623.

Willow, R. (2008). Lived experience of interracial dialogue on race: Proclivity to participate. *Journal of Multicultural Counseling and Development, 36*, 40–51. doi: 10.1002/j.2161-1912.2008.tb00068.x.

Zane, N., Bernal, G., & Leong, F. T. L. (Eds.). (2016). *Evidence-based psychological practice with ethnic minorities: Culturally informed research and clinical strategies*. Washington, DC: American Psychological Association. doi: 10.1111/j.1471-6402.2000.tb01019.x.

Chapter 8

Social Justice in Prevention Psychology

Healing with the Community Readiness Model

Pamela Jumper-Thurman, Barbara A. Plested, Kateri D. Coyhis and Hanna Moore

EDITOR'S INTRODUCTION

This chapter was written by four individuals, two of whom are young professionals. One young author, Kateri Coyhis, has led a traditional Native lifestyle while also completing a university degree. She is now an administrator of an international nonprofit charitable agency. The second young author, Hanna Moore, also recently earned her bachelor's degree. She spent much time throughout her life with Indigenous people. In their university educational studies, these two young authors majored and minored in history, classics, politics, and government. They conducted extensive literature reviews and wrote about the impact of colonization—in particular, boarding schools—on American Indians/Alaska Natives. These authors—our youth and future elders—share important insights about the impact of the history of the exploitation, colonization, and genocide by Indian boarding schools on Native American children and subsequent generations. They explore issues such as intergenerational trauma, and they write about their hopes for future decolonization initiatives in order to heal the traumas caused by Indian boarding schools.

Two seasoned professionals, Drs. Pamela Jumper-Thurman (Western Cherokee) and Barbara A. Plested, who have backgrounds in international cross-cultural research, coalition building, university teaching, and mentoring new professionals, join them in their chapter. They contribute their wisdom, educational training, and experiences from decades of research, mentoring, and teaching. Drs. Jumper-Thurman and Plested are part of the Colorado

State University team that developed the widely used Community Readiness Model. This writing team of four authors produces remarkable reflections from both current and future elders.

> "When a war between nations is lost, the loser we know pays the cost. But even when Germany fell to your hands, consider dear lady, consider dear man, you left them their pride and you left them their land. But what have you done to these ones?"—Now That The Buffalo's Gone, Buffy Sainte Marie. (Sainte Marie, 1964, Track 1)

It is impossible to discuss Indigenous populations in the context of social justice without acknowledging the historical and current impact on colonization. For American Indian populations, the aggressive act of colonization has shaped the environment, the political systems, the economic challenges faced day to day, and even the cultural and spiritual lives of American Indians. These injustices have permeated Native lives in various ways. Literature indicates that prior to the arrival of Columbus to the Western Hemisphere, there were an estimated 4.4 to 12.25 million Indigenous people living in what is now the United States (Thornton, 1987). Thornton also estimates that after approximately 400 hundred years of colonization, the North American Indigenous population reached a nadir of only 250,000 in 1900. Fortunately, the Native populations revived somewhat after 1900, and currently, according to the 2010 census, the nation's population of American Indians and Alaska Natives, including those of more than one race, is 5.2 million or 1.7% of the U.S. population (U.S. Census, 2010). These numbers reflect self-identification of Natives.

The decimation resulting from colonization left deep scars that have crossed generations and continue to impact Native people today. Duran and Duran (1995) aptly refer to this trauma as the *soul wound*, a profound spiritual trauma inflicted upon Natives. This *soul wound* reflects a multitude of demeaning actions and policies by the U.S. government and various religions as well as politicians and presidents. All of this has contributed to the tragic decline in the health and well-being of Indigenous people and to the theft of Native lands and resources.

REMOVALS AND RELOCATIONS

There have been other destructive traumas inflicted on American Indian populations, traumas that attempted to destroy Native culture. One of the most destructive of these traumas resulted in the breakdown of both the culture and the economic resources—the forced removal of Natives from their homelands, their families, and their properties. Today, it is likely impossible for someone to even imagine that a government could come into your lives, take your home, scatter your family, and take your children. Yet, this was the reality for Native people in the 1800s. One of the most well-known removals was the Trail of Tears. Native families were forced from their homes and farms and made to walk through harsh weather to new locations. On May 28, 1830, President Andrew Jackson signed into law the Indian Removal Act (Library of Congress, 1830). This forced relocation began in 1831 with the removal of the Choctaw. In 1832, the Seminole were removed, the Creek in 1834, and the Chickasaw in 1837. Finally, the Cherokee were removed from their homelands in 1838. It is unknown just how many Native people died on these journeys due to sickness and the harsh weather. It has been estimated that approximately half died along the trails (Ehle, 2008).

The Navajo/Dine' also experienced the hardship of a removal in 1864, the long walk. In the harsh winter months, they made a 300-plus-mile walk to designated military internment camps. Bosque Redondo was well documented (Baily, 190). For four years, they suffered severe mistreatment while housed in the camps until the historic United States-Navajo Treaty was signed in 1868. Following the signing of the treaty, the Navajo were allowed to return to a small portion of their former land base, and they began the long walk back home.

"KILL THE INDIAN IN HIM, AND SAVE THE MAN"

While the taking of homelands was devastating, even more destructive to the community and family circles was the taking of Native children from their families. The children were literally stolen and placed in government boarding schools, forbidden to speak their Native languages, punished harshly and forced to "assimilate." It is important to note that assimilation did not include acceptance by the general population. This forced assimilation was a cruel U.S. government driven policy. "Kill the Indian in him, and save the man." This iconic quote from Captain Richard Henry Pratt symbolizes the era of forced assimilation, loss of cultural identity, and the devastating effects of intergenerational trauma that began with Native American children at boarding schools (Pratt, 1800–1900). General Richard Pratt began the "Indian School Experiment" to build the boarding schools. In 1875, he moved 75 Indian prisoners across the country and taught them English, Christianity, and trades. In April 1878, he moved 62 of the younger and more intelligent prisoners to the Hampton Institute. Pratt published before and after pictures—the "savage" versus the "civilized" Indians. In the 1860s, the government set up 48 "day schools" outside the reservations and hoped the children would in turn teach their parents what they learned. The government then moved them further away and turned the facilities into boarding schools to keep the parents away from the children. In 1879, Pratt went to the Pine Ridge and Rosebud Sioux reservations in the Dakotas and convinced parents and elders to send 60 boys and 24 girls to a new boarding school in Carlisle, Pennsylvania.

The horrifying effects of Native American boarding schools continue to impact communities today because this legislation took away the opportunity for traditional transmission of Native American values and cultural knowledge. This destruction of families resulted in the inability to parent in traditional ways, to pass on stories, and to teach indigenous values and histories, and left the child to survive on his/her own, virtually without the strength of an identity. This attempt toward destruction of Native culture and the sense of Native community only served to strengthen the effects of intergenerational trauma.

Throughout the 1950s, the U.S. government made attempts to force Native people to assimilate into the European American mainstream culture. The first such attempt was the termination directive of the Termination and Relocation Act of 1954 (Public Law 959), which eliminated the recognition of several Native American groups across the country. The second component, the relocation, encouraged Native people to move to certain government designated cities and acquire vocational skills. The relocation directive of the Termination and Relocation Act of 1954 subsidized the immigration of Native American people from reservations to metropolitan areas, with the stipulation that they would not return to their reservation or home area. This act severely threatened Native American cultures by coercing individuals to, once again, permanently separate themselves from their cultural groups. In fact, it also failed to integrate Natives into the mainstream culture; instead, it only contributed to the formation of Native American ghettos in urban environments (Vernon & Jumper Thurman, 2005).

Finally, it is significant to note that many people in the majority population say these are all events that occurred in the past and many even believe that the impact is not relevant today. That belief is incorrect. The resulting traumas continue to this day. Much of this history is not taught in mainstream educational settings and yet it is a holocaust committed on Native people.

The ongoing exploitation of Native lands to utilize the resources that exist on the land, or the lands themselves, continues. For example, literally thousands of Native people and allies have rallied across the United States to protest the Dakota Access Pipeline as well as increase awareness of Indigenous rights (Wickstrom, 2017). The pipeline crosses sacred Native land, and should the pipeline leak, it will contaminate the drinking water for a number of tribes in the area.

The wealth of resources and land stolen from Native lands has provided only minimal, if any, compensation to the people who live on the land (Nies, 1996). Further adding to the complexity of the economic devastation to Natives are the federal government's current policies, specifically restrictions, on Native property rights (Riley, 2016). Reservation land and other lands within tribal jurisdiction are held "in trust" for Native people by the federal government. The historical impetus for this policy was to keep Natives/ tribal nations contained within designated lands. Then, the reasoning for continuing the policy shifted to preserving the lands for Natives. Still, today, the result is the same. Many Natives cannot actually own land; therefore, they cannot build equity. They are prevented from reaping numerous benefits, a factor that only adds to the economic challenges faced by many Native people (Riley, 2016).

INTERGENERATIONAL TRAUMA

It is essential today to understand that these events have not had isolated impact. They are not buried in history. The total control of Native land, the destruction of the family and the continued federal policies that exist to curtail ownership of resources and land have created ongoing intergenerational trauma. Perhaps this is the most devastating social injustice to Native people throughout the United States. Historical trauma has been defined as the "cumulative emotional and psychological wounding across generations, including the lifespan, which emanates from massive group trauma" (Yellow Horse Brave Heart, 1998). As a Lakota woman, Yellow Horse Brave Heart wrote about intergenerational trauma through an essentialist lens. She is a descendant of Sitting Bull, a Lakota leader, who led a resistance against the U.S. government. She began her work on trauma through the realization that she suffered from immense grief in her own life, which started her on the path to research on the topic. Armed with a background in clinical social work, the main motivation behind her research stemmed from a desire to help Native people heal. Dr. Yellow Horse Brave Heart conducted extensive research on Jewish Holocaust survivors and their families. She also conducted research on Japanese-American internment camp survivors and survivors of the bombing on Hiroshima, Japan. She examined research on psychoanalytic approaches to grief, the history of federal government policies on Native Americans, current Native American social systems, and research on Native American health disparities.

There are many individuals in powerful and policymaking positions who still do not accept the reality of intergenerational trauma and historical grief in spite of the fact that scientific studies have established the reality of intergenerational trauma and the cycles that are passed down. There is even an environmentally induced phenomenon now known as epigenetics, the ability to directly regulate how DNA functions (Skinner, 2015). Skinner's research shows that epigenetics have a major impact on trauma being passed down to generations, and that DNA can be altered by environmental factors. Skinner identifies this as epigenetic transgenerational inheritance, or an epigenetic footprint that remains.

As a result of these continued traumatic experiences, the symptoms associated with intergenerational trauma have become pervasive in Native American communities, resulting in higher rates of alcoholism, depression, domestic violence, sexual abuse, and even suicide. There has been a tearing apart of families because they no longer have the same set of values and teachings (Yellow Horse Brave Heart, 1998).

However, tribal nations are strong. They are in the process of healing. The literature on the identification and definition of intergenerational trauma and historical grief (Yellow Horse Brave Heart, 1998) established a pathway to recovery from the "de-tribalization" that has been inflicted on Native people and they have begun the journey to retribalization (Speck & Attneave, 1973) and healing.

CULTURAL RESILIENCIES AND RETRIBALIZATION

Culture as Resiliency

Throughout history and continuing through today, assaults on Native American culture and identity have been launched on every level. In fact, it would be safe to say that the challenges that Native communities are experiencing today are the result of the assaults to generations that came before. Despite the efforts to eradicate the culture and the people, Native nations have survived, gaining in strength and increasing in resistance to continued assaults on the culture. Throughout the United States, many tribes are already implementing prevention, treatment, and recovery efforts that are built on traditional practices. In fact, research supports that one's participation in cultural practices and traditional healings in Native communities are a powerful resource to relieve distress (Hartmann & Gone, 2012). First and foremost, in order to retribalize for healing, efforts should be firmly grounded in culture. The challenge is that there are currently 566 federally recognized tribal nations and approximately 60 state-recognized tribes. Cultures, histories, political systems, and resources vary across those communities. Prevention or intervention efforts that work in one community may not be effective in another community. There is not a "one size fits all" to address the social injustices that history has given to Native people.

Retribalization

The need to break the long-standing cycle of social ills affecting Native nations is of highest priority. Intergenerational trauma theory suggests that the ability to heal comes through acknowledging the traumatic events that have occurred, seeking restorative justice and exercising forgiveness. It is equally important to engage in cultural strategies aimed at intergenerational resistance, resilience, and recovery. Given the *detribalization* that has been inflicted on Native people, it is also essential to acknowledge the healing powers of resiliency that comes from retribalization. The concept of retribalization was published by Speck and Attneave (1973). It involves the building of a strong social network that includes the nuclear family, and all of the relatives of those family members, as well as friends, neighbors, work associates, and significant helpers from churches, schools, social agencies, and institutions willing to be involved. The premise behind retribalization is that the social network serves as the point of intervention (Speck & Attneave, 1973). In other words, it takes a community to heal.

COMMUNITY READINESS, WELLBRIETY: HEALING SOCIAL INJUSTICE

The Community Readiness Model was developed in 1994 at Colorado State University (Plested, Jumper-Thurman, P. & Edwards, R.W., 2015, 2015; Jumper-Thurman, Edwards, R.W., Plested, B.A., & Oetting, E.R., 2003; Oetting, E.R. Jumper-Thurman, P, Plested, B.A., & Edwards, R.W, 2001; Jumper-Thurman, P., 2000; Jumper-Thurman, P. & Plested, B.A., 2000; Edwards, R.W., Jumper-Thurman, P., Plested, B.A., Oetting, E.R., & Swanson, L. 2000; Donnermeyer, J. F., Oetting, E. R., Plested, B. A., Edwards, R. W., Jumper-Thurman, P. & Littlethunder, L., 1997; Oetting, E. R., Donnermeyer, J. F., Plested, B. A., Edwards, R. W., Kelly, K., & Beauvais, F., 1995). The Community Readiness Model is both issue specific and culture specific, and aimed at building the capacity of communities/tribal nations so that they might recognize and build on the strengths from within to begin a healing process of healthy change from the social injustices created by colonization (Plested et al., 2015). The model mobilizes and rebuilds the sense of community, *retribalizing*, in an effort to strengthen the recovery from the harmful effects of removals and relocations, the boarding school experience, and all of things that comprise the intergenerational trauma and historical grief that is still felt today.

COMMUNITY READINESS AND WELLBRIETY

Another well recognized model for community healing comes from the Wellbriety Movement, White Bison (Coyhis, 2002). Wellbriety means to go beyond recovery from alcoholism and substance use, to live a life that is balanced mentally, emotionally, physically, and spiritually. Don Coyhis, the founder of the Wellbriety Movement, discusses the importance of recovery from the effects of colonization in his teachings about the Healing Forest and the Four Laws of Change (Coyhis, 2002). Community Readiness is also a well-established model of change, developed around the same time as Wellbriety. The two models are consistent in their philosophies of healing a community. Coyhis speaks of the Four Laws of Change as follows: the first law is that *change is from within* (Coyhis, 2002)—the philosophy underlying Community Readiness is that if a community is to bring about healthy change, then that change must come from within the community; the second law is that *in order for development to occur, it must be preceded by a vision*—Community Readiness teaches that programs have a beginning and an end, usually set by funding streams, but a vision inspires, motivates, and sustains a community; the third law says, *a great learning must occur*—Community Readiness maintains that one must learn the perceptions of the community and be guided in the development of strategies by the knowledge gained from those perceptions; and the fourth law says, *you must create a healing forest*—in which Coyhis discusses a concept consistent with retribalization (Speck & Attneave, 1973). Community Readiness maintains that the building of strategies specific to the issue, the readiness, and the culture of a community is necessary for change to occur and sustain. The philosophies are consistent in their teachings and they align well with the concept of retribalization.

THE COMMUNITY READINESS MODEL

The concept of community readiness evolved in the early 1990s from studies conducted at Colorado State University that explored the development of effective drug abuse prevention programs for youth in rural Mexican-American and American Indian communities. The model is based on two research theories: psychological readiness for treatment (Prochaska, DiClemente, & Norcross, 1992) and community development theory (Warren, 1978). Although the Community Readiness Model was initially developed specifically for alcohol and drug abuse prevention, it was also created with a broader aim of assessing readiness for a gamut of issues ranging from health and nutrition issues (sexually transmitted diseases, heart disease, diet, etc.), to environmental issues (water and air quality, litter and recycling, etc.), to social issues (poverty and homelessness, drug abuse, and violence), to personal problems (depression, suicide, etc.), and over the past two decades it has been applied to many different social issues and health issues.

Why use Community Readiness in the context of social injustice? There are several reasons. First, there is great variance across tribal nations in resources, locations (rural, urban, reservation, pueblo, rancherias, and reserves) histories, and political and health systems. Therefore, an intervention that is effective in one community may not be culturally consistent or appropriate for another community. Second, although addiction might be a priority in one community, violence or child abuse may the priority in another community. Third, readiness for action varies across communities as well: one group may be rich with volunteers, community involvement, and energy, while another group may be struggling for input and visibility or even afflicted with apathy. The Community Readiness Model takes all of these factors into consideration and assesses readiness levels based on community perceptions of the issue.

Because of these variances, building the capacity of a community to address the social and health issues that have evolved from the many social injustices inflicted on Indigenous population is not an easy process. If prevention or intervention efforts are to be sustained, they must be practical and utilize the resources that already exist in a community.

Another challenge is that, when efforts are launched, all too often they meet with failure after a relatively short period of time. The general belief is that this is so because the program was poorly planned or not strong enough to change the status quo of the community. Maybe the feeling was that people were not sufficiently trained, or they just got bored waiting for results and moved on. Perhaps it has appeared that the community just was not interested. Frustration rises. If those efforts worked well in the neighboring community, why didn't they work here?

Communities are fluid—always changing, adapting, and growing; *they are ready for different things at wholly different times*. Readiness is a key factor to consider. The Community Readiness Model is a nine-stage, multidimensional model that facilitates community-based change and prepares the group for better integration of an intervention. It is designed to build capacity, investment, and cooperation, that is, establish connections, among systems and individuals, retribalizing the healing system in a process that is grounded on the local culture. Its greatest strength is that it builds a culturally responsive model of intervention consistent with the readiness of the community, alleviating the burden of wasted resources.

The Community Readiness Model is unique in that it assesses and measures *the community's perception* of a social issue. To effectively intervene in a community, the perceptions of those who live in that community are the best point of intervention. The Community Readiness Model utilized a semi-structured interview format gathered from key respondents (community members and providers). It does not utilize a sample, but rather an ethnographic style that requires fewer interviews to establish a point of repetition in the information provided, making it an easy and inexpensive process for a community to launch. The interviews are then scored on a research-tested anchored rating scale. A stage score is calculated for each of six basic dimensions that identify the factors related to the level of readiness. One gets both qualitative and quantitative information from which to build a strategic action plan. General prevention/intervention strategies have been developed and tested to coincide with each stage so that the user knows exactly what level of intensity to apply to increase readiness on each dimension.

The six dimensions are as follows: (1) *What efforts currently exist* (i.e., current policies, programs, data collection, and research.); (2) *Community knowledge of efforts* (i.e., awareness of what is occurring in all segments of the community); (3) *Leadership* (i.e., involvement and support of leaders, both formal and informal, and active leadership in programs); (4) *Community climate* (i.e., community energy, ability to address social problems, etc.); (5) *Knowledge of the issue* (i.e., extent of knowledge about the problem and why it needs to be addressed); and (6) *Resources* (i.e., availability of people, time, money, space, etc., to address the issue).

The model identifies nine stages of community readiness within these six dimensions. The stages are as follows: (1) *No awareness*—the issue is not viewed as a problem that should be addressed; (2) *Denial/resistance*—the issue needs attention, but "it's not our problem," or "we can't (or don't want to) do anything about it"; (3) *Vague awareness*—the issue is a concern that needs attention, but there is little motivation for effort; there is, however, interest among some for a team to be formed; (4) *Preplanning*—identifiable leaders feel that change is needed and the community climate would support efforts, though focus may still be lacking; (5) *Preparation*—practical decisions are being made, training programs developed, and people recruited to serve different functions; (6) *Initiation*—enough information is available to justify action, and action is underway; (7) *Stabilization*—programs are running perceived as stable, ongoing, and necessary; (8) *Confirmation/maintenance*—community support is constantly tracked and enhanced where needed; and (9) *Community ownership*—prevention or intervention activities continue at a high level with a high degree of community support.

The Community Readiness Model has been used successfully in several thousand communities, many of which were tribal communities, nationally and internationally to bring about healthy change. Many have shared their successes in articles, book chapters, videos, and news articles. It has been well established that community healing efforts that are based in both the readiness stage appropriate to the perceptions of the community members *and* the local cultural traditions and resources meet with less resistance for healthy change. By knowing the perceptions of community members and then aligning the intervention to that readiness level, the community is far more likely to engage in and invest in making healthy changes. Sustainability of the efforts is increased because the prevention and intervention efforts utilize local resources (volunteer effort, environmental resources, language, culture, etc.) and basic human spirit to guide the successful implementation of the work plan. Daniel Quinn (1996) said it best: "If the world is to be saved, it will be saved by people with changed minds, people with a new vision – yet if the time isn't right for a new idea, it will fail. If however, the time is right, an idea can sweep the world like wildfire. The measures of change are not ease or difficulty, but readiness or unreadiness."

SUMMARY

Although the story of intergenerational trauma is incomplete, it is important to acknowledge the elements of survival, strength, and resiliency of Native nations. Intergenerational trauma and historical grief have taken a great toll on the Indigenous people of North America; however, like other groups—the survivors of the holocaust, the internment of the Japanese prisoners, and the attempted genocide of the Maori people—Native people also have an innate capacity for healing. Although tribal communities were torn apart or *detribalized*, many now continue to *retribalize* for healing and many use Community Readiness to facilitate that healing. Some combine readiness with the Wellbriety Movement, the Healing Forest. The authors of this chapter believe that a community approach for retribalizing the healing process is essential to address the social ills that have resulted from colonization. The Community Readiness Model is a strength-based model and is well grounded on the culture and resiliency that exists in each community to more successfully implement prevention and intervention efforts. Through the strength of community and culture, we know who we are, as Indigenous people. Though we may have challenges with historical trauma, we also have great strength in the knowledge that we can find healing through historical wisdom.

REFERENCES

Bailey, Lynn R. (1970). *Bosque Redondo: An American Concentration Camp*. Pasadena, CA: Socio-Technical Books.

Coyhis, D. (2002). *The Red Road to Wellbriety*. Colorado Springs: White Bison, Inc.

Donnermeyer, J. F., Oetting, E. R., Plested, B. A., Edwards, R. W., Jumper-Thurman, P., & Littlethunder, L. (1997). Community readiness and prevention programs. *Journal of Community Development, 28*(1), 65–83.

Duran, E., & Duran, B. (1995). *Native American postcolonial psychology.* Albany, NY: State University of New York Press.

Edwards, R. W., Jumper-Thurman. P., Plested, B. A., Oetting, E. R., & Swanson, L. (2000). Community readiness: Research to practice. *Journal of Community Psychology, 28*(3), 291–307.

Ehle, J. (2008). *Trail of tears, the rise and fall of the Cherokee Nation.* New York: Knopf Doubleday Publishing Group.

Hartmann, W., & Gone, J. (2012). Incorporating traditional healing into an urban American Indian health organization: A case study of community member perspectives. *Journal of Counseling Psychology, 59*(4), 542–554.

Jumper-Thurman, P. (2000). In D. Bigfoot (Ed.), *Community readiness: A promising model for community healing. (Native American topic specific monograph series).* The University of Oklahoma Health Sciences Center, U.S. Department of Justice.

Jumper-Thurman, P., Plested, B. A., Edwards, R. W., Helm, H. M., & Oetting, E. R. (2001). Using the community readiness model in Native communities. Health Promotion and Substance Abuse Prevention Among American Indian and Alaska Native Communities: Issues in Cultural Competence, Center for Substance Abuse Prevention, *Substance Abuse and Mental Health Services Administration, 9*, 129–158.

Jumper-Thurman, P., Edwards, R. W., Plested, B. A., & Oetting, E. R. (2003). Honoring the differences: Using community readiness to create culturally valid community interventions. In G. Bernal, J. Trimble, K. Burlew, & F. Leong (Eds.), *Handbook of racial & ethnic minority psychology* (pp. 591–607). Thousand Oaks, CA: Sage Publications.

Library of Congress. (1830). Indian Removal Act. Retrieved 6/26/17 from https://www.loc.gov/rr/program/bib/ourdocs/Indian.html.

Nies, J. (1996). *Native American history: A chronology of a culture's vast achievements and their links to world events.* New York: Random House Publishing.

Oetting, E. R., Donnermeyer, J. F., Plested, B. A., Edwards, R. W., Kelly, K., & Beauvais, F. (1995). Assessing community readiness for prevention. *The International Journal of the Addictions, 30*(6), 659–683.

Oetting, E. R., Jumper-Thurman, P., Plested, B., & Edwards, R. W. (2001). Community readiness and health services. *Substance Use and Misuse, 36*(6&7), 825–843.

Plested, B. A., Jumper-Thurman, P., & Edwards, R. W. (2015). *Community readiness manual: Creating a healthy forest for Community Readiness.* Ft. Collins, CO: White Bison Publishing Company in collaboration with National Center for Community Readiness, Colorado State University.

Pratt, R. H. (1800–1900). *"The Advantages of Mingling Indians with Whites," Americanizing the American Indians: Writings by the "Friends of the Indian" 1880–1900* (pp. 260–271). Cambridge, MA: Harvard University Press, 1973.

Prochaska, J. O., DiClemente, C. C., & Norcross, J. C. (1992). In search of how people change: Applications to the addictive behaviors. *American Psychologist, 47*, 1102–1114.

Public Broadcasting Service. "Indian Boarding Schools." Retrieved from http://www.pbs.org/indiancountry/history/boarding2.html; Internet; July 12, 2017.

Quinn, D. (1996). *The story of B*. New York: Bantam Books.

Riley, N. S. (2016, July 20, 2016). One way to help Native Americans: Property rights. *The Atlantic*. Retrieved from https://www.theatlantic.com/politics/archive/2016/07/native-americans-property-rights/492941/.

Sainte Marie, B. (1964). *Now that the buffalo's gone. On its my way (vinyl)*. New York: Vanguard Records.

Skinner, M. (2015). Ancestral ghosts in your genome: Epigenetic transgenerational inheritance. *Soul Wounds: Trauma and Healing Across Generations Conference*. Stanford University.

Speck, R., & Attneave, C. (1973). *Family networks: Retribalization and healing*. New York: Random House.

Stout, M. A. (2012). *Native American boarding schools*. Santa Barbara: Greenwood.

Thornton, R. (1987). *American Indian holocaust and survival: A population history since 1492*. Norman: University of Oklahoma Press.

U.S. Census Bureau. (2011). *Profile America facts for features, American Indian and Alaska Native Heritage Month: November, 2011*. Retrieved from https://www.census.gov/newsroom/releases/archives/facts_for_features_special_editions.

Vernon, I., & Jumper-Thurman, P. (2005). The changing face of HIV/AIDS among Native populations. *Journal of Psychoactive Drugs, 37*(3), 247–255.

Warren, R. (1978). *The community in America* (3rd ed.). Chicago: Rand-McNally.

Wickstrom, C. (2017, March 10, 2017). Native nations rise brings DAPL protest to Washington. *The Washington Post*. Retrieved from http://www.aljazeera.com/news/2017/03/standing-rock-tribe-takes-dapl-protest-washington-170310032032028.html.

Yellow Horse Brave Heart, M. (1998). The return to the sacred path: Healing the historical trauma and historical unresolved grief response among the Lakota. *Smith College Studies in Social Work, 68*(3), 287–305.

Chapter 9

The Issues of Identity, Self-Awareness, and Social Justice

Fred C. Miller

IDENTITY AND SELF-AWARENESS

I am an instructor at a community college in the Pacific Northwest. This community college provides a variety of postsecondary educational courses for a variety of different student needs. The institution I work at offers Associates of Arts degrees to students who wish to transfer to four-year colleges and universities, as well as two-year terminal career programs in vocational-technical and mid-level professional fields.

I have taught at the community college level for over 30 years. I try to help students better understand how psychological theories can apply to their personal and professional environments. I try to convey to my students the richness in the history of psychology and its value in applying its theories to everyday life. I consider teaching an honor, an opportunity to help shape students to better appreciate themselves using the science of behavior as their tool. I am also very aware that I may be their first African American instructor. I know that as they listen to my words, they may be validating many of the stereotypes they were exposed to during their past. I also am aware that my desires, beliefs and goals often are not the goals of my students. I wanted to retire as an instructor and I understood that I would be required to meet certain criteria to become successful. Success was getting a tenure assignment.

Unlike academic colleagues at major universities, promotion at my community college is not based on the "publish or perish" criteria often emphasized in graduate schools. There is no requirement and little encouragement to publish any peer-reviewed articles. There is a minimum two-year, and maximum four-year, probationary period for freshman instructors to pursue. This process involves having lectures observed by full-time instructors, written self-assessments, and discussions with the instructor's department chair and school administrators. This requires the academician to develop interpersonal skills not only with students but also with staff and administrators. Those instructors who satisfy their probationary periods are granted continuous appointment. Continuous appointment is equivalent to a tenure appointment. When one reaches level, there is a sense of accomplishment, job satisfaction, and a sense of competence. How does this academic accomplishment shape the instructor's identity?

In this article, I will explore various aspects of academia that have specifically shaped my identity formation. My academic discipline is psychology.

How did my identity develop for me? The formation of identity is an ongoing process (Simone, 2001). Both of my parents were raised in the state of Mississippi. My paternal relatives worked in the city, while my maternal relatives were farmers. I inherited a strong work and religious ethic from both. My father served as a medic in the army. I was born at an army base in San Francisco, and, six months later, I was put on an army transport ship with my mother and older sister and shipped to France, where my father was stationed. During this time, a French babysitter cared for me. As was the custom in France, I was introduced to the customs of French society, one of which included wine at every meal. I spoke French before English, and we lived in Europe for three years. At the age of three years—when most American children are learning English—I was learning both French and English. After the age of three years, I spoke more French than English.

One significant life-altering event that I experienced around the age of two was a traumatic accident while living in France. When my babysitter was carrying me across a street, she tripped over a curb and fell. I suffered a broken collarbone. This fall resulted in my left shoulder being significantly higher than my right. In addition to this physical abnormality, I was beginning the task of learning language. I learned both French and English. The problem was that I spoke primarily French blended with English. Since I was in France with my family and a caregiver, this was acceptable. However, when I returned to the United States at about four years of age, my world began to change.

My family returned from France to a small town in DeKalb, Mississippi, where my mother had been raised. My father was from Kosciusko, Mississippi. My family spent most of our time in Dekalb. This was during the time of racial segregation. I remember the segregated water fountains. I was told which stores in town to frequent and which to avoid. I began to understand and cope with racism and an awareness of being an African American male.

During this period, a more subtle awareness of racism began to emerge. This was the feeling of overt and subtle indications of behaviors designed to show the prevalence of superiority and inferiority. This subtle pattern of creating an inferiority complex has manifested itself throughout the history of an African person in the United States (Frazier, 1968, p. 239).

I began to understand and become self-aware of my strengths and weaknesses as an African American in Mississippi. I had early experiences of watching my grandparents completing the family chores regardless of the weather conditions. I remember trying to learn the technique of milking a cow and the need to avoid flies and the strong noxious stench unique only in the barn.

I also became aware of my family name and how important family was in this area of the city. My maternal family practiced a type of collective culture. Each family member—aunts, uncles, cousins, and fictive kin—worked and contributed to the survival of the family. Kin and extended family members always attended holidays and special occasions.

Most of my maternal relatives were farmers who planted corn and cotton. This family clan was concentrated in a small valley in the city in Mississippi. My relatives were a religious, hard-working group of people. Each family member worked as an extension of the larger group. External events such as clothes and makeup were not a major emphasis then. I learned that what you accomplish is more important than what you can purchase. External beauty is fragile and transient, while internal vales tend to be permanent

Living in a closed environment taught me to accept the physical challenges. These differences did not define me as a person. I remembere an old African proverb, "To stumble is not to fall but to move faster ahead." This belief that I was part of an indescribable, proud family provided the foundational strength to help guide me through many trying times as a child.

Most relatives thought I was mentally challenged since I spoke another language (French) and appeared physically disfigured. While my relatives was puzzled over the use of my spoken language of "blended French and English," my mother steadfastly stood by me with love and support while I struggled to learn English and adapted to a physically deformed image. I realized that my physical body was different in many aspects from my close relatives; however, I learned that I was loved even with these physical differences. I learned that our differences are what make us unique and genuine. I now see that differences should be viewed as an adaptation of who we are, not as deficiencies. With increased age, as my shoulder physical disfigurement subsided while my command of English language improved, I remained vigilant to better understand those outliers in our society who suffer from language or physical challenges.

I also realized based on my experiences in Mississippi that I was an American and an African American, two paths of stereotyped life. I began to understand and realized my need to accept and understand both paths in life. W.E.B. Dubois called this self-awareness "double consciousness" (Dubois, 1994, p. 5). I worked to understand the dominant culture's expectations. I learned later that for some a sense of self was based on the need to devalue others. Quality of life has been based on the devaluation of African American men and the simultaneous elevation of people of European-American descent (Pierre, Mahalik & Woodland, 2001). While Mississippi was at that time a prejudiced state, I began to learn that what you perceive in life is not what you have to believe. I experienced hate in one part of the city but togetherness and love in the enclave of our family. Later I began to understand that while blatant discrimination had been replaced with a more subtle form, it resulted in a direct impact on mental and physical health (Pascoe & Richman, 2009).

When I was in kindergarten, my father, an army soldier, was transferred to Presidio Army Base in San Francisco, California. My mother attended a community college in San Francisco and competed course work to work as a licensed practical nurse. Shortly after her graduation, the family moved to Berkeley, California, home of the University of California.

When I was an adolescent, I began to notice ads touting the magical association of sex appeal with the use of a certain toothpaste, wearing a certain pair of eyeglasses, or using a specific deodorant. During my formative years, I remember a commercial phrase—"Brylcreem—A little dab'll do ya and you will look debonair!" This commercial depicted a white male putting this mixture in his hair, and then combing it, resulting in his hair straightening. I clearly remember wanting to buy this product hoping for this magical transformation to occur. I quickly realized that this product was for the American sans African Americans.

I learned that our society now tends to place an emphasis on body perfection, which is impossible to fulfill. Society tends to emphasize physical beauty at a level that is unattainable (Kimmel, 2011). Many television commercials tend to imply that purchase of a certain product will improve this manufactured imperfection. I believe that these-self implied imperfections are what drive many marketing campaigns

I realized that wearing certain fashions, speaking the appropriate and correct dialect and being cautious about who I was with was a recipe for survival. I also understood that this contributed to a psychological strain that is common among African American men.

During the 1960s, Berkeley was an exciting time. This was a transiting time for young Blacks. This was a time of the "Black is Beautiful" movement. This was an exciting time since many psychological theories were discussed in class. One popular approach in Berkeley was Maslow's concept of self-actualization, which I viewed as "Be all you can be."

On many street corners in Berkeley, you would see Black Muslims state, "Do for self" as they sold their newspapers and bean pies. This self-awareness and confidence has been instilled in both my sister and me throughout our formative years. For some, this self-help stance forms a basic foundation for motivation when one enters another culture (D'Souza & Gurin, 2016). When students enter the academic world, they are entering into another culture with all of its expectations and behavior.

While I enjoyed Berkeley, I took a chance and transferred to Pacific University. I was thrust into a small college community in Forest Grove Oregon. This amounted to a culture shock. Unlike the city of Berkeley, the community was majority Caucasian and in a rural area. Berkeley is located in a large metropolitan area. Berkeley was a fast-paced community where various social activities were the norm. Forest Grove was complete with few traffic stops and little to no activities. It was difficult to adjust my first year. After a futile attempt to study Optometry, I settled down and majored in psychology. I liked psychology and began my trek to become a psychologist. I graduated with a Bachelor of Science degree in psychology.

I was able to obtain a position as an instructor at a community college after I graduated from Portland State with a master's degree in counseling. As a teacher, I gradually began to understand how self-awareness is a significant component in the role of both personal and professional development. As these significant events shape and mold one's thoughts, over time, I developed a sense of identity—a self-picture of who I am. I continued my education while teaching, earning another master's in psychology and a PhD in clinical psychology in 2016.

Students in a community college class often represent a wide diverge spectrum of society. Many students (some of whom already have undergraduate degrees) attend community college in order to develop skills that will enable them to become successful in their employment (Krupnick, 2015) or to further their academic endeavors.

Kiely (1999) stated that simply providing current or past information in psychology presents only part of the challenge in the pedagogy of psychology. How the instructor delivers this knowledge is often more important than the content of the information. I strive to convey to students an element of excitement, richness, passion, and curiosity as well. At times I feel as if I am more of a performer conveying information to students while employing a variety of methods. I have developed a gage based on how students respond to my presentations. Their behaviors vary from a low when they look at the clock to providing stimulating discussions on the current topic. Over the years these past experiences have helped me better understand my craft and how I present these topics to students. It has also shaped my sense of self.

This sense of self identity is a lifelong process of assimilating and rejecting one's experiences (Rice, 1992, p. 437). These significant events include learning ordeals inside as well as outside the classroom. Additional required commitments such as various committee meetings, administration reports, and personal issues can dampen the enthusiasm one carries into the classroom. One burden I am always aware of is my recognition as an African American male. I quickly recognized that I may be the only African American the students may have while they attend college; therefore, the student may be more likely to maintain their racial stereotypes at the time for faculty evaluation. Often a student's first impression tends to predict how the student evaluates the instructor at the end of the term (Babad, Avni-Babad, & Rosenthal, 2004; Buchert, Laws, Apperson, & Bregman, 2008). I realize that I often have one term to change the students' stereotyped views concerning their instructor stereotype. I strive to be an instructor who is African American versus the stereotyped African American instructor. This sense of identity is important to me. I realize during my tenure as an instructor, I had to work with many supervisors who harbored many biases and prejudices.

I believe that success at the community college level is based on strong pedagogical and communication skills. Instructors who are granted continuous appointment are required to receive an assessment review every five years. How does this influence one's identity? Identity is developed in part by one's sense of views about oneself and self-awareness.

I now realize that as an instructor at an academic institution, I am still exposed to many of the cultural ills of our society. I should assume that a significant percentage of my students will represent our society. The dynamics of a classroom represents a miniature society. These students, mostly European-American, may be facing an African American instructor for the first time in their academic careers. That challenge also gives us all opportunities for further self-reflection.

I also assume that many of my students might have histories of incarceration. The United States has a dubious distinction of having the highest incarceration rate in the world (Alexander, 2010, p. 6). The plight of those incarcerated represents a moral and societal crisis for those of color. The prison population in the United States consists of a higher proportion of people of color as compared to European-Americans (Hartney & Vuong, 2009). As a community college instructor, I realize that the role of education should result in reduced recidivism due to increase opportunities in employment and societal reintegration (Davis, Bozick, Steele, Saunders, & Miles, 2013).

I also realize that some students in class have obtained college degrees and are attending class in order to prepare for an advanced degree. I have had physicians, nurses, and attorneys in my classes.

Through the years of teaching I reflected on DuBois (1994) concept of double consciousness. Am I an African American psychology teacher, or am I a teacher of psychology who happens to be African American? How do I relate to students in a classroom in which both types of consciousness exist?

I have reconciled this ongoing issue with the realization that I now accept both types of consciousness not as an either-or situation, but as one consciousness adapting to another consciousness. I realize that my identity is both, and I choose the preferred one based on the situation in the classroom and life. My identity is based not on a feeling of inferiority or superiority, but on using the best communication method to communicate my needs. Self-awareness and an understanding of the situation are necessary components to help me as I navigate the life as an African American man.

IMPLICATIONS FOR SOCIAL JUSTICE

The act of teaching in a community college is in itself a social justice initiative. One of the missions of community colleges is to "serve all segments of society through an open-access admissions policy that offers equal and fair treatment to all students" (American Association of Community Colleges, n.d.). In an article entitled "Modeling Social Justice Through the Community College," DeBard and Rice state that the community college offers educational options to "historically disenfranchised sections of society" (DeBard & Rice, 2009, p. 118). They add that the community college "that has evolved in the US represents a model of social justice that can be utilized by postsecondary systems of emerging third world countries to improve their social and economic well-being" (DeBard & Rice, 2009, p. 117).

Many years ago, I worked with several other colleagues across the state to bring an international speaker on intergenerational trauma to my community college. Contrary to the high cost for most continuing education workshops for psychologists, the community college held the eight-hour workshop for free. This enabled many helping professionals to attend the workshop, who otherwise would have been unable to do so due to the usually high cost of psychology workshops. Although the state psychological association predicted that few would attend the workshop because it focused on intergenerational trauma for ethnic and cultural minorities, we had to close the workshop when more than 350 enrolled. Because of its size, the workshop was held in two auditoriums. The program evaluations indicated that the workshop enabled many of the participants to understand intergenerational trauma in new ways, with new perspectives. Because some participants traveled across the country to attend the workshop and were on very limited budgets, the community college even provided free parking, for which many participations expressed appreciation. Although we were surprised to learn that the mission of that state psychological association was not to provide community service, the association did offer us its mailing list. Thus, we were able to reach a large audience of psychologists across the state. In addition, several special interest groups advertised the workshop, resulting in participants enrolling who were not only psychologists, but also substance abuse specialists, social workers, psychiatrists, cultural experts, teachers, professors, community leaders, government officials, and administrators. The audience was extremely diverse, more so than was customary for that state's psychology continuing education workshops.

As I work toward social justice initiatives in my own teaching, the self-awareness concepts that I have discussed have factored into my interactions with my students, department heads, and administrators. I continue to apply the things I have learned about myself and society in order help each student reach her or his maximal potential through not only an increased sense of self-awareness but also an understanding of how to thrive despite the stereotypes that are imposed on us all, regardless of our culture, ethnicity, age, geographical areas in which we have lived, gender identity, sexual orientation, race, physical health, psychological status, and socioeconomic status.

During my lectures, I want students to appreciate and learn how various psychological and social justice principles help them in their identity development. This has resulted in many social justice challenges, but I meet them head on, as opportunities not only for my own identity growth, but also for the growth for the community college and its students.

REFERENCES

Alexander, M. (2012). *The new Jim Crow.* New York: The New Press.

American Association of Community Colleges. (n.d.). Community College Mission. Website: aacc.nche.edu.

Babad, E., Avni-Babad, D., & Rosenthal, R. (2004). Prediction of students evaluation from brief instances of professors nonverbal behavior in defined instructional situations. *Social Psychology of Education,* 7, 3–33.

Buchert, S., Laws, E. L., Apperson, J. M., & Bregman, N. J. (2008). First impressions and professor reputations: Influence on student evaluations of instruction. *Social Psychology of Education,* (11), 397–408.

D'Souza, J., & Gurin, M. (2016). The universal significance of Maslow's concept of self- actualization. *The Humanistic Psychologist,* 44(2), 210–214.

Davis, L. M., Bozick, R., Steele, J. L., Saunders, J., & Miles, J. N. V. (2013). *Evaluating the effectiveness of correctional education: A meta-analysis of programs that provide education to incarcerated adults.* Santa Monica, CA: Rand Corporation.

DeBard, R., & Rice, T. (2009). Modeling social justice through the community college. *Community College Models,* 117–134. doi:10.1007/978-1-4020-9477-4_8.

DuBois, W. E. B. (1994). *The souls of black folk.* New York: Gramercy Books.

Frazier, F. E. (1968). E. Franklin Frazier . . . on Race Relations. *The Heritage of Sociology.* The University of Chicago Press.

Hartney, C., &Vuong, L. (2009). *Created equal . . . Racial and ethnic disparities in the U.S. Criminal Justice System.* National Council on Crime and Delinquency.

Kimmel, M. S. (2011). *The gendered society* (5th ed.). New York, NY: Oxford University Press.

Kiely, M. C. (1999). ZA piece of good news: Teaching as a creative process. *Canadian Psychology*, 40(1), 30–38.

Krupnick, M. (2015, October 28). Graduates of four-year universities flock to community colleges for job skills. *Hechinger Report*. Teachers College, Columbia University. Retrieved 29 October 2015.

Pascoe, E. A., & Richman, L. S. (2009). Perceived discrimination and health: A meta-analytic review. *Psychological Bulletin*, 135(4), 531–554.

Pierre, M. R., Mahalik, J. R., & Woodland, M. H. (2001). The effects of racism, African self-consciousness and psychological functioning on Black masculinity: A historical and social adaptation framework. *Journal of African American Men*, 6(2), 19–39.

Rice, F. P. (1992). *Human development* (3rd ed.). New Jersey: Prentice Hall.

Simone, D. M. (2001). Identity of the university professor is formulated overtime requiring self-discovery followed by being an intellectual scholar and teacher. *Education*, 122(2), 283–295.

Chapter 10

Decolonizing Knowledge Creation

Moving Toward the Sacred and the Liminal

Mathew A. Poteet and Bonita M. Veysey

EDITOR'S INTRODUCTION (SOG)

In *Radical Psychology*, we have selected authors who reflect very diverse views about culture, the etiology and treatment of mental health issues, approaches to research, and the sources of knowledge. In some ways, this chapter diverges from the styles of Euro-American writing that are typically associated with literature reviews, case studies, empirical reports, theoretical approaches, or methodological reviews. Because it illustrates many worldview differences between Euro-American and Indigenous paradigms, the chapter may be challenging for Euro-Americans who are less familiar with Indigenous communications styles. At the same time, readers from other cultures may find that it resonates much more than do some of the other chapters in *Radical Psychology*.

The first author, Mathew A. Poteet, holds many traditional Indigenous worldviews while working in a contemporary educational setting. His expertise is in oral communication, political and social activism, and community building. The second author, Bonita M. Veysey, is a seasoned researcher who has conducted major national research studies that have been funded in, and supported by, Euro-American institutions and agencies.

Their chapter, written in the form of a formal discussion/interview, explores the contrasts between the two authors, their writing styles, the ways in which they learn about life, and their approaches to topics associated with historical and contemporary colonization. It reflects the editors' wish to "walk the talk" about honoring the diversity associated with other cultural worldviews and communications styles. We hope the readers will appreciate, respect, and consider with an open mind the authors' direct challenges to prevailing Euro-American research, educational, and clinical practices. The topics that the first author discusses are often mentioned only in private settings in which there are no members of the dominant culture present. This chapter opens the eyes of its readers about the passion, frustration, and insights a nonpsychologist has about the practice of psychology. Since this author writes bluntly and sometimes harshly, his comments give readers an opportunity to examine their own discomfort (e.g., aspects of White fragility; see DiAngelo, 2011). His "thick descriptions" of incidents in his life (Geertz, 1973) give insights about his harmful, direct experiences with Eurocentric counseling.

Complemented by the professional insights of the second author, herself a researcher who has also experienced similar frustrations about the inequalities imbedded in our formal systems that limit the creation and application of knowledge to benefit the privileged, the reader is exposed to both the insights of a psychologist and the insights of an outsider—both of whom are articulating not just their own views, but the views of many individuals both inside and outside of the profession of psychology. Since there are more than 302 million Indigenous peoples in the world (Hall, 2012), their discussions have cross-cultural relevance across the globe.

***

Es hört doch jeder nur, was er versteht.

– Johann Wolfgang von Goethe

"Everyone hears only what they understand" (Goethe, 1998). In this brief observation, the nineteenth-century German poet and statesman encapsulates the greatest perennial challenge facing research and the creation of knowledge more broadly. If we do not have a personal or professional frame for it, information will not be integrated into one's knowledge base. Thus, one might argue by extension that we seek to understand only that which we already know and can at least imagine. Our research is condemned to iterate and reiterate what we have the *capacity* to know within the frame of traditional positivist science. But there are other ways of knowing and understanding, and there are ways to challenge science to engage in the borderland spaces, the liminal, bypassing the limitations of what we think is possible.

Using the example of psychology, this chapter will grapple with the issue of knowledge that is created by a select few often by placing the burden of research on those who might best be described as "other," the purposes of systematic knowledge creation (i.e., research) and who benefits; how the exclusion of groups and perspectives results in limited knowledge and harm to members of those groups reproducing colonial injury; and how the inclusion of perspectives requires major overhauls in the ways in which knowledge is created or remembered and how that knowledge serves a broad and diverse people. We include a section discussing how to co-create scholarship that is driven by, imbedded in, and honors the communities of people who are the focus of the scholarship.

We should also state that this chapter diverges from the common presentation of Western/European scholarship, choosing instead to engage in a conversation about knowledge production and knowledge reclamation and remembrance.

WHAT BRINGS US TO THIS WORK

We come from different places, times and experiences. Because we believe that there is no such thing as true objectivity, it is important to know a little bit about us.

Mathew A. Poteet (MAP): I was about 10 years old when I realized things were not what they seemed. I don't have many memories of my childhood, and the ones I have are fuzzy, but I remember markers, the things that stood out, throughout my life.

My dad was in and out of my life from a week after I was born until I was four years old. He was in and out of jail from the age of 16, until I killed him when I was 29. Now, when I say I killed him, I mean that in the most loving way possible-and it is meant metaphorically. Just about everything regarding his existence in relationship to my life is metaphoric. He was never around, and I have no memories of him until I was 12, when I met him for the first time at a Denny's in Reno, Nevada.

Every now and then I would get on this kick and try to find him. I would search the prisons and parole boards first. He had a bad temper and a drug and alcohol problem. He liked women and money, usually in that order, as he was a career scam artist, and especially toward women. I would never talk to him though or engage in any sort of communication. Just knowing where he was somehow made me feel better.

Man, he messed with my head. Everyday. How I thought about myself, how I made decisions parenting, being a husband, acting accordingly as a man. Even though I had a couple other men in my life acting as that father figure, it still felt like I had been ripped off—somewhat like when I was circumcised as a baby. Many kids get left by their fathers, and they are left to deal with the "what ifs." I didn't really have the "what ifs"; I was simply trying to fight his legacy. I was constantly worried that if I didn't act a certain way, I would end up just like him. So, I had no choice or control in the matter. It probably would have been easier had he never been in my life at all.

We all leave a legacy though or, at the very least, a trail. Places we've been, the things we've done, how we act and behave; everything we do and everywhere we go, we make tracks. One could follow those tracks and learn about who a person is and what they did throughout their life. My dad's tracks left me unprotected, vulnerable, and exposed. He didn't do a very good job at creating a positive or beneficial path. Due to the severing of certain biological connections, I am partially insensitive, even with direct contact, and I am scarred and easily chafed, if rubbed the wrong way.

So why did I kill him? I was done thinking about him. I was done having people ask about him. I was done with his existence and interference altogether. I had given him almost 30 years, while he had given me, besides life, nothing. I am grateful to him for my life, but for everything else, he can kiss my ass. My mom called me one day and asked about him, as she sometimes did; she asked me if I had heard anything about him. I didn't even hesitate. I told her he was dead. I told her he died in prison, and that was it. Good riddance.

To me, it makes no sense. There is absolutely no valid reason and no excuse for anyone, man or woman, who is fully capable, or even halfway able to care for a child, to consciously and intentionally leave his or her child(ren). Of course, it's not easy! But I didn't do it to my son, and I'm sure he won't do it to his. In our home, we all made it the point that everyone is vital to the family structure and system. We work together as a team, as a family.

What if there were more community-based, family-friendly activities, available to everyone? Not just "special" programs, where availability and approval is granted only upon meeting some sort of low-class, high-risk status quo. Many of those kinds of programs are seriously antiquated and ineffective anyway, like court-mandated anger management classes for people who beat their spouses. They make a lot of money for the justice system, but, overall, they are ineffective. You can't make somebody do something, like sending people to prison; it doesn't always reform. Sometimes it just keeps people from doing what they want. Teach families how to raise their children. Show them how to do things, don't tell.

Bonita M. Veysey (BMV): It's interesting that you begin with a moment from your childhood. When I was around three years old, I remember sitting outside waiting for one of my friends to come out to play. I had a moment when I thought to myself, "I am a monster." I didn't understand why the adults who clearly were watching me would stop talking when I got close enough to hear. Obviously, they were talking about me and saw something that I couldn't. What was it they saw? I lived and continue to live with this feeling that others can see something "monstrous" in me that I myself am blind to. While I am White, educated, and middle class, I have always felt myself to be an outsider. I trust "outsiders" more than I trust those in the community from which I came. They were, after all, the ones who hurt me the most. Why is this important? As I reflect on my past, it becomes clear to me that, because I felt like an outsider, I could empathize with other groups of outsiders.

What do I mean by that? I grew up in the 1960s. As a result, I understood early on from a countercultural, but also personal, perspective that it was my social responsibility to challenge institutions that reinforce the (oppressive) status quo. For example, in high school, two things happened to me that made me know differently about an outsider group. The first was a school trip to Great Meadow Correctional Facility, a maximum-security prison in upstate New York, where I saw and spoke to a number of men who didn't seem all that bad (although the guards warned us otherwise). The second was my involvement with the Catholic Left and my admiration of Phil Berrigan, Liz McAlister, and their anti-war, antinuclear proliferation colleagues at Jonah House in Baltimore, Maryland. These people and others formed the core of the Catonsville Nine and the Plowshares Eight. These were the other criminals I knew. In fact, Fr. Carl Cabat, an anti-war, antinuclear proliferation activist and a chronic, repeat offender who served over 17 years in prison, is an example of, according to some, one of the most intransigent criminals. The take-home message for me was that "criminal" is in the eye of the beholder.

Even as I trained to become an insider, I tried to keep the outsider perspective firmly in the center of my work, trying to understand what people might experience during and as a result of my scholarship—the ways in which I could further these communities' well-being, but also worrying about the use of my scholarship to harm. This is the constant challenge in my work. Regardless of how much I learn or empathize, I remain an outsider and recognize that I am treading in spaces that I don't necessarily belong. I guess I see my place as a voice for folks who have a limited public platform.

Much of my scholarship now focuses on how people transform their lives. But, really, my scholarship is about creating a different narrative about people with conviction histories; providing hope instead of feeding the fear. This is true also of my work with others who have been systematically "studied" and thereby excluded, most notably people with psychiatric labels and people who have problems with substance use.

MAP: Thank you for sharing part of your personal life, Bonnie. I agree. I learned a long time ago that law is not always justice. Our justice system can be manipulative and oppressive, and it sometimes uses confusion-based methods and tactics using language as its tool. Law is not infinite, but it is constant, that is, until it is changed, amended, or altered to fulfill someone else's agenda. Man's law allows for natural law to be overstepped. Similar to owning land, charging to swim in a lake, or taking someone's children.

It is a very good thing that gay marriage is now legal in a few states. Man, to be told I couldn't marry my wife, because one or both of us don't fit somebody's criteria. What's really horrible though, is that it was illegal to begin with. Somebody actually has the audacity to think she or he has the power to allow someone else to marry another, like having a constitution that gives people the right to pray how or where they want to pray.

Do you, the readers, ever ask yourselves why we do some of the things we do in the United States of America? What are your rules at home for cleanliness? Do you clean up your messes, before making another? Why do we fight with corporations about the right to know what ingredients they are putting in our food, when we should be asking why some of those ingredients are even being used? Why can't they just use real food to make food? Why chemicals? Why, when we know we have alternative solutions for energy, other than fossil fuels, do we still drill, frack, destroy, burn, contaminate, and toxify our planet, our home? And why do we abuse people and use laws to push and force these methods of acquisition?

Why do we allow people from different races, cultures, countries, backgrounds, and knowledge to speak for others? Why do we assume that everyone from those different races, cultures, countries, backgrounds, and knowledge has the answers to our questions? Why does culture and ethnicity have to be unique or exotic? We all have our own ways. Why do we have to know everything? It's when the other person doesn't answer, or doesn't give us the answer we're looking for, that we just make up our own answers, through our own research. And then, we become the invader.

I, for one, don't feel the need to ask permission to pray. I don't have to go to school to become something or someone; and, most importantly, I became someone the second my heart started to beat. Many people in my life, family and friends, have been deemed uncivilized, criminals, felons, at large, wanted, high risk, enemies of the state, when, in fact, they were warriors. They weren't activists or even freedom fighters, because those words can be used as colonial, fascist terms to incite a negative, propagandist response from the mainstream population, just like "fugitive," "insurgent," or "rebel."

Many metonymies (figures of speech that call a concept not by its name but rather by the name of something associated with that thing or concept) exist in our world, and these metonymies affect how we think about the concepts, how we use them, and how we respond to them. You could almost say that English is a wizard's language, as it has and continues to shape-shift and change its form; it also has the means of causing great confusion or trickery, especially against those who don't understand its usage.

My first eye-opening experience with this happened early in my career. I was working for an organization that was involved in a long history of unfair practices with people of color. They said they "went by the book," but "the book" was under constant review and amendment. The book was always written in favor of control for the organization, not the people it served. This specific policy in question read that clients may have a specific religious item. I was told by a senior administrator, when advocating for a client regarding this policy, that, while it reads "may," it may also be interpreted as "may not."

BMV: You talked about the importance of language—the language of law, of bureaucracy, and of control in its many other forms. You talked about how language can be used to confuse and blind us to underlying meanings and purposes. It seems to me that this is the power to name and claim. As you said, criminals in one community are warriors in another. Who has the right to name and claim? This also points to a fundamental question about the relation of naming a thing and its independent reality. Is reality truly an objective thing that all people can acknowledge or is reality different for different people and communities?

MAP: How can reality be real for one, but not another? Is knowledge reality? Is it reality, or just simply perception or even perceptual realities? How powerful are naming ceremonies? Does naming create an existence, or do these things already exist, so we named it?

WHAT IS KNOWLEDGE?

BMV: Why should we concern ourselves with how we know what we know? How does it differ from opinion or belief? In regard to epistemology, the *Stanford Encyclopedia of Philosophy* (SEP; Steup, 2017) states, "As the study of knowledge, epistemology is concerned with the following questions: What are the necessary and sufficient conditions of knowledge? What are its sources? What is its structure, and what are its limits?" To unfairly reduce a whole field to a few sentences, three conditions are necessary and sufficient for knowledge: truth, belief, and justification. Knowledge, therefore, is comprised of an assumption that foundational propositions are true, a belief in those propositions, and some form of justification of that belief. What justifies a belief is (1) dependent on evidence with "a high objective probability of truth" and/or (2) is based on "reliable cognitive processes or faculties," including "perception, introspection, memory, and rational intuition" (SEP, 2017). And there is another form of justification that falls in this category: testimony. Testimony, first and foremost, is distinct from internal cognitive processes as it comes from an external source. Testimony includes knowledge such as content of ordinary conversation, information conveyed through social media, books, news and other media, expert opinion, and the products of research. It is here that we would like to frame the problem of colonial knowledge. Why are we so prone to assume that an accredited expert knows the "truth" better than someone with a lived experience?

MAP: Children love to tell stories. Some of the wildest stories I've ever heard came from the mouths of babes, and doctors' case/treatment files. When my daughter was about two and a half years old, I thought I was going to prison for child abuse. My wife and I took her to the doctor for a checkup, and during her exam, because of a few small scratches on her legs, out of the blue she told the doctor that her Grandpa threw her into a bunch of rose bushes. My wife and I were horrified! My daughter continued, that, because of a bump on her forehead, "My Daddy threw rocks at my head."

We learn at a young age to tell tall tales as we discover the incredible world of our own imagination. There are two basic types of pretend play: fantasy play and sociodramatic play (Lindsey & Colwell, 2013). "Pretend play" begins around age two and is predominantly mimicked behavior (talking on the telephone, cooking, "tea parties," etc.). Playing games, like "Let's pretend," teaches children to interact in different social environments (Navarez, 2014). All of it, association and imagination, contributes to cognitive and emotional development—and also, "the story."

So, can anyone make something up? If it's written down, does it make it more accurate or true? If a child's imagination, such as my daughter's, can change or alter someone's life, can anyone's life be changed or altered because of imagination, or simply, implied thinking?

That which comes from the natural world, like a mineral that is physical and also very real and is made to be a cell phone, a car, or even a gun, initially starts as a thought-seed, planted by curiosity, watered and fertilized by the imagination, and, then, manifested into physical reality. The difference is, it is no longer natural. It is still physically real, but it is now artificial, or synthetic. It has been removed and altered outside of its natural state and evolutionary process.

We live in a materialistic, scientific society, so biased views and distorted values are placed within empirical generalizations of reality and truth of things that can only be found in ways that are seen, heard, or felt. Due to the lack of evidence for all things—people, life, and existence, and the individual and unique differences among us all—should we then, as human beings, be considered a phenomenon? After all, in the struggle of understanding life, the limited understanding is measured by what can only be observed. Western psychology relies heavily on patterns of behavior, a potentially harmful approach to treating people.

How does one explain being able to manifest ideas and thoughts into physical being, when empirical evidence cannot support its totality? At what point do we admit that human existence, and existence in general, is a phenomenon, and through the generalization of this phenomenon called Creation, done only to create comfort with the "unknown," we lessen our spiritual connection and the relationship to life's sacredness?

BMV: It seems that you are both talking about our individual connections to the "real," but also challenging the typical way we know things collectively (empiricism and generalizability). While epistemology is the field of study about how we, as individuals, come to know or acquire knowledge, formal and collective knowledge systems, such as research, have the same epistemological foundations. In the natural sciences, empiricism reigns. Science remains largely based on observable measures (i.e., perceptions of sight, sound, etc.) derived from theoretical propositions (thus driven by hypotheses) and probabilistic statements of "truth" (perhaps ironically, as tools and methodologies have advanced, scientists increasingly build knowledge based on the unobservable [e.g., dark matter]). Understanding how our environment functions, from gravity to the movement of the oceans and air currents, to the composition of minerals and molecules, and to the behavior of genes, bacteria, and viruses, has led to major advances in the human ability to survive and thrive. In general, the observational methods upon which this type of knowledge is created seem to be more resistant to implicit and explicit biases. It is in the application that bias is evident. Consider how research into fusion has led both to new energy sources and devastating destruction.

One might argue that natural sciences are more resistant to the influence of cultural bias. However, in the social sciences it is hard to deny that the theories and the knowledge derived from them are heavily laden with cultural and historical assumptions. Like the natural sciences, social sciences are driven by principles of knowledge production based upon empirical evidence and prediction. While there has been a great debate over the past 30 to 40 years about the validity of various paradigms (e.g., positivism, post-positivism, and constructionism) and methodologies, as a field the praxis of knowledge creation has not changed that much. Social sciences, psychology included, still hold the experiment up as the "gold standard" of knowledge production, to understand, explain, and predict. Yet, evidence, even experimental evidence, in the social sciences is fraught with culturally based assumptions that lead to privileging certain topics that ask limiting questions and derive narrow conclusions. Who is allowed to participate in establishing the research agenda, and who vets the products of that research and in what manner, thereby defining what is "true," is yet another layer that excludes voices, perspectives, and other forms of preexisting knowledge. As Steup (2017) claims, "Since many view scientific facts as social constructions, they would deny that the goal of our intellectual and scientific activities is to find facts." Another example of, "we hear only what we understand."

MAP: Some truths are true, no matter the belief. Some truths are so powerful, they set people free. I remember asking my uncle, "So, if I believe in the

Sweatlodge, it is real and powerful?" Uncle Rob said, "Whether you believe in it or not, it is real and powerful."

In April of 1986, I was in the third grade. Along with every student in the school, I was given the Iowa Tests of Basic Skills. Out of 17 areas of scoring, I tested highest in the 90th percentile for usage and expression and, in fact, tested above average in all but three of the tests. In spelling, for example, I tested in the 79th percentile. My lowest score was in the 37th percentile for reference materials.

In 1989, I took it again. I tested in the 86th percentile for usage and expression; however, this time, I tested my highest in the 94th percentile for reference materials. And in spelling, I had climbed the statistical ladder to the 89th percentile.

On January 24, 1990, when I was 12 years old, the following was written about me by a school administrator: "Aaron, a transfer student, has been in trouble consistently since the beginning of the school year. He goes out of his way to agitate and cause trouble . . . He does not fear reprisal from either teachers or students and has been seen delighting in the negative response he enkindles from both peers and adults. The word 'masochist' was suggested . . . There are no indications of processing deficits or academic difficulties that one would associate with a need for remediation. He was also tested for GT [gifted/talented]. Although the results are probably not accurate—due to possible emotional interference—he did make a half-hearted attempt to comply, at least with the oral questioning. He is undoubtedly bright, if not gifted. His parent evaluation rates him highly on creativity. He is certainly creative when thinking of ways to get into or cause trouble."

April, 1990—In spelling, I tested again in the 89th percentile. This year, though, I barely made it on the chart for most of the tests. I scored in the 1st percentile for usage and expression and only in the 5th percentile for reference materials. The majority of the scores were below average! What happened? Why were they so inconsistent? What makes this different from any other assessment process?

Furthermore, how far does sarcasm and cynicism go when you're deciding the fate or destiny of another person's life? As a professional, such as the educator who wrote the abovementioned report with obvious personally biased opinions, I was undoubtedly framed as a safety and security risk, instead of focusing on the "fact" that I was "bright and gifted."

Why didn't he include a focus on that? Why didn't anyone ask the obvious question, not what's wrong with you but, instead, what happened to you?

BMV: Individual harm is how the dominant culture manifests itself through its agents. I don't know if this can ever be eliminated, but I believe it is much more likely to happen when those in power do not consciously reflect on their positionality when interacting with others not like them (not just cultural differences, but also, for example, adults to children) and take responsibility for their use of power. Certainly, you have personally experienced harm and pain from people who should have been caring for you and supporting your growth. When these individual harms are repeated over and over, this becomes a cultural assault, often based on unrecognized colonial knowledge.

COLONIZED KNOWLEDGE CREATION

BMV: If you are a mouse, asking how we can make a better mousetrap is tantamount to asking whether an efficient death is somehow "better" than an inefficient one. If one belongs to a traditionally studied group and does not have a voice in the creation of knowledge, including the questions of greatest interest, methodology, data collection, interpretation, and dissemination, one is much like the mouse. If research is conducted by the few for the purpose of prediction and control of the many "others," we must ask whether this is a practice that should exist at all. The practice of psychology and the research foundations upon which it is based historically have been created by and for people in power, in this case White Anglo-Europeans and men, with the general assertion that theories, principles, and practices are universal even if derived solely from White and/or male samples (see, for example, Kohlberg's [1981] theory of moral development). For example, with only a few exclusions (e.g., children vs. adults), mental health diagnostic schemas (e.g., DSM and ICD) are assumed to be valid regardless of identity or experiential differences. The professionalization of, and socialization to, the practice of psychology and, to a large degree research as well, means that the field of those recognized as "experts" is exceptionally restricted.

MAP: I used to work in an institution where I was continuously told, "You are not a clinician. You're not allowed to write or run therapy programs."

"No, Doctor, I'm not a clinician, but I'm telling you, the patient doesn't have a speech issue, and she's not FAS (Fetal Alcohol Syndrome). English is her second language." The patient, born and raised in the Alaskan bush, had a really thick accent. That's all. A diagnosis, that may have required medication, was reached simply based on how the doctor auditorily misinterpreted the patient's speech. Would that not be the colonial illness itself, condemning—I mean "diagnosing"—a client based on our own lack of foresight, awareness, or knowledge of other realities outside of our own understanding?

If you're not working on the mousetrap, they don't want you working.

That specific situation and conversation that followed, greatly concerned me. So, I wrote a music-based, culturally- informed therapy program (which included singing traditional powwow songs), and I included the required evidence-based materials and references. Additionally, I provided resources, which included tribal best practices and evidence-based music therapy research. It was denied, declined, and derailed. I added a colleague, a clinical psychologist who had never had a proposal denied by that institution, to the proposal as a supervising clinician, and it was denied again. "Everyone hears only what they understand."

BMV: So, despite playing the game by providing evidence from related fields and having a credentialed supervising clinician, it wasn't enough. "If you're not working on the mousetrap, they don't want you working." This seems to reflect many aspects of embedded and nonconscious colonial thinking. We have many examples of "foundational" nineteenth-century research that was used to justify male, Euro-centric, cisgendered, hegemonic structures. I am thinking about Stephen Jay Gould's (1981) descriptions of the advocates of American polygeny and craniometry, Louis Agassiz and Samuel George Morton, as an example as well as the nineteenth-century Lombroso study of the physical traits of "criminals." Once in a while, I think that we have moved beyond studying groups for the express benefit of someone else, as was done in the Tuskegee syphilis study, only to be confronted by a story of well-meaning scholars. For example, recently the British Broadcasting Company (BBC; March 18, 2017) and National Public Radio (NPR; March 21, 2017) covered a story, "Healthiest Hearts in the World," based upon an article published in *The Lancet* (Kaplan et al., 2017). The article is a summary of a traditional research study describing subjects, methods, and results. What interested me was the backstory that was not described in *The Lancet* study, but was reported in the audio interview. Briefly, an anthropologist became so enraptured of a small culture in Bolivia that he decided to live in this community. While there, he discovered that the people of this community, the Tsimane, have exceeding low rates of heart disease. In fact, he was soon to find that they had the lowest recorded levels of atherosclerosis ever, anywhere. He invited scientists (specifically, cardiologists) to join him to try to understand what was going on in this population. Using a sample of Tsimane, ages 40 years and older, "coronary atherosclerosis was assessed by coronary artery calcium (CAC) scoring done with non-contrast CT" (Kaplan et al., 2017). If my understanding is correct, this involves a nonintrusive CT scan. Okay. So a small community with few contacts with the outside world is now a part of a medical experiment conducted by outsiders that involves a CT scan that will in no way benefit them. Further, the findings do not truly advance our understanding of the heart health of those who benefit from this study (i.e., the greater Western public). "These findings suggest that coronary atherosclerosis can be avoided in most people by achieving a lifetime with very low LDL, low blood pressure, low glucose, normal body-mass index, no smoking, and plenty of physical activity" (Kaplan et al., 2017). Under what rationale can and should we be doing this? Science, writ large, has made us promises to improve health and quality of life for all. We know, however, that these are often qualified promises, improved outcomes for some and sometimes at the expense of others, including our environment and the other life that inhabits the earth.

MAP: True, Bonnie. Too many studies and experiments have been performed, with little to no benefit to the population being studied and/or experimented on. Scientific findings seem to be the objective, not the solution, and certainly not the implementation of the outcomes/solutions. Furthermore, as you mentioned regarding the Tsimane, there is a total disregard for indigenous prevention aspects. It becomes a scientific anomaly, not a universal reality. "Making two possibilities a reality. Predicting the future of things we all know . . . Science fails to recognize the single most potent element of human existence . . . Science has failed our Mother Earth" (System of a Down, 2001). It's not the fault of science, though, that creates these problems. It's how it is used.

Despite the differences in treatment, what is being treated, and how it is treated, psychology still follows the same model as medical practice. One of the challenges with this, is it appears that the medical model tends to focus solely on illness and the treatment of illness, rather than focusing on health and wellness, and the treatment of health and wellness. When we talk about naming and claiming, this is where, in my opinion, it gets dangerous, or even foolish.

Michael Grinder, author of *The Elusive Obvious: The Science of Nonverbal Communication* (Grinder, 2016), said to me, "Imagine you go to the doctor, and they tell you that you have 'X.' They invite you in to a quiet, private room, and with so much genuine concern and compassion, staring you right in the eyes, and maybe even putting a hand on your shoulder, they tell you exactly where your disease is. And they practically hand it to you, and you, you willingly accept it."

When I heard this, it was like thunder hitting a window. So explosive. It was, to me, a sacred naming ceremony for illness.

Doctors are medicine people, right? They are educated, taught, and trained to work with illness and disease. Their focus is illness and disease. Many are very compassionate human beings and went into their profession to help others. They have no intention of making people sick, killing them, or being a distributor of sickness and illness. But one could say that the practice of medicine is often performed foolishly and without proper knowledge of how to truly heal people. I am not a medicine person, and I know very little about a whole lot. But what I do know is that the medical model, despite being based on research, is still guesswork—trial and error. The scary and sad part is that when it errs, it affects lives in catastrophic ways.

The concept of "my way will better someone's life" is brazen, to say the least, and has put our society in an awkward place today. A "fog," as I have heard Don Coyhis (personal communication, n.d.) call it, for many people today, is a reality full of confusion, frustration, fear, uncertainty, and hesitation, all the while being conditioned and taunted with illusions of grandeur and schemes for lucrative lifestyles: achieve the American Dream, go to an Ivy League school, land a financially successful career, or all of the above.

We teach, enforce, and reinforce these things to the members of our society via colonial concepts. There are agencies and offices within our governments, corporations, associations, and institutions that seem to have little to no empathy, compassion, or interest in regard to humanity and/or social justice. Their legal and political fingers touch everything today, and it's the arrogant and bold intrusions, demands, and actions that continue to reflect and model the very same behaviors and actions of the original visitors to North America. As is the case in Bolivia you described, that same intruder disease is exactly what we're talking about here in America.

Is there really a disease living among us? Euro-America has created a culture of appropriation and exploitation, and at the very core and foundation we unwittingly celebrate that. What was the last holiday you celebrated, and how much did it cost you? How might people from other cultures view that holiday—as a celebration, solemn prayer, or even a cause for mourning?

We have taken (and continue to take) bits and pieces of other cultures and customs from around the world, put our own spin on it, and then sold it as an original idea. You don't patent culture, especially someone else's and definitely not without their permission, right? That's stealing, isn't it? Yes, it's one of the first "laws" that many of us were taught: Don't take things that don't belong to you and so on (unless you don't have one of your own). We tell others not to do things, then turn around and do the same. It sounds like a starter kit for classic cultural, Eurocentric narcissism.

BMV: When I think about cultural appropriation in the process of knowledge creation, I like to reflect on the three basic principles of ethical research described in the 1979 *Belmont Report*: respect for persons, beneficence, and justice. One would think that ethical principles would protect groups or classes of people from exploitation, but that is not necessarily true.

To summarize, respect for persons attends to two aspects: individual autonomy and special protections against inclusion in research for those with "diminished" autonomy (including children, incarcerated people, and persons with cognitive challenges). Respect, therefore, is about free choice to participate in research. Beneficence "is often understood to cover acts of kindness or charity that go beyond strict obligation." In practice, the *Belmont Report* focuses on two aspects of beneficence: (1) do no harm and (2) maximize benefits while minimizing risks of harm. What is interesting in this is that, while the general notion is that research should benefit society at large, there is a general agreement that some subsample might bear the burden of dangerous or intrusive procedures that will not directly help them, but will produce substantial benefits for "society at large," including similar others (e.g., cancer patients). "The problem posed by these imperatives is to decide when it is justifiable to seek certain benefits despite the risks involved, and when the benefits should be foregone because of the risks" (Belmont Report, 1978). If taken seriously, as Institutional Review Boards (IRBs) are called to do, this is an enormous challenge and responsibility. Finally, justice requires that the burdens and benefits of research are shared equally. That is, research should not be conducted on a population solely because it is easily accessible or cannot otherwise defend itself (e.g., children, prisoners); that is the burden. And the benefits should be accrued to all, including those in the group from which the participants were selected.

These three principles undergird what constitutes ethical research. I think that you can see in this formulation how we can justify the appropriation of cultural artifacts, practices, and techniques for the greater good. I recall a story that was told to me by a medical anthropologist of my acquaintance. He had conducted an ethnographic study of people who were homeless, and some of the report described how they survive in the subcellars and tunnels of the train stations in New York (see Baxter & Hopper, 1987). Fascinating idea and findings. People are so creative and inventive. The researchers' intent was altruistic and their advocacy for the homeless is unquestionable; and I'm sure that the IRB that reviewed the protocol found it benign. However, this report drew attention to things that might have been better left unknown by the public and authorities (see Johnston, 1981) and was used to find and expel those living in the station and its underground spaces; creating thereby substantial benefits for "society at large," including police, city management and strap hangers alike—but not for those people who were the focus of the study.

What do you think? Can we really know the essence of the natural world and our place in it through traditional research?

MAP: I think we can. Again, I don't think it's the science, I think it's user error. I don't think all aspects are considered, validated, or utilized. "To say that water consists of hydrogen and oxygen is to say nothing that relates to water generally or to all its characteristics. It is to say nothing that relates to the great oceans and to a drop of rain, to water's capacity to extinguish fire and to Archimedes's law. In the same way, to say that verbal thinking contains intellectual processes and speech functions is to say nothing that relates to the whole of verbal thinking and to all its characteristics equally" (Vygotsky, 1934, para. 4).

Raising the phenomena of the human experience to a general level creates the very decomposition to our humanness, which Vygotsky referred to in his thought and word research.

I think about this when I hear parents talking to each other about doctors' diagnoses of children. Having a baseline, in general, creates a very serious social bias. And "your child is under the baseline" is the type of diagnosis that destroys a great deal of potential naturally imbedded in the human creativeness of that child, and of the parent too.

An elder told me, "We all have our own ways. Just like the leaves on the trees or the snowflakes in a blizzard, each of us is different, in our languages, customs, foods, ceremonies, and our people and families. This is what makes us, us." We all have our own ways. Of course we do. None of us is the same. We know this all too well; on the very surface of our bodies is the empirical evidence that each of us is unique—as unique as our fingerprints. No matter how many billions of people there are on this planet, regardless that the process of procreation is the same, despite the fact that our physical existence is formed from the same liquids, gasses, and minerals as everything else in Creation, fingerprints are unique to the individual.

"A word without meaning is not a word but an empty sound . . . word meaning, then, is a phenomenon of both speech and intellect . . . it is a phenomenon of speech only to the extent that speech is connected with thought and illuminated by it. Word meaning is a phenomenon of verbal thought or of the meaningful word. It is a unity of word and thought" (Vygotsky, 1934, para. 6).

Simply from our imaginations and our thoughts, we have created an unnatural world outside of the realms of the natural world. We have expanded beyond the unnatural world by introducing virtual space. We have created an alter-space reality, a world that is unstable, unpredictable, disassociates us from the foundations of balance, harmony, and connection with the universe—and we have found the methodologies by which to validate and justify it. "If we assume man has been corrupted by an artificial civilization, what is the natural state? The state of nature from which he has been removed? Imagine, wandering up and down the forest without industry, without speech, and without home" (goodreads.com, n.d.).

BMV: This is a fascinating concept. You are suggesting that we have created and live in a largely unnatural world of our imagination (and have done so for as long as human kind has imagined unseen possibilities). I wonder about the connection between this unnatural world and civilization. Is there really such a thing as a natural civilization? It seems to me that civilization is created and sustained by communities and societies, generation after generation, often through long-standing institutions, such as education and religion. These same institutions are the tools through which we have been convinced that core foundational beliefs of "civilization" are real, natural, and good. We need to be critical of our assumptions, these inculcated beliefs. Without this, we can go so far afield with the best of intentions.

Since this chapter is about knowledge creation in psychology, I went to the APA (2017) home page to see what the membership of U.S. psychology presents as central values. Here's what I found.

"Our mission is to advance the creation, communication and application of psychological knowledge to benefit society and improve people's lives. We do this by:

- Encouraging the development and application of psychology in the broadest manner.
- Promoting research in psychology, the improvement of research methods and conditions and the application of research findings.
- Improving the qualifications and usefulness of psychologists by establishing high standards of ethics, conduct, education and achievement.
- Increasing and disseminating psychological knowledge through meetings, professional contacts, reports, papers, discussions and publications."

The APA has nearly 100 journals dedicated to both practice and research covering dozens of topic areas. Here, we must think about experts and knowledge creation and the championing of this disciplinary knowledge. To further underscore this, the organization's goals are also explicitly stated, "APA aspires to excel as a valuable, effective and influential organization advancing psychology as a science. The core values that guide our mission include pursuit of excellence, knowledge, diversity and ethical action.

Our strategic plan goals are to maximize the association's organizational effectiveness, expand psychology's role in advancing health and increase recognition of psychology as a science."

Sounds good, right? "To benefit society and improve people's lives." Except that the language seems to be more focused on building a knowledge (i.e., practice and research) empire that is privileged over other disciplines and forms of wellness and knowing. When we grapple with knowledge creation and dissemination, how do we uncover these more covert messages and structures; and should we even waste our time?

MAP: I believe it's worth it. I don't think it's a waste of time. I think it is needed and necessary. [But, they need to be done with the consideration of creating and implementing solutions.] Federal research is colonized in the ways that the government influences and intrudes into research. For example, the Government Performance and Results Act (GPRA) was created to improve government performance management. The Substance Abuse and Mental Health Services Administration (SAMHSA) grantees are mandated under the GPRA criteria to collect and report data using the GPRA's measurement tools (GPRA Modernization Act of 2010 Tools, SAMHSA, n.d.). In regard to research, the problem with this is that it puts the U.S. government in the position of setting the standards and criteria and, ultimately, controlling the results. The research of human beings, for the balance and progress of mental health, resides under the confinements and rule of a public policy/agenda—colonization at its finest.

There are personnel issues and active resistance toward nonclinicians working within this field, as I have repeatedly experienced, while all the while, there are nonclinicians creating and enforcing many of the standards (e.g., those insurance case managers who are not psychologists, but do dictate to psychologists the amount and type of care that is authorized for a certain client). That is "God save the King!" thinking right there, nonpsychologists dictating to psychologists. Protecting something that you can't even participate in; you're not good enough.

Basically, nonclinicians are being told by clinicians, "Anyone can help you with your mental health needs, but only clinicians can really help, as long as the clinicians follow the steps by those (some of whom may be nonclinicians) who have developed the standard."

How can these methods and processes be effective and successful, when standards of care, treatment, and assessment are misguided, misinformed, and misunderstood? This is a serious conflict of interest. Or, at the very least, a conflict of qualification and competence.

So, who is the expert? What even makes an expert? What determines qualifications? Is it experience, time served, education, or all of the above? For years in institutional settings, I have been unfairly dubbed, "the expert," and have been asked by administrators to create standard operating procedure manuals for ceremonies, such as sweat lodge. My answer has always been the same, "If you want to know about it, or are curious to what goes on, please join us. You are more than welcome to come inside. There is no one way to conduct a sweatlodge ceremony—we all have our own 'ways,' and you are welcome to learn the way I was taught. To that end, I will not create a Standard Operating Procedure Manual for ceremony."

Under most circumstances, NASA would not hire a barista to evaluate their aerothermodynamic programs unless that barista was competent in the process. Through the means of gaining this knowledge, or competence, though, that barista could then be qualified, and NASA may hire that person. Many agencies, corporations, organizations, and franchises recruit their employees straight out of high school, because they see qualities that fit their mission. If we are truly invested in full participation, or inclusion, as most clinicians encourage their clients to do, how is it that we continue these paths of colonial injury? Exclusion, discrimination, segregation, classism, hierarchy—oppression from all angles—I thought you talked about moving forward.

Before the research is even started, it's already infected. Researchers, your research is about your agenda, and what you want to know about me, through your eyes, your experiences, your intelligence; it's not about me, or what you really need to know, in order for us to effectively and successfully work with each other. The standards and criteria are biased, with no apparent real interest or understanding in who I am.

The research conducted follows the current practice, which is colonial by nature (Duran & Firehammer, 2015); it does not lead it, which it should. The standards, practices, and baselines are tainted from the beginning, resulting in inaccurate results.

What are the questions? What are you going to study? Who does the research? What is to be done with the solutions, recommendations, interventions, and so on?

You research what you already know about me, or what you think you know.

"If the research proposal must be substantiated by what already exists in the research literature, then the foundation of the proposal is research that is based on western empiricism and underlying that method is western philosophy, which in many instances is felt as a tool of social control and colonization" (Duran & Firehammer, 2015).

BMV: It is clear that we live in a society with interlocking institutional messaging that excludes many from full participation. I openly acknowledge that, as a person who has benefitted from others' exclusion, I am complicit sometimes without awareness, but I am always complicit when I engage with others without challenging basic assumptions. How do we move forward?

MAP: In my opinion, in order to change systems, we should be reflecting and creating those changes within ourselves first, right? Not just expect change to occur on its own. We have to think and act in accordance to the change being sought, and not just hope it changes. If our children act in a manner that is not a positive reflection of the family or the community, and we want our children's behavior to change, then, in most cases, the behavior of the parents must change first, right?

BMV: Mathew, you are so right. We need to do the hard work of changing ourselves before we can begin to think about working with others. And facing our potential complicity is a never-ending process. As we begin to think about whether we can indeed create knowledge that is inclusive and reflective of the issues and questions of most importance to each community, it is helpful to me to struggle with whether we should focus on decolonizing knowledge structures or democratizing knowledge creation. It seems to me that decolonizing requires deconstructing—literally, taking apart and maybe never putting this particular structure together again. Democratizing implies creating equal access and equal voice. Of course, we have had historical problems in our "democracy" that challenges the notion that egalitarianism can actually happen. We have issues with this word. The original meaning of the word is the rule of government by the people. Extending this to research, the oligarchs would be us, the researchers and the leadership of organizations such as the APA. The people would be, who? The studied, the ones in the majority who worry about the studied? Can we propose that we leverage the system? If we were truly committed to democratizing knowledge and knowledge creation, what would that look like?

DECOLONIZING AND DEMOCRATIZING KNOWLEDGE

BMV: To democratize knowledge, we must create broad pathways for the persons from underrepresented groups, expanding who has valid voice and expertise; embrace different ways of knowing that are valued by different identity groups and extend how knowledge is created and transmitted, including the artifacts of that knowledge, moving from a cult of the expert to a community of experts.

I really like how Syracuse University's Democratizing Knowledge (DK) Project (2017) formulates this concept. "Our aim is to construct ways of 'democratizing knowledge,' revitalizing and transforming the reach of these knowledges to address difference, identity, equality, justice, citizenship, and democracy and making these knowledges more visible, more sustainable, and more institutionally public on the campus and beyond."

How do you think about the challenge of democratizing knowledge in your work?

MAP: I worked in an institution that had an overrepresentation of Native American clients, who were requesting sweat lodge ceremonies. Especially for Native American clients and other people of color, the institution wasn't providing cultural services, as the sweat lodge that was up and being used had been ordered by the superintendent to be torn down. Four days after it had been torn down, two children under the institution's care committed suicide. Not long after I was hired, the administration said it needed someone to start running ceremonies for the clients. They came to me and said, "So, you're the Native American staff. Our clients are asking for sweat lodge ceremonies, and we want you to start providing that for them."

I told them that I wasn't allowed to just start running ceremonies; I had never officiated ceremonies' and there were specific cultural protocols; so I needed to talk with my elders first.

They replied, "That's fine, but you are being detailed to the sweat lodge on Saturdays, beginning next week, and it will be added to your position description. You are expected, as part of your regular duties, to follow this directive and expectation."

I said to my uncle, "They want me to start running ceremonies here. They asked if I needed a certificate or license to pour water in ceremony. Strange, isn't it? I don't know what to do, though, Uncle, I've never poured water before. What are your thoughts? It's a lot of responsibility, and it scares me. I've spent a lot of time with you, and I would like to know what you think."

Uncle said, "It's not how long you've been doing something, Nephew. It's what you've gotten out of it, since you started doing it. The people up there where you're at need somebody to help."

There was little to no understanding, awareness, or sensitivity from the administration as to ceremonial protocol. They assumed that I could run the ceremonies. When I told them I needed to talk with my elders, it surprised them. There was the assumption that because I held Native worldviews, I could automatically do these things.

There is something, however, very powerful about saying, "I have to talk with Grandma first." We do what our elders tell us to do. They have much more life experience and wisdom than us younger ones.

BMV: As a person who has Native beliefs, you have faced repeated challenges. It is fascinating that persons in control of these places and spaces put you in this impossible situation of being an expert, but not according to your professional (i.e., psychology) legitimacy. In some ways, this seems like the epitome of White privilege (and I am White). I am truly asking you, can we find a place where First Nations and traditionally trained psychology researchers can partner for the benefit of the people?

MAP: Of course there is a place. As Rumi wrote, "Out beyond the world of ideas of wrongdoing and rightdoing, there is a field. I will meet you there" (Barks, 2005). And yes, I too have witnessed a great deal of privilege. But I am not the one to answer this question. There are many others out there who can. I would be out of line to think I could. Again, we all have our own ways. There are many people in the world, who all have their own voice and can speak for themselves. I think it is a little unfair to think that one person can speak for or have the token answer for an entire race.

DEMOCRATIC KNOWLEDGE CREATION IN PRACTICE

BMV: Thank you for raising that point. Recently, I had a long conversation with Krzysztof Czyżewski (Kris), the director of the Borderland Foundation (for description, see Zaborowska, 2009) in Sejny, Poland. Several years ago, he told me two things that I will never forget. I asked him recently to remind me of the details one more time. The first story is about working in the borderland. For two weeks in the fall of 2003, some of the best professional European musicians came to Sejny to conduct concerts and workshops with the local residents to acquaint them with the work of Arvo Pärt. Pärt's work is tranquil, beautiful, and minimalist. Kris told me that he had some worries before the first concert. Should he tell the audience about Pärt's music to prepare them? Would they not understand or would they be bored? Would the musicians object to the small church venue? He had nothing to worry about. The people listened with an untrained but authentic ear. The musicians reflected afterward that they had never had such a receptive audience. I asked him, "Why did they say that?" Kris said that most audiences are acquainted with various musical forms. They have preconceived notions about music and, as such, tend to be critical. These audiences cannot engage with the musicians and the music without their music knowledge getting in the way. I asked him whether the musicians knew what they were getting into when they came to Sejny. Yes, they knew. They came because they were the best. Unlike others, they no longer worried about climbing the professional ladder and meeting professional expectations. They were interested in sharing with this particular community and having an impact. Through the additional concerts and discussions over the next few days, together the musicians and the local citizens explored music and place. This is what it is to work in the borderland. Finding a place to change and be changed by deep engagement. One might argue that as much as the musicians and local citizens changed each other, the place and Pärt's music, as interpreted by the musicians, were also changed.

Kris also talked about the concept of problem-solving. He said when we focus on a problem, we seek the direct causes of that problem. As he said this, he used his hands to reach out to grasp this problem. "We can never solve the problem this way. When we reach beyond the problem to an imagined future," stretching his arms out and encompassing the problem, "we no longer need to focus on it. The problem will not exist."

When I think about working in the borderlands between cultures (of any sort) to solve problems through understanding/knowledge creation, I think about the liminal. I love the definitions of the word in the *Merriam-Webster Dictionary*:

(1) of, relating to, or situated at a sensory threshold: barely perceptible or capable of eliciting a response
(2) of, relating to, or being an intermediate state, phase, or condition: in-between, transitional

It is that uncomfortable space between states or cultures, a place of unknowing between two (or more) knowns. It is also a place of shadows just outside perception, but perhaps, if we have the courage and perseverance, we can indeed peer into that place just beyond the light to discover a shared space and a new way of knowing.

MAP: My uncle once told me about a visit he had at a doctor's office. When he walked into the lobby, the receptionist said, "Hi, good morning! Welcome to our practice!"

He said he looked up, with a smile, and said, "They're practicing? I don't know if I'm comfortable with that. Don't they know what they're doing?"

She smiled back, and replied, "Yes, they do. You're here to be seen? Which doctor?"

"Well," my uncle said, "I'd like to see the Witch Doctor!!!"

My uncle always liked to use humor. He was incredibly sharp, with a quick wit and impeccable timing. He loved contrast, and presenting it to others through comedy and storytelling was a talent of his. He was a funny guy, but he was serious, too.

When I hear the term "borderland," I think of contrast. Humor also plays into the contrast. Living in a world that is sometimes difficult, stressful, or lonely to live in, humor can build relationship, decrease stress, and make conversations or topics easier to deal with. To me, the contrast is that experiential reflection of what you, your mind, and your body already know. I remember hearing Don Coyhis (n.d.) say, "When you are at a point in life where you don't know what you don't know, with hard work, you can move to a point where you know what you don't know."

Sometimes it's the contrast that shakes things up for us. And, when you know what you don't know, so much work can be done. Is that the borderland? There is contrast in everything we experience, every day, reflected from what one is taught or learned. It can be a place of incredible discomfort, and it can also be a place where great personal development, knowledge attainment, and relationship growth can exist. Is that the borderland?

BMV: Yes, I think it is that, but I think it is something more. As I ponder the meaning, given that Sejny is near a border, I imagine that it is also like the experience of folks who live along the U.S. borders. They come and go between countries. They don't see the rigid boundaries of place or citizenship or status. And the culture that is derived from this borderland space is a unique combination of both cultures; like Tex-Mex.

MAP: Yes, the term "borderlands," reminds me of border towns, the border, and boundaries. And it has the word "order" in it (do what I say) and lines—people being put into those boxes, and cages, and containers, and capsules, and I hate when things are put into boxes. I was put into a box before, and I didn't like it.

In this borderland place where we meet, I think it just simply starts with respect, acknowledgment, and honor. Honesty is a good place to also begin.

Being honest with oneself first. And listen to learn. Tell some stories. Be genuine to the person, not the position.

I don't think we have to name that place you're talking about either. I think it is more like the bridge. And I think it just is. I think it's a place where everything moves how it's supposed to. Balance. You have your ways, I have mine. You know who you are, I know who I am. I respect, acknowledge, and honor your ways, and you do the same. You don't interfere with things you don't understand, and I'll do the same. You don't take what doesn't belong to you, neither will I. You don't sell what's not yours, neither will I. If either of us have questions, we'll go to the source. We won't assume or just observe. We will engage; we will ask questions.

We have to stop romanticizing cultures, quit being so aggressive and confrontive to one another, stop going to war (good God, the blanket of anxiety and fear that has gripped our nation), and we need to stop being delusional about the real problems in our world. Things are a mess out there, but there are ways to fix things, but again, I'm not the one to ask. I have no answers to any of the current problems. That's why I decided to write. I know nothing about a lot. And we'll probably disagree on most subjects!

BMV: That's interesting. Disagreements seem to me to be the fodder of imagining the possible. I think we need disagreements and different ways of understanding to solve those complex problems that we share. In fact, Scott Page calls this the 'diversity bonus.' Better solutions are achieved when people representing cognitive and identity diversity come together to solve problems (Page et al., 2017). It is great that you mentioned bridges as well. Kris also talked about both problem-solving and invisible bridges. When talking about problem-solving, Kris used the example of shooting an arrow at a target. "If you focus solely on the center point, you are bound to miss," he said. "You must take everything in, like air currents, the distance." He reflected that our world has been fragmented by identities. If we want to create true multiculturalism, we have to think beyond the celebration of each culture. We need to be inclusive. To do that, everyone must have a place. If we try to name each group, he warned, we are bound to miss someone or some group. There is nothing wrong with the sharing of stories, histories, music, but it must go further. People must come together to co-create something new, something that continues the story forward that also represents all participants.

Bridges are interesting. In fact, many of the Borderland Foundation's projects use the symbolism of a bridge as a catalyst for shared creative endeavors. Anchored on both shores of two cultures, walking onto a bridge requires a letting go of the known and a willingness to engage in the unknown. But at the same time, Kris shared, in our culture we think that crossing a bridge is heroic. We cross a bridge, immerse ourselves in another's culture. Amazing, courageous, certainly mind-bending. It's heroic, like climbing a mountain. The hiker succeeds when she/he/they achieve the summit, but, Kris asked, how many people lose their way on the way back down that mountain? How many are lost because they did not prepare for the return journey? Just like the return journey from a mountaintop, the importance of the bridge is to cross and then to return. Assuming that the others from across the bridge are on the same journey, one can imagine that the travelers are changed, that the travelers affect the communities to which they journey and that they impact their home communities when they return. Are we ever not changed by experience if we engage authentically and fearlessly?

MAP: A friend of mine, consultant Miguel Valenciano (n.d.), said, "When it comes to life, we have to become comfortable being uncomfortable."

Those who practice meditation say it can take a lifetime of practice, dedication, and discipline to reach Nirvana, and still they may never reach a complete understanding of what it is. Furthermore, my uncle, who practiced martial arts, said that in over 30 years of his practicing multiple arts, he had still not learned everything. His personal understanding of each Kata had developed, changed, and evolved throughout the years, continuously expanding his own relationship with the art. Much like the musicians you mentioned, even though they had achieved so much, this was an opportunity to continue their learning and the relationship with the music.

To say that simply living in the borderlands provides the solution, though, is not enough. The change requires a major shift in thought—a radical shift—and the thought must be reflected in ways that differ from the current knowledge base. It's a balance, and, honestly, some things do not or should not belong.

BMV: Mathew, this is so true. The first question, then, is, "when, with whom and under what circumstances should we pursue knowledge creation together, and when should we agree that this is not a shared space?" If we choose to move forward together, what do borderlands and bridges have to teach us about research and knowledge creation? How do we really co-create knowledge that is meaningful and benefits the communities that pose the questions and seek the answers? How do we move from being open to others to true inclusion and seamless partnership?

BEING COMFORTABLE IN THE LIMINAL: MOVING TOWARD THE SACRED

BMV: To be honest, there have been a lot of discussions and techniques/methodologies about how to increase voice, including a greater focus on qualitative methods, engaging peer researchers, and actively engaging community members in all stages of the production of knowledge. There is also an ongoing conversation, usually negative, about scholars studying members of their own identity group(s). I particularly like one innovation that is happening in the Newark community in partnership with a faculty member (Gluck, personal communication, 2014). The community now has its own IRB. This IRB is focused on making sure that any research (1) benefits the community, and (2) if a program is implemented in order to test the effect of an intervention, there are plans to make that program sustainable over time; that is, it doesn't go away when the research is completed. While these are important, I would argue, democratizing knowledge creation is not about methodology, but about values change. And the values change must be authentic and not just rhetorical window dressing.

Further, there are other important issues to consider here. First and foremost is the fallacy of the community. There is no such thing as a monolithic, homogeneous community. The very idea undermines the uniqueness of each individual and the intersectionalities that exist in every geographic and intentional community. How then do we engage with these places and groups to represent voices? What would those values be?

MAP: The values used and exercised should reflect the values of the community.

BMV: As a preliminary list, I would suggest at a minimum, every knowledge creation endeavor should ask the following:

- What are the questions driving the project and do they lead to greater inclusion and broad benefits?
- Who is the target of data collection (if any) and how does this project serve them and the group that they "represent?"
- Is this knowledge for knowledge sake? Is it really necessary?
- Who benefits the most from this project: the investigator, the field, the society (and exactly which segments of society), the subjects, or the subjects' group?
- What are the unintentional, but predictable, negative outcomes of the scholarship?
- How are multiple voices included across all stages of the project?

MAP: I like this list, and I would be willing to bet that each community it was brought to, there would be additions or subtractions to the list. *We all have our own ways.* We have to remember that. According to region, culture, beliefs, and customs, each client is different and each community is different. These questions need to be asked.

SUMMARY AND CONCLUSIONS

BMV: It is ironic that we write this chapter in a book entitled, *Radical Psychology*, a book whose readership is likely to be economically advantaged, highly educated, and English-speaking. The venue alone is a colonized space. How do we create and support democratic knowledge creation, when the book form itself and its content are not accessible to the many? Likewise, how do we radically transform the field of psychology, when its very foundations are built upon theories and propositions created by a privileged few imposed upon the many "others?" Like a stack of pennies, when the bottom ones are not centered, the column is unstable and can only grow in a crooked manner. Is it possible to correct the column without toppling it? Do we believe that research in the field of psychology can be democratized and made more inclusive, such that the "findings" are meaningful and have positive impacts; that those who are the experts, and who ask the questions, create the scholarly outputs that represent broader (i.e., all) communities and voices; and that all are the beneficiaries of knowledge? The short answer is yes, but it is a qualified and complicated yes.

Long-standing institutions often have explicit mission statements that are benign. Yet, the unspoken goals of these institutions, including those whose rhetoric are the most beneficent—religion, education, and medicine to name just a few—are often focused on socialization (i.e., social control) and use techniques that range from soft influence to coercion to ensure that citizens comply with normative beliefs and behavior and that those who don't are identified and controlled. To extend Chenelle Jones' (2013) article title, "The system isn't broken, it was designed that way," our institutions are not broken, they are designed to do exactly what they are doing. This is a huge problem. We are suggesting that we shift the implicit institutional intents and goals to serve the many and not the few.

Putting aside the issues of funding and political support, how do we take on this challenge? Taking a page from the book of higher education, we are now in an unprecedented time when our constituents are demanding visible outcomes. Some institutions are eagerly embracing the challenge and reflecting back to the call of the Morrill Act (Cantor, 2012; Ensign, 2017) for institutions of higher education to be sources of innovation and engines of social mobility for their local communities. Can psychology and psychological research take up the same challenge?

MAP: I don't think it's a matter of "Can psychology and psychological research take up same challenge?" I think it's a matter of, "Will psychology and psychological research take up the same challenge?"

We have a choice to be responsible or irresponsible. We have a choice of doing the correct thing or the incorrect thing. We have known for a long time that many of these systems/models are not inclusive on the global scale. We have known for a long time that specific information/knowledge that is inclusive is ignored or deemed bias.

BMV: I guess I have to go back to my personal foundations. I believe, to substantially change these institutions without destroying them, one must be an "insider with outsider values," as Anita Hill so eloquently argued in her 2002 op-ed piece. She attended poignantly to the impact that insiders, in this case women in the FBI, could have on the institution of the FBI and its leadership. We encourage the body of the APA with its vast diversity to challenge the organization and its membership to think inclusively and broadly; to consider who is expert, what scholarly products are valued and how to engage "non-experts" (i.e., those with lived experience) as full partners in knowledge creation.

FINAL COMMENTS

BMV: This chapter really is not about transmitting facts or providing the silver bullet for "decolonized" and collective knowledge creation. It requires the reader to work, and to observe, analyze, and reflect. If you get it, great. If you walk away and think, "what the devil was that about," go back and read it again, note the structure and the voices, and think about the liminal and the sacred and how engaging in these spaces requires different goals and values.

This is an uncomfortable space for me as a researcher. To be honest, I have conducted studies that I worry about a lot. I know that my intent is to create a different narrative, particularly for formerly incarcerated people. But I also understand that knowledge created can be used in many ways; for good or ill. I believe in leveraging research for the good of the populations who have so graciously participated. If misused, I sincerely beg your forgiveness.

MAP: This is the amazing part of what we are doing. Acknowledging the discomfort that a researcher can feel as they conduct a study is powerful. Acknowledging the harm that may have been caused to people being studied, and later treated based on the results of the study, is even more powerful. It is all a recipe for change in how business is conducted.

Editor's comment (SOG): Recently, at the end of a mandated university workshop on cultural competency that Mathew, the first author of this chapter, and I conducted, a White, female faculty member said, "What do I think about today? I am upset now. I came here because I thought it would be an upbeat discussion about cultural competency. Now, I am feeling very sad about many of the things we discussed. This isn't what I wanted to hear." She was the same individual who had expressed great surprise to hear that a Black faculty member stated that she saw herself as a "token" at the university, and this faculty member added that at each staff meeting, when she entered the room, she always first looked for other attendees who were people of color. The White attendee stated, "Really? Well, I am White, and I never look for other White people at any meetings. You really do that? I find that hard to believe."

After hearing the White faculty member's expression of discontent with the workshop because it raised so many uncomfortable topics for her, Mathew waited for her to finish reflecting about the fact that she was shocked to hear that there was still a sense of pervasive inequality among faculty members at that university, many of whom still experienced inequity and many forms of microagressions on a daily basis.

He then replied, "Medicine sometimes hurts before it heals."

REFERENCES

American Psychological Association. (2017). American Psychological Association Homepage (www.apa.org/about/index.aspx – accessed July 22, 2017).

Barks, C. (2005). *Rumi: The book of love: Poems of ecstasy and longing*. San Francisco, CA: HarperOne Reprint Edition.

Baxter, E., & Hopper, K. (1981). *Private lives/public spaces: Homeless adults in the streets of NY*. New York: Community Service Society.

Cantor, N. (2012, September 6). What shall we do? Higher education's existential crisis. *Huffington Post*.

DiAngelo, R. (2011). White fragility. *International Journal of Critical Pedagogy, 3*(3), 54–70.

Democratizing Knowledge Project. (2017). Accessed March 10, 2017. http://democratizingknowledge.syr.edu/.

Duran, E., & Firehammer, J. (2015). Story sciencing and analyzing the silent narrative between words: Counseling research from an Indigenous perspective. In R. D. Goodman & P. C. Gorski (Eds.), *Decolonizing "multicultural counseling" through social justice* (pp. 85–97). New York: Springer Science + Business Media.

Ensign, M. (2017). http://www.chronicle.com/article/Let-s-Train-Extension/240664.

Geertz, C. (1973). Thick description: Toward an interpretive theory of culture. In *The Interpretation of Cultures: Selected Essays* (pp. 3–30). New York: Basic Books.

Goethe, J. W. (1998). *Maxims and reflections*. London: Penguin Books.

goodreads.com. (n.d.). "Quote by Jean-Jacques Rousseau." https://www.goodreads.com/quotes/602062-if-we-assume-man-has-been-corrupted-by-an-artificial

Gould, S. J. (1981). *Mismeasure of man*. New York: W.W. Norton.

Grinder, M. (2016). *The elusive obvious: The science of non-verbal communication.* Battle Ground, WA: Michael Grinder & Associates.

Hall, G. H., & Patrinos, H. A. (2012). *Indigenous peoples, poverty, and development.* Cambridge, MA: Cambridge University Press.

Hill, A. (2002, June 6). Insider women with outsider values, *New York Times.*

Johnston, L. (1981, March 11). A journey into the city's Netherworld. *New York Times.* N.Y. Region.

Jones, C. A. (2013). *The system isn't broken, it was designed that way: A critical analysis of historical racial disadvantage in the criminal justice system.* Clifton Park, NY: The Hampton Institute.

Kaplan, H., Thompson, R. C., Trumble, B. C., Wann, L. S., Allam, A. H., Beheim, B., Frohlich, B., (. . .); & Thomas, G. S. (2017). Coronary atherosclerosis in indigenous South American Tsimane: A cross-sectional cohort study. *The Lancet, 389*(10080), 1730–1739. Also, listen to: http://www.npr.org/sections/goatsandsoda/2017/03/21/520565500/who-has-the-healthiest-hearts-in-the-world http://www.npr.org/sections/goatsandsoda/2017/03/21/520565500/who-has-the-healthiest-hearts-in-the-world.

Kohlberg, L. (1981). *The philosophy of moral development: Moral stages and the idea of justice.* San Francisco: Harper and Row.

Lindsey, E., & Colwell, M. (2013). Pretend and physical play: Links to preschoolers' affective social competence. *Merrill-Palmer Quarterly, 59*(3), 330–360. Retrieved from; http://muse.jhu.edu.proxy.library.nd.edu/journals/merrill-palmer_quarterly/v059/59.3.lindsey.html

Nagai, C. (2009). Ethno-cultural and linguistic transference and countertransference: From Asian Perspectives. *American Journal of Psychotherapy, 63*(1), 13–23.

National Commission for the Protection of Human Subjects of Biomedical and Behavioral Research. (1979). *The Belmont Report. Ethical principles and guidelines for the protection of human subjects of research.* Washington, DC: Department of Health, Education, and Welfare.

Navarez, D. (2014, April 1). Is pretend play good for kids? Retrieved from *Psychology Today.* https://www.psychologytoday.com/blog/moral-landscapes/201404/is-pretend-play-good-kids.

Page, S. E., Lewis, E., & Cantor, N. (2017). *The diversity bonus: How great teams pay off in the knowledge economy.* Princeton, NJ: Princeton University Press.

Rouseau, J. J. (n.d.). Retrieved from goodreads.com.

Substance Abuse and Mental Health Services Administration. (n.d.). *GPRA Modernization Act of 2010 tools.* Author: Samhsa.gov.

Steup, M. (2017). Epistemology. In E. N. Zalta (Ed.), *The Stanford encyclopedia of philosophy.* (Spring 2014 Ed.). https://plato.stanford.edu/archives/fall2017/entries/epistemology/ (accessed 7-14-17).

System of a Down. (2001). "Science," featuring Arto Tunçboyaciyan. Track 10 on *Toxicity.* Columbia. Compact disc.

Vygotsky, L. (1934). *Thinking and speech. Lev Vygotsky 1934.* Retrieved from Marxists: https://www.marxists.org/archive/vygotsky/works/words/ch07.htm.

Zaborowska, M. J. (2009). The Borderland Foundation in Sejny, Poland. *The Journal of the International Institute, 16*(2), 14–15.

Conclusion

Moving Forward in Social Justice Initiatives

Susan O. Gelberg

WHEN WE BEGAN

From the moment we, the editors, began to conceptualize the vision of *Radical Psychology*, we understood that we would be asking each other, the publisher, and our readers to "step outside the box" of contemporary Euro-American academic theoretical premises and writing paradigms. Seeking to infuse into our book a diversity of worldviews, theoretical outlooks, writing styles, and professional disciplines, we knew that we would strive to write directly and openly in order to inform, challenge, and support readers who wished to better understand current issues associated with decolonizing contemporary Western psychological teaching, training, research, theory, and clinical practices.

We asked our authors to write about their social justice passions knowing that this might mean presenting paradigms that were radical departures from contemporary Western psychological worldviews. Also understanding that those topics might create conflict with readers, one of our editors cited an Indigenous tenet, "Conflict precedes clarity" (Don Coyhis, personal communication, undated). In seeking to accomplish the above, we would strive not to proselytize but to present culturally informed views for our readers' consideration.

Being radical in our approach to this book, we incorporated the word *radical* into the book title and used it as an acronym to describe some of the qualities we thought that radical psychologists might have. Those qualities bear repeating. In chapter 1, we suggested that radical psychologists:

R: Realize that there is still much that they don't know and much that "they don't know that they don't know."

A: Accept that because of blind spots and information gaps, the imposition by psychologists, researchers, counselors, and educators of Euro-American worldviews and practices on individuals and groups has a high potential for being harmful to populations that do not subscribe to traditional Eurocentric worldviews.

D: Make efforts to decolonize psychological formulations, practices, theories, and research through the

I: Inclusion of colleagues and consultants who endorse and practice other worldviews.

C: Develop counterhegemonic (opposition to status quo) initiatives including

A: Social justice action and

L: Legal protection for all regardless of the diversity of culture, ethnicity, socioeconomic status, health, physical or mental ability, spiritual or religious beliefs, educational background, sexual orientation, gender identity, sexual biology, age cohort, and ancestral backgrounds.

We selected authors who practice cultural humility (Shaw, 2017) in their self-appraisals and demonstrate through their professional work that they embrace many RADICAL qualities. Our authors realize (the *R* in *R*ADICAL) that there is still much they don't know. In addition, our authors have experienced what Woodson (1933) calls "miseducation," which refers to the impact colonization has had on the distortion of historical accounts. Miseducation results in the denigration of racial and ethnic minority cultures or other worldviews. Understanding this, some authors of *Radical Psychology* incorporated into their chapters historical accounts that corrected what they perceived as biased Euro-American historical accounts of a particular topic. In doing this, our authors hope to help readers understand the ways in which a more accurate knowledge of traumatic historical cultural factors can be better incorporated into psychological research, teaching, and clinical activities. We view this as an important step to help Western psychology develop into a profession that is less harmful and/or irrelevant to more and more people as world demographics change (Grayshield & Mihecoby, 2010).

Throughout their professional careers, the authors of *Radical Psychology* accept (R*A*DICAL) that Eurocentric psychological practices can be harmful to those who endorse non-Euro-American worldviews. Our authors have frequent ongoing dialogues with contemporary psychologists and counselors about what they see as potentially harmful therapies (Lilienfeld, 2007). In addition, the authors have sought to decolonize (RA*D*ICAL; Goodman & Gorski, 2015) harmful practices through their writing, research, teaching, professional services, and social justice activities.

Radical Psychology strives to reflect diversity through the inclusion (RAD*I*CAL) of a multitude of worldviews in regards to colonization and decolonization. Many of our authors collaborated in their writing with colleagues who reflect differing cultural or ethnic worldviews. In each of their chapters, the authors develop counterhegemonic (RADI*C*AL; Greenleaf, Bryant, 2012) approaches that challenge the status quo. Finally, their professional activities illustrate many types of social action (RADIC*A*L), including political and legal (RADICA*L*) professional activities.

WHERE WE WENT

As a first step in increasing knowledge of social justice, the Introduction and chapter 1 include a focus on historical Euro-American colonization: what it is, what individuals and institutional systems it affects, and how it is reflected in psychological practices. The acronym *radical psychology* was introduced. This writer suggested conceptualizations about how social justice might address colonization within the profession of psychology through a deeper understanding of historical factors and historical trauma.

Chapter 2, "The Existential Change in Perspective in the Diagnostic and Statistical Manual of Mental Disorders – Fifth Edition (DSM-5)," was written by David D. Moore, one of the editors of *Radical Psychology* and an academic scholar with a long history of conducting culturally informed research. Dr. Moore's work includes many collaborations with Indigenous leaders.

Chapter 2 discussed the evolving *Diagnostic and Statistical Manual of Mental Disorders* (DSM; American Psychiatric Association, 1952, 1968, 1980, 1987, 1994, 2000, 2013) and the resulting conflicts that occur among psychologists and between psychological associations and interest groups.

Dr. Moore is also a practicing clinician, and he has developed strong community coalitions. He included in his chapter insights about how he integrates cultural sensitivity into the services he provides for ethnically and racially diverse clients.

Chapter 2 offers an opportunity for readers to explore their own responses to Dr. Moore's discussion of the history of the different editions of the *DSM*. His frustrations in overcoming Eurocentric roadblocks while conducting research and developing clinical services are evident throughout Chapter 2, as are the ways in which he addressed these roadblocks.

Chapter 3, "The Psychologist and Allied Behavioral Health Facilitators Retrained as Humanistic Firestarters," was written by two of our editors, David D. Moore, the author of Chapter 2, and Don Coyhis, an international leader in Indian Country and the founder of White Bison, Inc. White Bison is a substance abuse treatment program that has received federal research grants. In this chapter, theoretical and methodological research issues that continue to challenge Euro-American paradigms were discussed. The chapter discussed new ways to evaluate psychological practices, research, evidence-based practices, and education based on Indigenous healing paradigms and the research they have done. Chapter 3 included the personal and professional insights of Dr. Moore when immersed in the healing practices of a different culture. The processes Dr. Moore went through have relevance to psychologists who are immersed in other cultural paradigms.

Chapter 4, "Treatment Interventions for Intimate Partner Violence in the Lives of African American Women: A Social Justice Approach," was written by Carolyn M. West, who has won many awards for her research. In writing this chapter, Dr. West drew on her personal experiences, professional training, research, and peer-reviewed professional writing to relate violence to social justice initiatives. Her chapter is especially relevant given the current political climate of the MeToo and Time's Up movements as well as other social justice activist movements that have included a focus on intimate partner violence. Given the statistics of the high prevalence of intimate partner violence, it is likely that some mental health professionals have experienced some type of violence in their own lives. Dr. West showed how those experiences can provide a clear focus for professional activism in the area of domestic violence.

Chapter 5, "Immigration and Social Justice," was written by Alfonso Mercado and Amanda C. Venta. In this chapter, Drs. Mercado and Venta illustrated how conducting culturally informed research, developing a community outreach project, and engaging in professional leadership activities within a state psychology association furthered their professional endeavors and social justice goals.

Chapter 6, "Moving Beyond Culturally Competent Services for Vietnamese Americans: Working Toward Social Justice," was coauthored by Drs. Kim Nguyen-Finn and Jerome Fischer. Drs. Finn and Fishcher have a long-term professional mentor-mentee relationship. Chapter 6 focuses on Asian American social justice issues. This chapter exemplified how two people from two different backgrounds worked together to develop writing that shows inclusivity and takes advantage of differing worldviews. The information they shared about common Asian American traditional values, behaviors, and communication styles will help readers from other cultures understand Asian etiquette and develop stronger rapport with clients through a deeper understanding of Asian history, communications styles, and values. It will also help researchers avoid misinterpretations of Asian American verbal and nonverbal behaviors.

The case histories in Chapter 6 offered a deep understanding of individual, family, and cultural traumas as experienced by many Asian Americans. The detailed anecdotes were crucial to help readers understand trauma through the eyes of the traumatized individual. The description of their experiences exposed readers to very emotional passages while asking them to avoid responses that might be characterized as showing white fragility (DiAngelo, 2011) and thus reduce readers' ability to absorb the material.

Beyond knowing about cultural historical colonization, social justice requires deep introspection by activists in order to become more aware of implicit and explicit biases and stereotypes they may hold (Boysen, 2009). Chapter 7, "Adventures in Intersectionality: The Journey of an Early Career Psychologist", by Jessica L. Binkley, illustrated the use of self-reflexivity and critical consciousness (Shin, 2015) by a young professional who applies the concept of intersectionality (Shin, 2015) to her self-analysis. Dr. Binkley discussed supervision issues, White fragility (DiAngelo, 2011), and identity factors (Meyers, 2016) as they affected her work with diverse clientele in a Euro-American mental health agency.

Chapter 8, "Social Justice in Prevention Psychology: Healing with the Community Readiness Model," was written by Pamela Jumper-Thurman, Barbara A. Plested, Kateri D. Coyhis, and Hanna Moore. Two authors, Kateri Coyhis and Hanna Moore, are young professionals. We selected these young authors in order to reflect the respect that other cultures have for the voices of youth, who are seen as tomorrow's elders. Given their immersion in a non-European cultural background, we see Kateri Coyhis and Hanna Moore as experts who can give readers a firsthand knowledge on how the young can provide a crucial voice in challenging the Euro-American psychological paradigms to which they have been exposed.

Kateri Coyhis led a traditional Native lifestyle while completing a university degree from a Euro-American university. Hanna Moore spent much of her life with Indigenous people. In their university studies, these authors studied and wrote about the impact of colonization—in particular, boarding schools—on Native Americans. These two authors shared their insights about their hopes for future decolonization initiatives.

Joining Kateri Coyhis and Hanna Moore in this chapter were two seasoned researchers, Pamela Jumper-Thurman and Barbara A. Plested, who have strong backgrounds in cross-cultural research studies as principal investigators, grant writing coalition builders, university professors, and mentors for new professionals.

These four authors worked together to write a chapter that represented the voices of our youth accompanied by the reflections of seasoned researchers. The authors' combined insights are helpful to those who work with populations that have experienced other forms of Euro-American colonization.

Chapter 9, "The Issues of Identity, Self-awareness, and Social Justice," focused on social justice issues for African American males. It was written by Fred C. Miller, a psychologist who has conducted federally funded research with elderly African Americans experiencing cognitive impairments as they aged. Dr. Miller is a culturally competent researcher and educator who consistently infuses social justice factors into his educational and research practices at a community college. In Chapter 9, he wrote candidly about the identity issues of a Black man living in a White, Eurocentric society. His insights help readers understand how developmental issues affect the personal and professional identities of individuals from a nondominant culture.

Chapter 10, "Decolonizing Knowledge Creation: Moving Toward the Sacred and the Liminal," was written by Mathew A. Poteet, one of our editors, and Bonita M. Veysey. Mathew Poteet received his traditional learning from Indigenous elders. He directly experienced the damage of Euro-American psychology when he was a boy as Eurocentric psychologists, and mental health practitioners assessed and treated his childhood traumas. His cultural history was not considered relevant. At best, his cultural background was considered superficially and with considerable stereotyping and scorn. He suffered greatly throughout his early life because of harmful interactions with contemporary Western psychology. In Chapter 10, he wrote from his perspective as an individual outside the system of psychology and as a person whose thinking has always been informed more by traditional Indigenous histories than by Eurocentric education.

The other author of Chapter 10, Bonita M. Veysey, is an experienced researcher, author, mentor, and professor. The two authors' discussion about the democratization of knowledge challenged readers to understand the perspectives of two writers who have both witnessed and experienced colonization and are now social justice activists. This chapter provided readers with an opportunity to reach beyond ethnocultural biases that may arise when reading texts that significantly differ from traditional Euro-American academic writing styles and content. The writing and content styles the authors selected show how cross-cultural conversations benefit through inclusion. Readers may then better appreciate how they can also communicate more inclusively with colleagues from other cultures.

Chapter 11, written by this author, summarizes a few highlights for each chapter. Chapter 11 also presents additional research relating to the developmental nature of social justice initiatives. Social justice mentoring is discussed, as are several Western psychological approaches that reflect many of the social justice values that our editors believe radical psychologists should endorse. Chapter 11 invites readers to read more extensively about psychological paradigms that reflect cultural best practices and provides warnings to those in the dominant culture to avoid a number of common cultural transgressions that may occur when professionals work in areas in which they are not cultural experts. Finally, extensive resources for further study are suggested.

WHERE WILL WE GO? THE DEVELOPMENT OF SOCIAL JUSTICE ACTIVISM SKILLS

Because radical decolonization imperatives often involve changing the status quo, they may pose individual personal and/or professional difficulties for social justice activists and for the individuals or agencies they are challenging. In order to effectively address these conflicts, advocacy requires skills not only in cultural competency with individuals, groups, and communities, but it also benefits from strengths such as cultural etiquette, self-awareness (Teo, Gao, & Sheivari, 2014), problem-solving (Eskin, 2013), skillful goal-setting (Emiliussen, & Wagoner, 2013), conflict resolution at the interpersonal, intergroup, organizational, and international levels (Deutsch, Coleman, & Marcus, 2014), knowledge of the complex psychological issues that affect assertiveness (Soule, 2016), stress management (Linden, 2005), self-care (Cardozo School of Law, 2016), and politics (Lee, Smith, & Henry, 2013).

Lewis, Ratts, Paladino, and Toporek (2011) write in depth about social justice competencies as delineated by the American Counseling Association. They developed a workshop to help participants apply advocacy principles to their practices. The workshop was conducted in 2010 at the National Multicultural and Social Justice Leadership Academy, which is housed in Division 17 (Society of Counseling Psychology) of the American Psychological Association.

Lyons et al. (2013) discuss best practices in social justice qualitative research, including sections on research design, data collection, data analysis, data interpretation, and application of findings. Ponterotto (2010) reviews qualitative research best practices and ethical issues as they relate to multicultural research.

These advocacy competencies are many of the same strengths psychologists seek to develop or assess in others when formulating their teaching objectives, treatment care plans for clients, supervision activities, or research objectives. Just as psychologists encourage their clients, students, or research subjects to do, mental health professionals must learn to tolerate and avoid terminating discussions that become uncomfortable and challenging to themselves or to others (DiAngelo, 2011; Sue, 2015).

For mental health practitioners who have personally experienced the impacts of colonization, additional issues may arise, some of which are described by Grayshield (Grayshield & Mihecoby, 2010) and in the beginning of Chapter one of *Radical Psychology*. These individuals must learn to stop enabling Euro-Americans to avoid or end uncomfortable discussions about colonization, Euro-American microaggressions, potential problems with Eurocentric psychological paradigms, and other social justice topics. They must also learn to recognize the organizational dynamics that stifle challenging discussions about colonizing agency policies (Ho, 2007).

MENTORING

Mentoring and the Zone of Proximal Development

In understanding the personal and professional difficulties social justice imperatives pose for individuals and institutions, it is helpful to view social justice activism within a developmental framework. Just as there are developmental tasks throughout the life span for personal development (Learner, Lamb, & Freund, 2010; Overton & Learner, 2010) and professional development (Orlinsky & Ronnestad, 2005), social justice advocacy involves developmental tasks for advocates and mentors (Adams, Perry-Jenkins, & Tropp, 2014).

Developmental theories of clinical supervision (Stoltenberg, 2005) can be used to help advocates learn how to best increase social justice skills. In addition, mismatches between the skill levels of the supervisor and the supervisee can cause harmful impacts on the professional development of supervisees (Barnett, 2017; Stoltenberg, 2005). As an example, for heterosexual social justice activists who are seeking to address heteronormativity, this author and a colleague once proposed a developmental model for heterosexual allies and their mentors (Gelberg & Chojnacki, 1996). Heterosexual allies/mentees benefit from different levels of challenge depending on their experience. Dr. Chojnacki and this writer proposed developmental tasks for cognitive, behavioral, and affective domains at each stage of ally development. We also suggested specific supervisory behaviors for differing stages of ally development.

In formulating those developmental tasks for allies (Gelberg & Chojnacki, 1996), we used developmental concepts such as the *zone of proximal development* (ZPD) and *optimal mismatch*—concepts which can be applied to ensure that mentees are not either overwhelmed or underchallenged by their mentors in setting their goals for advocacy. The goals of both mentors and mentees can be placed within a developmental framework based on ZPD principles.

The ZPD framework was initially used to in educational psychology to study children's cognitive development. The concepts were first introduced by Lev Vygotski, a Russian developmental psychologist (Vygotski, 1978). Wood, Bruner, and Ross (1976) formally labeled the concept as the *zone of proximal development.*

Vygotski (1978) proposed that there is an optimal learning task level that lies in between the level of a task the learner can do independently without help (the learner's *actual level*, Thompson, 2013), the task level that a learner can do with help (the learner's *potential level*; Thompson, 2013), and the subsequent *realized level* that the individual can then do independently (Thompson, 2013). The middle zone of proximal development (the learner's potential level; Thompson, 2013) represents those learning experiences that can be mastered by the learner with assistance from another without being too difficult or frustrating for the learner. Contemporary educational practices have expanded these concepts by introducing the concept of *scaffolding*, which refers to the guidance provided initially, to help children learn (Verenikina, 2003).

At the University of California, San Diego, Ferholt and Lecusay (2010) studied the zone of proximal development as it promoted learning between child and adult. Results indicated that learning was bidirectional in that both adults and children experienced simultaneous development.

The implications of ZPD for social justice are intriguing. Research has shown that both the learner and the mentor benefit from engaging in learning activities that are in the ZPD—namely, in the area and level that the learner can master the task with the assistance of the more experienced mentor (Ferholt & Lecusay, 2010).

Other Mentoring Recommendations

In "Social Justice Mentoring: Supporting the Development of Future Leaders for Struggle, Resistance, and Transformation," Neville (2015) discusses the balance between affirmation and challenge as it applies to students of color, who are often routinely either hyperscrutinized or neglected in clinical supervision. She provides personal and professional recommendations for mentoring social justice mentees. Ali, Liu, Mahmood, and Arguello (2008) also discuss the theoretical and practical implementation of a social justice agenda in psychology training programs.

In the *Canadian Journal of Counselling*, Palmer and Parish (2008) write about educational, research, and training on social justice issues for counseling psychologists. They recommend that training include foci on feminism, critical psychology, and multiculturalism.

Motulsky, Gere, Saleem, and Trantham (2014) discuss nontraditional teaching approaches to promote social justice consciousness for future counseling psychologists. They suggest pedagogical techniques, experiential exercises, video resources, and opportunities for self-reflection as ways to train counseling psychologist as future social justice advocates.

Developmental Approach to Social Justice

Looking at the objectives and populations discussed by each author in *Radical Psychology*, it is easy to imagine how one may become overwhelmed in selecting goals that are appropriate given a particular work situation, developmental level as a social justice advocate, and individual interpersonal skills or weaknesses. For some individuals, that is, those who still reflect the *Nice*

Counselor Syndrome (Bemak & Chi-Ying Chung, 2008), joining into an honest one-to-one dialogue with another professional by the introjection of social justice issues into the conversation may be the first step in addressing social justice. A more advanced step might be to become more public about discussing social justice perspectives in an agency staff meeting or at a conference. For individuals who excel more in writing than in spoken communications, the initial discussions might be through journal articles or other forms of professional or lay writing about social justice.

Mentoring and the Developmental Nature of Self-Efficacy

Psychologists are educated, supervised, and otherwise trained in their fields so that their sense of self-efficacy (Bandura, 1977) as professors, researchers, or clinicians increases over time with additional professional experience. Since social justice is not routinely part of psychology curricula, and since mentors and supervisees may not be as culturally competent in social justice activities as is the student/new professional/mentee, self-efficacy as a social justice advocate may remain low for even seasoned researchers, educators, or clinicians. For some psychologists or counselors, the ability to receive feedback may be challenging, uncomfortable, and unsettling—especially if the feedback is from an individual who has cultural expertise credentials other than Euro-American credentials.

Low self-efficacy can prevent social advocates from initiating meaningful social justice initiatives. Just as psychologists help clients, students, or research subjects address low self-efficacy, they—the mental health professionals—can benefit from using those same techniques to avoid passivity due to their own low self-efficacy. The inclusion of the support of culturally competent allies can help activists set developmentally appropriate social activism goals and, through success, raise social justice self-efficacy through meeting those goals. The opposite problem may also exist, in which Euro-Americans overestimate their self-efficacy in multicultural or social justice activities.

Mentoring and Self-Assessment

In an article entitled, "Unskilled and Unaware of It: How Difficulties in Recognizing One's Own Incompetence Lead to Inflated Self-Assessments," Kruger and Dunning (1999) found that individuals who were incompetent in areas such as logic (as judged by consideration of the bottom quartile of test performance of their research subjects) lacked the self-monitoring skills to know how well they were doing. That is, in certain social intellectual domains, their low-performing subjects could not accurately determine whether they are accurate in their judgments and when their judgments are in error.

When we apply the findings of Kruger and Dunning (1999) to situations in which Western psychologists who have had only superficial training in multicultural topics and who are also minimally effective in the eyes of mental health professionals from other cultures, there is a good possibility that those self-assessments will be in error due to faulty self-monitoring skills. Mentors who have been immersed in the particular culture that is of interest to the Western psychologist can help provide feedback to that psychologist so that self-assessment then becomes more accurate. This would increase accountability so that there was a reduced potential that the services provided by the Western psychologist were potentially harmful to students, clients, or research subjects.

CULTURAL RED FLAGS

We have spent much time in *Radical Psychology* encouraging individuals in the dominant Euro-American culture to reach out to those in other cultures. There is, however, a major issue that Euro-American psychologists may not be fully aware of—an issue of which others in racial and ethnic minority cultures are more often acutely aware. This is the issue of exploitation—both intentional and unintentional. At the same time that self-efficacy develops in social justice advocates, advocates from Euro-American cultural paradigms run the risk of overstepping their boundaries if they do not receive constant, direct ongoing feedback about exploitation from cultural mentors. For example, psychologists who learn about Native American ceremonies can become overly confident—having an inappropriately high sense of self-efficacy—and incorporate Indigenous ceremonies into their practices without thinking to consult Native elders about the appropriateness of this. The practice of non-Natives conducting Indigenous ceremonies violates major ethical and legal Indigenous codes. Native American ceremonies are not to be performed by outsiders, and they are not to be sold.

Similarly, the ceremonial services of other cultures are not for sale. For psychologists whose paradigms still reflect colonization, this may be a difficult concept to grasp or accept. They may automatically feel that they have the "right" to use those ceremonies, when, in fact, they don't. One culturally acceptable solution would be for elders from that culture to offer those ceremonies for free (or for a donation that would be determined by the person invited to the ceremony). For those psychologists who place a high priority on materialism and financial gain, this option may not be attractive, especially since any donation would go to the individual providing the cultural service, not to the mental health professional.

INCLUSION ISSUES

We have stated throughout this book that ethical violations by Euro-American psychologists often occur unconsciously (Dunning, Johnson, Ehrlinger, & Kruger, 2003) and can remain so indefinitely without regular consultation with cultural elders. This highlights the need for the inclusion of cultural experts and cultural leaders as mentors for Euro-American psychologists who seek to provide cross-cultural counseling—or for any psychologist who does not possess the racial and/or ethnic cultural expertise to work with a particular client.

If cultural leaders agree to assist, it is essential that they not be placed in a "one-down" decision-making position. This may require strong assertiveness by mental health professionals who are working in Euro-American institutions that only accept Euro-American credentialing (e.g., masters' degrees, doctorates, and some type of Western licensure). One can see how the act of including a cultural expert as a leader in clinical programming often leads to a need for skilled advocacy at both individual and institutional levels.

EXPANDING THEORETICAL HORIZONS

Searching for Current Research in One's Professional Field

We have emphasized the need for the inclusion of cultural experts in decolonizing psychological services, research, and teaching. There are a number of branches of psychology that share many principles helpful to the under-served. There are 54 divisions or interest groups in the American Psychological Association. Some are clinical subspecialties (e.g., clinical psychology) and others focus on topical areas (e.g., ethnic minorities). There are many more psychological theoretical approaches such as cognitive behavioral therapy, existential humanistic tradition, object relations theory, and psychoanalytic theory. Whatever areas of expertise or clinical specializations social justice advocates have, advocates can benefit by first investigating whether social justice principles have been discussed or researched for the particular theoretical orientation they use in research, clinical practice, or teaching. For example, in a recent article entitled "Motivational Interviewing and Social Justice," Miller (2013) encouraged those who specialize in, or use, motivational interviewing techniques to consider how the inclusion of social justice considerations helps the focus of motivational interviewing expand outside of the therapy room.

Liberation Psychology

One psychological theory that strongly endorses social justice values is liberation psychology, founded by Ignacio Martín-Baró, a psychologist, professor, and administrator at El Salvador's Universidad Centroamericana. Baró coauthored *Writings for a Liberation Psychology* (Martín-Baró, Aron, & Corne, 1994). Following Martín-Baró, liberation psychology was further developed by Montero (2009) and Montero and Sonn (2009). In an article in the *Interamerican Journal of Psychology*, Tate, Rivera, Brown, and Skaistis (2013) provide a comprehensive summary of the theoretical underpinnings of liberation psychology and its principles (which include the importance of the recovery of historical memory, consideration of colonization, and liberatory change for oppressed populations). The article is an excellent introduction to the principles of social justice as implemented by liberation psychology theories and practice.

Jungian Psychology

Jungian analytic psychology is a theoretical orientation that reflects many non-Western worldviews. Carl Jung was a Swiss psychiatrist who founded analytical psychology. His principal theories included archetypes, the collective unconscious, and the process of individuation. In "Medicine Wheel, Mandala, and Jung," Eduardo Duran (2012) discussed the above Jungian concepts and commented about the striking parallels and key differences between the principal theories of Jungian psychology and Native perspectives. Jungian workshops sometimes include a focus on how Indigenous theories and perspectives intersect with Jungian psychology. Jungian principles support consideration of the unseen, dreams, archetypes, and other psychological or spiritual aspects when providing assistance to clients or patients. Jungian principles thus often resonate with individuals from other cultures.

Positive Psychology

Positive psychology is the "application of scientific methods to identifying key antecedents, correlates, and consequences associated with living a good, full, and meaningful life" (Chang, Downey, Hirsch, & Lin, 2016, p. 3). Positive psychology is a strengths-oriented psychology model, in contrast to other psychology models that may be deficits oriented. *Positive Psychology in Racial and Ethnic Groups: Theory, Research, and Practice* introduces "positive psychology within the context of race, ethnicity, and culture" (Chang, Downey, Hirsch, & Lin, 2016, p. 7). Chang et al.'s book focuses on the application of the tenets of positive psychology to multicultural theory development, research, assessment, and interventions developed for different ethnic and cultural populations. Chang et al.'s book also discusses ethnocentric biases and controversies about whether positive psychology is universal and culture-free or relevant only when placed within cultural contexts.

HOW SOCIAL JUSTICE MOVES US ALL FORWARD

The first two chapters of *Radical Psychology* discuss the potential harm that Eurocentric contemporary Western psychology principles and practices can cause when imposed on individuals or groups that do not endorse Euro-American values or worldviews. The chapters that followed discussed many approaches to addressing social justice issues and cultural competence in psychological practice, theory building, research, and training. For each of the authors of *Radical Psychology*, the benefits of working on cultural competence and social justice initiatives have been unique and numerous. Similarly, for each reader, the benefits and challenges of reading *Radical Psychology* will differ depending on that reader's professional identities, cultural background, availability of social justice and multicultural mentors, person-environment matches, and developmental level as a social justice activist.

Writing this book has been an immense challenge but provided a sense of accomplishment as the authors and editors have worked to provide readers with an optimal balance between challenge and support. As editors and authors, our gratifications are many, and include the following:

- Gaining new knowledge in both the field of social justice and cross-cultural counseling
- Challenging each other to conceptualize "outside the box" of contemporary psychology practices
- Working together on unified objectives as a team with diversity in thought and action
- Challenging the status-quo of contemporary Western psychology to improve its cultural competence levels and social justice foci
- Suggesting new research, teaching, practicing, and training paradigms
- Pushing ourselves to our best efforts in advocating for vulnerable populations
- Writing in a way that is relevant to readers across time, disciplines, cultural backgrounds, and levels of knowledge on social justice and cross-cultural counseling topics.

We, the authors and editors of this book, are not alone in noting the many benefits of social justice advocacy. As discussed in *the Praeger Handbook of Social Justice and Psychology, Volume 2: Well-Being and Professional*

Issues (Johnson, Friedman, Diaz, Franco, & Natasi, 2014), research has documented important benefits to both the advocate and the underserved or non-Euro-American individual or population being served. In their chapter entitled "Well-Being, Justice, and Social Change," Prilleltensky and Huygens (2014) write about direct ties between wellbeing and social justice efforts that include "organizing for economic prosperity, for health promotion, for effective functioning, for freedom, for equity, and organizing for participation, Inclusion, and dignity and mental and physical well-being" (Franco, 2014, p. xi).

One of the themes of *Radical Psychology* is the power of stretching beyond contemporary Euro-American psychological writing and reaching toward the knowledge of other disciplines. Paul Hawken (Paulhawken.com) is an activist, author, environmental activist, entrepreneur, and architect of corporate reform in regards to ecological practices. In 1965, he worked with Martin Luther King Jr.'s staff in Selma, Alabama, prior to the March on Montgomery; assisted with voter registration drives; photographed the Ku Klux Klan in Mississippi; and was assaulted and seized by (but later escaped from) Klan members. He recently said:

> When asked if I am pessimistic or optimistic about the future, my answer is always the same: If you look at the science about what is happening on earth and aren't pessimistic, you don't understand data. But if you meet the people who are working to restore this earth and the lives of the poor, and you aren't optimistic, you haven't got a pulse. What I see everywhere in the world are ordinary people willing to confront despair, power, and incalculable odds in order to restore some semblance of grace, justice, and beauty to this world. (Paul Hawken, undated, Paulhawken.com website)

We wish you, our readers, power, support, and courage in your quest for multicultural competency and social justice.

REFERENCES

Adams, M., Perry-Jenkins, M., & Tropp, L. R. (2014). Pedagogical tools for social justice and psychology. In C. V. Johnson & H. L. Friedman (Set Eds.), *The Praeger handbook of social justice in psychology: Vol. 2. Well-being and professional issues* (pp. 227–247). Santa Barbara, CA: Praeger.

Ali, S. R., Liu, W. M., Mahmood, A., & Arguello, J. (2008, Spring). Social justice and applied psychology: Practical ideas for training the next generation of psychologists. *Journal of Social Action in Counseling and Psychology, 1*(2), 1–13.

American Psychiatric Association. (1952/1968/1980/1987/1994/2000/2013). *Diagnostic and statistical manual of mental disorders (-1/-11/-111/-111-R/-IV/-IV-TR/-5).* Arlington, VA: American Psychiatric Publishing.

Bandura, A. (1977). Self-efficacy: Toward a unifying theory of behavioral change. *Psychological Review*, *84*, 191–215.

Barnett, J. E. (2017). Becoming a clinical supervisor: Key ethics issues and recommendations. *Journal of Health Service Psychology, 43*, 10–18.

Bemak, F., & Chi-Ying Chung, R. (2008). New professional roles and advocacy strategies for school counselors: A multicultural/social justice perspective to move beyond the Nice Counselor Syndrome. *Journal of Counseling & Development, 86*(3), 372–382.

Boysen, G. A. (2009, October 1). A review of experimental studies of explicit and implicit bias among counselors. *Journal of Multicultural Counseling and Development, 37*(4), 240–249. doi: 10.1002/j.2161-1912.2009.tb00106.x.

Cardozo School of Law. (2016, October 30). *Coalition building for our communities: A social justice and self-care training.* Conference: NY: Cardozo School of Law, Columbia Law School, Fordham University School of Law, New York Law School, New York University School of Law, Seton Hall University School of Law, and the Perception Institute.

Chang, E. C., Downey, C. A., Hirsch, J. K., & Lin, N. J. (2016). *Positive psychology in racial and ethnic groups: Theory, research, and practice.* Washington, DC: American Psychological Association.

Deutsch, M., Coleman, P. T., & Marcus, E. C. (2014). *Handbook of conflict resolution: Theory and practice* (3rd ed.). San Francisco, CA: Jossey-Bass.

DiAngelo, R. (2011). White fragility. *International Journal of Critical Pedagogy, 3*(3), 54–70.

Dunning, D., Johnson, K., Ehrlinger, J., & Kruger, J. (2003). Why people fail to recognize their own incompetence. *Current Directions in Psychological Science, 12*, 83–87.

Duran, E. (2012, Summer). Medicine wheel, mandala, and Jung. *Journal of Archetypal Culture, Native American Cultures and the Western Psyche: A Bridge between, 87*, 125–153.

Emiliussen, J., & Wagoner, B. (2013). Setting goals in psychotherapy: A phenomenological study of conflicts in the position of the therapist. *Psychology & Society, 5*(1), 16–36.

Eskin, M. (2013). *Problem solving therapy in the clinical practice.* London: Elsevier.

Ferholt, B., & Lecusay, R. (2010). Adult and child development in the zone of proximal development: Socratic dialogue in a playworld. *Mind, Culture, and Activity,* 17, 59–83. doi: 10.1080/10749030903342246.

Franco, Z. (2014). Introduction to volume 2. In C. V. Johnson & H. L. Friedman (Set Eds.), *The Praeger handbook of social justice in psychology, Vol. 2: Well-being and professional issues* (pp. xi–xxii). Santa Barbara, CA: Praeger.

Gelberg, S., & Chojnacki, J. T. (1996). *Career and life planning with gay, lesbian, and bisexual persons.* Alexandria, VA: American Counseling Association.

Goodman, R. D., & Gorski, P. C. (Eds.). (2015). *Decolonizing "multicultural" counseling through social justice.* New York: Springer.

Grayshield, L., & Mihecoby, A. (2010, Fall). Indigenous ways of knowing as a philosophical base for the promotion of peace and justice in counseling educationand psychology. *Journal for Social Action in Counseling and Psychology, 2*(2), 1–16.

Greenleaf, A. T., & Bryant, R. M. (2012, Spring). Perpetuating oppression: Does the current counseling discourse neutralize social action? *Journal of Social Action in Counseling and Psychology, 1*(1), 18–29.

Ho, K. (2007, September). Structural violence as a human rights violation. *Essex Human Rights Review, 4*(2), 1–17.

Johnson, C. V., & Friedman, H. L. (Set Editors), Diaz, J., Franco, Z., & Nastasi, B. K. (Volume Editors). (2014). *The Praeger handbook of social justice and psychology, Vol. 1: Fundamental issues and special populations; Vol. 2: Well-being and professional issues; Vol. 3: Youth and disciplines in psychology.* Santa Clara, CA: Praeger.

Kruger, J., & Dunning, D. (1999). Unskilled and unaware of it: How difficulties in recognizing one's own incompetence lead to inflated self-assessments. *Journal of Personality and Social Psychology, 77*(6), 1121–1134.

Learner, R. M. (Editor in Chief), Lamb, M. E. (Volume Editor), & Freund, A. M. (Volume Editor). (2010). *Handbook of life-span development* (Vol. 2). *Social and emotional development*. Hoboken, NJ: John Wiley and Sons.

Lee, M. A., Smith, T. J., & Henry, R. G. (2013, Fall). Power politics: Advocacy to activism in social justice counseling. *Journal for Social Action in Counseling and Psychology, 5*(3), 70–94.

Lewis, J. A., Ratts, M. J., Paladino, D. A., & Toporek, R. L. (2011, Spring). Social justice counseling and advocacy: Developing new leadership roles and competencies. *Journal for Social Action in Counseling and Psychology, 3*(1), 5–16.

Lilienfeld, S. O. (2007). Psychological treatments that cause harm. *Association for Psychological Science, 2*(1), 53–70.

Linden, W. (2005). *Stress management: From basic science to better practice.* Thousand Oaks, CA: SAGE.

Martín-Baró, I. A. (Author), Aron, & S. Corne (Eds.). (1994). *Writings for a liberation psychology.* Cambridge, MA: Harvard University Press.

Meyers, L. (2016, December). Investigating identity. *Counseling Today*, 24–30.

Miller, W. R. (2013). Motivational interviewing and social justice. *Motivational Interviewing Training, Research, Implementation, and Practice, 1*(2), 15–18. doi: 10.5195/mitrip.2013.32.

Montero, M. (2009). Methods for liberation: Critical consciousness in action. In M. Montero & C. C. Sonn (Eds.), *Psychology of liberation: Theory and applications* (pp. 73–91). New York: Springer.

Montero, M., & Sonn, C. (2009). About liberation and psychology: An introduction. In M. Montero & C. C. Sonn (Eds.), *Psychology of liberation: Theory and applications* (pp. 1–10). New York: Springer.

Motulsky, S. L., Gere, S. H., Saleem, R., & Trantham, S. M. (2014). Teaching social justice in counseling psychology. *The Counseling Psychologist, 42*(8), 1058–1083.

Neville, H. A. (2015). Social justice mentoring: Supporting the development of future leaders for struggle, resistance, and transformation. *Counseling Psychologist, 43*(1), 157–169.

Orlinsky, D. E., & Ronnestad, M. H. (2005). *How psychotherapists develop: A study of therapeutic work and professional growth.* Washington, DC: American Psychological Association.

Overton, W. F. (Vol. Ed.), & Learner, R. M. (Ed.-in-Chief). (2010). *Handbook of life-span development, volume 1: Cognition, biology, and methods*. Hoboken, NJ: John Wiley & Sons.

Palmer, A., & Parish, J. (2008). Social justice and counseling psychology: Situating the role of graduate student research, education, and training. *Canadian Journal of Counselling, 42*(4), 278–292.

Ponterotto, J. G. (2010). Qualitative research in multicultural psychology: Philosophical underpinnings, popular approaches, and ethical considerations. *Cultural Diversity and Ethnic Minority Psychology, 16*(4), 581–589.

Prilleltensky, I., & Huygens, I. (2014). Well-being, justice, and social change. In C. V. Johnson & Harriet L. Friedman (Eds.). *The Praeger handbook of social justice and psychology* (pp. 3–31). Santa Barbara, CA: Praeger.

Shaw, S. (2017, January). Practicing humility. *Counseling Today*, 41–45.

Shin, R. Q. (2015). The application of critical consciousness and intersectionality as tools for decolonizing racial/ethnic identity development models in the fields of counseling and psychology. In R. D. Godman & P. C. Gorski (Eds.), *Decolonizing "multicultural" counseling through social justice* (pp. 11–22). New York: Springer.

Smith, L. T. (1999). *Decolonizing methodologies*. New York: Zed Books.

Soule, R. (2016, Feb. 2). *Transforming conflict/compassionate assertiveness*. (PDF). Vancouver, BC, Canada: University of British Columbia Learning Circle, Centre for Excellence in Indigenous Health. Available at med-fom-learningcircle.sites.oit.ubc.ca.

Stoltenberg, C. D. (2005, November). Enhancing professional competence through developmental approaches to supervision. *American Psychologist, 60*(8), 857–864. doi:10.1037/0003-066X.60.8.85.

Sue, D. W. (2015). *Race talk and the conspiracy of silence: Understanding and Facilitating difficult dialogues on race*. Hoboken, NJ: John Wiley & Sons.

Tate, K. A., Rivera, E. T., Brown, E., & Skaistis, L. (2013). Foundations for liberation: Social justice, liberation psychology. *Inter-American Journal of Psychology, 47*(3), 373–382.

Teo, T., Gao, Z., & Sheivari, R. (2014). Philosophical reflexivity in social justice work. In C. V. Johnson & Harriet L. Friedman (Eds.), *The Praeger handbook of social justice and psychology* (pp. 65–78). Santa Barbara, CA: Praeger.

Thompson, I. (2013, Feb.). The mediation of learning in the zone of proximal development through a co-constructed writing activity. *Research in the Teaching of English, 47*(3), 247–274.

Verenikina, I. (2003). Understanding scaffolding and the ZPD in educational research. Proceedings of the International Education Research Conference (AARE-NZARE), 30 November – 3 December 2003. Auckland, New Zealand.

Vygotsky, L. S. (1978). *Mind in society: Development of higher psychological processes*. Cambridge, MA: Harvard University Press.

Wood, D., Bruner, J., & Ross, G. (1976). The role of tutoring in problem solving. *Journal of Child Psychology and Psychiatry, 7*, 89–100.

Woodson, C. G. (1933). *The mis-education of the Negro*. Washington, DC: Associated Publishers.

Appendix

Reflective Questions

INTRODUCTION

1. The Introduction begins with the negative implications of psychological practices that still colonize. Do you feel that this topic has received adequate treatment in the professional literature you read and/or in the discussions you have with your colleagues?
2. How would you respond to Cirecie West-Olantunji's university teaching example?
3. Do you belong to any special interest groups that focus on culture, ethnicity, race, or other nondominant worldviews? Why or why not?
4. How often do the continuing education programs you attend focus on the implications of culture, ethnicity, race, gender, sexual orientation, socioeconomic background, and so on, on the workshop topics? How often do you openly respond as an attendant to these issues that have the potential to colonize the topics of the workshop?
5. If you are Euro-American, how often do you attend workshops in which you are among the minority? What reflections do you have about these experiences?

CHAPTER 1

1. When you are exposed to topics that you find difficult to discuss because of your own emotional pain, anger, confusion, depression, anxiety, or other feelings, how resilient are you, so that you do not end those conversations because they are too difficult for you? Have your work behaviors ever reflected the "nice counselor syndrome" (NCS) in that you take a

neutral stance or give positive feedback when confrontation is required in order to avoid upsetting others or the system (Bemak & Chung, 2008)? How strong are your anger management skills in responding to these conversations? Your stress management skills? Your communications skills in avoiding any premature ending of a difficult conversation?

2. Given that 50% of Americans believe that their culture is superior to others (Pew Research Center's Global Attitudes Project, 2011), how effectively do you practice cultural humility (Hook, Davis, Owen, & DeBlaere, 2017)?
3. When you are working with individuals whose worldviews do not match yours, what is the impact on your self-esteem? Does this lead to any transference for your client or countertransference for you?
4. How do your religious or spiritual views affect your own countertransference or your client's transference in working with those who hold different worldviews? *In God is Red: A Native View of Religion*, Vine Deloria, Jr., a widely renowned Indigenous scholar, researcher, and educator, writes about the contrasts between Christianity and the spirituality of the American Indians. This classic work helps psychologists examine their transference and countertransference issues and stereotypes in spiritual areas (Deloria, 2003). How do you respond to the book's title, *God is Red . . .* ?
5. In pursuing your social justice or multicultural competence development, have you assessed your own family background of intergenerational trauma and historical trauma (Brave Heart, 2013; Brave Heart, Chase, Elkins, & Atschul, 2011; Elhai, Gray, Kashdan, & Franklin, 2005; Hooper, Stockton, Krupnick, & Green, 2011)?
6. How much do you know about—and integrate—consideration of factors related to intergenerational trauma, genocide, and historical trauma into your professional work as a researcher, clinician, or professor/teacher?

CHAPTER 2

1. DSM-5 has introduced the context of a person's diagnostic profile as arising through a developmental process. This chapter contrasts this new paradigm to DSM-IV's medical model of matching the person of today to a static, norm-referenced, diagnostic checklist. Using Section 3 of DSM-5 (American Psychiatric Association, 2013), the Cultural Formulation Interview, one model for diagnosing and treating persons who engage the services of psychotherapists, construct your own developmental narrative about your fit in the world of psychology. From what you have read thus far, how might you deconstruct your narrative to embrace postcolonial psychology?

2. Dr. Moore presents the Cultural Case Formulation as the methodology which bridges the standardized description of mental health disorders to the phenomenological measurement of diagnostic criteria. Using the Cultural Formulation Interview from Section 3 of the DSM-5 (American Psychiatric Association, 2013), write your own autobiographical essay about how your life, or the life of a family member, has intersected one of the DSM-5 disorders. How might your reflections shape your professional behaviors as a mental health professional?
3. Utilize this chapter to reflect on your own fields of research. In future professional endeavors, how might the developmental paradigm of assessment and use of phenomenological measurement affect the way you shape the Methods, Results, and Discussion Sections?
4. Using concepts presented by Durans' writing about what the era of post-colonial psychology could be (Duran & Duran, 1995), how do their reflections impact your own beliefs about moving into an era of postcolonial psychology? How well do their ideas resonate for you as a Prologue to the DSM-5 (American Psychiatric Association, 2013)?
5. How does the writing style that Dr. Moore uses in this chapter reflect postcolonial psychological writing? He incorporated a developmental perspective of how he encountered the professional field of psychology. Subsequently, he applied a phenomenological approach to measure events on the timeline between publication of DSM-IV and DSM-5. How did this impact your understanding of the parallel issues presented in the changing area of patient diagnosis? Using a writing style that best reflects the content of your writing and cultural background, write a few paragraphs to discuss your own thoughts about DSM-5's role in postcolonial psychology. How might your style differ from contemporary Western psychological writing styles?

CHAPTER 3

1. Vignette: The chapters in this book describe intergenerational change in postcolonial psychology. This chapter describes the lives of two men and their connection in community drug abuse prevention research. One man, Dr. Moore, joined this national research from the path of White privilege and the network of colonial research and inquiry embodied in the nation's major universities. The other man, Don Coyhis, came from the knowledge of nations occupying North America long before the arrival of the European population that founded this university research network. Reflect on the content of this chapter in light of the formative event in their relationship. Postscript: In prevention conferences at the turn of the century,

there were youth and adult research dissemination tracks. Returning from a conference, Dr. Moore's elementary-age daughter spent the plane ride home explaining to him the life and wisdom of a new friend she had just made: Don Coyhis of the Mohican Tribe.

2. In the beginning of Chapter 2, Dr. Moore writes, "The issuance of DSM-5 (American Psychiatric Association, 2013) calls for you to re-think your entire vocational life and your plans for living in a healthy way among clients, colleagues, patients, peers, and the broader community." He then presents the Wellbriety framework to illustrate how he has reeducated himself to meet increasing demands for more culturally informed research and treatment programs for substance abuse. How have the new demands made by DSM-5 shaped your own vocational behaviors as a mental health provider?
3. To better understand the examples Dr. Moore gives, view the Journey of Forgiveness document produced by Don Coyhis. This video includes Native elders discussing the traumas they experienced and continue to experience because of cultural genocide. It also discusses the culturally sanctioned treatments developed to address those traumas.
4. Write a short essay to describe how you have incorporated the teachings of cultural leaders that are relevant to your personal background or professional interests into the multicultural research, clinical services, or teaching you do.
5. Chapter 2 describes a number of psychometric techniques and psychological assessments that incorporate DSM-5 recommendations. Research one or more of those instruments or psychometric techniques and determine if it (or they) would be helpful to you in decolonizing any psychological assessments you are currently using.
6. Dr. Moore continues to work very closely with Don Coyhis to ensure continuing feedback and professional development for the services Dr. Moore provides. Develop a plan for you to consult with cultural leaders, who can provide direct feedback about the relevance and importance of the clinical services you provide for clients, students, or research subjects whose backgrounds reflect the experience of those cultural leaders. What suggestions did they provide? Did you experience any signs of White fragility (DiAngelo, 2011) while interacting with those cultural leaders?

CHAPTER 4

1. In the beginning of the chapter, Dr. West describes three pivotal experiences that shaped the development of her professional goals. Looking

back at your own psychosocial-cultural development, describe several personal and/or professional experiences that had a strong impact on your development as a mental health provider.

2. Dr. West presents a culturally informed assessment protocol for intimate partner violence. How closely does this parallel your own assessment of this topic? When you read about domestic violence research or treatment, how comprehensively does the article or book cover the issues she describes as being crucial to a full assessment?
3. If you or someone you know experienced any type of physical or emotional violence, how limited or comprehensive was your understanding of the research findings Dr. West presents in this chapter? How might this knowledge have helped you better understand that violence?
4. Dr. West describes her current professional activities as they include social justice activism. Drawing parallels with your own background of critical life events, how much have those events impacted your current social justice activism?
5. In reading about extreme violence in this article, what reactions did you have that might be considered to reflect your own countertransference about those topics? Or reflect "White fragility" (DiAngelo, 2011)?

CHAPTER 5

1. Why is social justice a psychology concern? Give specific examples of the integration of social justice in the field of psychology. Name some social justice initiatives the state and national psychological associations have developed.
2. How would you described the relationship between immigration and social justice?
3. Name some clinical strategies clinicians undertake to ensure an evidence-based intervention is delivered in a culturally appropriate manner.
4. What are the implications of the Hispanic Health Paradox for clinicians serving Latino clients?
5. How should we integrate Hispanic Health Paradox research with the health disparities and social justice literatures?

CHAPTER 6

1. What are some factors that account for differences within the Vietnamese American population?

2. How does migration trauma impact the mental health needs of individuals?
3. How does culture influence domestic violence situations among Vietnamese American?
4. How might the traditional Vietnamese beliefs and interventions of mental illness impact help-seeking behaviors?
5. In the professional supervision you have received, was there a focus on social justice and/or multicultural competence?
6. How might the ideas in this chapter change the supervision you would provide for new professionals?

CHAPTER 7

1. Consider your training program or place of employment. How are conversations about culture approached? Which cultural identities (e.g., race, sex, gender, and sexual orientation) are privileged in these conversations? Which are marginalized or silenced?
2. What are some ways in which you have observed or participated in white fragility? In what ways is White fragility reinforced and/or addressed in your training program or place of employment?
3. Who has served as a mentor or guide to you in your professional development? If you are a mentor, how might you approach conversations about how your own intersecting identities influence your mentor-mentee relationship?
4. Hardy and Laszloffy (1995) discuss identifying organizing principles for your culture(s) of origin as a part of creating a cultural genogram. What are some organizing principles in your culture(s) of origin? How do these principles become apparent in your clinical work?
5. Kliman's (2005) AVAF model requires the privileged party to consider six specific tasks when attempting to repair injuries caused by performances of power and privilege. Consider a time in which you have caused injury to another person. Which of these tasks did you find easy to address? Which tasks were more difficult?

CHAPTER 8

1. What is the psychological significance of an apology to a cultural group like those we have discussed?
2. How do the examples of American Indians/Alaska Natives being abused in American boarding schools qualify as genocide?
3. How has intergenerational and historical trauma continued to impact Indigenous communities?

4. How can The Community Readiness Model benefit American Indian/ Alaska Native communities?
5. Why is the concept of decolonization important to the American Indian/ Alaska Native population in particular?

CHAPTER 9

1. Go the Association of Black Psychology's website.
   a. Critique any commentary (using the Commentary Quick Link),
   b. Respond to the president's message on the home page, or
   c. Review an article in the *Journal of Black Psychology*.
2. Dr. Miller writes about childhood reflections that arise from his interactions with the Euro-American culture. Drawing from your background, state what childhood experiences from another culture shaped who you are today?
3. Looking at your own professional interests, how might the principles of Black Psychology shape your social justice actions?
4. Looking at the institution in which you are employed, the university in which you are teaching or attending, or your own independent professional activities, how might you be a better advocate for psychologists of color?
5. Review one of the classical research articles in your area of interest. How carefully does the research design attend to multicultural competence and social justice ideas?
6. Should lectures contribute to social justice?
7. Can psychological theories reflect and capture behavior from all aspects of our society?
8. Should psychologists be the moral authority of society?
9. Do you think most people of color process "double consciousness?" Should this aspect of behavior be eliminated?
10. Should there be a community college in incarcerated institutions?

CHAPTER 10

1. This chapter reflects on Goethe's statement, "Everyone hears only what they understand" (Goethe, 1998). Drawing from the knowledge you gained in your own professional education, how might this concept have shaped the teaching curriculum to which you were exposed? How might it have influenced the understandings you took away from your education and/or professional experiences? How can you correct any biases you may have encountered?

2. The editor's introduction to this chapter mentions the role of "thick descriptions" as a writing style that contributes new knowledge (Geertz, 1973). Discuss a multicultural or social justice topic with a colleague (preferably one who has a very different worldview) and record that using a writing style that might approximate a type of thick description of the issue. What were your emotional responses during this process? How might those reactions give you insights about the strengths or weaknesses you might have as a social justice advocate?
3. Speak with an individual who has another worldview about a psychology topic of interest to you both. Write a summary about that person's unique perspectives, and then ask for feedback. What concepts did you easily grasp? What did you not understand? How could you address the latter issue?
4. What have you been taught culturally about knowledge creation, the topic of this chapter? Have those concepts conflicted with what your educational training taught as the criteria for evidence-based research?
5. What steps can you take in your own professional development to democratize the knowledge you have about your profession?

CONCLUSION

1. Using the acronym RADICAL presented throughout the book, write a summary of your professional endeavors or future visions for yourself for each of the vectors.
2. The first paragraph of the section, "Where Will We Go? The Development of Social Justice Activism Skills," discusses the need for mental health professionals to strengthen such factors as cultural etiquette; self-awareness, and reflexivity about cultural issues; culturally informed problem-solving; culturally competent goal-setting; stress management; self-care; knowledge of culturally based politics; and conflict resolution at the interpersonal, intergroup, organizational, and international levels.
   a. Pick several of the above skills, knowledge bases, or factors that you think you need to further strengthen.
   b. How can you develop a "treatment plan" for yourself using such resources as supervision, mentoring, coursework, immersion in another culture, liaison with another colleague who possesses those skills, and/or participation in professional interest groups? What might be your short-term and long-term treatment goals for yourself? How might you select assessment tools to measure your improvement in these areas? How can you utilize the ZPD principles mentioned in this chapter to develop your treatment goals for yourself?

c. How does your self-efficacy in these areas change as you strengthen those factors?

3. Select a field such as Liberation Psychology, Jungian Psychology, or Positive Psychology and review one of the cited references. Are there any principles that have relevance or applicability for the current professional work you are doing?
4. How active have you been in your workplace or in participating in a professional association to increase the factor of inclusion as discussed in this chapter?
5. How often does a discussion of decolonization occur in your interactions with other mental health professionals? In the professional reading you do? In the clinical services you develop for clients, the research you conduct, the supervision you have or provide, and/or the courses you teach?
6. In your particular field, what are the immediate needs for decolonization and how can you begin to address them personally or professionally?

Index

About the Contributors

Editor's Note: All the contributors have very extensive professional backgrounds. Below is a brief summary of their qualifications relevant to this book. We have included both Euro-American types of credentialing and other forms of culturally sanctioned expertise and training.

Dr. Jessica L. Binkley is a psychologist at the Portland Clinic in Beaverton, Oregon. Her predoctoral internship was at the Center for Multicultural Training in Psychology at the Boston Medical Center, and her postdoctoral residency was with the Latino-Bilingual Track at Pacific University-School of Graduate Psychology (SGP). She is currently an adjunct professor at Pacific University—SGP, where she supervises a team of bilingual (English/Spanish) doctoral students and teaches classes in Human Diversity and Sexual Orientation and Gender Identity. She has been a panel member, a guest lecturer, a presenter, and symposium speaker on topics including cultural humility and intersectionality. Her areas of clinical focus include child and family work, trauma, and Latino/a mental health. Dr. Binkley is of a mixed racial and ethnic background (White, Eastern Band Cherokee).

Don Coyhis, Mohican Nation, is president and founder of White Bison, Inc., an American Indian nonprofit organization located in Colorado Springs, Colorado. Over the past 26 years, Don has developed a series of culturally based programs to address substance abuse recovery and treatment, youth prevention and treatment, programs for healthy families, and healing from unresolved grief and traumatic loss due to intergenerational trauma. The teachings of White Bison's Wellbriety Movement go beyond being sober to include thriving in the community and being balanced emotionally, mentally, physical, and spiritually. These programs have been implemented throughout the United States and Canada. Don Coyhis has authored several books that address recovery, treatment, and prevention of alcoholism and substance abuse for adults, youth, and families. He has been called upon to provide technical assistance for national policy organizations such as the White House Office of Drug Control Policy, Substance Abuse and Mental Health Services Administration (SAMHSA), as well as other national recovery organizations to develop social justice, prevention, and recovery programs for Native American communities.

Kateri D. Coyhis, BA, Mohican Nation, is director of White Bison's Wellbriety Training Institute. White Bison, Inc., is a nonprofit 501c3 charitable organization. She has over 15 years of experience in the nonprofit field. She is also assistant to the executive director and assistant to the chairman of the board at White Bison. She recently graduated from the University of Colorado at Colorado Springs with a major in history. She is a certified Daughters of Tradition trainer and a certified Medicine Wheel and 12 Steps Facilitator. As one of our future elders and young professionals, her insights about social justice and multiculturalism are highly relevant to the planning of future social justice initiatives.

Dr. Jerome M. Fischer, RhD, CRC, LPC, is professor and department chair of Rehabilitation Counseling at the University of Texas Pan-American. He has held many administrative, teaching, extension, and research appointments at the University of Texas Pan-American, the University of Idaho, and Eastern Montana College. He has taught undergraduate and graduate courses in rehabilitation services, multicultural diversity, educational research, substance abuse, global counseling, assessment, research methodologies, vocational rehabilitation, ethics and law in counseling, and grant management. He has chaired dissertation committees, has made many local, state, and national presentations multicultural issues, is a graduate student mentor, and is a highly respected researcher in rehabilitation psychology topics.

Susan Owre Gelberg, PhD, comes from four generations of authors, all of whom wrote about social justice, cultural diversity, and health. Dr. Gelberg is president and a cofounder of Cross-Cultural Counseling and Consulting, Inc. With more than 25 years of experience, she has worked in a research institute, universities, hospitals, a state hospital, a penitentiary, community mental health centers, large and small private practices, and a substance abuse center. Dr. Gelberg has consulted with medical professionals, community agencies, small businesses, corporations (including several Fortune 500 corporations), universities, and mental health agencies. She received recognition (Blanket Ceremony) for her work with Native Americans. She has made many presentations at professional conferences and published in referred journals on multicultural and social justice topics.

Dr. Pamela Jumper-Thurman serves as a senior research scientist affiliate faculty at Colorado State University. Dr. Jumper-Thurman is the co-director of the National Center for Community Readiness at Colorado State University. She is also co-owner of Council Oak Training and Evaluation, Inc. a female and American Indian owned company with offices in Colorado and Oklahoma. She is a co-author of the nationally used Community Readiness Model and co-author/editor of Cherokee National Treasures: She has served as a consultant for agencies such as the Center for Disease Control and Prevention, the World Health Organization (which adapted Community Readiness Model to fund five countries for the prevention of child maltreatment), Substance Abuse and Mental Health Services Administration, Native American Center for Excellence, Children's Mental Health Services, Office of Minority Health Research Center, Roslynn Carter Foundation, and Ford Foundation. She has more than 150 professional publications, research studies, and symposia presentations.

Dr. Alfonso Mercado is an assistant professor in the Department of Psychological Sciences and School of Medicine Neurology and Psychiatry Department at the University of Texas-Rio Grande Valley (UTRGV) in Edinburg, Texas. He publishes regularly in peer-reviewed journals, studies empirically supported treatment interventions with culturally diverse groups, and makes peer-reviewed presentations nationally. He is a member of the Board of Trustees for the Texas Psychological Association (TPA) and co-chair of the TPA Diversity Division, and President of the Mental Health Coalition of the Rio Grande Valley. He has been awarded the UTRGV's Faculty Excellence Award for Sustainability Education and AAIDD Texas Chapter Knowledge Award for Excellence in Education and Research.

Dr. Fred C. Miller is an instructor in psychology at the Cascade Campus of Portland Community College in Portland, Oregon. He was recently the principle investigator and director of *African American Dementia and Aging Program* (AADAPt), which received an NIH Grant. He was a consultant for Family-Based Care for Frail Older Persons at the Oregon Health and Sciences University School of Nursing. He has published professionally on depression and substance use by students in a historically Black college. He was a principal organizer and panel presenter on a state conference on intergenerational trauma. He has been a speaker for community organizations and professional conferences on topics such as Henrietta Lacks, African American dementia and aging, autism, cognitive decline and acculturation, health disparities, and intergenerational trauma.

David D. Moore, PhD, EdD, has taught in the Graduate School Psychology Departments at Argosy University since 2007. From 2004 to 2007, he was a faculty member in the Department of Mental Health at Johns Hopkins University, where he researched the integration of behavioral health and primary care. He served as White Bison's program evaluator of the Wellbriety® national, Native-based, peer recovery support network. From 1985 until 2004, Dr. Moore taught graduate-level behavioral science courses in the College of Education at the Universities of Washington and Puget Sound. He has conducted 20 years of national field research as principal investigator or program director in developing school-community prevention and intervention systems funded by the U.S. Departments of Health and Human Services (Centers for Substance Abuse Prevention and Treatment), U.S. Department of Education (Safe and Drug Free Schools), U.S. Department of Justice (Juvenile Justice, Native American Wellbriety® Mentoring prevention systems), and U.S. Department of Housing and Urban Development.

Hanna Moore, B.A., received her Bachelor of Arts at the University of Puget, where she majored in classics and minored in politics and government. She was a member of the International Baccalaureate at Thomas Jefferson High School in Federal Way, Washington. Her senior thesis was "The Impact of the Emerging Science of Psychology on Boarding Schools." Her learning was informed by elders of the Tlingit (President and Mrs. Ed Thomas), Haida (Grandma Ruby, Mata Family), and Tsimshian Tribes (Tribe Carver, Stan Marsden). From fifth to eighth grade, she served as student representative to the Federal Way Drug Free Schools Coalition. This was a five-year SAMHSA project that followed Wellbriety strategies and used Dr. Thurman's Readiness Model for its goals.

Kim Nguyen-Finn, M.A., LPC-S, is working toward her Doctor of Philosophy degree in rehabilitation counseling at the University of Texas—Rio Grande Valley (UTRGV). Recent honors earned by her include many scholarships including the UTRGV Presidential Graduate Scholarship. She was also named Rehabilitation Doctoral Student of the Year for 2017 by the National Council on Rehabilitation Education. She is presently in private practice in Edinburg, Texas, where she provides psychological, supervisory, and consulting services. She is also a full-time lecturer at the School of Rehabilitation Studies and Counseling and consultant counselor for the Office of Victim Advocacy and Violence prevention, both at UTRGV. She has many peer-reviewed publications and conference presentations on multicultural and social justice topics, domestic violence, and sexual assault.

Barbara A. Plested, PhD, serves as a research scientist affiliate faculty at Colorado State University. Dr. Plested is the Co-Director of the National

Center for Community Readiness at Colorado State University. She is also co-owner of Council Oak Training and Evaluation, Inc. a female and American Indian owned company with offices in Colorado and Oklahoma. She is a co-author of the nationally used Community Readiness Model. She has served as principal investigator or co-principal investigator for numerous grants and cooperative agreements sponsored by such agencies as National Institute on Drug Abuse, the Office of Juvenile Justice and Delinquency Prevention, the Department of Justice, and the Center for Disease Control and Prevention. She has over 150 publications.

Mathew A. Poteet is the chief executive officer and cofounder of Cross-Cultural Counseling and Consulting, Inc., where he develops clinical and training programs that focus on trauma, healing, culture, and diversity. As a recreation specialist at Chemawa Indian Boarding School, he actively supports the cultural and ceremonial needs for 300+ Native youth. Mr. Poteet has worked for many years in mental health, educational, and correctional facilities to help people who are experiencing trauma symptoms, depression, anxiety, behavioral problems, addictions, and criminal behaviors. He achieved state recognition and served in the Oregon governor's office at the Statewide Program of Affirmative Action Department. Mr. Poteet presents at local, state, national, and international conferences on psychology, trauma, social justice, and Indigenous healing.

Bonita M. Veysey, PhD, is a Rutgers professor and vice chancellor at the Rutgers School of Criminal Justice. Her research focuses on behavioral health and justice issues, including police interactions with persons with mental illnesses mental health, substance abuse treatment in jails and prisons, diversion and treatment services for youth and adults with behavioral health problems, characteristics of justice-involved girls and women, the effects of early childhood trauma and conditions of confinement and reentry, and continuity of care issues. Dr. Veysey also works with state and local agencies to evaluate correctional programs and policies. She has more than 125 peer-reviewed journal publications, books, book chapters, monographs, monograph chapters, others, research and technical reports, funded research and evaluation, recent presentations (in the past five years), grants under review, and consulting activities.

Amanda C. Venta, PhD, is an assistant professor in the Department of Psychology and Philosophy and is Director of the Youth and Family Studies Laboratory at Sam Houston State University. She received her B.A. from Rice University and her M.A. and PhD in Clinical Psychology from the University of Houston. She completed her predoctoral internship through the Menninger Department of Psychiatry and Behavioral Sciences at Baylor

College of Medicine, where she remains adjunct faculty. Her research has been funded by the National Institute of Mental Health and the American Psychological Foundation. She has received more than 25 leadership awards, scholarships, travel awards, and fellowships including being named a Rising Star by the Association for Psychological Science. She has coauthored four book chapters and more than 30 peer-reviewed articles and has participated in more than 100 professional presentations.

Carolyn M. West, PhD, is professor of psychology and the Division Chair of Social, Behavioral, and Human Sciences in the School of Interdisciplinary Arts and Sciences at the University of Washington in Tacoma, where she teaches courses on family violence, sexual violence, and sex crimes. With more than two decades of teaching experience, she writes, trains, consults, and lectures internationally on intimate partner violence and sexual assault, with a special focus on violence in the lives of women of color. Dr. West is the editor of *Violence in the lives of Black women: Battered, black, and blue* (Routledge) and author of more than 50 publications. In recognition of her scholarship, teaching, and service, she was received the 2016 Distinguished Research Award, the first Bartley Dobb Professorship for the Study and Prevention of Violence (2005–2008), and the 2013 Distinguished Teaching Award.

Lightning Source UK Ltd.
Milton Keynes UK
UKHW01n0612260818
327810UK00007B/276/P

9 781498 553681